Transmedium

Transmedium

Conceptualism 2.0 and the New Object Art

GARRETT STEWART

THE UNIVERSITY OF CHICAGO PRESS [chicago and london]

The University of Chicago Press, Chicago 60637
The University of Chicago Press, Ltd., London
© 2017 by The University of Chicago

Published 2017
Printed in USA

26 25 24 23 22 21 20 19 18 17   1 2 3 4 5

ISBN-13: 978-0-226-50087-4   (cloth)
ISBN-13: 978-0-226-50090-4   (paper)
ISBN-13: 978-0-226-50106-2   (e-book)
DOI: 10.7208/chicago/9780226501062.001.0001

LIBRARY OF CONGRESS CATALOGING-IN-PUBLICATION DATA
Names: Stewart, Garrett, author.
Title: Transmedium : conceptualism 2.0 and the new object art / Garrett Stewart.
Description: Chicago ; London : The University of Chicago Press, 2017. | Includes bibli-
    ographical references and index.
Identifiers: LCCN 2017009026 | ISBN 9780226500874 (cloth : alk. paper) | ISBN
    9780226500904 (pbk. : alk. paper) | ISBN 9780226501062 (e-book)
Subjects: LCSH: Multimedia (Art) | Multimedia installations (Art) | Conceptual art. | Art
    and technology.
Classification: LCC N6494.M78 S74 2017 N6494.C63 | DDC 702.81—dc23
    LC record available at https://lccn.loc.gov/2017009026

♾ This paper meets the requirements of ANSI/NISO Z39.48-1992 (Permanence of Paper).

Contents

Aᴛ ᴛᴡᴏ sᴄᴀʟᴇs ᴏғ ᴀᴛᴛᴇɴᴛɪᴏɴ ɪɴ ᴡʜᴀᴛ ғᴏʟʟᴏᴡs, ᴀᴛ ᴛʜᴇ ʟᴇᴠᴇʟ ᴏғ ᴀᴇsᴛʜᴇᴛɪᴄ ᴇɴᴛᴇʀᴘʀɪsᴇ as well as of media theory, the way forward is in fact between. This book joins certain experimental works of the last two decades in resisting both the sweeping antimodernist assumptions of a "post-medium condition" in art practice and the implacable "convergence" in media study that takes as axiomatic a digital vanishing point for all processes. Between these two premises for the material basis of image production (and certain audiovisual projects as well)—between the release from medium specificity and the leveling point of no return in universal computerization, between aesthetic liberation and technological foreclosure—experimentation makes its frequent and, in both senses, *curious* way. Its inquisitiveness is likely to grow contagious in the viewing act. This is to say that aesthetic encounter in museum space can be, more than ever, a variably cued engagement with a work's own materialized "thought experiment."

But what in fact to think about the enlarged, repainted, and then rephotographed single frame of a celluloid film when ripped from its place not only in an isolated strip but also in the whole cinematic medium? What to think about a prewar film projector found screening, in loop-fashion on a gallery wall, the brief computer-generated image of celluloid's long-forgotten role as the plastic substrate for binary impress in the first primitive computer? About digital landscape photography generated by US Air Force reconnaissance technology and its virtual-reality software when applied to landscape paintings rather than topographic maps? About a drawing, then lithographic rendering, of a film strip caught in every sense—snagged and bifurcated between frames—in its secondary representation? And what about—what to think and say about—an apparent photo reproduction of a classic oil painting that turns out, on closer inspection, to be composed of 10,000 separate computer-searched images? What one can say may depend on how one begins by denominating such effects.

Naming is claiming. It is an attempt to grasp as category, to posit an understanding. Certainly the elective affinities of art, like electoral politics, have their own kind of "term" limits. But even before this book's elaborating on a second-wave conceptualism (including but not limited to the frequent art of its electronic wavelengths), another terminology may already have given pause in the bracketing terms of the book's entitling and slip-knotted formulation. One might rightly suspect that such tensility is meant to anticipate something materially taut, even fraught, in the works coming in for discussion. Still: Transmedium? Object Art? Not art object? Not, as seemingly flagged by the sense of "Conceptualism 2.0," new media and its objects? No, the newness of the art doesn't depend on electronic circuitry. Instead, there is a different grammar on call in the overall title— and a more specific circuit of response implied. The claim advanced by the prefix "trans" of "transmedium" refers to the "across" rather than the "beyond" or "over" of its alternate usages. Certainly no sense of mediation is transcended in the works ahead, as one might be otherwise led to assume from the latest models of "post-medium" theory brought into discussion. Rather, the medial interplay within certain composite objects is cognitively traversed—and, in the process, reconceptualized.

To respond transmedium: that's the invitation of such aesthetic provocations, where the heuristic coinage of that term is proposed less as a free-standing substantive (a transmedium) than as a slant or bearing of response—indicating, that is, a directed attention to the where and how of manifestation. Directed by the analytic stance of the image or installation itself, such attention is routed in this way across—and often in and between—the work's own material coordinates. This is the path by which such artifacts seek to bring production and reception into the closest possible alignment across "the concept" thereby put into transmission, often by some unexpected crux of divergent medial procedures. The logic of that transmission, sought at form's own inner reach, is the very art of the transmedial object or installation—so that not just grammar but also punctuation is kept in play by my subtitle. The logic of intention comes back as inference when concept is manifested less in the consolidated *objet* than in an unexpected force field of reciprocal technical determinations— their new object, art. This is an art, often enough, of destabilization itself: destabilization—and its diagnosis. Many practitioners in this line are termed "art researchers," often with the sense of their being archaeologists in action, probing the history of their present means and materials. Art objects tend to become, as a result, fine-grained reports on their own medial constitution.

Technical determinations do increasingly prevail where once, instead, there were emblazoned signposts of a revered, cultivated, and proudly reductive medium specificity. So there's no proceeding here without the art history behind these newer works. Approach it this way. That apogee of modernism in the medial purism of "abstract" expressionism was actually quite concrete, a matter always of material surface and stroked pigment. In this high modernist strain, paint all by itself made its presence felt, expressed itself. It was only the next step, in recoil—rebounding in a direction opposite to that of Pop art in its own comparably antimodernist swerve—that was in fact a true move away from concrete materialization toward abstraction, toward disembodied idea, toward discourse. The first phase of Conceptual art was in many instances all abstraction. But before this discursive resistance to the cult of pigment, stroke, and plane, it had certainly been the medium that made its first impression in the encounter with high modernist works: the medium of washed or dripped paint in Morris Louis or Jackson Pollock, say, or mediality's overt "mixture" in Jasper Johns or in Robert Rauschenberg's "combines." In these years and works, medium (even when pluralized) was what met the eye in art. Meaning, if that's even what to call it, came later, came out, came through. Half a century farther along in the evolution of art modes, meaning is more obviously at stake than before, but now for the way it comes not so much through as across, by negotiating material tensions that precede any notion of manifest formal balance. This book has in its sights numerous transmedium works operating in this way through a composite and impacted mediality that is kept more in question than in clear view.

That question has become an aesthetic agenda. My goal is to show how such querying has worked its way into a broad-based (but itself basis-vexing) program. It's no accident, then, that art projects are increasingly called aesthetic "research." Hypothesis, evidence, and interrogation are the framework for its new materialities, not formal design—with veritable position papers often issued to frame them, whether by artists or their gallerists. Making strange is one thing; these works often seem driven to make it first of all hard. And sometimes all but invisible. Even at their most intricate or occulted, however, the elusive image structures to follow can still appear designed to aggress rather dramatically upon our initial sense of sight—and ultimately upon our sense of seeing, its false confidences, its potentially enhancing confusions. And elsewhere upon our sense of hearing, often "baffled" in one way or another. Yet, in all cases, response is oriented by material cross-reference in the charged field of transmedium operation. So what, then, more exactly, is that deliberated prefix meant to fix attention on? What distances are at once gauged and crossed by its internal transit? And, for all this sense of the between, why the singular in its stem? Why not transmedia? How fully internalized—and thus consolidating—is the liminality that holds (together) a work at some mutual threshold of mediation? These are questions raised by the works under discussion more often than answered by them. Rejoinders are everywhere—but only in other works like (by being always, in their cross-mix, at least a little unlike) them.

Through it all, the techno-cultural context is impossible to miss. By stratospheric overload, we are bombarded lately by as much mediation as radiation. Ozone depletion and digital repletion. The rain of image and text is a steady surge, two-way but irreversible. We Net-book our tickets and our faces, load our data up, down, and everywhere in between, find ourselves linked—or say enchained—and unwittingly data-mined if not biometrically archived. Visual art's way of intercepting this flux and reflux of transmitted signal and its shackling fascinations—when art practice isn't just swept along by it in reproduced thumbnail samples or Vimeo clips—is increasingly to suspend itself long enough, between a received medium and its unexpected pairing with another, to delimit and somehow traverse the gap. And the gap is in this sense conceptual before physical: often merely the sensed chasm, or bridge, between plastic or electronic form and some new impalpable field (or differential platform) of medial recognition. The trans in such cases can be unduly volatile: active, trans-active, contrastive, dialectical, and often undoing. Not to mention multifarious. Never have I written on a subject whose selection of evidence felt more arbitrary, not just at early stages but right down to the publisher's wire. It isn't simply that there are far more objects and installations than I had space to discuss here (par for the course), but that there are, and as if by definition, more and more appearing every day. In our exponentially multimedia environment—and ultimately mediatized culture—these are works that summon, and then mull, art's often lone and sole role: to slow perception to the level of its own investigated lines of force, to capture layered aesthetic procedures as a thought process.

None of this hard thinking is guaranteed, of course. In the wider field yet of mixed-media art production, there often seem too many visual ideas thrown out, tossed off, without any pertinent material realization. Or, alternately, too much assorted matter thrown up for consideration without a compelling thought to "support" and mold it, whether the installed objects are hung from walls or ceilings or piled on floors or pedestals. In its media-savvy aspects, Conceptualism redux may thus seem designed to offer an antidote. Or at least a stopgap. This book's claim, in sorting through a spate of contemporary evidence, is certainly not that the most important work currently being done, conceptual or otherwise, is necessarily or inherently transmedial. The proposal is simply that transmedial work, with its premium on a formative conflation of means, is more than ordinarily prone to find meaning in its materials—and in the cross-play of their process. Rather than an indiscriminate mix of materialities, the transmedial work, in a new and more rigorous form of the "combine," gains its internal traction from a concentrated interaction.

The cultural and historical forces impinging on these works are different, certainly, from the earlier animus—both anti-establishment and counter-Pop—that drove the intellectual engines of first-round conceptualist thinking in the 1960s. But this current impetus is no more narrowly art-historical, no more hermetically aesthetic, than before. In contrast to a broad swath of aesthetic variety in the decades since, it isn't primarily that the cult of medium specificity is eschewed in works of this newer conceptual mode on behalf of aesthetic freedom: a blow struck against mimimalist constraint and stagnation. That's the least of it. Well beyond the championing of multifarious stuff in a "mixed"-messaging aesthetic, any such rallying cry is outstripped in Conceptualism 2.0 by a tacit address to a global historical moment with little breathing room outside the labyrinth of corporate and military-industrial media streams. Any genuine local innovation in the matter of printwork, celluloid, video, or installation practice is likely to be, in just these ambient terms, every bit as historicist as it is art-historical. Time and again, its internally contending means are pitted against a perceptual field of ubiquitous and undifferentiated electronic transmission in the alternating channels of display and surveillance, from Instagrams to satellite or drone feeds. What kind of serious retinal or audial work in gallery space would be likely to ignore entirely this fiber-optic backdrop? Neither purist nor ecumenical, then, transmedia objects set out neither to distill nor to swell, but rather to cloud—and sometimes defiantly to muddy—the waters of unchecked image flow.

In the last few years of gallery going, the frequency with which I've been captivated unexpectedly by work of this sort from artists I'd never heard of (entirely my fault, not theirs, for they have seldom been "obscure," and in some cases quite famous)—and not just captivated, but arrested, magnetized, challenged, called to a response that had often to begin in some degree of decryption—would have been motive enough for such a book concerning aesthetic experiments sometimes written about but never systematically compared. But the basis of such comparison can only be found, as well these works know by showing, within the broader heritage of Conceptual art and its second wind (also too little studied) under digital impetus—where they find their license, resonance, and edge, even when not their direct instrumentation. Two motives converge. As such inventive practice in itself serves to model, a balance in commentary needs to be struck between aesthetic materiality and its medial history. Not aggregated as mere spot checks in an appreciable tendency, then, but entered upon as extended test cases, the fabrications to come, in all their audacity and panache, are allowed to articulate their own terms as fully as possible within the media heritage they conceptually revisit and materially re(de)vise.

Within which, a remarkable spread of effects awaits us in all sorts of medial imbrication—and aesthetic implication. These include the pitched differentials of cross-platform works that achieve canvas imaging with digital imprint, landscape photography with everything from jpeg magnification to intermittent Web signal, faux-photography with printer's ink, cinema without recorded space or movement, and other more demanding collusions and subterfuges too involuted to reference in any such cursory listing. The question always: what is of pressing interest in the technical interplay? A question unavoidable when the medial cross-feed is so far from being expedient or conventional as to be the very point of the fabrication that confronts us. The trans in all this is the mark not of an advertised interchange of media but of an inner system or counterplay in a particular work, whose own intrinsic form of mediation rises to awareness not as unitary but as multifold. This is a system whose explicitness, whose explication—we will come to say whose internal "analysis"—is its work.

The transmedial line of sight evoked or programmed by such contemporary gallery objects and displays—or, more accurately, the transmedial angle of vision, always triangulated, sometimes tightly dialectical—is art's way of cueing perception to our multifaceted means of seeing from within even the densest and most contested images. For it is just this multiplicity, internalized, from which the work emerges. No less than in the medium specificity of high modernism (with a review of whose tenets the "Prelim" will necessarily begin), this mode of perception does indeed put a premium on means even while newly insisting on the inbuilt plurality of that noun, that substantive—together with the substances, or materialities, at play in its apprehension. It always feels too soon to say so, until one work after another comes before us, but the general logic is clear—and will be recognized, I trust, in its overt departure from once-canonical models of reflexive purification in modernist media practice. In

Conceptual art's response, the logic, the distinction, is this: whereas one may of course contemplate a medium in something like its quintessential form, one must increasingly learn to think transmedium. The focus of that thinking, its locus and prompt, is what I am calling the transmedial interface in 2.0 manifestations of recent experiment: the switch point between platforms and assumptions alike.

What results is an adjustment in conceptual scale from within the vocabulary of mediation itself. The "inter" of the term *interface* typically identifies both an embedded function and at times an extrinsic orientation. The likes of drawing paper, stretched canvas, mirror, audio receiver, movie screen, codex page, liquid-crystal monitor: these are all familiar interfaces in a generalized sense not held narrowly to an electronics model. In this broad acceptation, an interface is understood as the differential mechanism that facilitates either some ocular or sonic recognition (via a mirrored or screened image, a bank of audio speakers, etc.) or a more coded and opaque electronic transfer in the economies of communication. By scalar leap, however, when one entire medium is held up to the terms of another, rather than held to its own conveyance in action—or, say, reframed through the lens of another—the level of perceptual engagement shifts. What results is a zone of higher-order interface: a field or filter of conceptual investigation rather than functional transmission.

Since naming is claiming, it is good to remember from here out, as with the 2.0 of Conceptualism in its contemporary ventures, that the nomenclature of "interface" borrows its terminological aura from newer technologies without any inevitable digital insistence. An art of the vexed interface is not necessarily arranged to address or rework any such computerized operations in their own prevailing terms. The aesthetic charge is rather to rethink the whole media field in light of certain impacted examples of criss-crossed or jammed transmit and their conflicted signaling, electronic or otherwise: to rethink—or better yet rewrite—the terms of engagement with manifestation itself. Again and again, the response called up by such works amounts to entering a discourse, often studiously abstract, whose determinations are sometimes slow to emerge and difficult to pin down. This is a discourse articulated internally but also bolstered by the exponential volume of gallery text needed lately to "contextualize" works (or "researches") that no longer speak for themselves in method or thrust, let alone by title—at least not without some exegesis of their own internal trans-lations. To say so is to recognize that the aesthetic experience at such moments—first perceptual or cognitive, then conceptual—is in its own right, and often by trial and error, a coming to terms. This is where the transmedial border realms of reciprocal incursion and rethought liminality become themselves "preliminary" to any understanding of the works, or workings, in front of us. For these objects or installations are formal structures faceted in conception to register the suspended technical authority of their own otherwise separate but now conjoined interfaces. So it is that the works we are asked to think through in this way are indeed, in themselves, conceived transmedium. To catch the force of that interface—to appreciate that "between" or "among," notional even when not operational—is this book's object of attention in engaging with these variable objects of perception.

In sorting this attention across the various levels of inference involved—technological, historical, and media-archaeological as well as cognitive and social and often political—I've attempted, instead of a standard table of contents, more of a program or playbill. This brief Overture, with an introductory first act to follow, is rounded out in the end with a curtain call, bringing back for transmedium response the operations of traditional theatrical film after numerous gallery experiments in the layered, impacted, or altogether unexposed celluloid trace. In between, two crowded Scenes—concerning fixed and kinetic imaging respectively—are spanned by an entr'acte of sorts. This is meant to secure theoretical and historical relations between the main phases of discussion by introducing new work, bridge-work, that occupies its own clarifying transitional space between still frames and their engineered motion. And it should be noted, too, that this loose theatrical scaffolding is more than just a figurative armature or a structural convenience. Though the particular works in question are far from staging some featured specificity of aesthetic means under a stable spotlight, they do actually perform, rather than just depend on, their own transmedium shunts and relays in an ongoing theater of inspection: a theater often so far from histrionic as to seem downright cryptographic.

Or at least hard to decode at a naked, however quickly acclimated, glance. So a single early example recommends itself going in—as far from medium specific as can be conceived, and specifically conceptualized to that end. This is a work of paper-thin interface whose separate medial formats may appear outsourced to each other in mutual redefinition. Given pride of place, the example has at least the advantage of being world-historical. Almost two centuries ago, the advent of photography introduced a new possibility to the post-Gutenberg mechanics of transmission. Maximizing its potential, the mid-Victorian image maker and self-styled wielder of nature's pencil (his metaphor for photography's light-drawing) William Henry Fox Talbot envisioned his new mode of optical storage not just in relation to an aesthetic of representational sketching but in immediate conjunction with its mechanical predecessors in the recording capacities of codex and newsprint sheet. In this regard, one of his images in particular speaks (illustrated) volumes.

Typical of media history in aesthetic manifestations, a technical turning point turns inward here upon its own conditioning momentum. Where the "mixed-medium" of illuminated manuscripts, for instance, once gave way not just to print at the dawn of mechanical mediation but to an efflorescence of painted Bibles in easel scenes, so, three centuries later, does the next radical media breakthrough reconceive itself in terms of a millennial predecessor. More than just publicly advocating the new options of photography for accuracy and variable scale in embedded print illustration, Fox Talbot illustrates his point by cross-mapping one medium with the other, photographic imprint with typeset impress, via a triangulation with their shared "negative" substrate in reversal per se. In 1844, in a contact paper "print" raised to reflexive identification as such, the Victorian photo artist records three lines of set type (rather than its eventual lettering on the page) that thus spell out in reverse—legible only in the attention of a second look—the phrase "Imitation of Printing." (period included). So indicated—not inscribed by nature's pencil alone but templated for reproduction—this materialized concept does more than register the innovator's technical and commercial brief in a print-work embodiment not needing to pass through hand set-up and mechanical pressure. More to the point, the image in itself emblematizes the artist's leading idea by summoning the shared inversion necessary to each visual prototype separately—and does so in two completely different typefaces for each noun.

The aesthetic force of Fox Talbot's "textwork" thus anticipates, by well over a century, the lexigraphs, including photostats, of Conceptual art that it so much resembles. In his transmedial figuration, the inherent reversal straightforwardly—if backwardly—posited by

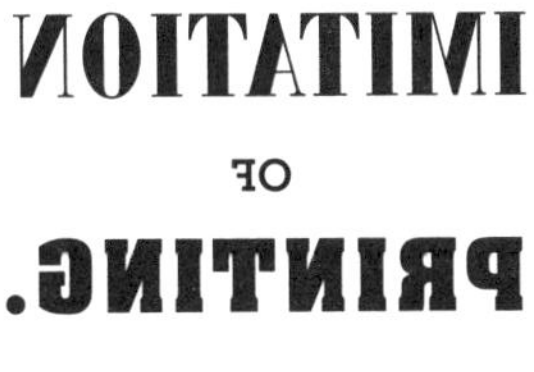

IMITATION

OF

PRINTING.

is not just proposed by discourse but, via a slippery interface, materially thematized, say thematerialized: a launching instance of transmedial conceptualization 1.0. Media history has had its usual way of catching up with such invention. For this single contact photograph, on its matte-paper backing, is not only displayed in a rare manuscript exhibit at Oxford's Bodleian Library as a separate artifact alongside an open page of glasswork illustrations from Fox Talbot's breakthrough work, *The Pencil of Nature*. It is also now available (the museum having acquired it and its copyright from the Talbot family in 2013) in so alien but nonetheless descendent a mode of access as the remote print-online version made possible through the library's "museoteca" service (only of course available, given copyright protection, when not intended for further print publication). Such, then, is simply the latest destiny, deconceptualized, refunctionalized, of Fox Talbot's transmedial seedbed. What can otherwise be seen indirectly germinated from this one-sheet interface between print-work logics—and can be found proliferating across subsequent skewed excerpts from the very book of modern media history—is our coming topic.

 Conceptualism 2.0

Like everything else media-historical, an emphasis on the conceptual object or installation has a rich—and oppositional—backstory over the last half century. It could be said that the cult of "the medium" arose when there was suddenly too plural a sense of media, dissipating any one provision, any one aesthetic mission. This is all the clearer in retrospect, from the vantage of our contemporary media barrage. Officiated over most pontifically by Clement Greenberg, late modernist "purity" must be partly understood against the backdrop of what literary scholar David Trotter delimits as "The First Media Age" of the interwar years, followed, of course, by media's rampant postwar proliferation.[1] For Trotter, cinema was by no means the only machinic challenge to written art. Literature also confronted the telephone as a new means of verbal intimacy and address rather than detached impersonal representation. Radio, too, posed its alternative models—and challenges. And then in the postwar period, though this is not Trotter's subject, a Second Media Age of remote video swept across popular culture with a momentum unabated down to the present, where it has only been exponentially enhanced by computerization. No doubt, though, that at the turning point to which Trotter's work implicitly leads up, medium specificity in the fine arts was, especially in the 1950s and early 1960s, proudly digging in its heels.

Conceptualism, in response and by contrast, entered the fray in the mid-1960s to process the discourse of both high and low culture together rather than to cordon off presumed impurities.[2] Subsequently, what Fredric Jameson, writing in the early 1990s, termed the "mediatic system" of postmodernist art is still widely apparent.[3] But since he wrote, what I am calling Conceptualism 2.0 arises to address, not redress, such mediatic orientation in the works of a newer cultural production that has been specifically influenced by the digital eclipse of certain forms of materiality, analog representation, indexicality, and the rest. Late in the second decade of Conceptual art, Jameson saw its defining feature as a general field of mediatic self-consciousness rather than any intrinsic functions or features of a work's disposition. His chief example (to which we'll soon return) was a gallery assemblage by Robert Gober that involved a freeform quadratic relay across separate formal elements of the installation: architectonic, sculptural, painterly, and textual. It was not exactly multimedial in the usual sense, but its manifold array kept little more than medial distinctions in view. More recently, in the era of universal computerization, any such adduced "mediatic system" has repeatedly gone inward, reformatted by isolated display pieces as their own *systemic* interplay: an inbuilt oscillation of means rather than merely a knowing conjuncture of media forms. Just this much hinted in overview of the announced contestational "backstory" is enough to suggest a superficial oddity of this book: namely, how—and why—its "preliminary" glance at the lay of the land constitutes one of its longest chapters. With so much prefatory aesthetic ferment built up behind the turn-of-the-millennium projects on which we'll be concentrating, this second sustained burst of conceptual experiment already has considerable wind in its sails, the cross-currents of which it is necessary to delineate from the outset. Certainly the works themselves regularly depend on the tacit media archaeology of their own revisionary processes.

Where the antipictorial bias of early Conceptual art, especially in its unabashed lexical forms, once oversaw the exile of image by verbal ideation, the thrust of Conceptualism 2.0 is a return to complex seeing, to visual image, but in the now-disaffected form of materialized idea. And in the special case of transmedial cross-purposing, the force of that ideation—in precisely its transverse slant—has one consequence first of all: no matter how hard you look, you are never quite seeing straight. The angle, the triangle, of perception is always deflected from one medial realization by (and across) the interface of another, whether conjured by visual association or couched in an actual technical source. That inherent give-and-take is our topic. But before tracing such resituated perceptual energies, how first to define "mediatic"?

Any such definition, of course, and not least its variant in "transmedial," inevitably bears the weight of the art history it would help crystalize in the very act of revising. Instead of the abstracted *idea of art* displacing execution and display, we look to recent projects in Conceptualism redux that stress, yet more fundamentally, the very *idea of mediation*—but do so from within its deliberately impure material instances, in all their social and political as well as cognitive ramifications. It is only then that works of this sort (of this internal sorting and transfusion alike) yield up their potential impact. For whether by optical allusion or actual material collusion, through secondary representation or technological cross-activation, the transmedium channels of such conceptual experiments route perception across collaborative formats from which some new specular (and speculative) force field is thereby generated.

[medium::specs]

Short of this marked betweenness, there can be no specifically transmedial charge, only separately deployed means: no felt interface of separate "medium specs." Concerning the odd typographic cast of this first among similarly punctuated subheads, much is to be unfolded over the course of their interpretive accumulation. And interpretive they are meant to be, investigating the procedural, often dialectical, tension of a given local structure or its broader conceptual horizon. In this first case: mediality at large understood over against the specifications achieved, and only in reciprocal interplay, by a work's own materialized speculation. Or, in the next instance ahead: mediation rendered systematic by the reflexive counterplay (adduced on this score by Jameson) of certain installation practices rendered *[system::mediatic]*. The double colon thus operates less as a revolving door at the point of material interface than as a lynchpin serving to split the transmedial difference. This is the difference that remains inherent to the noncoherence of the material field when tapped and manipulated by such cross-conditioned works.

Complementing (and enclosing) the colon format as a means of further yoking the pertinent terms in play, the typographic bracket—less a confident demarcation than a momentary conceptual holding action—serves as a kind of tentative and expandable ad hoc frame. Suggesting both a tight buckle and a loose hinge at once, such combined indications are a response, as for instance in *[medium::specs]*, to indeterminate rather than settled parameters. Such are categorical boundaries not dictated by a given brand of mediation but only gradually specified in its present anomalous instance. This shorthand can at times include, as below, the linguistic toggle of a shifting lexical interface evoked by homophonic waver to model certain divided pulls of the *[concept::dual]*. But the graphic logic of these inwardly reversible subheads does not depend on any such loose phonetic conflation (even when emblematically present). Rather, the abutting terms are designed to evoke a material tension in the works themselves kept active across a disjunctive gravitational field of percept and concept. Many hairs will be split, phrasal expectations bifurcated, even single terms minced and cross-worded, in the cumulative roster of these self-divided subdivisions, each of them roughly derived from a paradigm of tacit conditions and their irregular materialization that will be given fullest analysis in "Endscapes." Organizing them all is a logic made unmistakable in the reversibility of the noun/adjective shift (from founding dichotomy to featured effect) in a phrase like *[platform::manifestation]*, where the support is made apparent in the perceived result. This is just where a latent facilitation returns from the repressed or, say, from the inexplicit, in the form of materialized disclosure.[4] More needs to be laid out soon, even by way of preliminary sketch, about the binarist logic underlying this byplay (derived from the so-called semiotic square of structural analysis). For it is just the dyanamic such a template helps identify—where a tension noted at the surface of perception infers a deeper breach of medial continuity—that prompts a fuller negotiation of polariaties.

First, though, we can draw for comparison on two closely aligned accounts of mediation that arrive in the same year, 2013, and that might be said to resemble each other right up to the point where the present study begins. The company they part, if just marginally, opens the door on a third way. Each sees mediation as a social condition rather than (or before) a material determination, contextual before artifactual. The work of Conceptualism 2.0 doesn't challenge this general emphasis, only its implied priority, by foregrounding the technical substrate, the material means, within the communicative or contextual frame. But this is only to say that the transmedium force of such conceptualism is, often enough, a social diagnosis in itself rather than just the selective implementation of an aesthetic effect, its ironies contextual in the very materiality of their execution.

One definition of mediation (from Conceptual poet and theorist Craig Dworkin) sees it as a function of "networked objects in specific social settings," the other (from art critic Hal Foster) as marked by "social conventions" determined by "technical substrates" when understood "in a cultural field."[5] Objects in social linkage; technical supports in conventionalized recognition: in each critic's emphasis, therefore, the same resistance to the cult of high modernist specificity, indeed to any and all predetermined criteria, as well as the same insistence on shared cultural assumptions in the zone of reception. Each definition, when expanded by examples, thus stresses the relativity of "networked" understanding rather than some quest for material autonomy. So the same difference? Not quite. Distinctions rest unspoken in the mode of uptake, phenomenological in Foster's case (with architecture his main emphasis), cognitive and conceptual in Dworkin's (textuality and music his chief evidence). But what, then, is the relation of "networked objects" in Dworkin to the "cultural field" in Foster? A ream of blank paper makes a book in Dworkin, or blank vinyl a record, even at zero-degree mediation, when imaginatively configured with comparable intertexts in a minimalist iconography of the codex or phonographic form. In Foster, a sheath of artificial light takes on architectonic recognition in a global "cultural field" of surface display rather than built space. That's the contextual common ground that can be so differently marked—and sometimes actually paced—off.

Foster is a sociologically oriented art writer steeped in the long debates over the inalienable materialities and essentialized conditions of postwar art practice. For him, the pitched battles about medium have long been "stalled over the opposition between a modernist ideal of 'specificity' and a postmodernist strategy of 'hybridity.'" According to Foster, these positions in fact "mirror each other," dubiously assuming a "fixed nature" to the *objets d'art* in one mode or another—"with artists encouraged either to disclose them or to disturb them somehow" (xi). For him, instead, and in the grammar of a suitably plural definition (according to which one might say that the instability or "disturbance" is constitutive), "mediums are social conventions-cum-contracts with technical substrates; they are defined and redefined, within works of art, in a differential process of both analogy with other mediums and distinctions from them—a process occurring in a cultural field that, vectored by economic and political forces, is also subject to continual redefinition" (30). You can't determine the medium without knowing the parties it mediates between, the social axis it delineates, the forces that "vector" its betweenness.[6]

The alternate definition by Dworkin places yet more emphasis on the ideational, but always as linked to the material—not surprising in a book (*No Medium*) about artifacts that often appear reduced entirely to a materiality without active mediation (like the blank page or the silent audio disk). Dworkin begins with a basic "predicament": the problem of knowing when and how a given material is actually part of a communication circuit, or, in other words, when it is actually and already mediating. His recurrent example: paper, which is a material thing in its every appearance, but a different medium when sold as writing "material" or displayed under a vitrine as text object or bound in the form of a blank stack as a faux (or pure?) codex; or just held in the hand as part of an everyday book. Two "lessons" descend from this "predicament"—first, one's sense that a medium cannot be located "in isolation" from the mode of relay by which its data (its contents) are offered for transmission (30). The second lesson is that a medium is neither an "object" nor its "materiality" per se. We might call it instead a means. For his part, Dworkin offers another plural definition (of "mediums") like Foster's, avoiding any primary emphasis on individual specification—let alone on the fetish of specificity. Here is Dworkin's full proposal for the conditions of mediation, as excerpted and condensed above: "Taken together, in parallax, these two lessons permit us to glimpse the operations that constitute a more robust definition of media. Media, from this perspective, consist of analyses of networked objects in specific social settings" (32). For the Conceptual art theorist, it would seem, media are themselves conceptual before the fact: the implemented and interpreted *idea*, the "analysis" itself, of social connectivity rather than (even if via) the isolated materialities that might manifest it.[7]

For Foster, once more, mediums—in contractual acceptance by the receiver—are "conventions . . . with technical substrates." For Dworkin, mediums consist in the "analysis" of the conventions, not their material givenness as established and self-asserted—with communication keyed instead, at every moment, to their reconception in response. And if such media are means, always in contact or "contract" with reception, then, on Dworkin's understanding, we are to be confronted in what follows by works that perform such "analysis" on themselves—and do so by internal differentiation. For these are transmedial works that operate their own "parallax" (his term again) or triangulation. To say, then, that mediums (my own plural definition here) are the means by which, in the case of museum display, artifacts are found contracting with their own material preconditions in eliciting our perceptual and cognitive attention—this is not at all to insist that a medium must in some sense keep faith with itself. The contract in play doesn't require any "full disclosure" of medial essence. Rather, it implies an instigating—and, in many cases, still ongoing—transaction. Adapting Foster's metaphor, it is not just external cultural "vectors," whether economic, political, or otherwise, gendered or regional or transnational or whatever, that can be found to intercept and shape the receptual field of those entwined conventions that particularize a given (but never taken for granted) medium. Instead, and at base, a work's own technical substrate may in itself be vectorized, criss-crossed, divisive, if sometimes dialectical. Which is why I stress *transmedium* as the realized field of a *direction*, adverbial to a work's material predication: or, in other words, a differentially generated trace of its collateral means. So that the "parallax" of auto-"analysis" to which the coming works are prone returns to the etymological sense of "analyze" as "to loosen up":

in the recurrent cases ahead, to unbind for determination the transfused medial effects that have been put into differential play. It is just this that the twin colons of mutual redescription are meant to capture and encode in the punctuational parallax of the subheads throughout.

There is, in short, for Dworkin and Foster both, no predetermined allegiance to the medial convention-cum-contract. The issue of the substrate is one of material support, not purity—not a given unity of means but the effort at a contingently unified aesthetic field. It is in this sense that both Dworkin's and Foster's definitions fall roughly into line with Rosalind Krauss's emphasis on the "post-medium condition" after modernism.[8] The whole shibboleth of the intrinsic has been dispensed with. It is no longer a matter of the unadulterated versus the composite, the pedigree versus the mongrel, but rather of a perception itself hybridized by the combinatory associations unlocked from either mixed matter or, all the more often lately, cross-wired technology.[9] It is in this sense that one approaches mediatic embodiment less as homing in on an essentializing specificity than as generating an orchestrated medium specif*ication* across immanent differences and interchanges. But this remains an aesthetic issue before a technological one, if indeed a materialist issue before either. For this reason, the explorations to follow—focused on contemporary work that is often electronically "derived" even when not computer-driven—gravitate for their interpretive context toward art-historical theorizations of means and materials. This is their contested round—more than either the philosophy of new media and its video manifestations, on the one hand, or, on the other, the digital moment as conceived more broadly by communications and media history.[10] It is within the conceptual static of competing aesthetic forms—and formats—that these works find their definitive transmedial register.

[system::mediatic]

Transmedial register—or zone, or interface. In any case: *systemediatic* in its own discerned stress, a material impaction rather than relaxed mix. In that elided or "portmanteau" formulation (again triggered by the audiovisual interplay of alphabetic language itself), such an adjusted touchstone for what I am calling Conceptualism 2.0 takes us straight back to the treatment of Conceptual art and the broader "mediatic system" in Jameson's *Postmodernism, or the Cultural Logic of Late Capitalism*.[11] In what is for him the unstable "Utopian" (and socially escapist) impulse of postmodernism, which often finds temporary root in the fungible dimensions and delimitations of gallery space, the "transformation of social relations and political institutions is projected onto the vision of place and landscape, including the human body." Jameson adds in clarification: "Spatialization, then, whatever it may take away in the capacity to think time and History, also opens a door onto a whole new domain for libidinal investment of the Utopian and even the protopolitical type" (160). Indeed, his dead metaphor in "opens a door" takes on a more literal and dubious sense in that particular postmodern installation, *Untitled* (Robert Gober, 1988), submitted by Jameson as representative focus of his extended critique.

The parameters of this immediate example of "bad or nonpolitical Utopianism" (160) are not difficult to reconstruct, though the Concept may at first defeat response. I alluded to their quadratic function earlier, and it's time to step it off. As we walk into a demarcated museum space, a putative "room" that is only a zone of tacitly cross-referenced objects, we do so through a portal whose entrance door is not just unhinged but transferred to the opposite wall, though not *in* but merely leaning *on* that far wall—as if we have wedged our way into a non-space, a wholly liminal aperture. Between us and that displaced door—angled against, rather than opening into, the facing wall, with no exit thereby implied from the circulatory space into which we move—we see first, directly in front of us, the modest mound of an artificially installed earthwork (contributed by a separate artist, Meg Webster, unmentioned by Jameson). Next to it, a nineteenth-century landscape painting hung traditionally on the wall. And nearby, a book, lifted as it were from the very book of postmodernism (by appropriation and pastiche artist Richard Prince, cited by Jameson simply as notably "postmodern"). Together, then, the sculptural mass and the painterly vista cohabit the field of exhibition as two compromised and displaced versions of the thing itself, natural formation: one in 3-D dirt by a minimalist sculptor, one in 2-D oil by Albert Bierstadt from the Romantic archive of the nineteenth-century Hudson River School.

Joining those two "instances" of the American landscape in mounded earthwork site and oil-painted hilly scene—say its trace and its representation, index and icon—is thus the third sign function in classic semiotics, an arbitrary symbolic text. In this inner sanctum of museal space, then, deconstructed architecture houses the sculptural, the pictorial, and the literary in a way that lets the signature postmodernism of the last seem almost—Jameson doesn't quite say this—to "textualize" the whole furnished space, in the interplay of its ensemble, as a discursive network.[12] In the resulting mock *summa* of the sibling arts, rivalry is leveled to their

reflexive common denominator, with meaning emergent only in the rico-
chets among these selected instances of medial activity, not in the made or
shaped things themselves. Such is the clinching point of Jameson's broad-
gauged assessment. Under postmodernism, "the traditional fine arts are
mediatized" (160, emphasis added), since "they now come to consciousness of themselves as various media within a mediatic system in which
their own internal production also constitutes a symbolic message and
the taking of a position on the status of the medium in question" (160).
Even (and especially) Conceptual art must form its ideas from within the
preconceptions of media, operating therefore "from a place not above the
media but within their system of relationships: something it seems better
to characterize as a kind of reflexivity rather than the more conventional
notion of 'mixed media'" (162). Modernism's involuted purist watch-
word has become postmodernism's convoluted byword: reflexivity without
specificity; transpeciation, as it were; the "mediatic" per se. Yet this last is
a category that has undergone a notable evolution since Jameson wrote.
More and more often, the "mediatic" has come to be materialized in the
transmedial features of given composite works that may be said, if only
locally and ad hoc, to have *resystematized* their own medial contexts—and
often in an media-archaeological fashion quite foreign to the ahistorical
settings Jameson examines.

To account for the ethos as well as the aesthetic of such production, this
book is drawn to works of inbuilt media history that serve to reprocess
the longer traditions they variously raid, honor, empty, or replenish. What
we'll be focusing on, then, is often the diametrical opposite of medium
specificity—yet along a shared material axis—in works fully preoccupied
with the nature and grain of aesthetic means but without being moved to
occupy, disclose, and valorize only one at a time. That's the *trans* in play.
Other going terms point elsewhere, even when apposite both to this new
mode of Conceptual practice and to its avant-garde lineage. *Remediation* is
a technological function. *Mixed media* is a material description. *Multimedia* is cross-modal amalgamation. *Intermedia* is a disciplinary framework.
Within their orbit, *transmedium* names instead a materialized idea in process, a reversible vector of recognition. The transmedial object, as a kind
of open system, renders this idea, this inferred correlation, immanent in
a given work's own admixture of modes. Such manifestation, it is worth
repeating, is so far from medium-specific as to be—and on two or more
counterpoised fronts at once—*diversely* media-specifying. As distinct from
what is designated as "transmedial" or "multimedial" practice, the works
of Conceptualism 2.0 we'll be exploring locate a more integrated (if still

unsettled) effect instead, both in execution and recognition.[13] Call it a triangulation from within, entailing the reciprocal traverse of overlapping substrates—whether materially present or merely conjured under erasure. In either case, as too often minimized in "post-medium" theory, these invoked substrates are more than instrumental or material supports; they are the work's structuring function, its conceptual architecture, its explicitly manifold interfacial template. Here, one might say, is an art that singles out its inferences by pluralizing their process from within its own coordinated display. The result is a transitive materialization of effect whose object is precisely the art of such rethought composite manifestation, such cross-grained integral transaction. But a new term is deserved only if there are indeed "transmedium objects" out there worthy of the name, deserving some such efforts of taxonomy or at least comparative investigation as expended in the coming pages, and repaying the categorical attention thus bestowed—whether in art-historical or media-theoretical terms, or both. We'll have to see.

But you yourself don't have to wait. What is "preliminary" in this section is not its necessary prelude to illustration but its consideration of those inner liminalities—or again technical before social interfaces—from which a given work is conceptually generated. If one wants an initial dose of exemplification, that reader may go straight to the crowded Scene One of still-image works—dynamized along their transmedial paths of back-and-forth recognition—and then return later to these early pages for premises, art-historical contexts, and speculative horizons.

[concept::dual]

Conceptualism redux—wired or otherwise—is the topic. But where does one think to find it—and then how does one think with it when one does? How is duality its very concept? Or sometimes, beyond the twofold, a further multiplicity? Transmedial works are often devised so that oblique conjunctions of more canonical museum technique arise in various ways to quiz the image before us. The manifold can at times seem like a duel for priority in recognition. In the face of such experiments, even when works of ink on paper, the image is not so much drawn—or drawn out—for us; rather, the idea dawns. Slapdash newsprint collages, complete with sectors of faded and paint-splattered photo-offset, that are in fact meticulous photomechanical simulations in recycled and hand-applied printer's ink. The video of a revolving Victorian thaumatrope that is in fact the digital simulation of such a precinematic optical toy. An abstract painting that is in fact a photograph of deskilled industrial paint coverage digitally printed on canvas. Such are made or taken images received in double-take. And nothing in this spectrum of surprise holds these effects to two dimensions—given a sculpted vase in experimental and contorted form that is in fact the 3-D digital "printout" of human sound waves in electrographic transcription.

But the cognitive splaying of a single planar display is more common. And no electronics need be involved for such mediations to keep conceptual company with that explicitly digital work whose inferences are thereby ramified across a broader swath of contemporary art practice. The transmedial is a category whose aesthetic exceeds its technics. Sometimes works can seem to implode medial assumptions in ways that are not just pre-electronic but premechanical. An enlarged photo negative that is in fact an illusionist exercise in two-tone acrylic paint. Word/image collages that are in fact painted replicas of the celluloid interstices between advertising text and "illustration" in old-fashioned movie trailers. Such twofoldness is widespread on our current gallery walls—and to each of these foregoing provocations, as to all the rest anticipated up front here, we will be returning by title, maker's name, and the analytic rumination they incur.

Incitations to second-thought sighting are rampant in these and other such works, and not least in explicitly new media platforms. Famous paintings and photographs in low-resolution pixelated blow-ups that are in fact 10,000 separate and visually unrelated Web-sourced increments each. A video simulation of a striated abstract expressionist canvas, all vertical color bars like an electronically generated Gene Davis painting, that is in fact a computer dilation of the pixel tints that would ordinarily composite the DVD reissue of a commercial color film. High-resolution but out-of-focus wall-wide photographs that are, on approach, in fact brazenly pixelated enlarged jpegs of international violence captured from the Internet. The almost cinema-scale blow-up of a grainy analog TV image that is in fact a woodcut print. The "in fact" of all these self-correcting perceptions is exactly what measures the distance that such teasing works of on-site (re)conceptualization are meant to close. And just that closing up, that optical wising up, marks the transit across medial assumptions that delineates this book's attention. Often distant kin (or even close cousin) to classic trompe l'oeil, still many of these works do not so much trump the eye as trope perception itself as contingently mediated, indeterminate, epistemologically slippery, and entirely a matter of the viewer's stance, distance, glance, and ocular presuppositions. In such "twofoldness," the "in fact" writes itself out—one level up in the abstraction of response—as the more dialectical "either/or" in palpable transit to a perceptual "both/and."

What you see and what you "get" (inferentially) tend therefore to diverge in these conceptualist effects. Even on the near side of a medium's patrolled limits, formal features once tending to shore up an art work in categorical terms no longer hold firm. The result is that many aesthetic events seem reconfigured from within by an alternate but incorporated set of technical coordinates. These works seem, that is, transmediated. Such aesthetic events do not transgress borders; they ingest their own alternatives. It's a question of definition, as usual. But the art in these cases does the initial questioning and categorizing work for itself. That's what's conceptual about it. That's the new art's *work*: a matter of how these constructs arrange to *objectify* (exemplify for consideration) their own medial determinates, materialize them in the very process of their collaborative application. Yet they don't speak entirely for themselves—or set exclusively their own terms. As I began taking notes on these gallery surprises, one after the other, I found that to pinpoint the accomplishment of such optical procedures and ocular reversals, and give full weight to their own ambition, a broader spectrum of aesthetic mediality and its manipulations was called for. The latest experiments may in this way help rethink the very tradition they outstrip, the assumptions they repurpose. That's part of what they are there to reconceptualize: medium itself surveyed anew in the rear-view framework of "new media" formations and their trans-actional open circuits.

[support::system]

The emergent axis of comparison, then, is between the particular transmedial interplay inherent to quite different modes of presentation and display, whether audio/visual (cinematic), plastic (both painterly and sculptural), ambiguously photo/graphic, or more recently, let us say, pix-illusory. That's the axis. But the reason for the comparison is, first of all, the conceptual charge this level of apprehension distributes across various media engagements—and cognitive entanglements. The *idea* of the medial support is certainly as ubiquitous now, though no longer so narrowly insistent, as at the height of modernist self-reflexivity in painting. Yet it is a productive idea only if and when it helps think through, and then past, its immediate objectification in a single artifact. Only when it conceptualizes the systemics of aesthetic mediation itself. Time and again there is a sensed transit, turned contrast, between medial conditions that gets engineered from within the coordinated and sometimes deceptive materiality of the works in question—works, that is, putting their own means in question. So this book isn't a genre study, but more like a platform study. Rather than being aimed exclusively at new medial transfusions, it takes a longer view of (from within its closer look at) the whole enterprise of medial experiment. Ex-surrealist poet Marcel Broodthaers, in his installation and film work from the 1970s, and certain postmillennial digital artists are recognized here to be speaking the same discourse in different languages. Gerhard Richter's out-of-focus photorealism in oil, from the 1960s and 1970s, and works of video simulation in diverse graphic media, pencil or woodcut, share a certain syntax of reception in different material lexicons.

What therefore begins to sort out certain electronically inflected or ironized works into the category I'm calling Conceptualism 2.0 isn't predominantly their computerized aspect in itself, as in the commercial vernacular for second-generation technological upgrades like Web 2.0. What's decisive, instead, is the way these diverse works (internally divergent in their medial orientation) build on the resisted expectations and displaced visual procedures of the original postwar conceptual turn in museum practice. Stress falls on what new media have newly—and sometimes with shrewd results—helped artists draw into the open about mediation all told, as well as on what these latest medial operations have helped a viewer formulate about composite ocular and conceptual experience in works of an earlier vintage. The topic at hand, then, the issue at eye's reach, isn't the repurposing of one medium by another into which it disappears. That's ubiquitous, and well accounted for. We've learned long ago to call it "remediation."[14] Nor, even in the most unabashed and involuted cases of illusionism, is this book's topic mainly the *representation* (rather than functional incorporation) of one medium by another. The issue is instead, and visible only to varying degrees, the co-*production* of art by simultaneous medial systems—and more centrally yet, a co-*conception* of the resulting artifacts across medial platforms.

This is a matter, first of all, of reception—before a more materialist inquest into execution. In simply looking long enough, of course, you may "get it"—or not. Yet often more is needed—and seeded—in the gallery presentation of such manifold artifacts. There is certainly no underestimating the explicitly discursive parameters for many such works. I mentioned a moment ago how the latest transmedial objects may have "helped a viewer formulate" the work's own art-historical vantage. But they just as often require considerable "formulation" of their own motives in advance: explanation, decoding—even decryption seems at times more like it. On wall or flyer or catalog page, this can involve extensive ancillary notes of explication, both as regards a deliberately obscured process and even its inferred aesthetic purpose. Sensed here is a kind of 2.0 Conceptualist irony in the genealogy of abstraction from paint to paratext.[15] Long after overcoming the creed, turned cult, of medium specificity under the banner of abstract expressionism, certain art practice has evolved so that its own complexities of internal differentiation have grown in their own way occulted, optically abstracted, in the very process of their cognition, requiring technical as well as intentionalist glossing. Such is the front-loaded neoconceptual discourse in which a study like this can only strive, with further contributed reflections, to participate.

As you've gathered at a glance, the present book is an experiment in the conjured inferences of visual art mostly without its images, to say nothing of audiovisual installations without their sounds. In a roundabout way, this suits the tendency it surveys. (Even the inserted folio is more an optical table of contents than a sparse gallery of highlights.) The book proceeds, that is, not in the predominant absence of such images exactly, but in that conceptual space where, even *in situ*, their picturing or audition grows figurative for something else. Requiring explanatory captioning to make itself known, this extra something is often released between media substrates or platforms not so much in synthesis as (to use a verbal metaphor) in dialogue. As on-site glosses may suggest, such works are in themselves discursive—because conceptual. And by "on-site" I mean on website as well. But the fact that every image or installation I reference for discussion is by now available on-line—I've double-checked—is not some mere excuse for a mostly unillustrated prose and a more affordable monograph. The ekphrastic effort of these pages is a heuristic exercise in deciphering rather than derivative picturing. The tactically suspended sense of what we are seeing in these conceptual works, even face to face, often marks their ironic management of just that flood of manifest "data" otherwise netted (in its contrasting blatancy) by new media technology. The patient articulation of response—indeed the *process* of one's response—takes due precedence over the potentially abbreviating convenience of visual reprint (where you wouldn't necessarily recognize from a still image, anyway, what was "going on" beneath the surface in its transmedial pressures). For all the visual or audiovisual fascination of these material devisings, it is fair to say that sheer discourse still has a way of responding to their provocations in kind. Let's hope the reader, of these pages as well as those objects, agrees—or, better, sees it (sees them, sometimes hears them) this way. Indeed, when moved to flip between page and website, you are only replaying the gallery experience of finding these images framed for you by extensive discourse in wall text or catalog.

[process::art]

With the object being art, then, how are the differences of mediation kept in play to this end? That is the ongoing line of inquiry. It's hard enough to phrase the question properly, let alone answer it decisively. That's why I have settled upon the aptly unsettled grammar of my title, which, again, leaves behind the security of a noun form to operate as a variable modifier, naming both a material configuration and a sensory response. To be sure, the first reason why that all this is compelling is because it is: work by work, many notable pieces as fascinating as they may at first seem baffling, as suggestive as initially congested in their effects. With remarkable variety across a potentially leveling "mediatic" environment, such art vests its own interest as we look—as we take it in, take on its implications. The reason for writing about it, however, lies elsewhere, just to the side of its ingenuity, its often minimalist captivation, and its curious demands. Some writing, yes, is often required by it in explanation, right there be-side it on wall or catalog page—at least in the most complicated of such constructions. But more than this, responsive writing—discourse—is an answered interpretive expectation of the works themselves, the final stage of their process, their processing. Where Conceptualism 1.0, in its militant deskilling of art, strove in part to democratize art's function through the medium of pure discourse, in Conceptualism 2.0, by contrast, many works of technological density and sophistication—or works at least evoking the elusive world of computerized electronics, virtuality, and the mobile simulacrum—are reskilled in a different way to exclude from any easy grasp of their mastery the viewing subject they at the same time tutor back to recognition.[16] Where early wall works of Conceptual art could seem like deliberately arid footnotes to a subtracted visual display, certain experiments in the mode of Conceptual 2.0 would go begging for comprehension without some kind of extensive footnote. Further writing about these works is, therefore, part of their strange pedagogy. And other lessons are learned in the process, about less technically complex but no less multiplex works of mediation and display.

Such is the broad new curatorial curriculum in which any serious attention to these conceptual objects and machinations finds itself enrolled—and where, on a single museum syllabus, one encounters divergent works of zany electronic intricacy as well as meticulous artisanal craft. Such different productions, the latter often conceived in derivative if skeptical light of the former, are found grappling in their own complementary ways with the same reconfigured questions of image, index, retinal legibility, and display in a culture of electronic saturation. The invitation, sometimes the more aggressive incitation, is, as stressed in the "Overture," to *think transmedium*—across convergent purposes—from one material ground or field to another. Not as one might exist transgender or reside nationally transplanted or mobilize for political action transrace—but in a manner speculative and internally reversible, comparative, reciprocally indeterminate: a conceptual transposition initiated from within the material disclosures of the single (if not, again, singularly mediated) work.

Electronically inflected or "ironized," was it, several paragraphs back? How so? Verbal irony: saying one thing and meaning another. Visual irony: showing one thing while asking us to see another—to see through the manifest image plane to some other dimension of its visibility. In this respect, Conceptualism 2.0 has returned a decided imagistic prominence to the art object within the implicit discourse of its manifestation. This amounts to a retinal intensity withdrawn in good measure from the earliest 1960s and 1970s production in a conceptualist mode. It thereby constitutes a certain reversal in the work of denaturalization, whose lineage is important to bear in mind. In the first wave of Conceptual art, the most influential characterization of such an aesthetic agenda—regarding its negative thrust against a late-modernist medium purity—was the sense of conceptual works as "dematerialized."[17] Not strictly true, of course—since they had to consist of something. But true in categorical effect. The materiality of a received medium was no longer what came first to view in the space of exhibition—even when kept uppermost in mind by way of its removal. Dematerialized at least in regard to the canonical sense of medium-determined, then, what in many conceptualist works was *posited* by any such *negativity* was, as we know, an ideational (rather than idealist) notion of aesthetics. This was a notion involved first of all in a discourse of reception, institutional as well as cognitive and epistemological, rather than bent on some insistent denigration of matter. In this sense Duchamp was certainly the forebear and model. There's nothing dematerialized about his 1917 urinal, by *Fountain* or any other name. Just something funny about calling it art, about "installing" it not as a plumber would, but as a curatorial intervention.

So, again: a function twofold and conceptual in its irony, *[concept::dual]*. But even art's militant occupancy of a valorized perceptual field (like abstract painting) might recognize an inward strain in its own purist logic, one in which substrate and visual effect, material and application, are, though inseparable, still far from identical. Put it that, under canonical auspices, only certain materials "support" the category of "art." Such is the complex ideological *[support::system]*, when congealed in a narrowly institutionalized aesthetic, that is under what we might call *notional* (but not dematerialized) attack and travesty by Duchamp. With all such interlaced registers, my habitual double punctuation in the itemization of subtopics is, as already suggested, meant to put some further space between terms beyond the normal use of the colon for appositional restatement, let alone the hyphen for stable admixture. The twinned colons are inserted here to be more differentiating than the traditional i.e. of "that is" or "namely," more than the placeholder for a second wind of restatement. This typographic turnstile (turned reversible vector) marks, instead, a mutual interplay and recalibration, a conceptual transit back and forth across medial determinants. The material "support," for instance, is not just part of art's "system"; the system is part, not least when parodied, of a given work's reconceived (and often plural) support. This is because art's definition-in-progress is often a deliberate switchback of *redefinition*. As with *[process::art]* here and *[equip::mentation]* next, designation is caught on the cusp of a materialized ideation, reverbing between schema and technique.

[equip::mentation]

Though variably obvious from case to case, what in general the squaring-off of my double colons is meant to implant for eventual discussion is indeed captured by the square brackets, as well, that set them off as if in a loosely containing frame. Full explication will arrive only with the four-point graphing of such give-and-take when conceived on the model of the semiotic square. But there before us all the time will have been the format par excellence—when imagined diagonally vectored—of a structuralist dialects in this mode: in short, [::]. In art criticism, the most influential appearance of this analytic template is in Rosalind Krauss's *cognitive* and theoretical regridding of the high modernist grid itself, where she identifies the mode of logical analysis as the Klein group, but stresses her debt to Jameson's use of it (designated by him as the Greimasian square) in *The Po-*

litical Unconscious.[18] For Krauss it maps the eponymous *Optical Unconscious* of her study. For us, it will help foreground the material unconscious—or, say, the split subconstituencies—of transmedial operation.

In brief and in prospect, then, such squaring discerns a structural logic behind certain representational manifestations and their superficial polarities. In Krauss's application, the foursquare breakdowns of such methodology (to which we will return in "Endscape") are what permit her deconstruction of the figure/gound binary into those balked representational habits supplanted by an assertive modernist grid. This is the gridwork that, in its refusal of picture, is neither one nor the other: neither figure nor ground. For us ahead, at a level one notch more materialist in its coordinates, any worrying of the founding dichotomy between material and image must also confront not just their consolidation in the both/and of the proferred artifact. Analysis must engage, as well, the "double negation" resulting from the neither/nor of twofold contradiction in respect to some foundational medial (or transmedial) preconditions.[19] Parallax again. Neither a confessed material process nor a reified artwork defines the poles of conceptual response to certain exploratory conjunctures (as located in the top axis of the logical square). Rather, attention must probe to the double negation involved in grasping the neither/nor of transmediation itself (in its bottom axis of logical dichotomy). When actual graphic diagrams of this squaring process appear at the end of this book, by then they will have fuller evidence to illustrate—and illuminate. En route, the four-pointed paired colons are intended to keep this complex dichotomization in something like a collapsed linear (rather than geometric) view—and recurrently in mind. Along this very route, an earlier epistemological priority is thus encountered in a new and often electronic key: conception above execution. This is elicited especially by works in which one function of image engineering (*imageering*) may disrupt another, rub it the wrong way, abrade the channels of transmission, produce the static of stasis itself in the moving image, disarticulate seemingly found images into their thumbnail aggregates, simulate photography and video by other means, cross-weave VHS and HDTV images in their variant grain and resolution, or loosen the very apparatus of cinematic projection to the sheer beam and flow of light.

Why? I mean: what motivates this tendency of thought in so much recent art practice? Why do so many works probe in this way to the inner rather than outer limits of manifestation or transmit: those moments that, folded back on themselves, confront either their own potential or impasse in an interface with some alternate (though often simultaneous) system of mediation? In this sense, it is precisely by their not being tightly delimited according to the tenets of medium specificity that they assert their true internal liminality. Examples to come divide between static configurations generated from convergent operational platforms on the one hand and, on the other, kinetic imagery somehow conceptually cross-wired between medial expectations for the moving image, whether mechanical, electronic, or both. In the two phases of their deviance, the works characterizing these paired Scenes are rendered up—such indeed is their *[techno::logic]*—so as to revise, separately and together, all staid notions of picture gallery and picture show alike, including at times the very etymology of auditorium.

By this point in the dovetailing of aesthetic and technological history, then, the former epithet "dematerialized" has little place in either the artisanal or electronic modes of Conceptualism 2.0. Materiality is not dismissed here but investigated. Investigated and cross-referenced—yet not always according to immediately obvious commonalities. What did 1960s photorealism, for instance, in the cool vehemence of its craftsmanship, have to do with, or have to say to, the Conceptual art that proliferated around it in the antithetical deskilling of gallery practice? How could the two together, in recovered dialogue, speak to works based on the equivocation of actual photographic indexicality, digital and otherwise, that have flourished since? And how might the anti-cinema of the same early Conceptual art period, in the 16mm montage of a multimedia provocateur like Marcel Broodthaers, illuminate the kinetic platform work of new media video artists? Or give us, farther afield (but within a related optical system), a useful framework for coming to terms with the projected light sculpture of Anthony McCall, the latter's work being first filmic, now (much later) digital? Then, too, by what logic do early ventures in a black-and-white photorealist blur in the oil work of an artist like Gerhard Richter both foster and inform his own recent computerized analysis (and resultant digital repicturing) of an intervening abstract canvas from the middle years of his oeuvre?

Diachronic and dialectical at once, such questions are rhetorical only in the sense that they inquire into the rhetoric of the image systems under deployment in such works. Given what Vija Celmins sets out to accomplish in miniaturist ink, acrylic, or oil and, three decades later, what Christiane Baumgartner returns to in overscale woodcuts—each proceeding to isolate, denature, and reconceive the TV or video image, including its latent or overt violence—how could these *optical allusions to* (and illusions of) the broadcast image fail to resonate with each other at a level of conceptual irony intrinsic to their separate mediums but clarified together in triangulation with predigital screen transmission? Why wouldn't the pixelated break-up of the monumental jpeg photographs of Thomas Ruff, playing between cyber input and archival imprint, inevitably bear comparison with the intermittent sampling, in digital freeze frames, from the continuous webcam streams of Wolfgang Staehle? Or to put the case most strongly, because negatively: take Catalan photographer Joan Fontcuberta's career-long work in the epistemology of the automatic image, from cameraless photograms to his current digital ingenuities and internet composites. If these images do not speak to the exacting but deliberately lackluster painterly trompe l'oeils of LA artist Paul Sietsema, including some simulated photo negatives, all of them minimalist and reflexive, as well as to Sietsema's digitally untinged 16mm films (the two chief modes between which his work alternates, each in its own way transmedial), then wouldn't the very Concept of such artists' separate investigations be less compelling than otherwise? Wouldn't such efforts then be caught up in the hermetic ironies of their individual agendas rather than penetrating from distinct material practices to a common stratum of contemporaneous inquiry? Looking at such separate enterprises together is, at the very least, a way of seeing each anew. Any one of them may seem to epitomize the logic of a tendency and a trend. Enough such works, I am trusting, make for a claim, an argument, not ultimately bound to their particular descriptions or limited by their example.

The works in (and under) question are often revealingly codependent even when not manifestly code-dependent. Often they negotiate their imaging somewhere quite explicitly between superseded and dominant platforms—even if cast back, as if by analogy with present upheavals, to some earlier moment of technological transition. Synthesis isn't always the point, but antithesis doesn't explain the inbuilt tension either. Such works are not just half photochemical, for instance, while half digital; nor is it a matter, when moving images are concerned, of the videographic and the cinematographic by clear turns. The execution of such works is not just poised against alternate paradigms, but stretched *between*: a difference made immanent.

[trans::ception]

These works, one comes to sense, are best grasped—odd though it sounds—as *intercepting themselves* in their material specifications, often by way of exposing a gaping discrepancy. This is where definition can only come forth from the press of evidence, and where terminological discriminations, broached earlier, can be further shored up. "Transmedial" emerges as category by sheer distinction—to set it off from other "impure" modes, already mentioned above, in the modern history of art. "Mixed media" art, by contrast, puts one material next to or above (nonhierarchically) another, as flagged by title in a 2013 show at the Hirshhorn: "Over, Under, Next." Here was a comprehensive exhibit on just that: superimposition, underlay, and adjacency in hybrid forms, from Cubist photo-collage forward. In another terminology, "intermedial art," as suggested, like interdisciplinary scholarship, applies one method in view of or alongside another, relational more than conflationary. What, instead, I am calling transmedial practice more actively *pictures the difference*: negotiates it, traverses it. The *trans* functions, as we may now sense, much like the prefix in the etymology of metaphor as *trans-fer*: putting something across by crossing between registers.[20]

Operating neither in "no medium" (Dworkin's focus) nor in an immediately familiarized new one, such work hovers between, recalibrates, analyzes. In any effort at tracking the convergent terms of such practice, it grows more and more obvious that anything like definition must be left to the interpenetrating functions of each piece in turn. Only inquiry is called for, not advance categorization: an attention that waits on the particular details laid bare for comparison in the unique axis of transmedial reflection involved from work to work. Given their ancestry in Conceptualism 1.0, the hoary questions of "purity" or "essence" are addressed in such art, rather than dismissed, by the hyperspecific internal contrast of reciprocal liminalities. Another way to see this—if one is really looking—as well as to say it: whereas mixed media projects are everywhere, and often perfunctory in their material interplay, transmedium works, in a concerted force field of their own, are instead defined from within by pressures of the *inmixed*.[21]

But how, when encountering such transmedial works, is materiality to be registered as meaningful rather than just a means? Or coming at this question from the reverse direction: how is mediality made *material to* conception? A writer very far removed from the media-historical instinct that animates my "reading" of these artifacts has in fact a distanced view of aesthetic formalization that is particularly instructive in this regard. German social philosopher and Systems theorist Niklas Luhmann stresses the materiality of any medium in question, with form being what particularizes it into visibility as such: "The material is allowed to appear as material; it does not merely resist the imprint of form."[22] Say: rather than resist, it *takes* form, and as such becomes, again, material to the artwork's recognized effect. "Whatever serves as medium becomes form once it makes a difference," which is to say, for Luhmann, with his emphasis on communications networks rather than human expressivity, "once it gains an information value owing exclusively to the work of art" (109). Exclusively—or say: specifically.

Narrowly distinguishing medial ingredients from formative inflections of the art object in this nuanced way, through the *informative* circuit of its communicative address, can help us sense what is at stake and at play—and at reciprocal self-variance—in transmedial operations. For this is where collaborating materialities may be found to *inform on each other*. Revising Luhmann, then, for the special circumstances of such cross-specificity, let us say that whatever serves to distinguish *between* media becomes a formal element in this particular respect only at the point when, by doing more than just make a difference, it makes a particular, ingrained difference come to view. At which point, in the still-oscillating zone of optical support rather than retinal image, we would find configured something like the *[material::manifestation]* dialectic—rudiment of any conversionary *[material::means]* semiotics. And we would, at the same time, find articulated the conceptual interface operating in so many of the images and visual constructions taken up in these pages. When a particular work is sensed as actively crossing between alternate substrates rather than just alternate manifestations as image, then one may intuit its productive double negation: neither one medium nor its obvious contrary. And there may locate, in turn, the often ironic *content of its form*—the inference of its platforms—in generating exactly the transmedial seesaw, or whiplash, in question. In this sense, something like a given *[techno::logic]* can get processed as the meaning rather than the mere manifestation of its own instrumentation or technique, and with the retrospective history of such mediality very much in mind.[23]

[skeuo::morphography]

And that rearward glance, it should be added, has quite other manifestations outside of gallery space. In fact, the transmedial irony often entailed by such ingrown historicism can be usefully considered as the direct conceptual opposite of "skeuomorphic" commercial design. That term names the process, in a thinly McLuhanesque way, that makes the conjured form of the old medium into a sign for the accessible content of the new: as when a cellphone photo icon is, for instance, fashioned to resemble a standard camera with extended lens, or the "Windows Photo Viewer" is designed to recall the four-cornered insert tabs of old-fashioned photographic albums.[24] And beyond the explicit "skeuomorph" or retro icon—think, here too, of the play or pause "button" on a computer screen operated only by the lateral slither of a strictly metaphoric "mouse"— the transmedial reflex is even more broadly to be distinguished from a blanket culture of remediation. Digital transfers of theatrical 35mm film allow its images, of course, to screen alternately on home TV or by way of digital projection in a theater auditorium or to be downloaded on a tablet (another skeuomorphic term from scriptive culture). Same with the chip camera image, which can be screened, streamed, attached, Instagrammed, or digitally printed. These are transports across platforms, yet they don't make the image itself transmedial, but only its imagined (rather than actual) use. The two-dimensional commonality of canvas and tablet scarcely exhausts their description, nor does the loosely shared nomenclature of brushstroke and keystroke. The works ahead are entangled in a more deliberated formal systemics. To which one might rightly give the name *[plat::formatics]*.

The skeuomorph has certainly seen its heyday in the "remediations" incident to computerization and its "convergent" platforms. This book is written not in objection to the concept of "convergence culture" in popular media studies, which as a technological fact is incontestible, but written, rather, in contemplation of art objects posed against such indifferentiation: works that inscribe the gap between systems rather than leap it invisibly.[25] Under the aegis of convergence, posited as a clear mercantile imperative, computerization may properly refer away questions of medial essence to matters of platform or format, when in fact these materialities locate only one stratum of the pervasive (and entirely extra-aesthetic) condition shared by art and everyday mass culture in the age of blanket digitization. This is just the leveling condition, moreover, that art may in fact define itself as meant to refigure, allegorize, parry, or even gainsay.

The claim for convergent delivery systems does, after all, go only so far—especially when seen in media-archaeological terms. Cinema is not reducible to photography just because each was once mechanical in registration, chemical in processing, immediately monetized, and is now equally digitized. Cinema was born of this earlier shared condition, but was no less able to outgrow its photographic rudiments than was photography to imagine cinema's pending ingredients (like off-frame space)—and even to evoke the staggered chronographic phases of filmic motion from within its own time-calibrated but still-frame apparatus. Earlier yet in media history, just because photography and painting involve one-sided and two-dimensional picture planes, this didn't (and doesn't) prevent them—though sharing at times certain phenomenological horizons—from retaining and enhancing a carefully guarded realm of separate constitution and mastery. Distinctions keep asserting—inserting—themselves.

Audiobooks on disk, for instance, may be every bit as digitally delivered as an e-reader, but there is still a difference between listening and the outer silence of phonetic reading. It is a difference that no skeuomorphic recourse to "book" culture—digital page-turning or dog ears, simulated binding, and so forth—can entirely erase. Alternately, operating in reverse, the digital files generating mass-print fiction may be recruited by bibliographic craft—and medial tropology (recently dubbed "metamedial mimesis"[26])—to simulate, for instance, some earlier mode of imperfectly aligned and pitted lead typesetting. Viewed outside of its aesthetic context in experimental fiction, such an allusive typographic gesture could be thought to constitute yet another skeuomorphic domestication of page file by pictured sheet, impress simulated by computerized ink-jet. Skeuomorph: the (etymological) "tool-shape" of some operable function in the simulation of its obsolete predecessor—like (for further examples) the ring binder on a computer's desktop calendar, to say nothing of the term "desktop" itself, or the splutter of video interference on a DVD chapter menu for a film about either television anchormen or NSA surveillance, or theater curtains for the scene selections of a backstage movie musical, or for that matter the very term "scroll" for the arrow function of a movie's more particular searching in uploaded and fast-forwarded form. The metal siding on the so-called woody stationwagon, with it faux artisanal look, is a classic example, wagonizing the covered vehicle by simulation as well as nomenclature.

Although a technical term from product design, nonetheless the skeuomorph has immediate resonance, so we've started to see, for a certain range of strictly materialist intertextuality rather than actual engineering features. The very format of skeuomorphic remediation—in false etymology, skewing one medium toward another—is itself, loosely enough applied, a latent transmedial point of entry.[27] For now, it is enough to think of the skeuomorphic model as either the reductio ad absurdum or the halfway house of transmedial stucturation. To make visible—to emblemize, to iconize—the relation of present manifestation, however facile that relation in commercial forms, to its precursor or prototype: that is the gesture. Yet for a clear distinction between the functionalist and the formalist mode, so to say, of "retro" iconography, recall, from the

"Overture," Fox Talbot's wry turn (inversion) on his new photo processing when its mechanical imprint was conceived as an update of Gutenberg's textual impress. In his mirror reversal of *Imitation of Printing.*, the long glance back over technology's shoulder is not a concession to ease of use but a deeply probed common ground. In the broadest terms, as applied at times in the pages ahead, the skeuomorphic effect is conceived to bring into the new function (or, alternately here, aesthetic effect) the vestigial symbols of a former workability (or mode of art work). When this allusion to past functionality is no longer part of a serviceable remediation, but is instead depurposed and introjected as an aesthetic gesture—tendering not pictograms of utility but an integral grammar of concept—the history of imaging is read in the image less as a kernel of actionable recognition (click here!) than as an inferred cross-weave of perceptual cues. Once again, in their strain and estrangement rather than facilitation: their new object, art.[28]

[art::works]

It is upon such a surcharged field of crisscrossed modeling and transformation—where the work of art is the work it *does* in regard to its own conditions—that we now enter along an inevitably selective, but I trust suitably representative, trajectory. Scene One opens upon the precincts of single-frame imaging and its mutations in various planar (and sometimes screen) surfaces. Scene Two then raises a curtain on the moving image similarly reconceived. Across each phase of investigation, the comparative transit *between* impacted presentational composites serves repeatedly to alert us to the intriguing medial palimpsest—or kinetic transit—*within* them. Cued by such gestures of material inquest, one finds that the keenest interest of the examples gathered up rests with their broader exemplarity. Their transmedial effects are at once deeply dredged, inquisitive, and edgy. Whether cross-wired in a new media vein or simply unsettled in their cognitive grooves, such works have obdurately forestalled their own material and conceptual predetermination. Which is, after all, simply another way of characterizing the object art.

I referred, awhile back, to recent theoretical efforts to "conceive mediation in the abstract." Yet, truth be told, mediation has often grown *too* abstract in this discourse to recognize as such, too socially determined as well as obviously determining. This one may sense even in the emphasis on "context," on social framework, in the definitions of Dworkin and

Foster with which we began—though not so much in the close-grained execution of their analysis. Abstraction often holds sway, as well, in the work of other critics and theorists (Luhmann already included) to whom we'll later be turning. This gauge of mediation tends, if at the propositional level only, to back away from texture to contexture in a way pointedly resisted by the artworks themselves in their labor with materiality. They operate, therefore, in something of a pronounced, if productive, vacuum. Under reigning disciplinary paradigms, with media or medium now defined first of all as transactional, if not explicitly interactive, any baseline understanding of the mediatory has become dominantly communal in its bearings: transferential, maybe, but in the sense of an interpersonal and largely monetized "exchange." Vehicular rather than intrinsic: a medium more *for* than *of*. This book looks instead to artists who recover the materiality of imaging from within the broad modern traffic in image culture. Stressing the mediality itself of media, they do so by a *trans*-action that precedes and vexes reception rather than becoming just another name for it in the trans-port (and new electronic portals) of image relay as social commerce. Art of this disposition tends, for instance, to relocate new media's interface study within the mediatic reflex of a given *objet* or installation that has gone to work on its own (I repeat) *systemic specifications*. Which is where, and on terms however slowly emerging from a given work (together with its paratexts), any aesthetic response must try to encounter the effect in question. And precisely in the "context" of other works relevantly like it.

But the widespread and variable parameters of that relevance also need anticipation here. This is because, for example, the first extended demonstration of a low-tech transmedial initiative—after a brief look at certain high-tech curiosities in the sculptural objects of 3-D printing—comes in Scene One with the simulated 2-D remediated print work known as photorealist painting. Neither computer-derived nor computer-driven, as contrasted with so many later works in the vein of Conceptualism 2.0, this mode of postmodern craft may seem so low-profile in its cross-medial force that it is merely a case of taking photography as a facilitating adjunct and intertext for painting. It is that, but more. And that more is paradigmatic for the subsequent category under proposal here. If mediation's latest theorists understand mediums as the operation or analysis—rather than concretized instance—of material relations in an interlinked social context, and therefore never detachable from present use, never essentialized, this sense of "operational analysis" can extend to materials summoned but unworked by a given aesthetic venture. As is the nature of photography when called up in its translation to paint.

A particular medial interface may be either technically constitutive or merely conjured up by visual approximation. Photorealism as a genre of painting is perhaps the clearest case of this tacit and noninstrumental cross-reference, with its manifest but intangible return from effect to only probable cause: from painted exactitude to photographic model (whether or not an actual print image has in fact been enlarged, gridded, and projected over the canvas, as is often the case in the execution of such images). And so, though coterminous with the first resistant ingenuities of Conceptual art, photorealism's own holding action between mediations— or say its own *[photo::realist]* bracketing of technology and art-historical mode—anticipates more closely the inner dynamics of Conceptualism 2.0. In such work, on which the opening chapter will concentrate, painting transfers its "authority" to automatic record, as if by "citation" of the latter—and, in the process, spurs its own analysis of this transfer. In a more rudimentary mixed-media gesture, actual photographs plastered into an impasto might or might not trigger such analysis. Determinations here involve a kind of sliding scale. From the late 1980s and early 1990s, for example, Gerhard Richter's overpainted color photographs ("acrylic on photograph on board," one might generalize) certainly would count as an unexpected variant not just of mixed media but of transmedial experiment, yet the latter no more so than in the case of the same artist's "underpainted" (blurred) black-and-white images from the 1960s, the out-of-focus photorealism in paint alone for which he is more famous. This is to stress again that the inmixing of the image format in transmedial work can be either directly material or conceptually materialized, or sometimes both, and that its inferences come to the surface—however equivocated or variably colonized that surface may be—only under an analysis that the work's own internal (systemic) tension is the first to enact, to prosecute.

To prosecute, cross-question, invert, warp, disarticulate, what have you. Or in terms of reverse skeuomorphism: to *inconvenience* rather than naturalize and facilitate, making transmission pay its newly exorbitant way. Until you're not sure what you have in front of you. Or just why. I should certainly admit that what awaits reception in these chapters are case studies often so exacerbated in their fascination, so extreme, that their very service as *test* cases may seem limited. What intrigues us in their constitution turns more on their separate testing of inner limits than on some comparable fit with any prevailing model—except the unstinted mediacentric intensity of their renderings. Certainly their dialogue with other works is not always easy to overhear at first. That's what this book is there to audit: the tacit and building resonance among these knowing anomalies and one-offs. Yet despite this field of conceptual interplay, what is transmedial in their operation—it can't be overstressed, even when they are—remains internal to each work, systemic rather than programmatic. That alone is their guaranteed ground of comparison.

Transmedial "in their operation," yes—but, more broadly, in reflexive assessment of such operative procedures under a medial investigation not just interpretive but internal. So it is important to make plain at the outset, as motivating our pending return to photorealism in relation to the first phase of Conceptual art, that Conceptualism 2.0 in the examples here (as deliberately pliable as that categorization is advised to remain) is still only a subclass of transmediation—rather than, as it might sometimes appear, the other way around. For transmedium response is a disposition and a process, not a subgenre or a movement, let alone a "period style" or its high-tech revival.[29] Beginning with the work itself and its material valences, the idea of transmediation locates a structured habit of attention that can look not just *around* at what's out there by way of new transmissive functions, but *back* over art-historical evolution with new eyes for a former—if perhaps still formative—process in its defining conjunctures of manner or material. Initiated from within individual aesthetic composites, the transmedium outlook (or lookout) thus amounts, above all, to an analytic slant, an angle of perceptual uptake—a mode only in the sense of a posture of attention—in respect to the inmixed features, many of them computational lately, that might call it up. Such attention recognizes how the *content* per se of certain material conjunctures emerges as the very manner (in a vectorized sense again) of their *coming across*. With a majority of the fabrications awaiting us here, it is clear that a transmedium view, coached by the structure of the works themselves, offers the prevailing line of sight by which such experiments of Conceptualism 2.0 come into focus.

Inflected in this way by the gestures of Conceptualism 2.0, materiality does not just show forth in the seen, it *tells*. And within this further quotient of transmedial practice, it makes its mark more fully yet: it *argues*—and not just argues its own case but, in an almost ontological quarrel at times, contests other material and audiovisual incursions in a shared cultural surround. This is how its art works. To appreciate how *often*—on how many different fronts, across what an array of internal and shaping interfaces—is the task ahead. And the result of such scrutiny should make at least one art-historical tendency hard to ignore. For all the supposedly emancipatory energies of a widely vaunted "post-medium condition" in contemporary art practice, with its open field of materially unconstrained experiment, nonetheless certain rigorously investigative works turn inward upon their own convergent means or orientations in gestures that might rather be called *ultramedial*. The issue of medium, in short, doesn't vanish along with its former dictates and strictures. Intrinsic transmedial collisions spring its renewed—and intensified—aesthetic force.

Image Frames

CHAPTER ONE: *Hyperreal*

Spatially delimited versus time-based: that's the rough division that organizes our two Scenes. First the fixed picture (whether chemically fixed or just affixed to the wall) in the form of an image that won't stay put conceptually; then, in Scene Two, the moving luminescence that can at times put either picturing or motion, or both, up for debate. Although stasis within a hung frame may sometimes be as illusory as the fixed image (the "freeze") fabricated by the iterated frames of celluloid rotation, distinctions remain. We therefore take up the "single" picture first, however optically destabilized in presentation. The "image frames" of the Scene title can be photographic or painterly, pictorial (representational) or not, digital or hand-made. In a reception aesthetics, the image is as the image does—or, in Conceptualism 2.0, as it often undoes, by tricks of the eye electronically sourced or otherwise. Hence the plausibility of a zone of volatile, though still static, counterplay like *[image::frames]*, where the double colon would be lodged in this case to denaturalize an optical plane and unlatch it from its very demarcation—at least long enough, that is, to infer a subliminal transaction, a conceptual rebracketing in process. Transmedium notice would thereby identify the image *function*—its framing function, however composited and multiple, often reversible—that articulates a given retinal field as such, be it altered mirror or tricked canvas or elusive digital assemblage. In the grammar of such aesthetic attention, the substantive format turns to conceptual predication. Image frames in this sense, and reframes, more than it pictures.

Similarly, regarding the second Scene of this study, the double punctuation one might exert in a rubric like *[motion::captures]* would conjoin its terms so as to confront the reciprocal features of a medial interplay between fixity and process, often chemical fixity and motorized process. These are aspects brought together most often in the "moving picture" as traditionally conceived, but also in merely the moving of images—and sometimes in just the inching forward of light itself (as in Anthony Mc-

Call's installations), or elsewhere its seizing up in the jammed flickering still. And in another ocular syntax, sometimes motion captures not only a prerecorded event but even viewers themselves in motion. This happens as well in those transmedial though not programmatically interactive light sculptures, the "solid light films," of McCall (at once "drawn" and projected and, years after his first breakthrough works, now digitally edited): his rotating sheaves of beamed, misted, and viewer-encircling glow. Cinema, however, remains in his work, as we'll see, both the origin and the continuing touchstone—even when there are no longer any celluloid frames left at the point of beamed linear emanation. Yet the full transmedial effects (cinema / drawing / penetrable sculpture / performance) of such mobile traced light—without the moving image per se—will assume more clearly their place in a contemporary resistance to sheer display, along with many other 16mm and 35mm projections, once certain close cousins in graphic but not time-based practice have been contemplated within their arrested but variously equivocated frames of conceptual reference.

In moving first from recent and modestly photorealist image-texts by Ed Ruscha and Raymond Pettibon—about precisely the photographic increment of cinema—back to earlier canvases in a more full-blown "hyperrealist" mode, with its simulated automaticity of image, its faux-photography, we will be passing, for contrast, through a newer "realism" (or reality-manufacture) of indexical technique in the machinic simulacra that result from so-called 3-D printing in polymer accretion. For such is a process more deserving yet of that "hyper" intensifier: a whole new realm of the real in electronic contrivance. From a subsequent return to the procedures of photorealism, then, we move to work that excavates its own medial surface rather than exceeds it—and does so by probing *under* (*hypo*) the manifest to its contingent and often electronic gestation. But before this opening to the "hyporealm," undermining and predominantly ironic, we look to variations of the so-called hyperreal in ink and paint and even computer-sprayed plastic.

[movie::still]

Conceptualism 2.0 is, as noted, a conceptual before a technological category, an aesthetic stance influenced by latter-day platforms but not necessarily implementing them. Here is a second-wave conceptualism, then, legible as such even when unplugged. To make such a category clear when manifested in the still image and its quite explicit frame capture, we take up what one might call, in both senses, a motion-fixated example from the height of the digital moment. It is a hand-drawn rather than photochemical (let alone computerized) image, reproduced in multiple variants. As far from electronics as possible, the image serves to (im)mobilize an ironic nostalgia for older, rather than "new," media. Called *The End* in its various iterations, the work operates in this way as a reflex of obsolescence pitched in transmedial relation to other image forms caught up in a comparable technological transition. Picturing two of the last frames of a film strip as if they had slipped out of sprocket alignment with the aperture, this ink drawing—in lithographic transfer—catches the dialectical tension between photochemical imprint and cinematic projection: reduced here to the still image versus the aberrantly stilled one.

That this opening instance has the added benefit of anticipating the second half of this study under an iconic suspension, in the simulation of a fossilized celluloid sequencing, is the least of it. More to the point, the drawing's evoked serial inertia results from being seized up in a fixed-frame anachronism—and media-archaeological analysis—that distills much to come in the first Scene of these explorations by way of intersecting medial features in conceptual overlap. Moreover, with its interface work of seemingly imprinted film frames on paper, it harkens back, in a further conceptualist reversal, to the early landmark of transmedial conceptualism in the inverted font of that paper contact print of Fox Talbot's with which we began: in that case, photographed print type rather than an imprinted celluloid simulation in lithographic duplicate.

Through a highly self-conscious conflation of means within a given set of simultaneous manifestations, Ruscha and Pettibon collaborated on this 2003 series of subtitled lithographs in order to invoke the force of cinematic succession (two senses again: sequence and its implicit aftermath) in the light of other technographic alterations in the culture of representation. The images of *The End* in fact redeploy a visual trope of Ruscha's from the early 1990s, when filmic cinema's fate was first sealed by creeping digital eclipse—images that were at that point uncaptioned in the vertical truncation of their represented film frames. Two of the more recent subtitled works (with legends now in handwritten caps) happen to converge, especially in light of Ruscha's earlier innovations in the experimental codex forms of minimalist artists' books, in ways that serve further, as we'll note, to reorient a whole swath of conceptual book and text art in these same postmillennial years, including Ruscha's own in 2013. This is the case even though the immediate optical allusion (and illusion) of the 2003 pieces by Ruscha and Pettibon is that of adjacent vertical transparencies, not pages, on a dated and scratched film strip, as if worn thin by time and cultural supersession both.

Here is the twentieth century's signature medium—its distinctive imprint medium—caught between serial photograms in what, for a particular but unspecified film, may be the penultimate frame cell and its closural successor. What we see, that is, includes the lower half of "THE END" appearing on exit in the vanishing upper frame, with the emergent (but going nowhere) top half of the same two monosyllables edging up into the bottom sector of this en-route bifurcation. In part, the effect is to record not just the "Fin" of a given (or rather ungiven) screen text but of film itself as a discretely serialized rather than a bit-mapped medium, complete in these renderings with the accumulated vertical scratches resulting from celluloid wear and tear in the projector. Moreover, evoked here is an "end" transcribed in yet another, earlier, and now itself gradually eclipsed material form: ink on paper, reduced in this case from drawing almost to sheer writing, at least to a represented serif print font, in the minimalist rendering of two distressed backlit rectangles. Then, too, in this transmedial glimpse of a filmic strip (developed in visible liquid treatment [ink] rather than mere developing fluid), one senses a return from industrial production to the handmade simulacrum thereof.

In this very layering or dovetailing of material self-consciousness, these works of worded image serve to rehearse yet again the end of medium specificity. They do so by retracing the postmodernist departure from the goal of purity into what we've seen Jameson identify instead as the "mediatic system," which might well find one spectrum of its intertextual range (from incremental script to cinematic motion) telescoped and internalized in these individual (if twofold) word/image pieces. Twofold, because no sooner do they picture the motion picture's iterated inscription in frozen lock-step advance than they reinscribe this marker of cinematographic textuality within a hybridized graphic layout all their own. Given that *The End* insists in this way on recording its finality in so many (severed) words, imprinting it discursively as well as pictorially, the two most telling captions from this series of frame-line lithographs, these *cinegraphs*—etched by hand in slanted uppercase lettering, red and black respectively—read as follows. First: "AS MY EYES CLEARED, I FELT THE DIZZINESS OF NOT KNOWING WHICH END I WAS AT THE END OF." A text (visual or verbal)? A medial era? The uncertainty is secured by another of such epitomizing captions in the series: "THE ANALOGY BETWEEN THE ART OF THE ARTIST, THE NOVELIST, AND THE PRINTER IS, SO FAR AS I AM ABLE TO SEE, COMPLETE" (fig. 10, given closing pride of place in connection with the cinematic focus—and terminal mediation—of "Endscapes"). Especially complete, one might add, if by "printer" we are meant to include the processor of the cinematic print—how could we not be?—and if by "so far as I am able to see" the premium on the visible is made clear under idiomatic cover. Which certainly it is. Shades, again, of Fox Talbot's *Imitation of Printing.*

In all such "analogy between," then, lies the generative intertwine of such imagined material constituents. These subsisting conditions are offered up in this case as one key to the reading, transmedium, of any and all conceptual play between pictured frame advance and framed inked picture, each reduced to a unique variant of high-modernist "flatness." Yet beneath what one might call the cross-genre thematic of printwork that bonds artist and bookmaker with cinematographer in *The End*, all on collective exit from the last century, the real transmedial grip of this image lies within the split-frame image as originally conceived, without the captions, by Ruscha alone. It rests at the representational level, that is, with the image's own arrested sprocket traction, caught between photographic emulsion and kinetic projection. For sequence is already trapped and deactivated there between two contributory mediations *held up*, temporally and spatially at once, in mutual "analysis" and breakdown—and thus scanned like a vertical comic strip. Imaging in this way the foreclosure of photoprint cinema is a transmedial gesture, even before any verbal caption is introduced, achieved by centering on the intercepted bar between coherent frames—whose motorized elision alone produces the filmic image in the first place . . . when there is any image (other than two shorn and forlorn words) to project. It is in this sense that present representation in *The End* comes to us from the resultant distance of a third (rather than a second) medium—with the generative tension between photographic unit and spooling track traced in stasis by line drawing. Reframed in turn by lithographic imprint multiples, this syncopated fumbled "grab" is thus a double negation of the screen image, not first of all by printer's ink rather than photochemistry but, at base, by the glimpse of what lies between glimpses in the recovered (even while canceled) transmedial relation of photographic still to projected kinetic mirage: a relation returned here in belated recognition to its modular constituents. As happens, as well, in more recent work by Dutch-born, British-based photographer Mishka Henner in his 2016 *Film Stills* series, operating in a different transmedial crossover: between cinematographic frame and painted sculptural mass. His quasi-engraved images include—in homage to a previous century's medium, and perhaps to Ruscha as well—one titled *Breathless*, composed of "enamel paint on sandblasted Star Galaxy granite": the "Fin" of Godard's last frame rendered as its own tombstone at approximately 20 by 13 inches.

[end::papers]

After "the end" of "the printer" as both an artisanal job description and a machinic paradigm (in film lab as well as in artist's studio), display becomes, of course, exponentially digital. And precisely a decade after these graphic collaborations by Ruscha and Pettibon, based on the former's original images, Ruscha embarks on a further memorial homage to the art of "the novelist" or "the printer," either one, or rather to that of the bookmaker at large. And here again it is enlargement per se, more exaggerated and ironic yet, that is Ruscha's mode of choice. Shown first at New York's Gagosian gallery in 2013 is a series of almost trompe l'oeil open books—though too big to fool us about their utility, only instilling instead a hypertrophic sense of their one-time prominence in the very epoch of its surrender. These hypertomes are depicted blank volumes gargantuan in format and hovering at something like the wall-sized scale of the most expansive of Romantic landscape paintings—but with no scenography, no second space, represented, even through the sign language of writing. None, that is, but the horizonless plane of the contingently marked (blotched, yellowed, stained) but uninscribed—which is to say sheerly visual—surface of their simulated pages.

Seldom has Michel Butor's dictum been more fully and reductively realized (even at magnified scale) than in these works, as if they were huge mute footnotes to his claim that the one thing books have inevitably in common with painting is that all books (codices) are diptychs.[1] For this is never truer, or at least never more apparent, than when books have been stripped, demediated, of the very lettering that makes them work, makes them other than painted or sculptural works. Demediated of text, yes—but here *transmediated* as planar manifestations of canvas and page alike.[2] In the finesse of their execution, these giant books might masquerade as enlarged photographs from a preservationist's archive—might in this sense advertise their technique as "photorealist" bravura—except for the double estrangement of their wordlessness and their overwrought monumental (hence memorial) scale. Their hyperrealism reads instead as surreal: the final flaring of destined extinction—or at least as the inflated demotion of the book form to a gallery artifact rather than universal tool.

So when Ruscha, the former conceptual bookmaker from the 1960s and 1970s, gives us no page at all but only gold-tipped edges flanked by marbleized endpapers in one of these bulking works, *Gilded, Marbled, and Foibled* (2011–12), we confront the looming marmoreal tomb of the codex tome itself and its intrinsic medial service. As if magnifying the *fate* of the portable cellulose text as much as the felt texture of its surface— aspects of an object no longer the primary source of reading matter—all of these works, even when endpapers are not so histrionically included, seem almost like later iterations of *The End* series. For they hold ironically at bay, if only by scalar exaggeration, bookhood's own supersession by the legible backlit screen. As if in a magnified capstone, one might say, for this recent aesthetic tendency in biblio/graphic depiction, Ruscha's newest work offers pages so large, unwieldy, and weathered, even when not explicitly "marmorealized," that they communicate not any particular message but only the magnitude itself (even the enormity?) of a vanishing cultural hegemony. In this way most of all, perhaps, can these works over the last digital decade be placed in dialogue, valedictory at that, with the spirit of Fox Talbot's prescient conflation of typeset and photo offset. What the material surface of photography could once be advertised to do in enhancing book production has come round to what electronic imaging has done to coopt text processing altogether, let alone the filmic index.

Wholly unspoken, but everywhere in the air—as earlier with the case of Ruscha's dated two-frame film strips—is the long technical genealogy from manuscript through lead type to LED light: one of those many material declensions that transmediation is repeatedly, and on many different fronts, staged not just to render at aesthetic distance, but to reenter from the substrate up, archaeologically. Only some works, of course, are explicitly directed at their medial conjunctures in so many (blunt) words. Yet these can be unusually revealing. *The End* is thus, for our study, a fit beginning: the announced medium being lithograph on paper, but the art itself transmedial. Whereas this first exemplification across separate late works by Ruscha brackets in its way the entire history of imprint media—from the outmoding of manuscript illumination with the coming of mass print down to the breakthrough of Lumière—we turn next not to the digital overthrow of filmic cinema, but rather to the more extreme post-pixel materializations of electronic manufacture in the actual plastic fiber and fabrication of 3-D printing. After all of Western media culture has been tacitly surveyed in this way across one long and attenuated arc from Gutenberg through Google Books to print-on-demand objects rather than texts, we can return then to the postmodern rehearsal of an earlier, interim, and quite pointed "media war" in the clash between painting and photography over the claims of representational fidelity. For such is the nineteenth-century watershed (impressionism versus automatic record) that seems replayed in certain postmodern works—in the conflated photo/realist vein—by what comes to light as a sustained transmedial irony. Yet the far technological horizon is our checkpoint first—way beyond photographic imprint and its secondary representation—in the current realms of wholescale sculptural molding by remote control.

[print::matter]

We thus move from books and pages without print in Ruscha's latest wall-works to "print" without pages in a long-running exhibition that closed the next year at New York's Museum of Art and Design—by opening onto an almost imponderable future. It is no exaggeration to say that 3-D printing implicitly loops back through the very birth of humanism with Gutenberg to route us round instead to the eschewing of all paper text in the ultimate medial passage—wholly computational—from idea through plan (now electronic grid) to manifestation. It is in this sense that the current subhead takes shape—takes a newly subversive and potentially posthuman form—as an invitation to do just that, as impossible as it once, recently enough, would have sounded: to *print matter*, rather than words or images on a page.

Few technological functions in our current computerized climate are more disorientingly transmedial in nomenclature than the digital facilitations of "3-D printing." Nor more clearly marked as such than when several strictly aesthetic (conceptual, rather than practical) variants are placed on display together in that MAD show—with its punning idiomatic evocation of the imaginatively unmanageable, as well as postmanual, in the exhibition rubric "Out of Hand: Materializing the Postdigital." But the technical term is in its own right the true provocation. 3-D *what*? Naturalizing the strangeness of this phenomenon for those new to its possibilities, the term itself is another variant of skeuomorphic domestication. Without alphabetic or pictorial input of any sort, but rather via a graphic code either digitally copied from a spatial model or electronically self-generated, the printer jets out fast-drying liquid polymer rather than ink, building up surfaces and shapes of its own rather than just covering a page with language or pictures. Far afield from the raised lettering of braille, this dimensional printing is the newly computerized generation not of machinic signifiers but of incarnate signifieds: the coded generation of spatial form. Printing? Digital spray painting is more like it, in an impasto thick enough to count as digital sculpture—or in one remarkable transmedial (in this case audio-to-visual) leap, digital pottery (rather than poetry). We'll come to that.

In the meantime, there in the same gallery at MAD, a striking work throws itself immediately into theoretical relief. Or if not quite immediately, then after the catalog gloss helps us parse its formal anomaly. One foundational axiom (call it re-medial) from Marshall McLuhan comes vividly, indeed glintingly, into focus with this work of conceptual (as well as technical) bravura by the Scottish artist Geoffrey Mann, from 2010, called *Shine*, part of his "Natural Occurrence" series. It is as difficult to describe as it is easy to find on the Web. Without accompanying text, the illegible object would be incoherent and entirely perplexing. It is instead a riveting transmedial play between material and retinal recognition, the latter in fact objectified. And the McLuhanite lineage of media theory lends weight to its angular metallic flotations. In *Understanding Media*, McLuhan (unmentioned in the gallery's complicated explanatory note) famously said that the form of one medium, when superseded, is internalized as the content of a new form—as when light, medium of both illumination and of sight, is incorporated into the light bulb (McLuhan's launching example)—as in those further skeuomorphic versions, as well, in which the "chandelier" bulb is often shaped like a abstract candle flame. When, in Mann's work, the glancing beams of reflected light are converted to their own resculpted form, the principle is also backdated, in its own ornate way, to a pre-electronic instance.

[after::image]

As we slowly make out the jutting layered thrusts in front of us, we realize that these jagged cantilevered shapes that constitute *Shine* represent (or, more to the point, imprint) not the actual glow of candlepower but a laser-scanned trace of external illumination bouncing off the silver surface of an empty Victorian candelabrum. Here, in Mann's epiphenomenal displacement of source matter by its optic aura, his "printed" construction serves to reify the eponymous penumbra of one reflective object in translating it to another complementary form all its own: pure abstracted and rematerialized reflection without its fully discernible base, surface, or point of origin. As we gradually figure it out, what we are looking at is the result of a designer's remediation of a former design epitome, with digital processing turned upon artisanal Victorian culture not just in review but in a wholly oblique renewal. I grant the difficulty of picturing this, matched on site by the difficulty of decoding (and the word is indirectly applicable to its algorithmic mediation) what we see. But there it sits, bursting its own seams with whatever formal properties are left of an antique silver table piece that has been submitted, in bright light not its own, to a 3-D laser scan. The plastic manifestation has then been cast in bronze to freeze in place the encrusted spiked forms that register the vectors of its own reflection like some weirdly geometric thorny bloom atop a squat and warped decorative vase. The candles that once would have turned the decorative object into a source of light on its own are gone, with the metallic mold evoking instead the bounced rays directed upon it (rather than from it) as if they were, in the other sense, delicate architectonic beams in some structure of the ocular unconscious. Even with the initial bronze casting then encased in luxurious silver, the object is in no way returned to its original tabletop symmetry or function. Instead, it looks as if some phantom candle drippage has been skewed into windblown horizontal stalactites of represented light.

The process, and the thinking behind it—and the thinking it would induce in us—get spelled out on the artist's detailed website, with a video of this work in the various stages of its production. Once again in recent art practice, only discourse—a kind of retrofitted user's manual for perception itself—navigates the transmedium gesture as a trajectory of "interpretation": "*Shine* is a project that considers an object, its interpretation, mis-interpretation and reproduction back to object."[3] The circuit of reobjectification is rightly stressed. Further: "When we look at *Shine*, we need to consider the notion of what is a 'correct' reproduction. Sculptors and artists have had the opportunity to explore interpretation and abstraction, and *Shine* carries on this tradition in the digital arena where high resolution precision has been disrupted using the nature of the materials and processes themselves."[4] The grammar there is in its own way revealing: "When we look at *Shine*," we see shine itself, sheen and gleam, effect to a subsumed cause.

And the work has an archaeological as well as a technological dimension. Only new ocular machinations of electronic scanning can recover the retinal effects of such a Victorian tool and light source (candlepower)—an instrumentation preceding even electric energy, let alone digital tracing. In Mann's work, "transmediating" as it does between decorative antique thing and its shimmering optic uptake, a truer or at least "corrective" realism is broached. The eye's response to sheen is to distort the very surface it is reflected from; the digital scan's response to this is to "see" such distortion more clearly than the eye does, take it in and down, and then project it back (materially spew it forth) in sculptural form, rendering the otherwise unseen reverbs of sight in the form of a tangible incrustation. And in yet another transhistorical loop associated with this transmedial balancing act between optic index and 3-D trace, this experiment is a kind of impressionism in the round. For what is it that drives the cognitive brunt of this sculptural (rather than painterly) objectification of viewing (rather than of view) if not the urge to offer an electronic replay of the late nineteenth century's impressionist mandate in works of *perceptual* rather than objective mimesis, of *retinal* realism? What else could be uppermost in mind here but the notion, in this postrealist and neo-impressionist art, that how you see is what you get? In McLuhan's terms, the form of light has become the content of a new architecture of pure refraction, bringing subliminal optics to the surface as jagged thrusts of visibility itself. "Shine"—as manifestation rather than matter—has been recaptured as sculpted object in precious-metal replica, its object art: interpretive art.

[sound::shapes]

This same electronic print technology, in the mode of voice—rather than image—capture, can elsewhere, in this same exhibit, arrogate new powers to human sound rather than sight. This happens in an installation by François Brument that retools a classic interart tropology for a more radical transmediation. All actual phrasing in the literary mode of ekphrasis—verbal art representing visual form (think Keats's *Ode on a Grecian Urn*)—has disappeared here into a voice without referential input, a sound without speech or sense, that can nonetheless, as it were, declaim shape. (Full explanation still pending, I realize.) Whereas the typical 3-D materialization on offer at MAD is generated from a computerized optic scan of object or body that is then spewed forth in duplication, Brument's rarefied instance of such printing in *Vase #44* (2009) is a displaced form of audial-recognition that brings a potentially eclipsed materiality back to the prosthetic powers of an enunciating (rather than seen and laser-traced) body. It does so, one might say, in the bizarre electronic update of a dictograph from the preceding century. Think of it this way: voice-recognition software taken to a new digital extreme in voice-imaging, so that what is made visible from human sound is no longer just the peaks and valleys of a sonogram, let alone an irregular array of signifying letters, but a palpable shape. Where sound waves once merely displaced the atmosphere in spatial traverse, now they can make things *take* place out of thin air. What thus results from the audiovisual participant's recorded voice, wordless or otherwise—once engaging the mic and pressing the transmit button—is not a glass-blown speech bubble, for instance, but rather a digitally fabricated and freestanding piece of hollowed-out form in polymer build-up: a vase whose angles, shape, volume, and conical breadth constitute the 3-D translation of pitch, volume, duration, and the rest, in the productive (however meaningless) utterance. Fiat form; let there be matter: the Logos as wired (and polymer-loaded) Word.

In the case of Keats's urn, the poet's troping of the ancient vase's relief serves to vivify its sculpted surface, of course, along a projected emotional and phonological trajectory matched to an imagined 360-degree inspection of the material object itself.[5] But whereas Keats could only call out to the permanence and visual authority of an antique art in the supposed half measure of so-called word pictures, here, under the new digitized mediation of voice transcription, museum goers, however talentless with words or hands, can, by throwing their voices—it would seem almost the punning matrix of the entire work—thus *throw* a pot, or, in other words, render a vase in polymer replica. Interface/vase: a programmed transit whereby, as in all these works at MAD—even when far less obliquely purposed and conceptual than Brument's—we find software operating to transform image into a new hardware, a new utensil or *objet* all its own. And a further transmedial pun may dawn on us as actualized, literalized, in the case of Brument's vase: sound waves manifested, as if by another idiom given body, through the rippled and folded surfaces of a digital urn whose own spatial *volume* is only the material realization of a sonic one. In this transmedial throwing of the voice, ventriloquism has become *ventril-optic* in a new modality of, yes, plastic art.[6]

Traditional printing is often involved in translated works, of course. But these new digital processes can achieve at times a far more immediate transfer: a trans-slating of sheer accrued surface, layered, often as if slathered. But certain works of 3-D printing, as we've seen, are further sedimented with idea as well as plastic build-up. Closer to the general field of transmedial art, Brument's process of vox/vase translation—at least when conceived in the abstract—is something like the structural opposite (and conceptual complement) of Mann's bounced light rather than thrown sound. And Brument's work is related, in turn, to such sequenced audiovisual (hence transmedial) projects as those in the equally synesthetic practice of Max Neuhaus, as represented up the Hudson at Dia:Beacon rather than in Columbus Circle during this same period. These "mixed" conceptions include Neuhaus's installed soundworks in various architectural settings, to which the artist returns only much later, when the tactical labor of sonic placement and projection has been fully forgotten and only the music of ambient sound and echo remains. It is at this point that the artist makes drawings of the timbre and tempo—and *color*, another symptomatic transmedial matrix—of the once-constructed soundscape in pastel hatchwork and nonmusical notations. Such a latent structuring idiom of material determination (including "tone" as well as "color") is not simply a curious bonus of certain works, but rather an often concerted (and earned) structural model for the two-in-one of transmedial conception itself.

Back at MAD, of course, any such synesthesia is entirely computer-synthetic: the result of streamed data (literally spewed in this case) in an automatized circuit from algorithmic input to synthetic plastic output, from coded abstraction to objectification, that wholly bypasses human handiwork in the artifactual mode, replaced as it is by the sheerly digital keypadding of program cues. The transmedial synthesis is hardly just virtual, yet it is fabricated without any material fashioning aside from that of computerized instruction. And if such transmediation has taken us beyond a certain aesthetic horizon, it has also in some sense pointed back—to sensory correlations in earlier art making that have no imme-diate traffic with such futuristic machination. So we can productively start over, or at least round back, from the computerized asymptote of artifice at MAD. We return from there to an early antimodernist moment in a rethinking of the picture plane that is aligned with more abstract Conceptual art at least in that sense. This is a practice whose conflation-ary name, photo/realism, wears its transmediation on its sleeve: a clear case—normatively understood, generic, canonical—of a technopictorial imprimatur that verges at once on redundancy and oxymoron. Such is the thrust in painting to merge with the mechanical optic imprint, a move that thereby enters the perennial debate on mimesis long before the computer-extruded simulacra of 3-D printing might be thought to render it moot.

[photo::realism]

As two words, a pleonasm like "photo realism" would only be the name of the game in standard-issue indexical record. "It's almost like being there": the typical desideratum. But as one word for an aesthetic category (otherwise and more recently "hyperrealism"), the original term converts the nominal epithet "photo," via a momentary paradox in the context of easel painting, to an allusive intertext. It does so in order to describe a mode of realist facture that takes its model (for the most part actually, and always evocatively) from mechanical record.[7] What painting alone could once do to store retinal impressions over the time of laborious reproduction, photography could later do to render the ocular by precision optics over a briefer and eventually instantaneous exposure (as disclosure) time. In the mode of photorealism, the capacities interpenetrate in a lambent precision of technique. This is what the postmodern transmedium of such hyperrealism achieves by the painstaking—rather than instantaneous taking-down—of a picture whose realist allegiance is not to the scene as such but to the look of its precedent photographic capture. Instead of "that looks so real, so lifelike," the implicit response is "that really looks like a photograph." The whole basis of realist perception is caught in transfer to its mechanical trace—and then reverse-engineered in the mode of a dated artisanal craft of mimetic representation.

So let me return now, in transatlantic time, to a moment early in the conception of this book in which a dramatic confrontation between the hegemony of realist painting in the European Renaissance and its hypermediated revival in the conceptualist American 1970s was borne home to me from separate but strangely convergent Spanish sites. In the experience of art, some of the most intriguing conjunctions are often unscheduled. So it was with an award-winning Spanish conceptual photographer in whose work I had grown interested but concerning which I had anticipated no particular connection to Spanish classical painting, let alone to the accidental checkpoints of a traveling show on American photorealism, then and now, in its serendipitous Iberian venue. But a certain chain of connection, and historical declension, was hard to avoid. And so my own ad hoc comparative exhibit—or, say, exposition—here, over the next stretch of discussion: "Velasquez through Photorealism to Joan Fontcuberta: Toward a Transmedial Mimesis." This line of approach, via the impromptu gallery selection on my part below, is indeed meant to question how, and to what end, the layered ironies of Fontcuberta's latest initiatives in digital picturing reroute the double valence of the former photorealist gambit—automatized and artisanal (photographic and painterly) at once—round, not historically but materially, beyond all oil or acrylic mediation, into a reconception of the photo-electronic image per se. It is there that Fontcuberta presses the very condition of mechanical reproduction to an exploratory new limit. In an era of "global positioning" and universal transmit, connections are palpably made in his pictures not just, as we'll see, between media and paramilitary imaging, art and simulated artillery practice (as in other contemporary work as well, to which we'll be comparing his), but, more broadly, between the human sensorium and its increasingly virtualized fields of view.

But first, dateline Madrid: 1656, 1967–2012 (Velasquez at the Prado, the photorealists on tour). A mid-Spring conference at the Universidad Complutense on "American Voices" just over, there was time for the museums. Instead of sounds on page and stage, the seeing of some painted sights. There at the Prado for the first time, I came face to face with the legendary recess of personages in that apotheosis of an entire representational epoch (Foucault) that is "considered by art historians to be the world's greatest painting" (the guidebooks). Taking in Velasquez's *Las Meninas* (1656), and thus optically taken in by it, one peers through to that circumscribed and embedded exercise in painting framed as a mid-sized mirror on the far wall, where, in clear definition, the king and queen are seen (or, at least for many viewers, seem) to be holding firm for their rendering by the painter looking out past his back-turned easel toward us (in their prioritized place). That mirror will reclaim our gaze shortly.

But from the Prado and that early modern watershed in the Velasquez, it was, as it happened, a surprisingly short distance in Madrid that May—as well, of course, as a quantum aesthetic leap—to the postmodern case of painterly realism outbid, in its determining optics, by a technical, almost-mechanical perfection. This was a distance bridged from the artful rendition of an "automatically" (instantaneously) captured image in a mirror, as a framed painterly microcosm, to the evoked automatism of camerawork in the photorealist aesthetic. For only a couple of blocks, and the tree-lined width of a grand promenade, away, across the Paseo del Prado, waited the Thyssen-Bornemisza collection, whose richly sampled arc of European art history came to a fitting, if temporary, point of rest downstairs in a traveling exhibit called "Hyperrealism: 1967–2012," with all the usual (and mostly American) suspects in their fullest European exhibition ever.

Their high-fidelity and often magnetic executions, mostly in oil or acrylic on canvas and board—applied with an almost airbrush-smooth touch—brook no confession of surface whatsoever, any more than would, if available for display, the photographs that had frequently spawned them. These are not representations, like *Las Meninas*, in the form of painterly compositions; they approximate no visual rendition, *as art*, of the everyday urban or suburban world on which their scrupulous, their sometimes luminous, details are modeled. They are, instead, that other thing that emerged since the perspectival art of picturing in classic realism. They are (or aspire to be) sheer *images*, existing in this way on an undisguised continuum with the immediate capture of a mechanical snapshot. It is a continuum, of course, whose transmedial links are forged by labor, exactitude, finesse, obsession, and what can only be called a showy self-effacement. Oil stroke disappears into the look of transpicuous photo-emulsion in print transfer; unseen flicks of the brush substitute for the previous click of the shutter. What was once instantaneously taken is now given back over labor's invisible time.

On the very face of it, the contrast was extreme: beyond Velasquez, a Caravaggio in each museum, Goyas and El Grecos galore, and now Chuck Close. Between the realist and the hyperreal, intriguing *comparisons* came only slowly to mind. But a notable gain in seeing those photorealists together in a retrospective grouping was that their proclivities, their motifs, were accented by recurrence. One in particular came clear, along with the feints it entails. With photorealist framings, we tend to remember at random, I think, the individual topoi and locales, the street corners and storefronts, the motorcycles, the small-town movie marquees, the phone booths, the car lots, the Pop signage, the diners and their countertop accoutrements (bunched as institutional still lifes), the gargantuan portraits, and so on. But there is an intermittent stylistic impetus to many of the resultant effects: not just assorted cultural ticks and illusionist tricks, but rather a focal preoccupation. *Focal* seems just the word for it. Assessing en masse the bravura execution of several canvases in a row, one sees, in recurrence, how certain reflective surfaces—window glass, chrome, aluminum trailer siding, crystal vases, even ketchup bottles—are contours that test the finesse of the brush with their glint and sheen but that also accumulate toward another self-conscious relation to photography: the deliberately marked (by being optically unmarked) absence of the reflected instrumental source—namely (if perhaps anonymously), the original photographer snared by accident amid all that mirroring shimmer.

[mirror::art]

So back to the Prado, once again, for that ocular point of departure in Velasquez: its duplication, in recess, of the space that would be ours if the depicted mirror were not just what it so obviously is instead (that is, a represented framed surface under application by paint). What that set-back plane in *Las Meninas* helps set off is an otherwise encompassing fact of all less schematic paintings. This is the fact that we typically see not (as in this deviant case) the artist at work and the searching eye of his execution, but rather, more narrowly framed, what occupies his final gaze: not the peopled scene being rendered (imaginary or otherwise) but the marked surface over which the maker's attention has most recently pored. In this sense, Velasquez's summary masterpiece takes its place midway through the revisionary century of European art that, according to Michael Fried, was inaugurated by Caravaggio in the late 1500s.[8] For *Las Meninas* doesn't just infer, but also enacts, the innovative overlay of two "moments" in early realism that, according to Fried (though without reference to Velasquez), even if conceptually distinct, remain mostly simultaneous: the "immersive" moment of execution, where the artist plies his trade by applying his paint, and the "specular" moment, where the image is felt coming to him, as it later does to us, whole and finished. Such is the doubleness of which, for Fried, the self-portrait in a mirror is the epitome. Velasquez opens the curtain wider than ever on this kind of drama, and the world has always attended with rapt interest. But not always by noticing what I mean to stress here. The mirror within the painting isn't just the microcosm of realism, reflecting upon art's aspirations in the duplicating of a world. Rather, its delimited plane and bracketed double portrait is a painting-within-the-painting, noun and gerund respectively: a framed, if momentary and contingent, specular fixity (the royal pose) anticipating the encompassing moment of exhibition for an alternate canvas showing the painter still at work.

With this prototype in mind, we might say that photorealism arrives— holding the mirror up less to the world's objects than to their photographic traces—so as (by the evoked fidelity of automatism) to elide the difference, as if it were instantaneous, between an immersive technique and that moment of eventual specular reception in which the work is celebrated for looking just as real as a photograph. Aspired to in this, though with a certain high-handed panache, is the mere secondary image of an antecedent mediation. If the labor of painting is the picture's efficient cause in these hyperrealist executions, photography is (or is made to seem) its first cause. Whether based on an actual snapshot in canvas projection or not, the painting absorbs an ethos of mechanical duplication through and through. That's what distinguishes the hyperrealism of these works from the traditional form of trompe l'oeil. It's not as if you were there now, looking in on a sector of the real, your perception duped by duplication. Photorealism's frame is not a presumptive window in anything like this sense. You actually *had to have been there*, been there once before, camera in hand—or someone had to be—in order to have seized so precise an imprint of a now-absent reality. Such is the optic chain of association. So, too, with Velasquez at one remove. Only in the royal presence, long before automatic capture, could such a representation be effected, or at least initiated. It is something like that validating trace of the real—displaced in photorealism to the real of technological origination—that these postmodern paintings move to reinscribe.

Compared to the complex optic scenario of Velasquez's deep-focus tour de force, one finds in the nearby hyperrealism exhibit at the Thyssen the enforced flattening of the canvas plane to quasi-machinic rectangle. What we see in *Las Meninas* is a finished painting about the finishing of one, calling to mind the artist's unseen (though in another plane immanent) brushwork across the inner and averted canvas. In the Thyssen's rooms of photorealist work, any sense of facture or stroke, inventive composition and touch alike, tends to disappear into a battery of achieved photorealist precisions. In such a preformatted field of view, the laborious (under erasure) replaces the instantaneous with no advent of "impression" or subjectivity—just seeming imprint. Yet the metapictorial dimension persists: once a function of deep focus in Velasquez, now of auto focus. The mid-1600s and the mid-1900s: the twain meets after all at the plane of the self-consciously *virtual*. Yet the differences remain culturally determinant. Compared to painting in its late Renaissance heyday—allegorizing itself as a mastery of spatial disposition and surface execution—we find these contemporary paintings instead, though in no less reflexive a vein, evacuating any manifestation of technique within a crystalline *scenic* visibility all but mechanically vouched for. The immediate result, time and again, is to certify the work's unabashed participation in a contemporary *cult of the image* that has exceeded (and eclipsed) any local exhibition of a painter's specialized craft. But this happens not without bringing that same brandished craft—and its craftiness—to bear on a specific risk of automatism. Such is the flashpoint of secondary manifestation—as we are now to see in detail (or, more to the point, typically avoided detail)—that this style of painting's own flaunted transmedial legerdemain is able to summon from its photomechanical "pretext." Summon—and subdue.

[blind::spotting]

The recurrent nondetail I have in mind, that came suddenly to mind there (with collected evidence) in Madrid—a detail that tends to mark an absent center in the painterly field of view—bears lingering over in this context, since its minor wrinkle of execution may come to enfold an entire trans-medial logic. Here is where the withdrawn mirror in *Las Meninas*, beaming forward the king and queen, is indeed a crucial point of departure in the leap from Velasquez to the likes (and photo-likenings) of Richard Estes or Robert Bechtle or Ralph Goings. In Velasquez, the mirror (held up to nature or, higher in the chain of being, to sovereignty) is inescapably the rectangular emblem of the art that embeds it. Why, by contrast, does photorealism tend to withdraw altogether, or withhold, a yet more natural mirroring in the reflective surfaces it reproduces? Why go as far out of the way as these paintings often seem to do, these later hyperrealist "shots," to dodge the self-mirroring that some original recorder of the scene might have incurred? Why so much effort, that is, to occlude the apparatus? Or ask instead: why such a facile instinct to obliterate a work's own anchoring optical traces from within their very celebration? If these aren't exactly the right questions, they may still point at the right place: the internal van-ishing point not of the image per se but of its imaging—at once specular navel, blind spot, and transmedial breakpoint.

This, then, is what studying so many of these pictures in gathered his-torical retrospect tends to reveal—or rather to help us notice as implicitly concealed. Time and again the recessed accidental mirroring threatened by one or another reflective surface, in which the photographer's own image might contingently be glimpsed if this were a real snapshot (rather than the doctored duplicate of one), is denied us. The focal point of registra-tion is located roughly enough, that is, but only as its agency has already gone missing, whether from reflective storefront glass, from polished metal siding, from chrome bumpers or the deep acrylic glisten of auto-mobile paint jobs, from the vitreous curves of pitchers, goblets, or other incidental reflectors. Peer as we might, the origin has been disappeared in the finished product, the mechanistic work of record outplayed by the skill of surrogate rendering.

And there is more historical irony in this than might at first appear: a double twist of inference. In a return to the norms of the painterly tradi-tion so openly torqued by Velasquez, the recording hand in these photo-realist canvases—the hand of the cameraman in advance of the oil-paint maestro—is absent from their pictured spaces, even though their showy technical dexterity tends to advertise a technological grounding in some photographic original. This is just what locates the intended transmedial force of these works. About which no overstatement is required; at issue is a conceptual aporia only, not necessarily a documented anecdotal one. Maybe the original photographic image, by some luck of shade or surface slant, just missed snagging the shadow of its own captor. Yet in certain cases, surely, there may well have been at least some indistinct blotch of the photographer's reflection that—when projected for painterly rendition—might have been, as it were, "photoshopped" out of existence, overridden by a momentary infidelity of the tracing brush. Either way, actual or conjectural, real or theoretical, the chance remains of an extraneous and disenchanting stain, blot, excess, technical recess, call it what you will. And let "chance remains" stand (now that I come to reread it) as both clause and phrase, noting thereby both a persistent risk and its accidental trace or glitch. The threat remains, that is, of the image's retained source: haunting canvas after canvas at its very center of ocular gravity.

Following up, after Madrid, on my induced suspicion about this as a recurrent *felt* absence in many of these pictures even when there's no hint of it visible, I found what seemed—as amplified by further evidence since—a pointed confirmation of this structuring lacuna: an anomalous instance ultimately rule-proving in the exception of its optical candor. Represented by more than one early 1970s canvas in the Thyssen exhibition, Don Eddy's waxed Volkswagens on used-car lots, their silvery trim or buffed curves just missing the source of their photomechanical clarity in a reflected camera, often rivet the eye by pulling it in toward this abyssal point of no (mirrored) return. (Same, decades later, and displayed on the same Thyssen wall, with the huge, mirror-smooth, chrome-rimmed, maroonish Packard wheel-cover by Peter Maier called, by phrasal wordplay, *Plum Delicious* [2006].) There is, however, a work of Eddy's not represented in that traveling show, yet whose optical logic lurks tacit across the gleaming metallic curves of the rest. Leave it to the Web to turn it up digitally remediated. Called simply *Harley Hubcap* (1970), its titular shape, in full-frame close-up, is little more than a bent surface for an anamorphic self-portrait. Tightly framed there is a burnished metallic and all but semispherical curve, within which one sees the elongated lozenge of a standing body, arms lifted toward its line of sight, face blocked by an intervening small object: a body doing the deed redone by the painting in front of us, the latter a deed of exactitude in the simulation of mechanical capture. A locus classicus, the sixteenth-century *Self Portrait in a Convex Mirror* by

Parmigianino, has been updated from the obviously painstaking to the seemingly instantaneous.

[self::foto]

And a year later than the Thyssen show, in an extensive retrospective exhibit of Richard Estes' work at the Smithsonian Museum of American Art, one finds on display, from just the year before—and almost four decades since his first experiment in this mode (also on view in this exhibit)—the remarkable 2013 *Self Portrait* (fig. 1). Based on a photo taken on the Staten Island Ferry, the painting takes up the complex geometries of refraction on the glassed-in main deck. The most famous artist in this mode has thus bracketed a broad central span of his career with what it ordinarily made a point of suppressing. For the ferry portrait is answered via precedent, across the gallery, by a 1976 work also new to—and definitive for—my gathering private, now public, file on this crux of transmedial thinking across photorealist manu/facture. Far more explicit, more "realist" in features, than the shadow of recording in Goings' hubcap image, that earlier painting of Estes' (and Estes himself) is called *Double Self-Portrait* (1976). To be sure, semitransparent glass reflections had already become a trademark aspect of Estes' work by the mid-1970s—as if redoubling the canvas plane by the space in front of it and "behind" the spectator (the palaces lining the Grand Canal, for instance, hovering ghostly in the storefront windowpane of a Murano glass tourist shop). But his 1976 self-portrait does not simply include his own image—and not simply once only—on such a surface. What we see of the artist—as photographer rather than painter, alongside his tripod rather than easel—is more than one glimpse of the recording moment that is otherwise and typically "expunged" by Estes (as a catalog essay has it, as if more than just erased but aggressively interdicted).[9] Beyond the anomalous incorporation of the photographer's body in glass reflex, there is also, explaining its title as *Double Self Portrait*, a nontranslucent duplication from an actual mirror recessed within the space of the closed diner photographed head-on from across an empty Sunday street. At this distance from his own camera, the exact mirror image at half scale achieves approximately the same fidelity as the muted plate-glass reflection closer to us. And in each case the figure on view is the artist not as painter but as documentarian: phase 1 of his contribution—the *work* under selective photo initiation, not the *painting* in progress. In this way the use of the mirror for a painter's self-portrait (anamorphic or not), with all the "self-regard" this might imply, is adduced even while ruled out by the two-tiered automatism of instantaneous record before execution.

Thirty-eight years later, Estes' wry return to self-portraiture on the Staten Island Ferry allows him, by contrast, virtually to disappear from within his own avowed presence at the scene. This is no easier to describe than it is to figure out—as image even before further geometric figuration—when facing the actual canvas. For the apparatus in front of (rather than alongside) the artist's face this time—and, more important, the reflection it captures—all but entirely obscures its "authorial" agent. This happens when the photographer's mirrored image—through the weathered glass of the ferry—is occluded by the stronger optical dynamic induced by a row of opened sash windows on the other side of the boat. Coinciding exactly with his head and lifted camera, one of these small bifurcated windows is reflected as if in front of him in the much larger window seemingly through which—though in fact mostly at which—he is shooting. And this normal optical illusion installs at the same time a more pointed ocular allusion. At exactly the scale of his camera-blocked visage, the vertical disjuncture of that miniaturized window frame evokes in the other sense the adjacent vertical "frames" (and their barred disjuncture) of a cinematic (and thus more mobile) film strip: that same sequencing of stills that is arranged and numbered horizontally in a normal still-film roll.

Suggestions collect and condense. Many a photograph, whether or not destined for painterly transcription, and whether or not the point of capture is ferried along on a moving vehicle, is a kind of stop-action moving image. Transmediation is here triangulated through a held moment pitched at the intersection of cinematic momentum (evoked under arrest by the frozen frame), finished painting, and the photomechanism that preceded it. So it is that the artist—caught "on camera" at the outset of the work, of the *labor*, whose finish we perceive—is subsumed in front of his window by the miniature window apertures behind him. 1435, 1976, 2013: Alberti's famous "window," as model for painting, has returned in both these contemporary self-portraits as an embedded emblem of precision's own mission—and its ocular subterfuges. Moreover, that defining Renaissance figure of the mirror (Velasquez, 1656) abides as model even when no reflection whatsoever, let alone that of the artist-photographer, impedes the normative receding perspective of a photorealist canvas.

That's one defining historical arc. But once you find such images on the Web, or actual photographs of whatever description, paintings too, and enlarge them to the point of digital break-up, you have crossed an optical border that the coming works of "*hypo*realism" will transgress on their own internal—or systemic—terms. When what the "image frames"—what it actively enframes—is not, as here so far, its own precursion (operative and historical) in photography but its own substrate (as with Fontcuberta's pending work) in pixelation or computer fractalization (with each image amassed of its own rectangular synecdoches), one must, so to say, think again. Yet, in the works of this sort to which we're coming, the force of such Conceptualism 2.0, for all the differences in technological regress, exists very much on a continuum with those 2003 litho-cinemato-graphic frame disjunctures of Rusha's *The End* and the 2013 *Self Portrait* by Estes, with its layered study in the photographic contingencies of facial self-effacement. That continuum results precisely from the comparable transmedial axis delineated in each work separately. But of course what remains to be shown about these further second-wave conceptual images in their computerized context—what needs to be argued into the open—depends entirely on what waits to be seen in them.

[auto::mimetic]

The slow time of painting imitates automatism even while picturing its own difference: that's its transmedial automimeticism. Up to this point in our discussion, hyperrealism has been found to extrude in confession, at only very rare moments, what it normally excludes from view, what it takes as given: proof of the taking down—and then up again as evoked model—of an automated image rather than a sketch. By just such exceptions, as I say, is the norm secured: the photographer gone from his own realism. So let me sum up what seems at stake so far, as dawning on me in the Thyssen-Bornemisza, there within the gravitational pull of the Prado's Velasquez, and distilled since at the Smithsonian. Technological evolution in image science involves its own inbuilt hazards, which may of course be captured in secondary representation—not least the demotion of representation itself to a kind of voyeurism by means of some undue exposure (both senses) of the seer seen. But a residual medium may be recruited as a corrective to the new dominant. Before the actual procedures of electronic photoshopping, only hand-worked painting (if sometimes merely in the form of "touch-up") could once undo the primal flaw courted in certain cases by the indexical condition of all photography. It could do so by painting *out*, that is, the long sunset shadow of the photographer's body across the object of his or her reflection in some part of its surface.

And nowhere with more epistemological charge—or medial discharge—than in a predigital photorealism whose artifacts tease us with their aura of the automatic.

Art in the age of mechanical reproduction has reproduced in these works—over the time of patient craft—the instantaneity that once (at the advent of photography) threatened a received painterly medium on its two-dimensional home ground, its native plane. It has accomplished this while, in the process, erasing in paint the very oculus and agency of that primary photomechanical registration. The early modern logic of Velasquez's metapicture—with the facture of its hand-made mirroring, so to speak—has been turned inside out by postmodern irony. Under the aegis of the hyper, painting aspires to the look of wholesale involuntary replication; yet it may appear to achieve this through no less than the negation of automaticity's own founding condition in the unedited take. All this displacement takes place, then, in declension from a *[mirror::art]* paradigm where the mirror that *is* art and an art of the mirror, even under erasure, limn a shared conceptual interface. Riveted to its insubstantial manifestation in (as a rule) the unseen sighting *by* but not *of* the photographer in the blinding flashpoint of these *hyperrenderings*, the viewer's eye—in its attempt at penetrating the inferred technological origin of the picture plane—is typically rebuffed: submitted to a kind of conceptual reverse zoom in which the only sign of the photographer left to perception is the painting all told.

So a viewer's instinctive question has been, I am suggesting, as naïve as it is likely. How could so many shots aimed directly into a mirroring surface win free of the gratuitous reflex of the taker taken? They couldn't, because they aren't—aren't, in fact, photo shots. Just to raise the question, then, inaugurates the work of estrangement that attends certain of these hyperfamiliarized fields of view. That's the extra measure of realism (or candor) in their photorealism, dependent nonetheless on the frequent sleight of sight at the core of their bravura: the recuperated wound of their automaticity in an unwanted reflex erased from view. In the long run, the irony of such hyperrealism circles on itself in a sly ratification. And the images that just skirt the camera's own reflected sighting seem the quintessence of the mode. In the full flush of their histrionic precision and the hyped skill of their execution, these canvases have not edited out their painterly status after all, but only the surest clue to their claiming anything else. What is left for consideration falls between: again, the very question of the *image* in the optic deluge of contemporary life, a visuality set freer than usual here from all sense of an on-site source. It is a question thus vexed all the more in these canvases by the discipline of their own seemingly deferential craft. Neither photographed pictures nor pictures of photographs exactly, their curious interface between taking and making is there to keep a transmedial awareness actively in play—and, with it, a sense of the hypersaturated image culture from which they emerge.

One resists too much generalization too soon, however, chastened by the multifaceted nature of that one traveling exhibition. But what the viewer is undebatably drawn to, at the very least, in that traveling hyperrealism show—despite considerably different styles—is the common denominator of medial savvy in the flashiness of technique. Even when not implicitly referencing photography, that is, these canvases regularly impart an art-historical spin. Whereas abstract expressionism may have seemed in its day a true telos of modernism—the revelation of paint (its color and form) from within painting, or let us say of painting per se in the absence of all picturing—one of the photorealist canvases by Audrey Flack on display in Madrid can, in contrast, be read to send up this purism with a medium-deep in-joke. In a work of oil over acrylic, she paints the material cause of her representation's own effect: not an all-over layering of pigment, but rather a pile of half-squeezed paint tubes centering on one brand amid the rest, for which the painting is named, *Shiva Blue*. A long way from an Yves Klein abstraction in blue, here is painting rendering up to a studious realism its own physical base in commercial pigment. And next to it by the same artist is hung a yet more telling emblem of the whole hyperrealist aesthetic.

[photo::gravure]

In this second of her deadpan still-life renderings on display in the hyperrealism retrospective, Flack foregrounds an intermittent motif of the illusionist tradition (common elsewhere in her own work as well) when picturing, amid assorted knick-knacks and domestic debris in *Queen* (1976), a gold-plated photo locket with diptych portraits of two women in a snapshot mode no more realist in treatment—but no less—than the sundry articles heaped around them. Photorealism, that is, can on occasion wax real not just by capturing the moment and manner of automatic record (via auto-portraiture) but by including the material form to which the canvas aspires by association. Here the weight of art history, in the upper floors of the Thyssen, comes bearing down yet again on this postmodernist exhibit. Flack's canvas, unlike many in the show, elicits comparison (especially contrast) not simply with the broad genealogy of illusionist painting in the trompe l'oeil tradition but with a specific instance by John Frederick Peto on the museum's second floor, the unusually sparse canvas *Toms River* (1905).

As part of a late nineteenth-century dialectical backlash against the sketchy ocular flurry and blur of a post-photographic Impressionism, in the contrastive maneuvers of trompe l'oeil the receiving eye is fooled rather than pandered to by image. The eye's normal working is actually stretched and tested—rather than just manifested, as by an impressionist haze—in a simulated ocular process. Instead of *the way we see* being represented by the art we used to gaze upon perhaps more passively as pictured object, it is the case, in trompe l'oeil, that certain internally "hung" objects and their vertical supports are found deceptively substituting for the painted canvas and thus obtruding from the wall into gallery space—or dropping back from it into a fictive recess. The Peto at the Thyssen represents a spare hinged cupboard of some kind with a lone black-and-white photograph affixed to its wooden surface. In the other leading American and Victorian exponents of trompe l'oeil (John Haberle, William Harnett, Walter Goodman), photography is often a vested test case of duplication's art, including daguerreotypes rendered with the same exactitude as the envelopes and playing cards and ticket stubs affixed to a plane apparently not the canvas's own. Painting swallows rather than spars with its rival.[10] Peto's inlaid photos are often different, more sheerly differential: not half-hearted in execution so much as optically aloof, skewed to the dominant aesthetic, throwing it almost literally into relief. In the Thyssen example and elsewhere (though not always—and thus in each case a decision rather than a default), their sketchy cartoon simplicity, striking the eye like rough-hewn charcoal drawings, could fool no one. Only the material on which they are printed rises from its background as if with 3-D plausibility. With no internal depth to the picture plane of these embedded photos, they seem to be there almost ironically, so as to distinguish the flatness (if not the definitional accuracy) of photography at large from the greater—rather than the merely derivative—art of trompe l'oeil.[11]

Estes, Flack, then back to Peto and Haberle: all caught up in the play between surface treatment and image in what we might call the *[brush::shutter]* interface. Even in leaving the Victorians aside, a question central to the vocabulary of this whole study may arise here in the wake of extended hard evidence—and certainly bears reflection. Clearly less overt than in recent digitally inflected and cross-conditioned works, where exactly is the 2.0 quotient in the latent conceptualism I'm arguing for in the nearly half-century span of photorealist imaging? Broadly historicist rather than specifically genre- or period-bound, it rests with a flexible cast of perception rather than a defining mode of mediality or materialization. Derived in part, to be sure, from a habit of mind induced by the platformatic transfers of our own electronic moment, the true analytic (and ultimately reconceptual) force of transmedial attention comes from the binocular perspective, often the intense double vision, lately opened up for reviewing even such earlier hybrid dexterities as we've seen in photorealist technique—in all its flaunted pictorial interplay.

From this perspective, another artist's work offers itself in exemplification from that travelling show at the Thyssen. By contrast with Peto's earlier demotion of the inset photo, the effect of hyperrealism—its gestures often as excessive and self-imbricated as its own doubled *r*—is to lift all details to a comparable plane of fidelity and photo-literalist definition. And sometimes, most famously, a magnified one. The most recognizable artist in the Thyssen retrospective is undoubtedly the overscale portraitist Chuck Close, whose giant heads are mounted at the scale of public monuments after having been optically extrapolated from normal photo portraits by the gridding of the picture plane and its projected enlargement—and then painterly reconstitution—at outsize canvas scale. The historical contrast is immediately elucidating. Whether including snapshots or not in their frequent still lifes (Audrey Flack), or even filling their canvas frames with one such tacit portrait frame at a time (Close), these transmedial ventures, unlike their trompe l'oeil counterparts from an earlier century, aren't first and foremost *about* certain photos as painterly topoi (or competitors); they are themselves photo*graphic* in the very grain (or its lack) of their smoothed-out facture. Some inset photo isn't simply (even centrally) one among the tests of technique in this mode; rather, a sense of some precedent photo constitutes the aesthetic venture all told.

The one example of Close's work on view at the Thyssen show can sum the oeuvre, despite many variations on the theme in his evolving technique. His is a method best understood, perhaps, when seen to emerge by indirection from his early training. Close began following in the footsteps of Willem de Kooning, though already with a noticeable Pop sensibility, so that instead of his becoming an abstract expressionist, it is as if he sequestered this ambition in the underlay of his later facial hyperbolism. For he took increasingly to fissuring his magnified facial grids into scores of dabbed or finger-painted rectangular units—minor color-field abstractions in their own right—that disappear as sheer differential tones alongside hundreds of others like them in developing the neo-pointillist pixelations that accrue to the often greyer-scaled macro field of his photoesque blow-ups. These cellular dabs (these tiny bursts of miniaturized abstract painting) thus simulate the photogenetic build-up of the image all told. In Close's practice, an effect like the exposed comic-book discontinuity of Ben-Day dots in the photo-offset parodies of Roy Lichtenstein, for instance, has been rendered more assertive and integral at once, subsumed more fully to overall conviction at the right viewing distance. Realism, nonetheless, even facial realism, is exposed as an abstraction at base. Here is a perfect stylistic gesture for an artist who, once having been diagnosed with prosopagnosia (an inability to recognize faces), set out instead to collapse the "specular" moment of reception and identification (in self-portraits and otherwise) and the "immersive" moment of execution (Fried's dyad again) into the transmedial moment of photomechanical projection and canvas expansion simultaneously.

[reflex::action]

This twofold force in Close's work is all the more apparent in a curiously involuted variant of his photorealist mode (with strange retinal exactions all its own) on view in Melbourne at the National Gallery of Victoria in a 2013 sampling of contemporary art from a previous exhibition called "An Incomplete World." Nothing there was more incomplete than the graphic work of Close's *Self Portrait (anamorphic)* from six years before, which had no immanence as human image until warped into reflected compression. It is as if Close had begun with one of his enlarged snapshots—as gridded up by overhead projection into his pseudo-bitmap analysis—and then reverse-engineered its manifestation in shrunken form. For what one comes upon in a vitrine display is an anamorphic fan-out of an elongated honeycomb-like pattern, in pencil, stretched flat in an approximate semi-circular segment around the base of a small and highly polished chrome pillar—on which the bent drawing, its gridwork curved and oblong in a splayed and illegible geometry, is then "corrected" when mirrored back to the viewer looking in at the reflective tubular surface. The image comes to us reconstituted as neither a curvilinear abstract drawing nor an iconic face in some curved, silver looking glass, but as nothing more nor less than "a Chuck Close" in reflected miniature. Hyperrealist with a twist, the transmediation here, implicit as well as visible, takes a return route through reduced sculptural monolith to disembodied likeness. But Close's work wants further to suggest, in the more than ordinary distortion of the underlay, how much optical normalization is often needed to convert ingredient gradations into a coherent picture plane. That it accomplishes this only by an anamorphic transmediation between horizontal sheet and vertical curve is of course its further point: about vision's conversionary mutations made visible. And in the context of an avoided reflection of camera/man in standard photorealism—as if returned from the repressed in those two Estes works, or in Goings' hubcap mirror—Close's anamorphosis reverses the exclusion to a sheer exteriority. The mirroring ordinarily denied within the picture plane is, in this anomalous case, all that bends the flattened, fanned-out plane into plausible manifestation outside itself in something like the static (yet still loosely protocinematic) projection of an optical toy.

Many other mirrors make their (itself unmarked) mark in contemporary aesthetics, often equivocating the very idea of the made image. It is in this respect that their more or less "direct access" to reality, quite apart from their actual secondary representation on canvas, enrolls them as hyperreal objects within the conceptualist museum. Sampling them briefly, in their own version of an "automatic" (if nonmechanical) imaging like that of photography made available to evocation by paint, can round out this discussion of all such low-profile transmediation. We then turn, in the following chapter, to the computerized optics of photographic imprint more clearly related to the social context of Conceptualism 2.0 in its influence from new digital epistemologies. Earlier, among postwar mirror works, there is the quintessential conceptualist irony of automatic reflex in Ian Burn's 1967 one-sentence etching on a mirror surface: the eponymous "NO OBJECT IMPLIES THE EXISTENCE OF ANY OTHER." Really? Even, as an immanent counter-example, the surface on which another object's veritable duplication is made manifest? Is there no difference, then, as seemingly proposed by Burn's provocation, and either backed or parodied in its quote from David Hume, between ocular index and arbitrary referential sign? More to the point, isn't the ironic and ultimately transmedial (plastic and textwork) gesture of Burn's piece meant precisely to query the nature of mirroring as medium and hence the status of any other medium in its relative access to the real—as conveyed at whatever representational remove?

There may be, as well, a slightly earlier postwar history put into play by Burn's work. This history is one we are reminded of at a recent Guggenheim retrospective of German (proto-conceptualist) abstraction from the late 1950s through the 1960s, work constellated around the so-called Zero group. It may have been an unstated part of their whole project to insert so many mirrored surfaces into their wallworks and sculptures—as if the plane of auto-picturing were the "zero" degree of representational art. In any case, it is partly this very different premium on flatness, indeed on facingness—and its own borrowed depths—that again solidifies, if that is even the word for it, a very different aesthetic to that of *expressionist* abstraction in the same (American) years. For mirror art—mirrart, one might hear (and say)—transmediates surface and world at once. Heinz Mack gravitated frequently to the use of reflective planes, and there is also, in this same Zero show, Adolf Luther's *Virtual Picture (Mirror Object)*, from 1966–67, a deep-set frame containing dozens of slightly concave mirrored disks that reconfigure ambient space as a pattern on the wall: an ever-changing (because always viewer-"subjective") anamorphic kaleidoscope.[12]

In another turn of this spiraling Guggenheim retrospective, there are the vocal activations of the viewer/reader—viewereader—of Daniel Spoerri's 1959 *Auto Theater*, in which two imperfect, shimmering mirrors confront the spectator above three mechanically spooling scrolls that include, respectively, instructions for spectatorship, questions posed about art, and a rolling cascade of onomatopoetic German words—like *boink, plof, tonk*—that make their aural mirroring (their phonic mimesis) known only through the self-activated auditorium of private elocutionary theater. Even audiovisual art holds the mirror up to attentive response. One result is that a piece of unmistakable "mixed media" such as this, at a far pole from any focused and valorized specificity, operates its full effect only when viewed transmedium.

Earlier in the same year as the Guggenheim Zero exhibit, a very different kind of mirrorwork was on display, though equally composite, in a 2014 show at the Hirshhorn Museum called "Damage Control: Art and Destruction since 1950." Stopping just short of some graphic melodrama on the theme of psychological damage, one suite of images—in the mode of appropriated photography—reverts from the physical destruction of one medium (poster art) to the reflective power of its medial ground (mirror underlay) so as to vivisect the very construction of subjectivity in commercial image culture. To this end, Douglas Gordon comes at the issue of contained damage—in the mode of a quite literal (or somatic) de-facement—from a baldly allegorical point of view, turning the publicity images of cultural icons (from Dean Martin through Liza Minnelli down to Kurt Cobain) into an ironic iconology of narcissism's inherent feedback loop.

It is important to see the step into social satire, rather than just medial irony, taken by such conceptual laminates, advancing in this way beyond the numerous mirrored interfaces in the work of an artist like Michaelangelo Pistoletto, where figures painted on a reflective plane can thus seem to cohabit with the museum viewer in a virtual space of interaction rather than a mere plane of adjacency. Gordon flattens out the interaction in order to enact an identification. Addressed in first and second person along the ocular axis of fandom rather than gallery exhibition, Gordon's series of over a dozen singed (rather than signed) poster images is entitled *Self Portrait of You + Me* (with the celebrity's name as a kind of subtitle). Imagine the most blandly direct of medial specifications for these artifacts: burnt paper and reflective surface. Everything depends instead on the immanent transmediation of picture planes when one looks at or into—and then at oneself back from—enlarged star portraits with the general area of their eyes burnt out. Even as they seem blinded by their own spotlight, we stare only at ourselves *in them*. Surface damage induces here an in-depth optic collage. For these mirrors are planar supports on which, or from which— through the cauterizing of their subject's own represented gaze—we see our own. Not just see ourselves, but see our own gaze at work. What one catalog commentator, in reading Gordon's manipulation of visible burn and returned mirrored look, suggests as the hidden metaphor of stardom's "smoke and mirrors" is explored more fully than this phrasing might suggest in the transferential exchange of simultaneous self-projection.[13] Not merely a skewering of pop culture's idol-worship just where it thrives, in the eyes of exhibitionism and identification, such composite yet still bipolar works (you + me) are transmedial experiments, not just travesties, in the way they surgically isolate and then resuture image and picture, doing so across the pre-aesthetic ground of self-image and its mass-marketed transferences. Gordon's work thus signals the dialectic of the exhibition as a whole: by maintaining, that is, through citation and irony, a certain degree of *[damage::control]*.

Apart from this muted narcissism of an intimately distorted identification, and far removed as well from the specifically mass-culture horizon of Gordon's found and defashioned star "projections," the mirror has made other suggestive conceptualist returns since Burn—and every bit as much, though by different means, transmedial. There are, for instance, the treated mirrors from the mid-1990s by French painter Bertrand Lavier, in gold-plated artist frames, their surfaces almost effaced by broad off-white monochrome strokes reminiscent of French action painting—with only a glimmer of sheen, and no real reflection, squinting through the manipulated interface. Those works have their seductive optic appeal, no doubt about it, with something almost spectral about the play between stroke and reflective substrate, as in the cryptically titled *Domino* from 1995. But they enter into a fully conceptualized—as well as a further transmedial—circuit only when linked to the striking wit of Lavier's later work in digital printing, as for instance *Rue de Varennes* (2004). This is a "painting" named simply for the Paris street on which the image was initially captured. Here (once there)—in a new media trans-ference (no psychology this time, just art history) to an old-media format—the viewer is tempted to project upon sheer contingency the will of art: an arbitrary commercial expedience read out as a made work. This occurs when the whitewashed plate-glass window of a defunct business storefront has its picture taken, in the smeared occlusion of its paint-coated opacity, and then transferred to canvas by digital ink-jet printing. In this way, the broadly stroked glass seems translated, by reproduction itself, to the high art canon of gesturalist abstraction. The sequence is certainly more metapictorial than artisanal. Slapdash industrial whitewash on a window pane, transmediated to dig-ital imprint on canvas, rehearses—via the time-honored Albertian trope of painting as a window on the world—the last gasp of artisanal work in easel coverage. Here, then, is a mock photorealism: a mere photograph (and of an urban storefront, no less, topos supreme of the hyperrealist finesse) returned to canvas texture as simulated facture.

In connection with Gordon's damaged portraits, I spoke of the "pre-aesthetic ground of self-image"—in other words, the return of the gaze before the recognizant art of its irony. Transmedial works like his do seem mounted to exacerbate the hyphenate of "self-image," transforming it into the more conceptual ricochet of something like *[self::image]*. Same with the Saatchi gallery presentation, in the same year as the Hirshhorn exhibit, of the wall-sized work by Norwegian artist Jeppe Hein that might be thought—one of those underlying visual puns again—to give a different twist to the notion of an "installation view." For here the "picture plane" looks back at the room's spectators so as to transform our image in the very act of attention. On the wall nearby, in explanation: "*Mirror Wall* (2010). Mirror foil, wooden frame substructure, vibration system. 200 × 356 cm." Quite literally, the closer you look, the more (action) you see, since proximity triggers the electronic oscillation that ripples the zone of display with a narrow transmedial torque between reflex and alienating representation. In contrast to Gordon's pointed ironies of star transference and viewer "projection," Hein's concept is more straightforwardly museal: in the frequent self-consciousness of the viewing experience, one often sees something of oneself, or say one's own presence as spectatorial agent, in the planar displays of a gallery visit. With its typical transmedial play between mirroring and marking, here the broader mode of *[reflex::action]*, short-circuited to sheer *[refle ction]*, has been narrowed to the automatic index alone, even while equivocating in this case (by a distorting vibration) between image and the event of its notice. Yet Hein's work does so with the further suggestion, perhaps, that such is the implied fact of all aesthetic reflection—the never-settled image—in the eyes of a mobile spectator.

In its sensor-triggered machination, Hein's installation irony is all the more likely to take its rightful place within the mode of Conceptualism 2.0 if one looks back (and into) the many mirrors, besides Ian Burn's, deployed by the conceptualist successors to the Zero school. "Conceptual Art in Britain, 1964–1979," an extensive retrospect mounted at the Tate Britain almost four decades after that bracketed heyday of the movement, in 2016, includes notable mirror works that, in flouting the preconceptions of medium specificity, abrogate the borders between flatness and depth, display and participation, whether by mounting mirrors on canvas or redundantly "glazing" them in variably sized frames. In specific rebuttal to the modernist ideal of the monochrome, for instance, Michael Baldwin's series *Drawing (Typed Mirror)*, from 1966, imprints texts contesting Greenberg's purism on framed sheets of mirralon, a reflective foil-like surface, so that the lucid flatness of their own critique is impinged upon by images of the viewer and of other wall works in turn: a counter-manifesto compromised by its own contingent optics—and thus enacting by default the sheer fantasy of a "purified" plane.

So one may well think back to Madrid again—and, by contrast, to those blindspots of reflection in the Thyssen exhibit of hyperrealist canvases— but only this time to head north for the differently situated mechanical and fiberoptic intertexts of the Barcelona photographer Joan Fontcuberta: an artist on my mind throughout, though never on view. In one of his more recent projects, he offers the clear case of a digitally implemented Conceptualism 2.0 (as compared to Gordon's "hand-made" defacements or Hein's simple motor mechanics). This results from his having searched the Internet for the social-media equivalent of such *[mirror::art]* in the form of what he terms "reflectograms." What photorealism was typically constituted to avoid—the reflection of the lens whose work the painting simulates—is in this case the whole point. Fontcuberta's "grams" are to be distinguished from the typical Instagrams available to "social mediation." Rather, they are actual mirror shots (mostly self-portraits with reflex camera, often with flash flares, rather than reverse-angle cell-phone "selfies"), some 3,000 of them, mostly gathered from secondary circulation on surfed websites. Michael Fried's delineated tradition of the mirror self-portrait, from Caravaggio forward, is here thrown for a loop by photomechanics—and then once more by museum display. For Fontcuberta has optically projected these mirror photos—a transmedial displacement of their intended broadband pathways—onto twenty separate film screens in a 2011 exhibition called *Through the Looking-Glass*. They have become the public theater of private self-specularization.

This metaspectacle of projection puts an unexpected clarifying spin on this artist's previous photographic work. For in their original vernacular idiom, the exaggerated veridical nature of these automimetic images—bearing the confirming trace of their own capturing apparatus in the undoctored relay of the subject—is precisely what Fontcuberta's resistant agenda has called into question in his work over the last three decades. This latest trove of appropriations seems thrown on screen—extending the circuit of their narcissism and exhibitionism—for a transmedial comment on the residual indexical confidence (or contract) entailed by any such self-imaging voucher of presence. If, as in Gordon's work of Pop identification, the actual mirror is the most realist of all surfaces for the emblematic work of social representation, the fuller range of Fontcuberta's work gravitates more often to the elusive and illusory composite rather than an automatic reflexive planarity.

And in this "elusive" quality lies the need for extensive discursive clarification in so many of the constructions to come, Fontcuberta's among them. In contrast to the photorealist aesthetic, we encounter in these works a different quotient in the relation of cause to effect. We *know* that many hyperrealist works are produced by a gridding of canvas to parse the exactitudes of photo projection, but that stratum of production is gone entirely from the credibly realized shapes and colors of the resultant painted plane. In work like much of Fontcuberta's, however, with its typical practice of photo aggregation or transformation, right from the start we *see* something odd, off, oblique, or tacitly composite in the given image without knowing what causes it—or why. From which uncertainty, such unfixedness, the energies of closer looking—together with its secondary recognitions—are pressed into deeper service. In just this respect, Fontcuberta's experiments characterize precisely what the next chapter means—and means comparatively to pursue across several quite different practitioners—as the turn from the crowded spectrum of hyperrealism (wearing its technical associations mostly on its sleeve) to the more rigorous *undertextual* ironies of optical support or substrate: what I am calling the hyporealm of their unsettled mimesis.

IN REGARD TO FONTCUBERTA'S PRACTICE, WE HAVE MERELY SCRATCHED THE MIRROR SURFACE when considering so far only his multiscreen display of appropriated autoportraiture in amateur photography. This chapter soon returns to his earlier photo composites in their disclosed underlay (their hyporealization) as a simulated bitmap array—where undergirding comes clear as undergridding. A curious mirror work by another artist, however, can help secure the inferences of that return. The open secret of a standard mirror is that you are not there behind its surface when you seem to be. But how does one contemplate a substandard mirror, whose duplicating surface is itself crudely duped—from behind, beneath—in some dim matching of your shape and motion? This is the question raised by the technically ingenious (if technologically disingenuous) *Wooden Mirror* (1999) by Daniel Rozin: a transmedial work of wooden sculpture, digital photography, and computer electronics that reflects—across its own partially artisanal materiality—on the newer electronic protocols of optic recognition.

The counterintuitive effect is achieved as follows, with art arising from a battle with its own unlikely materials. Dozens of wired, honey-toned sawed squares are mechanically (and separately) rotated by servo motors under a raking overhead light so that the reflected brightness of their polished sheen when angled up, against their shadowed brown underside turned down, articulates the binary pattern of a quasi-digital mosaic. But what results is not just some abstract collage—or neomodernist grid. The effect, instead, is a composited version of the viewer's own image in shifting geometric aggregate, its simulated pixel "tiles" guided by a hidden digital camera whose lens is wedged between them at one central point. The upshot of such "shooting" is that the body and gestures of the recorded mobile spectator are fed to the invisible computer system, for processing in a "greyscale" format, so that the on/off (here up/down) array thus generated offers a mutating wooden checkerboard of mimetic shadowplay rather than a typical mirroring reflex—yet fully readable as "self" according to the deepest acclimations of pixel culture.

No denaturing 2.0 work, in its own throwback artisanal "carving," could cross paradigms—whole technical epochs—more openly. The most natural of all secondary images in a mediated but nonrepresentational reflection—or, say, the least arbitrary of all signs—is now fabricated by the *most* arbitrary of all signifying systems: the serialized 1-0 of binary code. The effect is once again a kind of reverse skeuomorph: the familiar mirror image (or webcam insert, for that matter) denaturalized by a folksy woodcraft simulation of its closed-circuit loop. Visuality's foundational "medium," light itself, has thus in its own right been translated from indexical vehicle to hyporealm code, as if indifferent to its own material conveyance. By a more direct use of electronic pictures, Fontcuberta's work brings the standard effects of digital imaging back to the surface—but only from its suddenly exposed underside.

[photo::genetic]

In the same year that Fontcuberta won the prestigious Hasselblad Award, an epitomizing work of his appeared in a 2013 show at the Met called "After Photoshop: Manipulated Photography in the Digital Age." Inverting an implied play on the etymological *manus* of the subtitle, the idea on exhibit in Fontcuberta's case might have been called "Manipulated Digitation in the Post-Photographic Age." His offering there was a reconstitution of history's first surviving photograph, an 1826 print by Nicéphore Niépce. This is point number 1 in what the viewer needed to know in looking, and was informed of by curatorial paratext. It is only further explanation that revealed the Web-searched basis of this transmedial composite as a textbook case of art's new "research" rather than "craft," with the archive of images generated in this case by a multilingual image search—incipiently "globalized," as it were—based on the terms "foto" and "photo." In this Googlegram work, as in Fontcuberta's other ironic adaptations of available technology, the processing of optical data files from key-padded Web searches is, by a further software process, configured into minuscule tiled patterns that serve to (re)generate—by adjusted fields of tonality, chromatic weight, and intensity—the pixel-like gradations of an overall master image. Unlike a traditional photo-collage, the parts, when taken in at the right distance, lose all separate status in their sum.

In another variant of such *[photo::genesis]* in an ironically anatomical mode, one of the most daring and least technologically predetermined works of this sort in the artist's catalog is the engineering—the wry ima-geering, from the micrographic ground up—that makes for a collage du-plicate of Gustave Courbet's *Origin of the World* (1866), with it scandalous vaginal close-up of a reclining nude. Whatever the debates over realism and its censorable limits in Courbet's day, the computer-produced com-posite of this notorious image has the look now of borrowing back from the latent (and often marketed) eroticism of early photography a reminder of those new pornographic conveniences (for ogling on Google and else-where) that have proliferated a century and a half later with Web imaging.[1] Later in this same decade of digital proliferation, in fact, such a transmedial zone between the received genres of art history and the new possibilities of networked imaging—again under the shadow of a global surveillance—finds another ironic manifestation in Fontcuberta's repurposing of found photographs. Reversing the bottom-up logic of the Googlegrams, in which the out-of-focus touchstone of Courbet's hypertrophic nude is composited of separately defined images, here Fontcuberta generates single murky images from Google Earth zooms of nude beaches for works in a series parodically called *Frontal Nude* (2010). In this play between Net.art and the history of painting—a history within which the naked first becomes "the nude"—remote satellite photography has rendered equivocal the whole notion of a global "frontality" from a God's-eye perpendicular. The new medium has thus compromised, by way of fidelity as well as privacy, the old mode. Canonical content is entirely unmade by upstart form. Yet by coming up against its own optical limits, surveillance returns the blurring veil of low resolution to sexually "private parts" across the transmedial blend of satellite capture and art-historical allusion.

[pix::elevation]

It is unsurprising that Fontcuberta would be drawn to Antonioni's film *Blow Up* (1966) and its problematic of scale in regard to the particulate molecules of a photo image. This interest takes shape in a 2009 instal-lation, *Blow Up Blow Up*, with the famous film's grainy evidentiary snap-shots of a suspected corpse enlarged yet again, beyond an almost illegible "life-size" in the film, to sheer blotches across wall-sized photographic planes: the image of the corpse become the death of all imaging.[2] But what may take us by surprise, in Fontcuberta's experimentation, is that the deeper computer logic eventually resulting in his Googlegrams, and then in *Frontal Nude*, had earlier—and quite beyond cinematic or even photographic allusion—sent him off in another and even more high-tech direction as well.

This earlier software manipulation—drawn more explicitly yet from military application than are the satellite scans of *Frontal Nude*—is even more drastically denaturalizing. In the remarkable *Landscapes without Memory*, he generates scenic vistas of the never before seen through a process his series title calls *Orogenesis* (named for the science of mountain formation). The resultant image plane derives (almost in the mathematical sense) from his feeding into an electronic conversion program the digitized data field of one or another canonical painting, often with its own two-dimensional approximation of three-dimensional space in the landscape mode—now a post-impressionist Cezanne, now a Braque, now an already surrealist Dali. These computerized images are processed through software designed by the US Air Force to "translate" flat topographic maps into the more serviceable form of pictured landscapes in simulated elevation. Cross-wired thereby is a virtual-reality apparatus issuing not in video simulation but in single mysterious prints (an André Derain, for example, spawning its wondrous electronically deciphered double).[3] This secondary "translation" from the urgency of military tactics to the purposeless redundancy of the aesthetic is so complete that all sense of the trained gaze of combat seems on the surface to disappear into the thrilling strangeness of such CGI terrain. What we encounter in the high-definition fantasias of these *Landscapes without Memory* are delirious eutopic/utopic marvels (the double etymology: perfect nowheres) rescued from artillery grids and repurposed for the energy of a disinterested electronic world-building. And yet, knowing the concept behind the precept, we can't help but sense ourselves at some few degrees of separation from "live-action" gunnery practice in a VR cockpit—or closer yet, in the spectator's own probable experience, to the flight-simulation video games descendent from the very software of Air Force experimentation. In either case, and beyond anything recorded or "imitated," or in any sense reconstituted, by these picture planes in *Landscapes without Memory*, it is instead their origin, their origination—not to mention (by that different etymology) their *orogenesis*—that derives from computer "memory" alone.

In this form of Fontcuberta's transmediation, the results are ad hoc procedural works. In his circuitous repurposing of this military software, the more or less approximate perspectival craft of the source painting is reinstrumented by an algorithmic regularity that distorts the painterly *imagined*—by an imposition of the electronic *virtual*—into the genuinely and disturbingly *unreal*. The sense elsewhere of the queasy hyperrealism that attends the too-close-for-comfort duping of human features in CGI animation, the dreaded "uncanny valley" of Hollywood computer engineers, has become quite literally the weird unpeopled landscape of a high-definition no-place. And beyond manipulations in this vein with actual landscape art, however far from realist treatment, Fontcuberta can disremember other more experimental work. When the all-over drips and squiggles of a Jackson Pollock abstraction are three-dimensionalized through such a software filter, one gets, in the digital printout, a landscape with rock-formation loopholes. There, as well as in the other works from this series, the hyperreal definition of these digital screenscapes—having passed through the underlying (itself invisible but definitive) electronic hyporealism that diverted them from military "realizations"—passes over into the implausible reaches of the surreal. The coded underlay—the substrate or, so to say, hypostrate—hails to the overplayed topography across the invisible conceptual ironies of electronic generation. Here is a transmediation that is all baffled interface.

From their origins in military epistemology, these works turn traitor to all accuracy of perception. They are visions of the mis-seen. Everything in the original image, even an intimate grove of trees in the Derain painting, gets mistakenly scaled to a broader geographical terrain by the intervening software conversion, so that the process is aptly named for a mountainous topographics. Moreover, in the second section of the volume that collects this work, called "Bodyscapes," Fontcuberta's procedure is also performed on anatomical close-ups in photographic black and white (veins in a hand, a nipple, nostrils, a penis) that generate equally unreal vistas of the world's geologic body in graded light and shadow. In this way are "humble epidermic maps that register the intimate topographies of our bodies" converted into "hieroglyphs" of the human anatomy denaturalized.[4] As Fontcuberta further explains, he has "tricked" (6) the computer system, constrained as it is to recognize only a narrow range of cartographic data, into the misrecognition of other visual input. The "trick," the trompe, doesn't extend fully to the viewer, however, since the spaces are palpably, even though sometimes not quite describably, unreal. The trumping of the eye, having passed through the machine, is thus all the more alienated from normal illusionism. This is crucial. For what is exposed here by the transmedial deception as de-perception—or deeper "ception"—may well be the "programmed" nature of all representation, if not all seeing.

Conceptualism 2.0 has thus entered into the semiotics of picture making by rendering the enforced ineptitude of a computer into an allegory of "recognition" itself and its hardly fixed or inviolate optic schemata. Same with the nude, in the reduced form of the naked body part, when parsed into corporeal detail so that its somatic contours are misperceived as uninhabited land forms. Writes Fontcuberta: "The representation of the world is here dependent not on experience but on a prior imaginary and previously codified experience that mediates between the viewer and a no-longer graspable reality" (6). Yes: "mediates between," and not just between work and viewer but, in those "unremembered" landscapes, between two starting points for computerized "elevation": the legible patterns of topographic notation versus the already pictographic conventions of mimesis—where the contrast is in fact a revelatory leveling. For of course landscape painting has its codes as much as does the military program designed to process the nonindexical abstractions of cartography. Given the fact that schema and realization involve noncommutable signifiers in the original Air Force software, one can marvel at the gap between chart and seascape, map and mountain range. All the more so in Fontcuberta's further conversion, where the attempt at transmediation in these images doesn't just generate unreal vistas but figures the virtuality of all imaging: call it not orogenesis so much as *oculogenesis*.

So it is that the shifting electronic tropes across Fontcuberta's whole recent career—not just his alternation between painting and body part as spur to regenerative transformation—emerge as tightly complementary. In his Googlegrams (as in his reflectograms as well, for that matter, first taken up in the last chapter), computer searching dredges the digital base of mostly analog imagery and binds its findings into another set of analog images. In the earlier computerizing of his virtual topographies—a related stage of his hyporealist trajectory—it is, of course, a yet more arbitrary collaboration between art history and CGI technology that serves to *transmediate* the aesthetic landscape, via military software, into a simulated and instrumental one: aesthetics reduced to tactics, but each deconstructed in the process as conflictually coded and mutually incommunicable.

[image::base]

For their "Beyond Photoshop" exhibition, the Met curators themselves were quite ready to call Fontcuberta's experiments since the 1970s a probing "deconstruction" of the myth of "objectivity" in photographic art. In the case of their chosen display piece, what is in fact dismantled is the coherent plane of Niépce's original—here reconstituted only by the illusory build-up of thumbnail images (fig. 2 and detail, fig. 3). Within the broader context of Fontcuberta's varied photo-epistemology, we can return now to this image for its fullest media-historical weight. Two figurative overtones, each called into question, shadow this electronic collage in relation to the photo's eponymous *View from the Window*. The first is the purported idea of a real-world "viewing" rather than a machinic image production. The second, inextricably, involves the longstanding trope of the Albertian "window," millennial figure for the very frame of mimetic representation—downgraded now to everyday trademarked functions of the Windows operating system. And just here lies its link to Lavier's occluded window image, *Rue de Varennes*, in chapter 1, his digital imprint on seemingly worked canvas. In Fontcuberta's composite image, the once famously photographed windowed vista on the Mediterranean is not now what it seems; the other streaked Parisian window (by Lavier) also dissembles its photographic status as a gestural painting. In a slippery phonetic enunciation that has a curious way of matching the convergent digital articulation of each work, it is the *[image::space]* per se, as imaged space, that is at once mounted, worried, and finally undermined by the irresolution of its *[image::base]*.

Whereas Fontcuberta's homage to Courbet displaces any myth of origination, optical or organic, onto the variable procedures of image generation, in *View from the Window* the artist has sought explicitly, according to the Met gloss, to relate "photography's chemical origins to its dematerialized, pixelated present." But the chemistry of that origin, and its availability to us now, is more complicated than the Met took space to explicate—and puts a further twist on the window as aperture. For this is a cameraless image recorded by camera obscura on a pewter plate treated with bitumen and exposed over several days' time. Its captured window was thus doubled by the nonmechanical pinhole of capture itself. But the much-reproduced image has come down to us in a further remediation (or doctoring)—well before the transmedial logic to which Fontcuberta submits it—that is central to an argument made by Kaja Silverman in her recent attention to his computerized troping on this image.[5]

Two main thrusts of Silverman's argument converge here: the minimizing of the camera itself in a broader definition of photo-graphy, obvious enough historically, and the more controversial preference on her part for a definition of photography not as index (say, trace) but as analogy (say, figuration, variable over time in its recognition value and cultural force). As touchstone for her revisionist "history," as for any account more traditional as well, the Niépce image is almost always displayed or printed in the format enhanced in 1952, through a kind of watercolor pointillism, by photographic historian Helmut Gernsheim, who had finally managed to track down the faintly visible original. Whether or not one would wish to claim an indexical basis for the initial murky "heliograph" (light-writing), with its double "window" (architectural and pinhole), still one might certainly accede in this case to Silverman's sense (though not phrased this way explicitly by her) that the print's afterlife is only an "analogy," aided by overpainting, for the scene represented—and indeed for the original exposure itself.[6] The chemical treatment, once used to retain the received image, has passed through another chemical treatment (watercolor paint) meant to retrieve its contours more vividly. To compromise with Silverman's claims, as one may wish to do, we can certainly grant that what we have here is no more than the analog of an index.

When Fontcuberta takes up the whole question of "the image," in its ubiquitously enhanced (or clarified) form, and passes it through the mosaic sorting of the Googlegram program, he is already transforming (analogizing) what might loosely be called the photorealist overlay of Gersheim's "restoration" with a new-medial analysis by automated and variable jpeg densities. The effect at this stage is certainly to dissipate photography's indexical aura (and authority) across a permutational array. The ghost of an original optic impress is built up in this case from cascades of inset backlit tiles matched to shadings of the black-and-white master image in a mimetic approximation according to density, luminosity, and hue (fig. 3 again). But this happens only once the subsidiary icons (or pixel-scale indices) are reshuffled from the interchanged lexical prompts of a hyporeal photogenesis. What thus splinters all organic integrity of image, shivers it to bits, is the same optic material that constitutes it, that underlies it (again: hypo=under). These are the same ingredient fragments, or Internet-sourced "excerpts," that may thus be felt to transmute the stylistic hype of hyperrealism to a new stratum of compositional irony and a new molecular grammar—beyond and beneath the gridded, sectored, and recopied photograph. This is a hypogrammar, an "under"-structure, whose "net" effect (both senses) is like an arrested motorization, by so-called search engines, of the overall image plane. What transpires is the demotion of photochemical art, at its very point of origin, to an operational expertise in digital graphics.

Again, the irony of scale: concordia in discord, with the constituent tidbit only gradually perceived within the gallery enlargement. In a mode of coherent lithographic printing rather than digital collage, one may recall—from the "Prelim," in a more directly photorealist mode—the enlarged rendering of sequential film frames, complete with time-worn scratches, in Ed Ruscha's *The End* (1993; redone with Pettibon in 2003), where the fixity of one medium refigures the closure (both narrative and media-historical) of the other. This is to say that the transmedial gesture operable in the photorealist project inheres in the hypermediation at work, for instance (1967–2012 again, as the Madrid show spans its development in chapter 1), in the absorption into painting of an alien mechanical optics and surface treatment. Photomechanical evocation in paint is, however, only one such transit point between medial determinations. And cinematographic evocation only another. Further screen regimes have followed, increasingly totalizing.

In Fontcuberta's case, and from the realm of automatic imagining itself rather than paint craft, we come upon pictorial formats that hover (and so in effect *cross*) between a ubiquitous and etiolated screen culture of digital relay and some other precedent form, like photography or painting. His Googlegram works aren't rescanned paintings or even rescreened photos. They are paintings and photos seen through ("across") the filter of their own either splintered or transfigured electronic aftermath. Yet Fontcuberta—operating at the subsisting stratum of the hyporeal— negotiates a further dematerialization of means. He does this in his simulated pixelations of picture planes that are in fact thousands of miniaturized (coherent but illegible—say, suppressed) ones instead. Computerized image searches are a cognitive facilitation, to be sure. When replayed by full-frame transmedial irony as photoprints, however, they install a figure for aesthetic belatedness from within the present artistic form. Under the thumb of the digital, as it were, these versions of the postmodernist rather than high-modernist grid can only, thus composited, suggest the material reliance of aesthesis on prosthesis. In being recognized as *hypo*realist effects for their dependence on underlying computer codes and their search results, Fontcuberta's extrapolations from one graphic platform to another optical plane are also leaps of transmediation that subordinate all question of technique to the new global premium on data technology and its algorithms.

Here, too, is where Fontcuberta's digital photography, even when not mobilizing military software in those *Landscapes without Memory*, intercepts the new global media ecology from another oblique angle of critique. One might readily want to follow the Met's lead, pointing us back into the precincts of photorealism itself, and see in the constituent color tiles of his gridded vistas a "deconstruction" not just of photography's objective basis but of its simulated indexical coherence under other medial circumstances. This is only to begin measuring what else is being taken apart by his work. The point isn't simply that every photograph is a disguised pointillism, every coherence a construct, optically groundless at base. The crux isn't graphic and optical so much as cognitive, ultimately social, which is to say political—and, as such, all but an optic allegory of the bottomless. In the latter-day reign of image culture, representation is entirely derivative, or say cumulative. You never seize upon a separable pictorial moment without sensing in it, if not quite seeing, all the other images that precede and feed it, infuse and muddy it, that in effect *secondarize* it. This recognition makes each arriving image just one evanescent rephrasing of a given *visual discourse*. In its strange scalar gestalt, getting us to see our inability to see otherwise is the schematic work of the Googlegram project. Just as Conceptual art originally gave ironic priority to discourses of culture over its privileged artifacts, so too in the Met example does discourse dictate the image. With its collaged homage to our first optical automatism, this redaction of *View* is a foundational image sprung from the archive by none other than lexical cross-reference (*f/photo*) and its visual redistributions. What looks like a dated photograph is lots of more up-to-date and datelined ones, arbitrarily rearranged within a broad thematic protocol of word-search functionality. The overall image is not appropriated so much as engineered in its arbitrary increments and rebuilt, its medium computational before visual.

The unmistakable (if scarcely straightforward) remediation of such a Googlegram work—optical information search-engineered into a multiplex iteration of its own original image—can nonetheless, in its ironies, only be assessed transmedium. This is perhaps most obvious, among Fontcuberta's experiments, when the transformation in play is, rather than a tapping of the photochemical archive, instead a matter of digital-on-digital realization. The notorious picture of the female US soldier dragging an Arab prisoner on a leash at Abu Ghraib—captured with the middle-distance neutrality associated with prison surveillance cams—becomes in Fontcuberta's treatment a toxic mosaic dredged and recemented from the name-searched roster of key players in the Iraq invasion: familiar and widely broadcast images of Bush, Cheney, and Rumsfeld prominent among them, yet revealed only on determined close inspection of that iconic viral image in its new cellular composite. Surveillance may thus be felt redirected from the torture site toward its strategic origin in the halls of power. In contrast to the inbuilt legacy of a surviving early photograph, the Internet here reconstructs the already digital image that it once distributed. And it does so this time, beyond the technological shift, in order to picture an ethics of cause in its effect rather than just, as with the Niépce, the technics of a visual destiny in its prototype. But to perceive the concept behind (beneath) the reconstituted scandal of this prison picture, we must look across mediations—and back again—from leaked exposure to its literal (as well as politically figurative) build-up, from incriminating document to the lies that underlay its long-festering perversity, from a rogue digital image of anonymous torture to the internationally recognized *features* of the self-serving imperialism that gave rise and shape to it: the manifold *face of power* recycled in miniature photo-ops. In inferring what we really *see* in looking again at such an image in its unprecedented electronic ubiquity, the transmedium vector of suggestion—by contrast with the Googlegram of Niépce's image—is expressly more political than epistemological.

And analysis needs to stress again the seemingly bit-mapped locus of the ocular gestalt. Faintly cracked and spackled on first notice, the flattened-out databank of text and image in these works is in the other sense banked, terraced, graded (by hue and brightness rather than height) in a unraised topographic scrim that is found ultimately resolving—at just the right full-frame distance—into one among many possible pictures quite other than any that actually accrete to contour it. The whole is, in fact, far less than the sum of its parts: neither an aggregate nor an average but a spread of sheer difference gelling to "crazed" shape (and not least in the etymological sense, from pixie, of pixelated).[7] As such, of course, Fontcuberta's image discloses the truth of all imaging writ both small and a bit too large at once—too large for quite overlooking this fact in an encompassing look. In the reconfigured Niépce, certainly, as a version of our "first" photo, the logic of the congeries shows through the gestalt with an unusual clarity of implication. The photonic composite is almost an optical rebus as well as an allegory. Who can see the Niépce *without* seeing its splintered legacy? How else to approximate its priority without reassembling some overloaded sample of photography's historical and international fallout? And where more trenchantly than, with the Abu Ghraib photo, in a gridwork of data registration that, with overtones of surveillance purview, resolves into picture only on a need-to-see basis? How else to understand the atrocity than to see the bigger picture—in all its fragmentary contradictions—that such ferocity symptomatizes? The bigger picture—and the small men of power whose portraits make it up. In both the first art-for-art's sake photo and the later evidentiary scandal, the image comes to us as the disclosed composite of its own possibilities—by future extrapolation or present inculpation, respectively.

Though a politics of picture circulation is often implicit in Fontcuberta's work, it is the epistemology of contemporary imaging that is the more unremitting keynote. Its timeliness is part of the irony it prosecutes. Inevitably conjuring up the more straightforward and seemingly holistic scans of Google Earth, Fontcuberta's mosaic images in this vein infer at times the ogled dearth of the real. It is by just such intrinsic scalar irony that the Googlegram image operates to fractalize one level up the microchip tilings of any pixelated image, webbed into view across its own bitmap array. Certainly Fontcuberta's version of Niépce's landmark vantage point, his *View from the Window*, offers up a window we don't think to see *through*. This is one destiny of the lens that doesn't lead us back to human optics. This is one illusion of an illusion, one transmedial picturing of a former visual index, that pitches us past spectatorship altogether to decryption and analysis, to reading, but with no coherent authority claimed for its discrepant checkerboard scheme. So this is one differential image surface—one like so many others we encounter lately (only more so, and insistently)—that actually yields up to consideration its strictly differential composite. With the philosophical stringencies of text-heavy Conceptual art hereby emptied out by mere image-search linkages to certain freestanding multilingual lexemes (foto, photo), and with the earliest mimetic irreverence of the modernist grid downgraded from revisionary conceptual scaffold to a sheer sorting mechanism, an impasse stands forth in its true dimensions. With automaticity lording it over invention, electronics has vanquished all retinal integrity once claimed by the optic field. Isolated by composite simulation itself, such photonic hyporealism has rendered, and so tendered to view, one fragmented photo plane—advanced in the name of many, and indeed riding on the backs of many separate image modules of its own—that won't stay put for spectation. Nor let us settle in for a stable view. Such a contrivance leaves the seeing human body nowhere definitively to stand. Well beyond any painterly repression of the photographic moment in hyperrealism, routinely eliding the photographer's reflection we might expect to glimpse in storefront glass or chrome hubcap, we have come to a place where the *electronic* blind spot is no longer optical so much as ontological.

[frotto::grammatic]

These digital works evince, as noted, a long-standing preoccupation on the artist's part with the dubious epistemology of the image that goes back to his precomputerized work of the 1980s. In a 2014 keynote lecture at the national convention of the Society for Photographic Education, Fontcuberta described his major projects, including his several public hoaxes (epistemological send-ups), as bent on the "delegitimizing of photographic evidence." And in the process, he gave a particularly vivid and crisp picture of conceptualism itself (its guiding logic) in describing his return to Fox Talbot's renowned trope, "the pencil of nature," and to the light-sensitive, camera-free imprints (photograms) that preceded photography. Distinguishing between their evidentiary uses in the first instance, and their formalist use in the high modernism of Man Ray and Moholy-Nagy, he explicitly describes his various photogrammic efforts as instead "conceptual": not documents on the one hand, not formalist abstractions on the other, but investigations into the image itself in its visibility.

And transmedial at that, with more than just a vaguely mystified sense of "light writing." The works come across as articulated by a stronger syntax of direct appropriation. For they fall between already reproduced images, whether commercial or aesthetically valorized, and the encroachment of real objects indexically registered. In this sense, these early works referenced by his lecture, for him a seedbed of later explorations, are for us a focal point in distilling the transmaterial ironies of his career. The name of this photogram series, *Palimpsests*, suggests a cognitive lamination endemic to image culture and here, yet again, undone. As paratextually disclosed, the procedure is everything. In picturings made in the period from 1987 through 1990, so we learn from wall or monograph, Fontcuberta treated his found objects—the mass-circulation prints of original artworks by painters like Matisse and Cezanne, along with picturesque catalog covers, wrapping paper, or realistically patterned wallpaper—to direct optical exposure, transferring their "likeness" (as immediate imprint) to secondary reproduction on chemically sensitized photographic paper. In the process of reproduction, rather than representation, such photograms also include the light-cast shadow of real objects previously depicted (referenced) and now actually overlain on the already patterned image surface—bird, leaf, whatever—with these borrowings from the real appearing only as dark blank silhouettes in the chain of reduplications. Conveying a sense of reproduction as an infinitely coded recess, these works arrange that the real and the artificial speak to each other by displacement and negation, image over against its optical blackout.[8]

Even apart from these directly indexical works, one is tempted to think of "frottography" as applied more widely to a career's work that is always rubbing the image the wrong way, in one canted direction or another. Aligning his specific experiments in friction and impress with his other experiments in the epistemology of record and the vagary of trace, one may come to understand the manner in which photo concept has exceeded its chemistry in Fontcuberta's thought, whether in the return to Victorian forms or in the sabotage of military-industrial ones. His is the work less of a cameraman than of a *photographist*. Index is equivocated or reprogrammed, automatism goes electronic, documentation compounded or imploded from within. All that remains, in various hypostrata of lamination, are the graphics of reflected light.

The strategies cohere even as they diversify across Fontcuberta's experiments. The transmediation at stake repeatedly commutes between affordances now aesthetic, now commercial, either disinterested or strategic—as if to expose a new and suspect continuum in our image culture. For in those *Landscapes without Memory*, Fontcuberta's resort to computer-enhanced military cartography in the service of virtual reality terrain, in tacit association with surveillance tactics and ballistic science, bears out German media theorist Friedrich Kittler's relentless paradigm for the harbinger in military decryption technology of all advances in media art and commerce.[9] Certainly the paramilitary dimensions of contemporary imaging are by no means incidental in the current practice of conceptual media art, well beyond Fontcuberta's sourceless, memoryless sites as travesties of tactical virtuality.

[scan::lines]

From these same years of medial transformation we're living through, and finding pictured back to us, there is the striking artisanal and conceptual work of German artist Christiane Baumgartner—with her own tangible debts to Gerhard Richter as landmark innovator in a concepetualist inflection of the photorealist mode. *Photographism*, again, one might say. Or perhaps better in her case to call it—in distant relation to photo-inset trompe l'oeil (Peto to Flack)—a new kind of photogravure, its waves of light and shadow submitted to a more fixedly engraved trace. More to the point yet: *[video::gravure]*. The illusionist effect of Baumgartner's TV-derived works results in manifestly transmedial artifacts, with woodcut delineations representing linear video signals—hence the conceptual interplay of *[scan::lines]*. Hers are images in which the notion of the postwar archive of combat cinematography and the postmodern media field ambiguously converge. And in which yet another underlying pun as matrix comes to mind in the materialized ideation of culture's *graphic violence*. This is especially clear when Baumgartner takes up as explicit topic—indeed as optical topos—the videography of combat imaging.

Approaching a major work of hers in the painting wing of London's Imperial War Museum (*Game Over*, 2011)—nearing it from the far side of the large gallery in which it is hung—one may think at first it's a video screen-grab of war footage photographically enlarged over a dozen times, losing any real fidelity in the process: an exploding aircraft from a bygone era in a grainy soft focus reminiscent of pre-HD documentaries on broadcast TV. Same with the attack planes in the 2009 work *Luftbild*. There seems in play an immediate allusion to Richter's World War II fighter planes caught as if in blurry stop-action by his out-of-focus photorealism; or, especially in the overhead "shot" of *Game Over*, his bombardier's eye-view of Dresden under siege (*Bridge 14 FEB 45 (I)*, 2000), with released bombs receding from overhead into the vertical distance in their assault on a bridge. But Baumgartner's images have been achieved not in scraped and smudged black-and-white oil, like Richter's often are, but in boldly carved woodblock prints whose rough-hewn table-knife gouges evoke— at least from the spectatorial distance necessary to mute their oversize jaggedness—the familiar striations of low-resolution video. In this way, at "heroically" enlarged museum scale (like landscape painting of old, or "historical" war tableaux for that matter), Baumgartner's reimagined image of attack planes works to "update" footage (or photographs) of World War II bombers into (twice tramsmediated) graphic transmissions. That woodcut treatment is typical of her work, whatever the setting re-pictured, but the specific intertext in Richter for the aerial warfare pieces (unlike her scratched-out capture, for instance, of the fixed-frame routine view of highway traffic cams in another print) gives a special edge to this particular skyscape—or skyscrape—as televisual image. And with *Game Over*, the odd interlaced patterns of vertical interference, traversing her characteristic lateral scan lines, have the uncanny effect of producing from within this image of remediated video—as if in a phantom telescoping of screen technology—the further transmedial evocation of a criss-crossed pixel grid.

One may also note a certain irony in Baumgartner's graphics associated with that other sector of recent German work mentioned above, the imbrication of military technology and the industrial media complex in Kittler's theoretical writings. For in Baumgartner's craft, if only in its implicit media archaeology, the innovative military science of real-time image transmission, leading as it eventually does to commercial television, is being reinvoked by a simulated TV image. This aside, however, there is the further logical irony of origin and aftermath inherent in such images. In the irregular, ridged cascade of her horizontal slicings, a sense of those former wars we normally see "classically" documented (archival photographs and film footage, like heroic painting before it) is overlapped, imposed upon, by a latter-day optic that, by extension, calls up war's current satellite- and drone-based video operations in its Mideast "theaters." The remote imaging that used to be part of war's effect as reported, its epistemological aftermath, as for instance its TV reminiscence in History Channel retrospects on World War II, is now, in short, part of its operational system, its electronic execution—as to some degree suggested also by Fontcuberta's paramilitary digital topographies. This is the case even while the meticulous labor of this inference in Baumgartner's art—the productive action of its transmedial irony—returns any such contemporary electronic overtones of an increasingly unmanned aerial targeting to the humanized realm of the strenuously hand-made.

With photorealism-derived work like this—in what might, were it a movement rather than a single oeuvre, be dubbed videorealism—Baumgartner's technique does have an indirect precedent in the yet more exacting pencil-sketched or oil-painted newsprint photos and TV images from the mid-1960s by Latvian American artist Vija Celmins, better known than Baumgartner in the United States. Celmins's oil-on-canvas reproduction of an eponymous *Time* magazine cover from 1965 on the LA riots—with its vertical triptych of photographed violence looking like jump cuts on a film strip—is preceded the year before by a work called *T.V.*: a dimly lit, almost monochrome, painting of an aerial crash suspended in mid-broadcast on a pictured monitor. Celmins's 2011 show at the Los Angeles County Museum of Art, entitled "Television and Disaster 1964–66," captures the transmedial nature of her de-realized photographic and cathode-ray images in pencil and paint. And when she is more recently featured in that "Damage Control" show at the Hirshhorn (chapter 1), the pieces selected—some of them almost obsessively miniaturized in technique—include a later pencil reworking of the former TV-themed imagery, now called *Airplane Disaster* (1968): a yet more realist sketch on a paint-treated rectangular field in the middle of a larger expanse of drawing paper that simulates (in trompe l'oeil fashion) the slightly raised shape and muted sheen of a photographic print torn as if from a magazine or book, with a few words of type visible at the upper edge: "caught by enemy fire and disintegrates." The medium: "graphite on acrylic ground on paper."

The transmediation: graphic violence by any other name, returning an instantaneous death into laborious impersonal memorial. As the Hirshhorn essay by Kerry Brougher suggests about these and other images "almost superreal" (68) in their effect, what Celmins accomplishes is a "desensitization of the image" (68)—as image. Light-sensitive paper is one thing, but what crossing the gap between document and craft achieves here, one would want to say, is to render the shock of such an event in a new, hardly aestheticized, but somehow publicity-cleansed form, rinsed of exploitation. The lack of sharp focus in the image—as of course with Baumgartner's engraved woodcuts as well—returns us with new force to the very *idea* of disaster rather than just its catalog.[10]

For what is painstakingly delayed by Baumgartner's technique is, as with Celmins's, not just the swiftness of the pictured motion but the motorized action of the video image itself in coming to view. Such is the full transmedial irony of Baumgartner's woodcuts: letting us experience one thing (conjured TV or CCTV "still") while showing us, otherwise, how differently its optics actually find manifestation. (A rough moving-image equivalent of this will arrive in Scene Two with the slit-scan breakdown of a DVD image by Cory Archangel.) At opposite ends of a scalar spectrum, Celmins's miniaturized and Baumgartner's inflated screen simulations (rather than traditional "screen prints") serve to illustrate yet again, in their reversionary artisanal forms, the transmedial oxymoron of "techno-primitivism."[11] Opposite in historical trajectory to the paintbrush as a "toolbar" icon (that term itself anachronistic), here are further skeuomorphic reversals of a dominant technology by a residual technique. In Régis Debray's terms, the videosphere and the graphosphere may be thought to interpenetrate in such works on the common ground, or contrived interface, of the fixed trace.[12]

In this respect, too, the re-visionary charge sprung by Baumgartner's work in combat video results, it can only seem, from exactly the double distancing, historical (World War II) and medial (from photomechanical imprint to block-print impress), by which such picturing connects with the machinic specularity of contemporary warfare—and, by further association (as we'll see below), in work like that of Mark Tribe's in the videogame graphics of combat's latent terrain. Each artist keeps implicitly in view the link between the optical and the tactical in the new global reach of remote ballistics, in everything from satellite reconnaissance to drone targeting.[13] In contrast, Fontcuberta's own version of such traversed specular orders is more entirely imagistic than, say, instrumental, concerned with the credibility (rather than the tactical operability) of picturing per se. In computerized camerawork rather than hand-carving, his pictures install no sustained recoil from the automated electronics of a surveillance, let alone a video-game, ethos. He is drawn instead to the deceptive undergirding of the image by its own refigured optic undergrid. In the work of Baumgartner, by contrast, emphasis falls specifically on the medial continuity between the videosphere of documentary record and the latently invasive deployments of a related imaging system, where visual capture, mobilized for surveillance, can be activated for aggression. Yet one might think to put it this way by generalization after all: warring claims for the most urgent form of contemporary museum imaging increasingly take other ocular modalities of contested terrain, like those of electronic warfare itself, into the picture. And beneath the fetishized commerce in media violence, we have needed to stress how—with Fontcuberta as well as with Baumgartner and Celmins—the hyporeal/m of a picture's labored remaking gets manifested as sheer composite (and entirely unweaponized) image. To materialize the image of violence in this way is not to aestheticize its status as such, but to analyze it from the (under)ground up: in its internal transmit from one medial form to another.

[bit::mapped]

Such analysis is no less incumbent on attention even when the images of violence on display come straight from the internet. Linked to Fontcuberta's Googlegrams in this sense, as well as to the very history of blur to which Richter's own early work contributes, are the new German "updates" of such procedures in the digital irresolution of Thomas Ruff's devastated landscape prints, before which we're about to take up our dwarfed (and politically diminished) position. And these, too, benefit from conceptual orientation. De(con)struction: that's one recurrent link between the shattering of the picture plane in the *[trans::cept]* of mediation and the violence often associated with such image systems—whether military software for Fontcuberta's *Landscapes without Memory*, or televisual hardware with Baumgartner's retreatment of air-warfare graphics, or Mark Tribe's work (below) with militarist virtuality. As has no doubt been amply apparent before now, the only way to compass the transmedial is to grasp it as a broader-band oscillation of means—and inferential relay—than that of a more stabilized form/content dichotomy, but often sharing with the latter a certain latent dialectic potential. In her knife-scored images of mechanical violence in electronic transmission, for instance, Baumgartner distances form from content to a high degree—even while obliquely reconvening them to just the extent that the wavy lines of woodblock inscription seem calculated to evoke both the invisible wavelengths and the manifest scan lines of video broadcast. Certain other artists operate the confrontation of form and content at closer range.

This is the case, to be sure, with Ruff's outsize photoscapes—mostly from the middle years of the last decade and the rubble of its War on Terror horizons. These are works whose version of appropriated optics is drawn not from the striated video screen, like Baumgartner's or Celmins's, but from the pixelated Internet. Instead of receding into a streaked commemorative distance, the irony of Ruff's gargantuan photo planes is that nothing comes clear in the real-time transmit they evoke even at exaggerated scale—nothing except disintegration itself and its figurative geopolitical murk. In monumental (untitled) jpeg blow-ups of found imagery, serially displayed, and regularly drawn from scenes of violent destruction—ranging, for instance, from the 9/11 attacks to bombed-out Mideast cityscapes—Ruff transmediates between low-fidelity screen shots and high-candor print technique. Asserted by these enlargements—beyond (or beneath) the indexed disintegrations they depict—is the fractured and faded optic field (the hypogrammar) that constitutes them. Up close, the quarter-inch fragments, bunched together in two-inch-square tile blocks of 64 pixels each, are multiplied a thousandfold across the huge photo plane, all of it, of course, automatically configured. It's rather like confronting a low-definition cellphone image on an IMAX screen. Paradoxically sharpened by high-definition chromogenic imprint, the pixel-shredded bitmap blur of these images is quite specifically (medium-specifically, as it were) different from the urgent flurried grain or frantic action of war photos in a predigital mode.[14] As such, the fractured patterning of Ruff's enlargements conduces to another kind of graphic allegory. Figured (rather than disclosed) to view is a certain untenable and artificial closeness. Troped, that is, by pixel break-up and its dispersed accuracy of registration is the underlying fragmentation of a globally networked culture of entirely remote witness—and this while regularly bringing to view violent conflicts for which, in the other sense as well, no clean "resolution" is in sight.

In Ruff's epic jpegs, the fissuring chaos and fragmentation are thus referred back from content to form—and then back again as a comment on media distantiation: not as an accident of capture but as the too-familiar constitution of net images both in an ephemeral, global, and therefore epistemologically removed archive and in a world of repeated splintering violence. Politics and optics again coincide—at just the off-angle of diminished clarity. It is, moreover, by a kind of poetic justice that the images don't work well for online manifestation at museum websites. They need to be seen, instead, in the transmedial interspace—or again interface—between pegged screen shot and expansive archival print. To have mounted two of these prints across nearly half a gallery wall each in the Hirshhorn's "Damage Control" exhibit is only to mark the failure of such "control" over the degradation of the medium and the destruction of the referent alike, where these blow-ups can't help but figure (in rendering metaphoric) the mostly out-of-focus nature of one's newly globalized purview. The transmedial, in the playback loop from Web to print, thus comments on any viewer's potentially attenuated grasp on things transnational. Certainly the daily dose of bit-mapped images secures no immediate access to a coherent geopolitical image, no global mapping in its own right. Far (in every sense) from it.

That's exactly the point of such medial anomalies in the practice of Conceptualism 2.0. Trans-acted again and again in transmedial work of this sort is a deep relationality articulating the image relay—as, for instance, in the unnerving relation between the jagged ridged tracings of televised archival footage in Baumgartner's woodcuts and the violence over which they stand watch and offer retrieved witness; or between the primal digital fragmentation of Ruff's images and the blasted cityscapes their surface can barely agglomerate into resolution at such remorseless scale. Artisanal versus high-tech: each equally techno-investigative in nature. We have seen from the start how the category of transmedial art needs, by definition, to exceed the latest cross-section of so-called new media. Yet in current experimentation, no doubt about it, the digital is likely to have considerable purchase. Just how so, or how much, is the question. Or one of them. And distinctions everywhere declare themselves. Yet to insist that the Googlegrams of Fontcuberta make their scalar transition—from jpegs to tessellated gestalt rather than from pixels to jpegs—across a greater platform gap than Ruff's hypertrophic optical expanses, even though enlarged to the breaking point, isn't to claim the former as any more determinately, even if more flamboyantly, disjunctive in their conceptual double vision. Nor, therefore, any more transmedial. Even marked scalar discrepancy in the material substrate of an optic display operates on a sliding scale of its own—and can at times, often all the more potently, go virtually undetected.

In a two-staged installation at Momenta Art in 2012 called *Rare Earth*, Mark Tribe mounts for gallery display, in traditional frames, eight large-format landscape photographs in the tradition of Constable or Corot, gently contoured and thickly forested, but somehow oddly untrammeled and spookily lit—what, misted?—with the pictured leaves at times almost translucent around the edges. More uncanny valleys literalized, as if preserving the faint haze of their own backlit origin. For as topography, they are a rarer earth yet than they seem at first look: indeed ersatz, secretly pixelated, wholly rarefied in the split between terra firma and its virtual double. They are in fact hi-definition frame enlargements from the background landscapes of combat video games, immobilized as if in wait for the targetings, the F/X artillery bursts, the digital zooms. True to their global electronic moment in the era of Google Earth, Tribe's landscapes are images under the sign of reconnaissance. What they most resemble, within the aesthetic of war-gamer simulacra, is surveillance in suspended animation, the scene awaiting the sighting—and then the on-monitor mayhem orchestrated by layers of choreo-graphic spectacle and interactive kinesis. Again, hyporealism: an apparently photographic image undermined as index by its own underlying digital generation as high-definition but still invisibly pixelated video frame. Once glossed by paratext in their mute strangeness, these fixed views offer an example (comparable to Fontcuberta's *Landscapes without Memory*) of the data-file as image bank in the simulation of paramilitary terrain—and its converted virtualities, translated from combat-game console to wall art. And when the gallery discourse brings all this to light, one may sense the further dimension of the series title: conjuring not just an earthly terrain rarefied by virtuality but those "rare earth elements" or minerals involved in the manufacture of many electronic image systems: the mining that precedes all data mining as well as so much computer simulation.

And these canvas-scale photographs are counterposed in another room of this same installation, within its express theme of "paramilitary fantasy," by a fixed-frame but moving-image video by Tribe (only the barest motion discernible, unlike most of the frame-advance art in Scene Two) of an upstate New York landscape, serenely deserted, eminently "peaceful." In its ironic reprise of an American pastoralism associated with the Hudson River School and its ilk, the recorded topography is identified this time, not as the computerized backdrop for some first-person shooter or other action video in whatever degree of enhanced graphics it parades, but as an actual paramilitary training ground temporarily unoccupied by the right-wing militia who regularly perform their armed exercises across its terrain (an event waiting in the wings of this video shoot). The too-nearly-real of so-called war games, their frenzy suspended, answers in "live" footage to the commercially staged scene of pending fictive violence in the combat genre mode of videogames, even as the former is neutralized, demilitarized, in its very status as all but static gallery video and the latter transmediated into a museum genre of its own as art print.

[stereo::typographies]

As staged by Tribe's twofold videographic parsing, the politics of vigilantism and its links to white supremacist paranoia are brought into at least visual association with the mass culture of video gaming and the CGI scenographies of violence, whether executed in cartoon graphics or "cinematic" verisimilitude. Such an associational optic can lead us back to the explicit racial politics of two overtly transmedial artists who also return us, in the process, to the discursive and textual register of an earlier conceptualist practice. In a 1995–96 suite of works called "From Here I Saw What Happened and I Cried," African American photographer Carrie Mae Weems reprints as portrait-scaled enlargements, in heavy red tinting, various archival mug shots of nineteenth-century slaves (from the Getty Collection). These black faces and busts are framed so that lettering etched on the glass—scored as if into the zone of represented flesh like chattel branding—offers up in its ghostly superimpositions, when closely approached, a range of all-too-legible prose stereotypes about the emotional profile and social function of the instrumental body on view in this sometimes quasi-scientific, sometimes erotic, imaging. In address to these early photographs, and completing the dehumanizing logic of declarative (almost imperative) clauses begun with "You become…," the results include "…an anthropological debate" and "…a photographer's subject." As with Ian Burn's mirror work, or Michael Baldwin's *Drawing (typed Mirror)*, the words are in something of a focal tug-of-war with the images—at the strictly optical as well as ethical level—with no way for the viewer to keep both text and picture in focus at once. To register the compacted irony at the level of text/image overlay, one has to conceive transmedium the reciprocal hypo-thesis—with its reversible impositions—concerning the underlying (and overbearing) coercions of label versus index.

With perhaps a double pun on the "colored" body (a wordplay used elsewhere in Weems's work)—and as if under a specific reframing here as red ("read") bodies—these tinted, culturally tainted works nonetheless align closely in their word-image shackles with the image/text laminates of Glenn Ligon from a decade later. In his works appropriated photos are again overlain with the wording of received attitudes, this time stenciled in ink and coal dust rather than etched or typed. Hyporealm and its alternate "reality" are once more pitted indiscernibly against each other in a retinal contest unresolved in the mediated event. Ligon's are works in which excerpts from the fiction of James Baldwin are rendered (partly in industrial debris rather than just artisanal charcoal) over crowd scenes in black-and-white from the Million Man March, producing more like a mottled confusion than a figure/ground gestalt. If Weems's portraits must be "red against" the demeaning incised markers of reductive racist taxonomy, Ligon's operate to expose the way black identity is often suspended in a densely overwritten (even when sympathetic) atmosphere of ethnic image co-constructed by discourse in a stereotyping whose traces it is hard to see past.[15]

Equally in Weems and Ligon, then, the transmedial conceptualism of each artist's project is designed to intercept—and, by way of visible mismatch and interference, thus unsettle—the imposition of terms upon persons. In each case, the legacy of 1960s wordworks arrives in this second phase of conceptualism when words, transcribed or audible, are either bonded in new ways to image or radically subtracted from its own ongoing force. As we move to the further kinetic screenings of Scene Two, we will encounter several other artists whose "deconstruction" of image culture (the Met's term again for Fontcuberta's Googlegrams) goes to work on the inertial momentum of film or video as well as the fixed-frame picture.

None more resolute—and esoteric at times—than the LA artist Paul Sietsema, whose participation in a 2.0 aesthetic of the conceptual can be sensed even in the wholesale absence of electronics in his work (either by instance or even allusion). Whether in drawings, painting, or film, his transmedial "displays"—pitched between the handmade and the machinic, or in other cases across the found, the fashioned, and the vanished—operate very much within the field of global image culture, but under an unusually stringent and minimalist investigation and constraint. His work thus addresses an ambient "videosphere" (or disembodied image regime) only from the bottom up, rendering uncertain the nature of picturation in even its least spectacular forms—as far from computer-generated, and even from seemingly (manu)factured at all, as it is possible to come. The result, especially in his unflappably bland and undramatic trompe l'oeils, is that their tendency toward the covert transmediation of the seen runs all the deeper for it. With his imagings in paint or ink, and precisely as imagings rather than pictures, surface and hyporealm (manifestation and underlay; sometimes in the strange form of recto and verso) reciprocally switch places until there is neither picture plane nor image left securely to distinguish, neither support nor optic product—except for the retinally manifested virtuality at their interface.

It is toward that recognized zone of the neither/nor, of course, that the both/and bracket of our ongoing subheads has been in part directed—most recently, with the racial stereotypes exposed or undone by typographics per se. Early in Scene One: the *[movie::still]* that is neither one nor the other, but rather their linked lithographic "interrupture," as it were, in Ruscha's *The End*. There is, further, the alienation of traditional *[print::matter]* by digital materialization in 3-D computer sculpting. Elsewhere, the realization of photography by painting as something of an internal contradiction; and then, within this *[photo::realism]*, a further and almost paradoxical crux: the tacitly perceptible occlusion of its own reflective *[blind::spotting]*. The resulting transmedial *mise en abyme* of the hyperrealist aesthetic is to be contrasted in this respect, as just explored, with Web-based or otherwise digitally inflected works in the composited photo plane. These are image structures that tend to dissipate into their own *[photo::genetic]* breakdowns in the mode of *hypo*realism. Thus, recurrently, has the typographic cast of such analytic emphasis been meant to register (and reframe) the off-kilter perceptual slant induced in the first place by these named or nameless works and their explanatory discourse. Discussion throughout is by no means wedded to the typographic shorthand of these subsections, just meant to leverage with it a cumulative pattern of response solicited by the works themselves.

Some of this solicitation involves, within the zone of *[reflex::action]* alone, even a strategic misrecognition at mirroring's traditional vanishing point, where support regularly disappears into image (Gordon)—or across its anomalous transmedial simulation by wired binary composite (Rozin). More pointedly in the experiments of fixed-frame transmediation, or let's say more *markedly*, treatment can be found displaced in its explicitly electronic iconography from pictured optical cause to surface effect—this, for instance, in representations of video imagery by pencil or woodcut in the *[scan::lines]* of an *[image::base]* equivocation (Celmins, Baumgartner). Or in the *[bit::mapped]* hyporealm of a digitized "imagespace" no longer *[terra::firma]* because establishing no stable ground plane or image plane (Tribe, Ruff, Fontcuberta in his topographic transforms as well as his Googlegrams). So it has gone, the bracketed poles of a demarcation often so fully polarized as to turn inward on themselves in a contrary new force field bred of their own denatured collusion—and collision. The same implied dynamic will organize our consideration of Sietsema's work next, whose *[event::marking]*, just for starters, marks no event but its own execution, and (also based here on his own title) whose *[brush::painting]* collapses its grammatical dyad into a pleonasm of sheer studio tool in reductive apparition: the mere painted brush. If in Sietsema's work, as proposed above, there is "neither picture plane nor image left securely to distinguish," only their reversible surfacing-to-view, then his is an exemplary case in recent art practice—especially in his simulated photography with pen and ink—of representational formats mutually derealized at their own transmedial interface.

CHAPTER THREE: *Derealized*

M EDIATION IS ALWAYS CONTEXTUAL, YES. BUT THE CONTEXT CAN BE POINTEDLY, EVEN AG-gressively, site-specific at times. In this way, the deliberate transposition of media may delimit its own conceptual field within the wider culture of the image. At the flashpoint of intersection and transfer, the process can subtract as much as compound. Instead of the mutually reinforcing inversion of Fox Talbot's *Imitation of Printing*, with its decisive punctuation included as a nonalphabetic print "character"—an image that served us at the start in locating an "overture" of its own to the entire transmedial tradition—certain latter-day interface evocations across discrete media can seem more drastically evacuating than conflationary. What they pare back to is what they lay bare.

Paul Sietsema is certainly not alone in this brand of resolute minimalism. His British contemporary Simon Starling, for instance, comes at once to mind in the medium of conceptual photography rather than paint craft. In each case, as evidence will show, much depends on the orientation of an image toward some presumptive origin in the real. If the *hyper*real (as in the latest vocabulary for photorealist painting) serves almost to exceed everyday perception, and if the *hypo*real burrows beneath the seeming image to its ingredients, its medial gradients, still another version of conceptualist prestidigitation may be said to unrealize its own constructions. This is the kind of intuition-rebuking work gravitated to by Sietsema. Repeatedly he fabricates an apparent plane other than its picture's mere surface, together with objects on it in low relief, in such a way that the resultant image operates only as a gradually unmasked disclosure of its own stroked or meticulously inscribed support. To this end, the transmedial gambit is often as flaccid a mirage as it is exaggerated in legerdemain.

Though best known for his unflinchingly antinarrative films in the conceptualist vein, two of which we'll be briefly "screening" in Scene Two (along with Starling's metafilmic work)—with their deliberate refusal of the digital and their return, in Sietsema's case, to the 16mm aura of the early conceptual avant-garde—Sietsema's other devisings, for wall rather than screen, directly pave the way. In his canvas rather than film work, as well as in his ink drawings, every surprise is that of mediation thrust into sudden prominence—and isolation. Through the deceits of pigmentation—in an almost parodic minimalism of trompe l'oeil—he pursues many of the same questions of ocular expectation and authenticity that are brought out in his celluloid projections: brought out, that is, by silent articulation in the play of image and text. In the tantalizing obliquity and defied immediacy of their every anti-illusionist detail, his audibly motorized silent screen images—accompanied by the projector's unboothed sprocket purr—cannot therefore be apprehended, let alone appreciated, when divorced from the seemingly contrary illusionism (but often stunted pictorialism) of his painting and drawing. Here—straddling our two Scenes of investigation as Sietsema's experiments so revealingly do (like those of Tribe, or Starling to come)—is cross-over work of a quite unflinching sort, with both still images and film courting the arcane within an unseductive cerebral brinksmanship. If Sietsema approaches a certain conceptual limit in his abstract motivations, it is only the far edge of a terrain elsewhere and variously trodden—if never quite familiarized. We've been retracing some of it. We turn now to Sietsema's curious footprints on this slippery turf, then later to his motion-picturings of it— where in both manifestations, as much as in Fontcuberta's longer career, the preoccupation is radically epistemological in its wit. And studiously epistemographic in its execution.

As represented among a wide array of his work in an early career retrospective at the Chicago MCA in 2013–14, it is Sietsema's own titular category of "event drawing" that gives us a first terminological handle on the relation of his gifted (if introvert) paint craft to his better-known moving-image practice. Sietsema operates from various studios in LA that become at times the *mise en scène* of his illusionist rendering. Yet technique in trompe l'oeil has never been more mutedly trumpeted—so thoroughly neutralized has its execution become in these works. It takes so long to realize what we are looking at, and why it commands attention, that the nature of the image ends up coinciding with idea by the time one makes it out. Who would bother simply to fool us with so little, and in such a "dated" expenditure of craft? This is art without the hook of any undue charm except for the lucid beauty of its minor surprises—and their major conceptual returns.

What most of Sietsema's canvases make us think we see is entirely unfetching at first glance. One isn't lost in some classic trompe l'oeil wonder over how the image of a folded newspaper, say, can look so much like the real thing—angled out past the edge of a painted mahogany tabletop—that it enters our space under conditions, all but palpable, of the virtual rather than the fictive. With Sietsema's pictures, one marvels instead, and only on minute inspection, at how even a real unfolded upside-down newspaper laid flat on (perhaps) an artist's studio table to protect it, and paint-splattered as expected, would be no more credible as such, its yellowing text no more legible, than the upright and all but imponderable rendering of the same in front of us in a gallery frame. For, remarkably, this apparently daft craftsman has actually taken the trouble to redraw the surface of the throwaway newsprint in a printer's ink of his own—and to trouble the very idea of purposive making in the process. It isn't what we thought we were seeing at first, and there's nothing to do now, once faced with its continued lack of show, but to think about it.

The gesture—including the many hours of nongestural precision drafting—results in what we might call a medial dossier as well as single simulated newspaper "issue," a fabrication art-historical more than just datelined and ephemeral. Where the Impressionists painted the blur of newsprint in the hands of café readers, and where Picasso brought actual newsprint into his collages, and where Rauschenberg painted on newsprint instead of canvas at times, and where Warhol (and later Gober) reduplicated in its own terms the mass-print medium by less ephemeral lithographic replicas, Sietsema returns to represented (rather than appropriated) print face without either the out-of-focus scene of its reading or the freestanding museal defiance of its lackluster simulacrum or magnification. Yet he does so by all but erasing—in the deceits of his exactitude—the difference between the found and the fashioned. In such a tacit allusion to printing as the *first* mass medium, newsprint similitude in Sietsema's works does indeed approximate mechanical reproduction, but only as "cited"—since in fact the legible surface is not mass-multiplied at all, but sedulously hand-copied. And up to a point, the longer it takes— and the more optical work—to realize this, the harder it is to see what the draughtsman's labor has been all about, here or in Sietsema's other trompe l'oeils.

Never eye-popping, the rigors of technique carry little visual thrill, with even the magic elevation of objects in apparent relief seeming still somehow flat, monochrome, affectless, and blank. What are these images fashioned to make us see about seeing? Among such faux bas reliefs, try taking up a position, for instance, in front of *Untitled figure ground study* (*white ring*), from 2008. With its thick white enamel circle on an upside-down newspaper sheet, as if it were the smear from a removed paint-can lid, this apparent refuse from the workroom would seem lifted into the vertical and framed as a museum object—in a Duchampian flaunting of subtracted craft—only by the wholesale irony of the most immediately findable of a studio's "found objects." For here is evidence of paint's own "containment," physical rather than conceptual: liquid "product" and its "packaging" rather than aesthetic production. That's one sensible first impression. Yet, despite the title, the "figure" doesn't in fact dominate the "ground" in any standard way. Rather, a transmedial position is marked out between pigment and newspaper imprint when each is realized to complement the other in a study not appropriated in a tongue-in-cheek fashion from an artist's makeshift environs but painstakingly executed there. The ground(work) is all figure this time, intricate but deadpan.

[event::marking]

Or take your bemused place before *Event Drawing* from the next year, where ink is again used along with enamel paint, and where what has putatively happened to the newsprint plane is more than random spillage. From a distance it may look like the parody of a drip painting by Jackson Pollock, executed on the paper-strewn atelier floor. Closer up, it resembles a mixed-media collage piece. Silver coins slathered with black enamel look to have been dropped on yet another upside-down newsprint surface, as if now glued to it by caked pigment and sent upright to the wall: an irony perhaps—and, if so, blunter than usual for Sietsema—about the imbrication of finance and fine art. Maybe—except that the coins are entirely artful in themselves, trompe l'oeil replicas, executed in ink along with the blotches of enamel. And under these circular driblets of black are hand-reproduced print columns not obviously sliced up for selective relevance like the newsprint snippets from a Picasso collage.

Yet such print columns do achieve a barbed autobiographical pertinence in one such newsprint work, this time involving an accidental splash of white on a folded newspaper shown upside down. This work is identified as another *Untitled figure ground study*—but constitutes an "event" of drawing yet again. Sequestered upended there, in proximity to an ad for a London antiques sale, is a half-favorable, half-dubious review by Roberta Smith in the *New York Times* (May 23, 2003), on the occasion of Sietsema's Whitney debut, calling his film work, in particular, "brainiac" and insufficiently "accessible." As in the work before us, however, access is entirely in the eye of the beholder—if only when aided by the apparatus of paratextual commentary in those captions, or catalog essays, or printed interviews with the artist so crucial to this kind of aesthetic production (identifying in this case, for instance, the incorporated further commentary of the press review). The issue here isn't biographic in the main, however, nor even first of all hermeneutic. We don't need the artist's *view* of the work, or its gestation, any more than usual. But someone needs to tell us what's actually happening on its surface (or in fact sometimes its backside as well, as the case may be) in order to help us figure out what is figured by it. Otherwise, the brandished densities stay opaque. Otherwise, for instance, who can read upside down, or would think to? Some Conceptualism, we find, may expect of us, in reaction, what is beyond any immediate conceiving. Unless of course the point in this particular case is—a point going without saying, only showing—that whatever may have been the reviewer Smith's quibbles in this now "recycled" printer's ink form, and whatever else might have been opined about or offered for sale in the *Times'* weekly Manhattan gallery centerfold, art is always *mounted on*—and here materially (and literally) *supported by*—the discourse, aesthetic and commercial both, that precedes and feeds it. And with a further optic pun as well in this case—for no matter what "coverage" the *Times* might give to experimental artists, however superficial or not, here the experimental wager of the replica outplays critique in its reduction of the latter to a workroom's protective surface *covering*, wholly expendable in its own right.

"Brainy" to a fault or just seriously reflective, Conceptual art can certainly seem to some more concept than art. Yet there is no denying the fact that—simulating an image falling somewhere between the already unorthodox poles of "deskilling" (John Roberts) and "no medium" whatsoever (Craig Dworkin)—Sietsema works his material inquisitions under the aegis of an exquisite technique.[1] Every exposed word of the *Times* font is as legible as if it were, not repainted, but printed in ink—as in fact it is, but in the other sense of a "printed" (as opposed to a cursive) inscription. This we learn by way of an (invisible) irony we're clued into only from the relevant paratext, since the rigorous "hand-writing" happens to be dispatched in Sietsema's favored medium—returning again to the source—of printer's ink itself. So it is that this leveled figure/ground execution, like that of *Event Drawing*, is gradually recognized as no more than an event or episode of tincture and line. In the reciprocated mode of *[event::marking]*, it installs its allusion to modernist newsprint collage while also rendering both its secondary representation and its further reduction.

Any sense of a definitive interface vacillates in reception. With image operating beyond the ordinary difference between a surface prepared *for* painting (like the dyed canvas support of other Sietsema images) and the surface *of* the painting as image, we are backed up in imagination (via an evoked studio scene) to a drawn print surface rather than a painting's stroked plane, yet with the newsprint replica already succumbed to the inevitable mess of paint. The apparent found construct as an aleatory collage is thus summarily *derealized*—but only to reveal the meticulous return of its own repressed treatment in a cousin medium. This sense alone, in the instant recognition of a newspaper's "colorless" everyday service as makeshift dropcloth, is what the exacting technique of Sietsema's trompe l'oeil is unabashedly lavished upon. Or put it this way: an antipictorial modernist epiphany of paint-in-action has been reduced—beyond the higher contingencies of drip—to the very picture of accident. Given Sietsema's other work, including a satiric film on Clement Greenberg (Scene Two), the force of all this is unmistakably art-historical. Hyperrealism has replaced abstract expressionism from within the latter's own foregrounding of pigment. And Conceptualism 2.0 (nondigital here, but caught up in the crisis of the image under universal dissemination) is one name for this displacement—this derealization—from imprint to a now hyperpictorial but unseductive facture. Certainly the virtuality thus perpetrated engages an epistemography not unlike Fontcuberta's or Tribe's, where images are materialized in the form of an inbuilt subterfuge, one whose interface only transmedium recognition can delimit or resist.

Sietsema's muted tour de force returns us to differences as pure and simple as they are visually obscure, differences best understood as a reductive doubling-down of transmedial ingenuity: between raw paint per se and painting, newsprint ink and ink drawing, surface and its coverage (or covering), and so on, including (as we'll see next) brushed lines and photochemical tracing. Such are the at once occupied and emptied zones not just of contrast and correlation, as in mixed media, but of cross-mediation. These works are spurs to materialist thinking in precisely their deployment as display pieces, conceptual even in their rigors of execution. Then, too, their minimalism questions the limits of the artisanal in the historical wake of modernism's religion of medium specificity. Just enough examples tend to be exhibited to elicit the principle. The slopped top of the paint can, in another canvas in this series, isn't really stuck to the newspaper. It's painted there instead in two dimensions. It thus appears in a simulated low (very low) relief on the indifferent spread of a newsprint surface (with advertising images and print text intermingled) that is not really there either, nor therefore prone to yellowing before our eyes, but, stunningly again, lettered and sketched in ink. Between machine technology and manual technique, we are caught momentarily off guard on the estranged common ground of visual productivity and its discursive inferences.

Everything is less than it seems—and more—and not least in the personal in-joke of *Untitled figure ground study*, with its implicit leap from studio preparation to critical response, worktable to published review. And back again. Such is the transmedial illusion of painted paint and hand-"printed" print. Or say this: that Sietsema's semantic separation between "figure ground" and "event drawing"—in those several works from the same series—involves in each a similar categorical overlap. Just as the "figuring" is that of a pure ground in the one case, with that spread newspaper, so, in the other linked works, does the "event" end up as the rendering of no episode beyond its own execution. Whether in that transcript of his work under review in the *Times*, with the review in turn under splattered white paint, or elsewhere in the rendering of those paint-slopped coins and their defaced signifying value, the event taking place is only a happening of the hand in its distribution of ink and enamel.[2]

[brush::painting]

With Sietsema's newsprint works, including the entirely stifled narcissism of that *Times* review, he takes several steps further into (deceptive) simplicities. When the paintings and drawings of this cryptic craftsman enter the transitional space between studio *work surface* and wall-hung *worked surface*, his reflexivity closes on itself in decidedly intertextual ways. If those splotched newspapers are an homage to Jackson Pollock, so might we think of *Brush Painting* (fig. 4) as an homage to the subsequent Pop cartoon aesthetic of Roy Lichtenstein. Sietsema's gambit is executed in matte grey-greenish enamel on dyed canvas, 2012; redone in flat grey the next year. A broad-stroke house-painter's brush, over six inches wide, seems soaked in off-green or pale grey paint and stuck to a canvas of roughly the same color, the paint dripping down from the slathered brush almost to the wall work's unframed lower edge, as if threatening the gallery floor. But here we go again—closer in. The brush doesn't stick out half an inch from the canvas after all. It is painted into it, or on it, not obtruding from it. It is, for Sietsema yet again, the trompe l'oeil twist of cause put forth as effect. The brush that does, the brush that is—*[brush::painting]* indeed.

In many ways Pop can be thought of as the opposite of Sietsema's neoconceptualist trompe l'oeil: a pilfered mass iconography over against a minimalist everyday (mis)perception. But that's only a start in considering the coterminous heyday of Pop art and Conceptual art as ironized by the redundancy and deceptive redoubling of *Brush Painting*. In the case of Lichtenstein's mid-1960s *Brush Stroke* series especially, his medial disclosure seems a direct satire of any purist modernism left over from the Greenberg school. If painting is the true subject of painting, why not make it more obvious yet as the sheer application of pigment? In *Little Big Painting* (1965), the scale of a single paint stroke exhausts the entire image field. It is a work that comes to us, hat in hand, for our chuckling recognition. This isn't painting, or even *a* painting: neither the act nor the object. No modernist distillation here, just a flip send-up. Lichtenstein's is the painted trace of brushed surface as simulated synecdochic cause within an equivalent and simultaneous effect. Synecdoche: the part standing for the whole, here in the explicit service of rendering such a whole parodic and deflationary. Lichtenstein's abstracted slapdash (and slapstick) brushwork is magnified to canvas scale only through the work of separate strokes for the representation of separate clustered fibers raked across canvas. There is "concept" in this scalar irony, but so blithely obvious—recalling another signature effect of Lichtenstein's—that cartoon thought-bubbles of knee-jerk exegesis might have been painted in to telegraph the blatant joke of this *[brush::work]* in its graphic hypertrophy.

Seitsema's probable debt to Lichtenstein, however, takes a further turn in this regard, since the earlier artist's own brushstroke series—so immediately right for the comic book mentality of the Pop juggernaut—took its own further turn, in the manner of Claes Oldenburg, into exaggerated site sculpture. Compare the latter's huge typewriter eraser at the Hirshhorn with Lichtenstein's floating brushstrokes at the same museum—not only in their shared wry gigantism but in their signal difference. Cast into the monumentality of obsolescence itself, the eraser is a freestanding object anywhere, awaiting only the now-dated surface of its ministration. But the brushstroke *requires* surface, and so, its striations floating thickly in thin air, it becomes a double parody of mediation—or of betweenness. It is seen levitating in the conceptual interspace between hand and canvas, tool use and surface—ultimately between sculpture and painting. Same stalled transit, same equivocated interface, in Sietsema's *Brush Painting*, but in reverse—in a work that, until decoded as painting, might well look like the sculptural bricolage of a found 3-D object soaked in its own fluid medium. In contrast to Lichtenstein's brush painting, Sietsema's invisible strokes—on a solid canvas surface—work to simulate the presence of cause from within monochrome effect: an actual brush stroked into pigment-soaked view. What results is the similitude of sculptural relief rather than, as in Lichtenstein's sculptural piece (and madcap part-object), the sculptural simulation of a detached yet implemented gesture.

Along the spectrum of transmedial experiment from Sietsema's optically deceptive paintings to his enigmatic film work in Scene Two, there's also his trompe l'oeil evocation not of gunked-up studio implements and paint-can detritus but of photographic imaging in the same workroom setting. This particular image is certainly as hard to describe as it is puzzling to make out in person. What baffles the eye at first as the pointless "deconstruction" of a disassembled painting grows no less mysterious on further information. An illegible trio of canvases or drawings is set apart from their potential single frame, its detached matting, a ruler, and a hammer—the latter an instrument with which perhaps to fix or affix the frame, rebuild or hang it. And this grouping is all the more perplexing for being enlarged as what looks like an outsize negative photo print of its tacit "event." Yet this is only to be identified on the wall plaque (to the viewer's bemused deflation and elation at once) as another drawing in ink. Our puzzlement is further redoubled here by the title *Painters' Mussel 4* (2011), which some further printed research discerns, for the uninitiated, as the East Coast nickname for a freshwater species known scientifically as *Unio pictorum*. Is this somehow—in some outré and unmentioned intertextual recession—Sietsema's allusive point: this pun on "pictorum" that has lost all "unity" of medial as well as pictorial effect in the spectral glow of its photo-derealism? Or is it just a passing allusion to the possessive epithet "painters'" for this irrelevant shellfish—linked perhaps by further permutation to the painting's own shell or exoskeleton in its now separate and intact frame? The point is only to wonder.

Before returning to Sietsema's experimentation, compare his mysterious deployment of an evoked filmic negative—caught between object and imprint, balanced on the transmedial cusp between manual and mechanical representation—to explorations at a similar interface in the canvases and prints of San Francisco artist Jordan Kantor. In one celebrated sequence, Kantor begins by rendering Manet's *Bar at the Folies Bergère* (1882) in the black-and-white full-sized painted version of a conservationist's x-ray image. Kantor then hangs alongside it a full-sized actual negative—in a chromogenic print version—of its already simplified and abstracted patterns. To complete a conceptual "triptych," this initial byplay of transmediation is followed at the same scale, and emptied out in the process, by a deep x-ray of Kantor's own original canvas image in abstracted black and white. This third image achieves a further and final reduction that, showing only the stretchers and metalwork of the hung support, is displayed in a lightbox format as if still under magnified backlit examination in receipt from the developing room—yet with no fashioned pigment left to inspect.[3] Repainting the painting as it never was, in its shaping patterns of tonal gradation rather than true color, is thus one step toward a demediation of image entirely. For there, beneath the medial patterns that underlie all representational force on canvas, we arrive at a final reveal of the sheer material platform that undergirds them. All underlay, no surface: the hyporeal at a new impasse, touching bottom, all picturation zeroed out.

Kantor's sequence of what we might call intensive *lateral* (or sequential) stratification stands as exemplary even in its unusual serial contortion. His extended conceptual tour de force shows how tightly internalized the medial explorations of contemporary practice can become while remaining fully legible (when and if, that is, discursively assisted) in their involution and self-displacement. No broader "mediatic system" of intertextual self-consciousness needs to be invoked beyond the self-systemic layering (or peeling off) of such a serial work. It isn't enough to have appropriated the artist (Manet) whose "facingness" (in Michael Fried's influential characterization)—whose typical pictorial flatness, with its avowal of surface as much as of representational space—is further essentialized, rather than corrected, by the curtailed mirror depth behind the serving girl at the bar. To have then submitted this work to a technological analysis of stroke and saturation on a separate canvas: this is certainly a transmedium extravagance.[4] On the face of it, or rather probing beneath it, the painted x-ray of a painting offers the rendering (up) of mediation itself under the analysis of pigment and coverage. And it does so (in a process to which the next subsection returns) by no less than a minor archaeology of visual technics, moving from ocular to radiographic visualization in two stages of optic penetration.

In that third stage of Kantor's closed system, radiography drives analysis beyond photorealist x-ray to a closer look beneath all "viewing." This subrepresentational attention is the sort invited—indeed actively elicited—by many works of dispersed picturing, many transmedial probes (like Sietsema's), having nothing to do with the technological penetration of x-ray. These are works concerned in other ways with the refusal of a surface's first impression. Beyond this, however, Kantor's subsequent image of the canvas substrate—with its wood and metal bracing—rounds out (while hollowing out) the derivative sequence by "dematerializing" the painted image altogether in recognition of its deeper (or second-degree) material infrastructure. The extremity of this penetration is in fact quintessential. We've been noting equivalent internal rigor in many other works. But here the reflexive suggestion seems unusually clear. Only such associated (call them decomposite) views of easel work can loosen the grip of any medium-specific aesthetics in the more strictly material apprehension of the framed support—in the form not of an oil work's typical picture frame but, minus all treated surface, of a canvas's *pictured frame* in its underlying scaffold and braced joints. In this case, what ordinarily goes unseen, let alone unviewed, has been submitted to a transmaterial forensics beyond all normal curatorial or conservationist scrutiny. The hyporeal, bottomed out, has induced its own derealization.

On the topic of lightbox display, a further example comes to mind in something closer to what one might call a hyperrealism not of painting but of photography itself. This is the not only staged but further transmediated image by conceptualist Rodney Graham from 2011, *Small Basement Camera Shop Circa 1937*. Graham's is a work of media metatheatrics in which the artist poses himself as a prewar photo clerk in front of promotional sign for "Verichrome Film" in this scene of digitally captured verisimilitude. The effect is not unlike the hyperreal (but differently transmedial) mock-ups, though always uninhabited, of sculptor-photographer Thomas Demand, where paper and cardboard reconstructions of often high-profile photographic settings, like the raiding of the Staasi offices after the fall of the Berlin Wall, are then re-shot in a high-definition version of the unreal.[5] What Graham has done is to take the lightbox dramaturgy of Jeff Wall's influential aesthetic, for instance, and pass it through a media-historical as well as just a performative irony, technical as much as situational. Hence the parallel with Kantor's backlit x-ray. The operation of the chromogenic print in Graham's piece—typically a digital file sent by laser process to photographic paper and then developed normally—is rendered uniquely, if retroactively, amenable to the kind of rear-projected lightbox treatment (in the mode of examination) that slide photos in 1937, to say nothing of color negatives, would have been subject to. Technological advance rehearses itself in this revisitation of predigital chemical development—and its plastic manifestation—from within a single transmediated frame.

[photo::ontology]

Where Kantor paints a denaturalizing forensic photography and then photographs painting's material support in an image-effacing gesture, Sietsema, like Graham in his quite different way, charts another kind of middle ground. He does so by simulating the material platform of photographic imprint with striking exactitude—and not just as a film negative, as seen above, but in "positive" paper form as well. His triumph in the latter mode, the diptych *Boat Drawing* from 2010 (which appears in later and variant iterations), faces off the apparent backside, on the left, of an aged, weathered, and crumbling sheet of large-format photographic paper with, on the right, and of course impossibly, its recto image, also slightly yellowed and fraying at the edges. The one blank though splotchy rectangle is tilted up to the right in its frame, the other angled just as slightly downward, to the same degree, as if to match the pitch of the "photographed" sailboat leaning into the waves on its imprinted surface. The optical chiasm opens a chasm in the logic of materiality itself. Immediately something is thrown off. How can we see the back and front at once of an antique found artifact? We can't. We are only seeing betwixt them, their noncoincident twain—and this via a sleight of secondary sight.[6] When we discover that these images, both of them, are trompe l'oeil ink drawings, minimal and maximal respectively, we are thus made to imagine the friable materiality shared between a photographic recto and its verso as part of their constitutive image plane, whether further treated or not. We are prompted to this contemplation, that is, from exactly the present fantastical simulation of their very difference in the time-worn and disintegrating material substrate shared by each.

Apart from the tacit irony of surface reversal entailed here, what is highlighted by the foregrounding on the left is an unshadowed (if stained) planar expanse free from emulsive image, as if it were the photo somehow demediated, bleached out, rather than its mere converse. And then in the right half of the diptych, there in its own more plausible frame—though slipped out of horizontal orientation—a photorealist drawing. Sietsema himself is quite precise on the medial recession involved in this: "I use watery acrylic inks, and I like the parallel of the brush in ink and the boat in water. I like the match-up of the flat white topographical field of the sails, the portrayed photograph and the paper the drawing is on." As a result of the likening and its liking, what we are therefore to see, to recognize, is "a boat captured in the ocean, captured in a photograph, the photograph captured in photographic paper, and the photographic paper captured in the paper of the drawing. The overall combine of aesthetics ends up consisting of the residual aspects of each."[7] Yes, the "residual aspects of each"—and the transmediation of the lot.

In stressing this medial "combine," the artist might also be describing the "residual" drippings of his splattered newsprint pictures. In residue begins re-estimate. His art is as much a back-formation, in fact, as is that nominalized predicate form "combine." Such a minor neologism implies hybridity, while the precipitant "residuum" suggests, in the case of *Boat Drawing*, not just the pictorial evocation of the sails' light-drenched and billowing fabric by blank flat paper but the conceptual pressure exerted on the viewer by an optical stripping down from image to the sheet of support—and then its build-up again in ink rather than traced light. Mutual "residuals" become laminates, transits, new mediations. But one must always loop back to rethink this, there in the gallery and here in commentary. Concerned with the content of their own (only slowly disclosed) form, Sietsema's trompe l'oeils are in fact works that induce in conception a hermeneutic circle that can feel, in crossing media registers, more like a spiral of unfurling redefinition. Although *Boat Drawing* is a work on paper rather than on "dyed canvas," his favored medium elsewhere—a drawing, in short, not a painting—those sails have nonetheless their transmedial relevance as stretched canvas surface. This is what Sietsema meant by the "match-up" of their "topographical field" with that of the paper out of which their image emerges. Before photography, the epic seascape was a thing of the painter's art alone. After technology, what now? Of course, the white sheet—the transmedial matrix and interface as it passes in perceptual apprehension from the look of imprinted, to the fact of discontinuously stroked, paper—is the medium of all inferential motion (the work of windblown canvas) within the representation. In its recognition first as photograph, then as drawing, that support is thus transferred from the time of capture to that of execution in a virtual pentimento of subtracted and reactivated craft. If, in the presumptive photograph, the surface of the sails is in part made automatically visible only by contrast when the sun's light falls effacingly on their angled expanse, this effect is replicated by Sietsema in the ink-outlined zones of unmarked drawing paper that "read" like the cognate white material under depiction. So it is that absence indicates (though no longer photographically indexes) presence—as if still, by association, within a binary logic related to the negative circuit of photochemical transfer itself.

So what concepts, to put it bluntly, are being entitled by the photo-simulation of *Boat Drawing*? The diptych is certainly drawn forward: not just from left to right, in the direction of the ship plunging ahead, but forward from imagined nautical scene, through photo plane, toward the depicted rendering of photographic precision in watery ink. The residue of one condition, in representational uptake by another, becomes a conceptual palimpsest. And this is only further complicated, in the diptych structure, when the logic of *[figure::ground]* is converted instead to implausible interface—where we see not just the look of photography in drawing but the look of its paper support from beneath and behind. Moreover, in the deceptively flat-footed title *Boat Drawing*, the gerundive overtone allows the sense of a motion through as well as a capture by—and this in the sense of a boat "drawing near" the shore, perhaps, or alongside another boat, from which it could be photographed in the first place, as well as in the more technical sense of a boat "'drawing' a specific depth of water necessary for floating" (a tertiary dictionary usage). As with the parallel *Event Drawing*, the title ends up playing between form and content in a double helix of association built on the initial hermeneutic spiral of its illusionist ironies. What or who is "drawing" what? All we're told is "ink on paper," in finer print than the title. By exactly this classic means, various segments of the imaged vehicular sheets of canvas, as set sails, seem set into optical regress within demarcated sectors of unmarked drawing paper edged (rather than internally sketched) into negative visibility as spread cloth. And all of this floats in a bizarre simultaneous distinction between image and its untreated reverse face. Side by side in their frames (of transmedial reference), illusionist recto and verso, time-worn paper and "imprinted" image, operate as a kind of recto/vers/ion of a vanishing material interface: an interface literally paper-thin and ultimately, in simulated division, nonexistent.

For all their internal density, it is clear that Sietsema's ironies far exceed those of execution and technique. So we return briefly to a theorist of "medium" in his more "practical criticism" of the conceptual object: namely, Craig Dworkin. Far afield though we are from the radical book sculpture that began my thinking along present lines, we round back here to effects promulgated—and made problematic—in work of just this sort, whose textual "demediation" often implies its own minimalist brand of transmediation. This is that "crossing" between print-ready surface and nonlinguistic mark, for instance, when each is recognized as linked but distinguishable means (vehicles, gestures) of figuring transmission under arrest. Discussing at one point in his own study, *No Medium*, certain similarly reductive paperworks, and building on Marcel Duchamp's notion of the "inframince"—the infra-minim or "ultra-thin" distinction in an etymologically related mincing of differences—Dworkin concentrates, among Duchamp's examples in an interview, on the "impression formed between two sides of a thin sheet of paper … something to be studied" (18). *No Medium* proceeds to just such "study" in relation to Conceptual nondrawing, nonwriting, and page-laminated illegible bookwork that, each in its own way, foregrounds the substrate of any writing—or its absence. It does so in the ultrafine distinction between vehicle and its inscriptive service, or say between surface and textual impress—as well as between recto and verso of the same tangible sheet.

In the transmedial case of Sietsema's photo/graphic "impression" (automatic imprint reseen as hand-made), *Boat Drawing* moves to inhabit that vanishing latter space, in Dworkin, between "two sides of" thinness itself. Sietsema's flat-faced but twofold work thus opens up this space as simply the contrast—the strictly conceptual space only—between two fields of a trompe l'oeil diptych: the simulated blank—if aged and stained—sheet over against (not actually turned over to) its equally simulated coverage. How narrow is that difference? In the medial traverse of this work by Sietsema—in the wholly lateral "flip" from rectangular plane to worked image—it's exactly the paper-thin difference between the real and the illusory. Each half of the diptych derealizes the other in its logical impossibility. More even than with the fused distinction of *[photo::realism]*, the epistemic limbo of hesitation in all of Sietsema's projects is a charged force field. Between the photographic surface dissembled and the drawings or paintings disguised, between what the image plane looks like and what it can't apparently be (until announced as such), between mechanics and craft, falls the transmedial interface—invisible, strictly conceptual.

In the modes of photo simulation sampled from Gerhard Richter (and his American counterparts in hyperrealism) through Vija Celmins, and for another and more recent point of comparison with Sietsema's "deceptions" (as trompe l'oeil was once officially designated), we can turn briefly to their histrionic counterparts in the grandiose "landscape paintings" of Swiss-born New York artist Rudolf Stingel. Nothing could be farther from the trompe l'oeil pencil work of Celmins—regarding the photo-ontology (the photontology) of depicted photographs—than the twice-remediated hyperrealism of Stingel's massive canvases, shown recently in Manhattan at Gagosian's Chelsea space. These works resemble 8×10 photo snaps of the Alps: but eight by ten *feet*—and only somewhat fogged by enlargement in oil. Landscape paintings as large as one is ever likely to see these days offer up black-and-white images of Alpine vistas whose chromatic restrictions fall halfway between a tonal hyperrealism of snow, rock, and grey skies, on the one hand, and, on the other, simulated black-and-white imprints, no longer in mint condition, of mostly monochromatic slopes. But as one approaches these vast canvases across the equally monumental gallery space, one sees that this is photorealism with a difference: the difference made by the *further* trompe l'oeil inferences of wear and tear. For these outsize images are speckled and flecked with painted imitations of abrasions and nicks here and there on the supposed photo surface, and occasionally a thin scalpel gash to indicate a scarring fold. The frozen time of the photographic moment has been twice simulated in its return to the coarsening course of time.

As if in reference to Richter's black-and-white smeared surfaces from the 1960s, Stingel has replaced the simulated blur of imprecise registration with the simulated vulnerability of postimprint duration. More than in the Madrid retrospective of idealized photo-real-ization, these are quite explicit paintings *of* photographs—though wildly more enlarged than in any normal treatment. But that's only the beginning of the effect, starting with the earliest one on display. Following this initiating work, and over the last couple of years in this series, the slight mirage of damage has been enhanced with spots of white paint that fall (as if literally fallen) halfway between snowflakes and splatter in various ratios across the canvas surface, or say halfway between the drips of an unprecedented monochrome Pollock and some imagined Richter snow scene. The remarkable result in these massive canvases is that the more the accidents of the studio seem to leave their incidental and potentially disastrous mark(s) on the simulated work of the camera—in other words, the more blatant the trace of splatter as blemish on the plane of exactitude—the more the underlying depiction looks photographic by contrast. Transmediation has achieved here, one might say, a new level—recalling Ruff's giant jpegs at the Hirshhorn show—in the optical "control" mechanisms provided by the damage/ mirage dyad.

In all this, whether passing between newspaper as found surface in Sietsema's sardonic rebus of critical counter-reaction (reviews being what a subsequent work "builds on") or newspaper as reproduced image—or between brushed ink and negative photo imprint elsewhere—the traditional gesture (outward) of trompe l'oeil is balked. That mode's canonical intent is to manufacture a third and all but tangible extra dimension beyond, as well as sometimes behind, the canvas plane—whether in the manner of conjured depth or thrust. This mission to breach the boundaries between the field of image and the space of viewing, if only by a few inches of foreshortened tactile subterfuge, is reduced here to a perplexing minimum.

Even the brush of Sietsema's *Brush Painting* hugs so tightly and thinly to the canvas that it hardly operates, say, like some tantalizing drawer opened toward us in the classic nineteenth-century simulation, or the closet cabinet left ajar and inviting, or the fully rounded grisaille sculpture in a Renaissance altar niche. Then, too, the newsprint and photographic simulations in Sietsema's catalog function as two-dimensional craftsmanship pursued on behalf of two-dimensional mass reproducibility. None of this has the least sheen or sensuous appeal. Despite the minimalist splendor of its execution, these works are the opposite of eye-catching, except in their obliquity. Rather than pandering to awe or ready amusement, they offer a retraining of the eye in the name of visual idea.

[pattern::inversion]

Instead of the ocular foolery of works jutting outward into gallery space, then, Sietsema's reflect back more directly on interchangeable—transmedial—forms of imaging: back so far as, in some cases, to resist the evolution of media. That's one force of their multiple gambit: to demachinate the image, which means here to write the newspaper back into holographic (hand-written) form, to turn the photograph back into a drawing, to brush the very brush itself into existence not as a commercial object but as an image of aesthetic possibility and first cause. Such works enter and occupy the zone of mediation rather than specifying their own privileged means. And in some cases—reversing the Greenbergian liturgy—they are not the revealing of paint from within painting so much as the disclosure of painting from within what looks like the mere slop or glob of paint. Sietsema's *Chinese Philosophy*, from 2012, may be named for its illustration of the Yin/Yang principle, in its freeform duplex patterning of black against white, but it also seems to borrow (in order to overturn) associations from a Chinese art of the disclosed brushstroke, here as *Yang* to the illusionist *Yin* of spilled pigment. Two small bottles have apparently tipped over on a once horizontal canvas, soaking the surface in equal puddles of white and black enamel cuddling up to each other. This perception holds until they are recognized, instead, in their illusionist draftsmanship, for their simulation of the same accident-on-purpose they at first appear to index—with the painting having achieved this mirage through the invisible dripping and stroking of what is meant to seem like autonomous paint flow.

That's the closer we get. And then there is the conceptual standing back, where what comes across is, let's say, transmateriality degree zero.

In a medial reflection burrowing beneath the fact of painting itself to the separate chromatisms at its base, *Chinese Philosophy* enacts, we've by now realized in contemplating it, a design behind the aleatory, a staging behind the happenstance, a meticulous illusionism behind a supposed if minor workplace mess. As in the Chinese principle, apparent foundational dualities are found co-constituting each other: not just black and white but event and its representation. But with a further irony in this case, a further material artifice, since black is more than merely the negative complement of white at painting's (sub)medial level of pigmentation. No clean balance of contraries can be sustained upon contact. If this were in fact a natural occurrence—a spill—rather than a trompe l'oeil irony frozen at a moment that resists commingling, what would most likely result from a momentary abutment, then blurring, of antinomies would be more like the greyish half tone in many of Sietsema's other paint-splat works, with the canvas or illusionist newsprint paper as mock-dropcloth. Neither the nature of the rendered paint puddles in *Chinese Philosophy*, that is, nor the logic of their illusionist depiction, operates under laws of verisimilitude. And if, in demurral, one might say that the so-called surface tension of the two enamel spills might keep separate their tints, then that tension is itself transmediated between executed brushwork and pigment contingency. In any case, the blocked crossing between Yin and Yang here, within the fundamental optical flip-flop of the deceptive canvas, comes through to us, if only on reflection, as a miniaturized and isolated form of an arrested blending, a purism that goes at least part of the way toward dematerializing the pigment base into abstract idea rather than flow.

Elsewhere in Sietsema's exploratory procedures, the abstracted inversions can be so complete as to be altogether invisible in their materiality. This is the last of his conceptual interventions to "come clear" when experiencing his work in exhibition. It's not only hard to convey here, but impossible to notice in person, since what look at first like found objects from the arbitrary debris of a studio are in fact appropriations in another sense—but only as canvas backing for painted effects on their reverse side. The impossible recto and verso of the same photo print in *Boat Drawing*, unless one or the other of them were photographically reproduced (remediated), may in this way be meant to refer us round to what only curatorial discourse makes known about the paint-on-canvas, rather than ink-on-paper, series of painted "deceptions": the fact that each image is itself the verso of a found recto. This is because the announced "dyed canvas" support of these works has required just this treatment, the saturation of a kind of primer coat, to be applied to the backside of found canvas reproductions, pallid and murky, cut out of second-hand shop frames: a process perhaps captured by the negative image of frame and hammer in *Painters' Mussel 4*. These include appropriated canvas copies from da Vinci to Cezanne to Norman Rockwell. We'd realize nothing of this process, seeing none of it, unless—though mysterious and laconic in itself—there weren't a multi-fold flyer accompanying Sietsema's show at the Chicago MCA, which, with further accompanying explanation, reproduces these faded color "originals" along with the title of the Sietsema works that flip and eclipse them in their new framed display. In this whole process of transmedial layering and invisible interface, these worked planes negotiate between multiple-print reproductions of fabled representations and, in the studio studies on their backside, the simulation of sheer material pigment and its tools either abandoned in isolation or defacing mass-print news text.

It would be only a truism if it weren't, again, a deep-seated visual pun: in whatever is left to the office of painting after modernism, its effort must be *mounted* equally upon the history of its forms (in found canvas homage) and upon the forms of discourse (print discussion and critique) that ground and contextualize it. To lampoon both assumptions, by putting them so baldly forward as Sietsema does, is only to make the point more, as it were, graphic. On the back of the reproduced representations of absent objects and their painted scenes, Sietsema produces the false impression of present objects from the studio—so that the inversion is, again, as much conceptual as tangible. In such a materialist and transmedial ecology, even the silent vandalism involved in this defiant recycling of previous reproductions enters into the hermeneutic circle of new productivity.

To reiterate: you don't see all of this in the gallery. You must be told it, as well as shown it, by the paratextual flyer. In the process, that dozen-fold catalog adjunct—the paratext as metatext—is in its own cryptic right, as sheer format, an apt gloss on Sietsema's methods, which are themselves only slowly *opened to view*. Usually, of course, with most conceptual work, the discursive gloss is merely functional, a straightforward parsing of technique in hinted connection with theme. Yet the anomaly here is also in its own way exemplary. For when the paratext is itself a piece of conceptual text art, its intimate relation to the thinking of the (other) visual artifacts to which it refers is all the harder to miss. An unfurling collage of found (and then overturned, reframed, and lost) reproductions, stretched to full broadside width in this flyer, occupies the backside in turn, we find, of an extensive interview with the artist without which those appropriations would still be entirely opaque. Hence the emblematic force of this particular recto-version as gloss. With a cross-medial discursive field like that delimited by Sietsema's experiments, it isn't that you don't know which side is up—which side, so to say, of the *inframince*—but that you must keep invisible idea and present manifestation, concept and object, in mind at once, folded over and into each other. Between tradition and the new image—or between the history of reproduction all told (including bland commercial reprints) and art's original enterprise—stands the shared platform that, in making it his own, Sietsema makes into a metaphor, a trope for its own production. Such is a trope, a figuration, which then you sometimes do *see*, or at least recognize—as for instance when, in that materialist rebus involving the simulated *Times* spread, "the idea is" that new work must be executed *over and above* the discourse of newsprint critique.

Maybe the ultimate propositional matrix for Sietsema's varied production emerges from his heady reversals in something like this discursive form: Conceptual art, so to say, is only the reverse face (the historical flip side) of tradition: the thought—and rethinking—of its own underpinnings. Or have it that conceptualism, as in the experimental film work that rounds out Sietsema's material preoccupations, is the narrative redescription of its own found—and thus inherited—materials. That lineage, that legacy—together now and then with its openly refused genealogy—is part of what remains to consider as we shift our gaze from the framed image to the frame-line paced manipulations of the tampered celluloid strip in "motion picturing." But as is already clear from the comparison between Stingel and Sietsema, we have moved well beyond the fused registers of technological and artisanal reproduction in the self-impacted canon of *[photo::realism]*. The epistemic limbo of hesitation in the works of these two artists (spectacular and minimalist, respectively) delimits a charged retinal field dependent on far more aggressive discrepancies than in that alternate mode—and twofold optical mold—of evoked mechanical exactitude known lately as the hyperreal. From certain photo-invoking images of Stingel and Sietsema—operating between what the image plane looks like (weathered prints) and what (so the eye asserts) it couldn't feasibly be—arises by inference the elided yet defining interface. No hyperrealism has moved unflappably to duplicate and trump another medium's precision. No hyporeal is brought to the surface on inspection from a separate realm of image making thus divulged. Instead, in these self-trumping trompe l'oeils, the work of the image is its own derealization as index, a seeming instantaneity laid bare as labor and its meditation. Such is the triple take induced with the productions of each artist separately: back and forth and back again from the apparent to the internally (or systemically) comparative. What's at work in the object of this art can thus only be seen, if seen is any longer quite the word, transmedium—where perception is certainly as much a deciphering as a glimpse, a gathering cognizance more than a recognition.

[surface::tension]

Always a certain negotiated conceptual discrepancy: between surface impression, that is, and the transmedial forces that can be gradually educed to define it. Again, the reciprocities of technical (if not technological) unmasking: exposing the medial tension that *is* the surface—in its fraught play between manifest image and the banked force of another medium's separate history. At this point such recognition tends to refashion the work as a kind of transmedial inventory—or even impacted archaeology. Take Sietsema's *Boat Drawing*, once more, as an epitomizing instance, where the nineteenth-century overthrow of drawing itself by photography (in the service of captured space) is poised—and all but posed outright—as a medial genealogy upended. Between the recto and verso, not of a found, but of a simulated photographic sheet, now surface, now image, there is no remediation, no before and after, no front and back, just the image plane's *pictured* reversibility—its total *materialization*—across the diptych interval (rather than intangible interface) betwixt and between. With paper and photo-imprint reconceived—and thus derealized—by paper and printer's ink, the conception of captured nautical progress is entirely transmedial.

This is where any one "making" (Sietsema's favored term) remakes assumptions about its layered means, and where the manifestation of any one surface—any one manifested image—is regularly put in tension with its confluent material work-up.[8] From the most straitened, almost cramped, of projects in Sietsema's wallworks, then, emerges perhaps our broadest view yet. It surely doesn't need further emphasis at this point that the whole *idea* of "Conceptualism 2.0" directs us not to some central revisionary idea *in* its putative artifacts, but rather to the continuance—for a different moment in culture, and in culture's art and media history—of the 1960s initiative, at least in one of its corrective impulses. In this phase of its trajectory and renewed agenda, as in the early backlash against essentialism, conceptual distancing asks us yet again, by making it necessary, to think before seeing, to read the visual rather than just receive it: to *cerebrate* in material terms, rather than celebrate, the mediation. Otherwise, a retinal complacency sets in with implications far beyond gallery experience. Passivities of the eye in looking: one common enemy in the half-century arc from Kosuth's photostats to Sietsema's faux photos. At base, the principle is clear. It amounts to a principled mission at the very basis of aesthetic transmission: only in differentiating media can a blow be struck against ocular indifference. Such is the case, to be sure, with the specific and often polarized transmedial recognitions in play so far—pitched between mirror and advertising graphics (Gordon), photographed whitewash smear and gesturalist monochrome (Lavier), pencil stroke and TV greyscale (Celmins), crafted scrape and video lineation (Baumgartner), pixel array and mounted frame grab (Ruff), website thumbnails and composite reproduction (Fontcuberta). This is the polarized case in Sietsema as well, of course, with this minimalist image maker operating his ironies now between ink and photochemical index, now between fastidious brushwork and illusory found brush.

The ongoing motive can be framed, of course, in dramatically different ways from one practitioner (or "researcher") to another. Unlike in Fontcuberta or Tribe or Baumgartner or Celmins or Ruff, each in their quite separate techniques, there appears to be no trace of geopolitics in the epistemological twists of Sietsema's studio ironies. Nor (with so little happening at all) is there the least trace of violence, graphic or otherwise, in either his paintings and drawings or his films. But what might therefore seem sedate or even numbed in the lackluster exactions of Sietsema's works on paper or canvas is, nonetheless, charged with a maximum of internal contradiction at the interface—concerning precisely the difference abstract expressionism hoped to brush away—between appearance and application. Yet here the contradiction is less between stroke and picture, surface and figure, than between found and fashioned. What is transmedial about Sietsema's laconic and demanding work, in the broader context of Conceptualism 2.0, transpires at the evasive interface, not between the digital scale of data streams and the stability of wall art, but rather between the very presence of material and its illusory doubling by representation. Yet this is only to realize that Sietsema's effort at visual "making" is very much in the line of work that plays, in quite different terms, between ocular input electronically sourced and its intercepted aesthetic transforms. This is because his making, too, his remaking—even amid the contemporary devaluations of an inflated image economy—sustains its own insistence, within an epidemic of looking, on making us see: see *harder*.

Sietsema's process is to be grasped in transit, reversibly, between minimal depth (brush, lid, coin) and the lesser build-up of ink or paint, elsewhere between the handmade and the mechanical (simulated photo negative, retrieved antique print), and everywhere between the found and the fabricated. These gestures sketch the transmedial torque of his own epistemography in the era of image overload. In just that regard lies his eccentric exemplarity. With Sietsema's devotion to the handmade in an epoch of technological (rather than just mechanical) reproduction, and to the preceding history of representation that his artifacts (like those of his compeers) are moved to inscribe, whether in painting and drawing or film, Sietsema locates his delimiting place in this study. He labors, we may say, at the lower frequency, the minimal bandwidth, of Conceptualism 2.0, responding no doubt to the digital—precisely by resisting its facilitations—in his pursuit of what after all, what first of all for a creative worker, can still be "made" rather than simply accessed or processed, what image forms can still be fashioned rather than just taken as given.

When fashioned around that "what" as an open-ended question, Sietsema's procedures make for an enterprise in new making that decidedly postdates the initial strictures of a 1960s and 1970s Conceptual art, concerned, as so much of that work was, predominantly with the *concept* of art rather than its fresh production. The influx of wordworks, the encroachment of language onto canvas to the exclusion of stroke or picture, the apparent usurpation of aesthetic practice by its theory, was, in those days, a deeply polemic way of insisting, among other things, on the inevitable discursification of all display in the public idiom of aesthetics. Against the former bastions of medium specificity, at least, the battle was no sooner joined than won. Artists since, and none with more resolute quirkiness than Sietsema, nor with a more decisive reversal of the "deskilling" imperative, have accepted the distinction—though not the mandated divorce—between the concept of art and its shaping force. They have done so by forcing ideas of art back *into* the wrought artifact rather than *instead* of it. When realized there in such contrapuntal material form—rather than simply as captioned absences, notional indications—these are ideas that typically require a good measure, as we know, of subsidiary explication. The tyranny of on-canvas notation has given way, on many fronts, to an arcane aesthetics of annotation.

Usually, too, and in time-based work especially (Sietsema's films included), the rejuvenated making that triggers such elucidating discourse is achieved not by some radical innovation but by a triangulated grappling— and hence transmedial engagement—with prevailing materials and ocular expectations. Cognitive friction is one intended result. Both in and beyond Sietsema's rarefied craft, such *[surface::tension]* can affect more than one medial axis in its structuring of the image: pulling not just across the manifest plane of rendering in its teasing of the eye (and its "derealizing" of the presumed image) but shifting between treatment and support in what should also be marked as a *[surface::depth]* counterplay. Such effects are to be contrasted with the less occulted manner—in other words, the manifestly *surfaced depth*—of hyporealism in such technologically mediated works as those of Ruff or Fontcuberta. What awaits in Scene Two are various interrelated modes of both hyporealm disclosure and surface derealization when found concentrated in the subnarrative screen experiments of time-based projection. There, too, under a renewed conceptual pressure, the idea of art has returned to practice and execution, not just pronouncement: to image-spanning rather than image-banning analysis. In projection 2.0, then, and in its transmedium gestures most clearly (and in none more *purely* than Sietsema's), ideation is carried once again, however automatized or not, by material technique.

Entr'Action

THE STRUCTURAL CHARGE AND CHALLENGE—AND PROBLEM—OF A BOOK LIKE THIS IS NO DOUBT
clear to any reader by now. In trying to survey, if scarcely fence off, such a
loose, unruly category and its rough historical determinations—namely,
transmedial art in the mode of Conceptualism 2.0—the chosen examples,
in order in fact to be exemplary, have needed to be rather disparate. Yet in
order to exemplify convincingly, demonstration needs at the same time to
secure comparisons along a commons axis. In arguing for the prevalence
of a free-form mode, rather than an established genre, there may be safety
in numbers—but only if they add up. So variety is at war with evidentiary
coherence, multiplicity with taxonomy, coverage with common denomina-
tion: the inherent trouble of coming to terms with such a multifarious art
practice under the pressure of clarifying illustration. We have done what
we can, and will continue to do so in Scene Two. But with what results so
far in the balance—or descriptive bargain—struck?

Transmediation: in spatial form as well as in time-based practice, a
manifold effect analytically decomposed. And in the process of this de-
composition: its epistemography. That much at least we can take as established at this point—and can let argument now turn on as we move to
kinetic imaging. It is, of course, a real convenience that the most important
exemplification I needed for pinpointing certain issues involved in the
strained counterpulls of recent transmedial art, and in netting something
of their range, do split about equally between still and moving effects.
But in its more or less arbitrary symmetry, this evidentiary split can't
be allowed to obscure a certain actual division, or transition, internal to
each half of the argument in its historical inferences—and ready now to
be spelled out in more detail: namely, the shift from Conceptualism 1 to
Conceptualism 2.0 (in however low-tech a format one sometimes understands that latter category). For this is a transition taking in, as it does,
most of the watershed decade that immediately follows Fredric Jameson's
evidence about late 1980s installation art and the a-historical "concept"

of its utopic topologies. Nor should one minimize the fact that such a transition in aesthetic practice has been nonetheless more gradual than the venture-financed and corporate-marketed escalations of international media culture in the same years, a perceptual saturation to which much art practice of this period lends at least implicit notice—or perhaps tries fending off with some latent resistance.

To put it this way is only to allow again that certain more seasoned artisanal gestures—of ink pen or brush, as of mirrors or photographs—can at times line up in their irony with rather divergent processes of electronic screening and even, as well, alongside the now-throwback operations of old-fashioned slide projectors (Kodak no longer making or marketing these "former" machines) in a work of Robert Heinecken's soon to be discussed. I anticipate, because the case is scarcely atypical. Lumped with the magic lantern along a spectrum of obsolescence that numerous works are eager to retrace in their own variable ways, slide technology is now mostly rendered only by skeuomorph, and then only by name at that (not icon), in the Powerpoint "slideshow" format. Whatever the place of nondigital artistic practices in the light—or backlight—of such electronic dominance, only a momentary standing back from example to pattern could hope to get this clear. To make room for summarizing this uneven genealogy, where new media platforms can be introverted or contested with the same conceptual irreverence that eschewed them altogether in related gallery art from the previous decade: such is the point of this current interregnum, before returning full tilt to kinetic instances.

For as the invoked theatrical term *entr'acte* is meant to call up, we are concerned with an abiding tendency, in aesthetic display, for an artifact to *perform* its own constitution as a virtual theater of mediation, whether mostly in fixed-framed tableau so far, or in the dumb shows of silent filmworks coming, sometimes even in audiovisual enactment: in all cases, given their impeded reality effects, as a technically conflicted metadrama of transmission. So the chosen term from stagecraft for an intermezzo between our major episodes—a term for both a pause and a playlet all its own—comes naturally to mind. But it does so not least at the level of its own enunciation in that widely borrowed French nomenclature—with the elided shared sound of its abutted terms (entr[e]act) arriving under more than ordinarily visible mutuality and suppression—indeed punctuated by apostrophe on just this score. Between the acts, then, or here between the extended Scenes, structurally as well as lexically, appears a conflationary act of its own, dovetailing, hopefully cinching: not a separate interlude but an analytic lynchpin. So that indicated in this way—by a kind of alphabetic rebus, and recalling Dworkin's borrowing from Duchamp's terminology—is not just the *inframince* of distinction as the "ultra-thin" border between flipsides of an issue but, more to the point here, the expository breathing space between them. From which certain generalizations may be invited concerning nothing less than the transmedial entr'action—the conceptual *traction*—exerted by works of divided material loyalties or appropriations.

In securing this midpoint breather for some brief review and achieved new vantage, I should mention a helpful crux in earlier reactions to my evidence. In a seed essay for this book, circulated for a faculty and graduate student seminar at Yale in 2014, everyone in the room (I discovered by a show of hands after the problem arose from one questioner) had read the following sentence as it was *not* in fact intended (though the point was implicit in my presentation as a whole).[1] I was expressly meaning to distinguish, in this phrasing, between works distilled to essence and those still in transmedial flux, works purified versus those oscillating with an indeterminacy as to means as well as meaning. The sentence was this: "What stands *contra* to institutional modernism, then, in these mixed pieces (and their often differential parts) is their exploration of contrastive rather than crystalized means: a function cross-fed and intrinsically tensed rather than essentialist." The unanimous sense of the meeting, to my surprise: that I meant, or should have meant, to highlight (with that last contrast of modifiers) how the works under examination—as opposed to being medium-specific—are instead media-historical, "tensed" in the grammatical sense: dependent on paradigms of past, present, and to come. This, rather than just uptight concerning their own medial input. My essay's chosen phrasing aside, there's no doubt about this historical dimension. So I can revise the proposal this way as a result, to keep both emphases in play: "Works in the social field of Conceptualism 2.0 are tensed, conflicted, precisely by their self-historicized sense of a transmedial play between superseded and emergent media regimes: that is, by their conveyed inference of 'tense' in image history itself."

And another thing there's no doubt about: the play between art and media technology in this history. With the switch soon to be thrown on the motorizations of Scene Two, what is clear so far is that mediacentric imaging is often arcane to precisely the extent that it negotiates with the "archaic," with previous and dated technical functions—however recent the supersession involved, all the way from Victorian black-and-white photography, say, to the last gasps of predigital filmmaking late in the next century. Such is the tacit and elusive archaeology of such works. In this way they depend upon, even while often upending, a certain sense of historical priorities. This in itself isn't surprising; it is simply part of their reminder, their inbred prod, about context, irony, historical memory, and art's intervention in the process of change, of loss. But often enough, as we know, any media memory of this sort needs some nudging, some active historical gloss, in order to be recognized as such. Exaggerated cases make the point most readily. You have to know (or would, in some future period, have to be told or shown) what a black-and-white photograph once looked like, not to mention the earliest one that has survived in the archives, in order to appreciate the washed-out greyscale of its simulation by 10,000 illegible color "shots" in a rectilinear webwork all their own (Fontcuberta's Niépce). You'd have to know what the now-dated intermediary step of the photomechanical negative once looked like (itself negated or overridden in digital camework) to appreciate its trompe l'oeil treatment in paint (Sietsema), let alone Fox Talbot's inverted Victorian rebus for the interchangeability of print and its photographic complement. Or need to remember the low-def TV image to register the irony of its woodcut manifestation (Baumgartner). Just as one day, perhaps all too soon, you will need to have your memory refreshed about the look of inked newsprint on paper, as well as about the fetishizing of pigment and surface per se in high modernism, before appreciating the simulation together of these two modes of display in their minimalist implosion as workbench leftovers rather than art (Sietsema again). Extreme in a different way, in the kind of work that often awaits us in Scene Two, you have to be made aware (by a fairly extensive explanatory gloss) of what the first prewar computer looked like, and roughly how it worked, to appreciate a simulation of it by its technological progeny in a CGI animation spooled past on an "antique" film projector (Simon Starling).

Conceptual practice of this sort, its summoned images residual in the age of a dominant electronics, can thus operate like an archaeology projected into the future. They can suggest, for instance, that one day we will appreciate hyperskilled drawings of long-defunct newspaper typography, let alone the elegiac ironies of codex sculpture—in other words, the uptake of defunct "mass-print media" by medium-dedicated work—as we now appreciate easel paintings of illuminated manuscripts done by former "illustrators" subsequently plying (reapplying) their trade in the first decades after Gutenberg. And beyond such a futurist historicism, there is, at times, almost a *reverse* archaeology in transmedial practice. Think, for instance, of that mode of hyperrealist painting we considered early on, where the artisanal form of brush craft confronts its own once threatened eclipse by the instantaneousness of photography, thus replaying an earlier century's crisis in representational media even in the act of flamboyantly overcoming it. For in such work paint stroke ends up achieving the fidelity of its proximate automatic cause (or model) in the snapshot. It does so by simulating, through optical allusion as well as illusion, the limpid precisions of the latter's photo-finish effect—so that the newer form (photography) may end up, paradoxically enough, feeling superseded by the precedent medium of paint. Call it another curious version of the reverse skeuomorph: the present painterly remediation "familiarized" by the simulation of its own former upgrade (rather than simple predecessor). In general, therefore, the transmedial quotient of these and other such works often makes them stand forth as experiments in auto-archaeology, where the fossil is never wholly laid to rest, but instead—to mix metaphors from the uncanny in the way these works themselves often do—where the vestigial effect ghosts the image so that the dominant remains haunted by the return of its own repressed. In view of this, when I say that such transmedial works are "tensed," this certainly does involve a time-coding grammar of their own metahistorical irony—and this as an integral part of their self-contestation across either evoked or activated medial supports. Yes, tensed in both senses, to be sure.

Which is why we needed, from the start, to see their difference from simply mixed-media exhibits as resting unsettled in the force field of the *inmixed*, its object art history as well as art. So far from unprecedented, such a sense of the aesthetic in these provocations—these *provoccasions* as transmedial events—is downright canonical when looked at from a certain angle. Concept here is born of disuse, of the inutile. It is generated—following Kant's very definition of the aesthetic—by a purposiveness without (surviving) purpose. This sense of art as the emergence of the made under the sign of the noninstrumental is no less applicable when the object appears aggressively stripped of a former purpose than when it seems invented in the vacuum of any utility, birthed free from use. Conceptual art, from Duchamp's *Fountain* (merely a urinal "unplugged") to Robert Gober's faceless, drainless sinks (in the era of an AIDS epidemic whose pollution was uncleansable by such invoked everyday hygiene), is thus the case of an artifact depurposed for a new purposiveness. This is not necessarily a strict remediation, just a rethinking.[2] Nor is such a logic far removed, finally, from the conditions of art at large. The point isn't simply that the thing on that plinth called *Fountain* is an appliance (purpose) suddenly "cited" as newly purposive but—and because—useless. What conceptualism does by such contextual transfers, and precisely on reflection, is to reconceive all art as a kind of depurposing, or say a defunctioning. Rolling hills that you can't rove, flowers you can't smell: this is the denaturing of landscape in its role as sheer representation. The naked beauty whom it would be too little thrill to kiss, she being made of marble: such is the defunctioning of the human anatomy as statue, the reduction of palpable body to "nude." The book whose page you can never turn, whether painted in two dimensions or sculpted in three. And so on. Remediated, demediated, depurposed, rendered sheerly purposive: that is one arc of conceptualist fallout in its wider application to a representational aesthetic all told.

[historio::graphy]

But how does this chart over time, over recent image history, especially in light of Jameson's claims for the historical dead-end of postmodernist— and would-be utopian—installations like Gober's earlier example from the late 1980s? One might think of installation art of this sort as the scalar exaggeration of the artist's "multiple" in the earlier years of conceptual work. There was, for instance, Joseph Beuys, in a prototypical Fluxus gesture, setting out the impressed copper "matrix" of a vinyl record on squares of his signature felt as if they were absorbing its sound, and then placing these in a vitrine next to a sundial-like sectoring of a wheel under the cognate German/English word "Mutter"—and all under the gallery title *Sun Disc* (1973), as if it were itself an archaeological find. The history of time, of warmth, of sound, of absorbency, all sprung by the proximities of the part objects. Enlarge them (or not)—and space them out across an entire gallery—and you have something more like Gober's *Untitled*, Jameson's negative case in point, with its "multiple" discrepancies calling out to each other across a space they all but arbitrarily carve out from the norms of instrumental meaning and commerce, from rationalization itself. To this end, a decade before his treatment of Gober, Jameson had made a broader point about the history of vision in *The Political Unconscious*, seeing in modernism a recognition of the "perceptual" itself as "a historically new experience"—when isolated from instrumental sensation. This is an experience whose "vocation," whose "Utopian mission as the libidinal transformation of an increasingly desiccated and repressive reality, undergoes a final political mutation in the countercultural movements of the 1960s"—since by then the ideological weight of "psychic fragmentation," together with its symptoms in perceptual dispersion, was "once more politically timely."[3] But never say "final," for it was only a decade later, on Jameson's own subsequent account, that the isolated perceptual ironies of this counter-praxis had mutated from unabashedly splintered cognition to the artificial "Utopian" assemblage of Gober's installation art, where an underdetermined ad hoc system elbows its way into a temporary displacement of the social, of history itself.

In Jameson's understanding, space doesn't exactly become a medium in such work, but its functionless parameters figure the utopian place of a posthistorical interaction: appropriated books no longer leashed to authorial identification, earthen plot denatured, dated painting retrieved by ironic juxtaposition, architecture deconstructed (Prince plus Webster plus Bierstadt plus Gober's own split portal by synecdoche for the whole interliminal convergence). Where have we come since then? If Conceptualism 2.0 is not meant to single out any functions exclusively electronic, as stressed more than once to this point, then what other second stage does its rubric mean to uncurtain? How has it gone beyond the late 1(.0) of Jameson's "mediatic system" if not simply by injecting electronics into its media field? One might respond that anything "utopic" about Gober's space itself, as well as the time it takes in solicited contemplative recess from historical time, could only be fully understood, even in its own moment, in terms of its temporary and bracketed departure from the escalating media culture of computerized video imaging. But only a live feed of the Bierstadt from some distant museum (forecasting a work closely approximating this by Wolfgang Staehle in Scene Two), or a motionless but "noisy" VHS loop of it from within a gilt-framed but low-resolution TV monitor embedded in the wall, would have introduced this new medial consciousness *systemically* (that crucial term again)—rather just than as an implicit part of the cultural surround under dubious utopian remission. That's, in fact, why Jameson is drawn with more enthusiasm, but without further commentary, to the direct media-historical confrontation implicit in Nam June Paik's videography from the same period.[4]

In Gober's *Untitled*, by contrast, consider the inclusion, again part for whole, of Richard Prince's appropriated book. We don't know from Jameson's mention which one it is, but let's say, for the sake of argument, it might be his simulated original cover of *The Catcher in the Rye* attributed not to Salinger but, in the same typeface, to Richard Prince. Whether or not there is now anything between its covers but blank pages, it is an artifact obviously defunctionalized at the level at least of auteurist recognition. If it were carved of wood, that would be one step further—as in the trompe l'oeil *bibliobjets* of Steve Wolfe, including the early summa of his method (now in the Fisher Collection at SFMoMA) in which he duplicates the trompe l'oeil cover of a scholarly book on the paintings of trompe l'oeil American master John Frederick Peto. Yet only if the Salinger/Prince novel as object were "caught" on a video loop—in a series, for instance, of spatial freefalls with alternating freeze frames—would the transfer between its reading and a punning subsumption of content to form be fully mediatized. But that's merely to circumscribe one level of distinction between stages of late-century conceptualism (between appropriation and video transform), without any of the historical determinations that seem lying latent in the notion of "2.0" when not tethered to a strictly technological definition. So the question remains: what has changed from preceding phases of the conceptualist project with the introduction (though not necessarily into the operation of separate works) of universal computerization? How are practices ("researches") that increasingly archive their own predecessors— whether in representation, imprint, or projection—somehow the shared result of an intervening history in the way that high modernist medium specificity could be seen as a first reaction to the postwar media age and the ever proliferating culture of the immaterial image in video broadcast?

On the good assumption that "nostalgia" or "elegy" wouldn't begin to exhaust the jostling ironic archaeology of such works, and in search of other metahistorical burdens they might be intended to carry, or attempt to unload, one can return to the place of historicity in Jameson's account of postmodernism itself, where, for instance, the "retro film" of the 1970s, as opposed to the genre of historical epics—from *Bonnie and Clyde* and *The Conformist* through *The Godfather*—was a kind of posthistorical pastiche of recycled "style."[5] Granting that, it is equally important to recall that such works were still executed in the contemporary media format of high-gloss color (and widescreen) cinema, the typical fare of Hollywood commerce. These exemplars of ahistoricity tended not to imitate '30s or '50s film in any manifest way, just '30s or '50s style in detached reification (cars, trains, fashion). Since then, and in distinction from such works, as well as from the more obscure configurations (like Gober's) of noncommercial art from the same period, what we might call the post-postmodern works we've been examining tend to press past the historical levelings of a digitally facilitated global capitalism to a specific investment (no longer to be cashed out as faddish and saleable) in a narrower band of historicism. One might say that these experiments move past the escapist evocations of the retro film to certain laminates of the retrograded image. They operate in this way not as an immersive pastiche but in a layered and (again) *tensed* stratification of historical forms, painting against photography, chrono-photography against cinema, codex against e-text. And so on.

In this sense one may contrast Francis Ford Coppola's *Bram Stoker's "Dracula"* (1993) to his *Godfather* trilogy (1972, 1974, 1990). The retro panache of his mafia narrative contains nothing like the transmedial moment in *Dracula* when the 35mm luster of the film goes suddenly intermittent, grainy, and sepia, spluttering with both jumpy splices and muted sprocket noise, just at the point when the count in London is lured to the bustling 1896 arcade by the announcement of "the amazing cinematograph" on initial display—the upstart mechanism of the Undead in perpetual motion.[6] Introduced the year before Stoker's publication, and unmentioned in the novel, cinematography thus waits almost a century for its full transmedial ramification in a narrative in good part about preceding modes of technological record.

Cineaste Coppola's is a spectacle, in the case of *Dracula*, that deliberately and famously resists the new 1990s dominance of CGI imagery—with all the film's special effects touted as strictly cinematographic, not computerized, developed in-camera and in lab rather than digitally input. Coppola's Victorian retro turn is in this case medial as much as it is costume-historical, attesting to the spectral powers of "old-fashioned" chemistry and optics in a century-long continuity with the first film screenings. Here, then, from the mainstreaming of popular art, and drawing on the technological annals of its own prehistory, is transmediation 2.0 without the least hint of the digital—except by dint of its avoidance. And this in a film (closely influenced by the Stoker novel in this respect) that is explicitly about, and punctuated by, Victorian photography's new-medial use for long-distance visual recognition (real estate sales)—as well as, on other technical fronts, by handwriting updated through stenography, the manual typewriter, and the dictograph, each mediation often appearing superimposed, in Coppola's metafilmic treatment, over the scene whose mysterious events it is in the process of transcribing.

So that the yet more disruptive pocket of screening-within-the-screen at the Cinematograph's debut in Coppola's plot—that most salient moment of transmediation between boxy 16mm and widescreen 35mm, between tinted stock and full color, between rudimentary flicker fusion and its later seamlessness, between sprocket noise and its eventual muting—is isolated in just this archaeological context with all the other prefilmic devices (and even protofilmic: arcade silhouette projections and their shadow-play, for instance) that the film goes out of its way to incorporate. To say the least, this garish, splashy thriller is hardly a conceptual work. But, read against *The Godfarther* trilogy, it can help mark for us (from its commercial distance) the *medial* rather than sheerly *stylistic* self-consciousness emerging, in gallery work, across the two or more decades in question between the heyday of Conceptual art's various estrangements and their audiovisual aftershocks in 2.0.

So where, in sum, is history in any such broad aesthetic transformation? The answer: both outerdetermined, in shifting technological contexts, and inwrought; both outside, that is, in the importunate media surround we began this book by scanning—with all its new catalytic pressures of display and surveillance arising since the earlier epoch of predigital Conceptual art; and inside, organizing the mediacentric works themselves in their own decentering, including their inmixed differential archaeology. Regarding the genre profile most recently discussed, whereas nostalgia film stages an escape from history into "period" style, conceptual projections, in gallery works rather than Hollywood narrative, shift the instinct for historical obsolescence to the level of audiovisual materiality rather than subject matter. Instead of anything resembling a nostalgia film, then, we encounter in museum space something like an embedded memory of film itself—even when the tone of certain works, in their baroque contortions, is anything but openly reminiscent or wistful. At stake, although only on obscure view at times, and bearing no resemblance to a retro film, is instead the retrocession of photochemical film all told. And the process can find itself manifested even in narrative film—and with further degrees of medial layering—as when Michael Haneke's 2006 *Caché* records in high-definition digital the embedded viewing of VHS tapes. Or when, with Haneke's later (and our last) transmedial film work,*Amour,* the on-screen events negotiate a material relay—radically *entr'acte* in its own right—back through photographic automaticity to easel painting. Here is a mode of thematized conceptual irony for which, by the time of "Endscapes," the less narrativized experiments of Scene Two should have uniquely prepared us.

For the most part, the arcana of the *arche* entered upon by such works, most of them far more circuitous and obscure, or at least cryptic, than Haneke's films, operate against the escalating pace of "convergence culture" (Henry Jenkins again). They do so by the refusal of all easy fusion—and all facile nostalgic evocation. By contrast with the Jamesonian pastiche of the retro, then, it bears repeating that, in the palimpsest of the transmedial, it is technological history that turns back on itself through mediation per se rather than through the detached accessories of dated cultural style. This occurs even when a work's conceptualist thrust resists time and succession long enough to layer and conflate separate perceptual regimes. If this is still to "spatialize" time, in Jameson's sense, it is not to cordon off and reconfigure the precincts of vision by installation, but rather to laminate in display a past transmissive process and its successor. Such is the new repurposiveness without purpose whose cognitive service is to *relativize* (rather than its anagram *revitalize*) media possibilities—this, instead of relegating one to the subsuming other as in standard consumer practice.

And all this, so we're seeing, transpires across a several-decades transformation in resistant art practice that moves from an initial undermining of medium specificity toward an increasing sense of mediations ever on the wane—with new ones always on the way. Until the endgame may now seem upon us in universal digital circuitry. Short of this, though often tacitly contemplating it, Conceptualism 2.0 frequently operates in transit from one media dispensation to all that has subsequently dispensed with its means. Yet this tends to be an outmoding intercepted in process—the earlier medium re-cited, resituated, residual, but still asserted from behind as a pressure on our understanding of the new. It is as if history is still in the works—or at least still in the work, churning there. So it is that the frequent looping effect of new medial projects develops a recursion historical more than just material and optical.

Whether the original conceptual agenda is seen as the dematerialization of the visual in art or, alternately, the deskilling of its practice, in either case its 2.0 incarnations return to materiality and technique—often in the form of sheer technological affordance—in the deliberate absence of technique's enshrined specificity. The temples of the intrinsic and its rituals are long gone. Scourged by idea, skill returns profanum in new retooled formats—and confusions. Yet the works we're continuing to examine don't just veer disarmingly between technology and craft, but rather align the variable "deceptions" of the latter (again, that Victorian term for trompe l'oeil) with certain deliberate roughenings and occlusions of the former. These are pieces that must be pieced out in the mind. Even with no text injected, the requisite paratext turns them discursive as we scrutinize and ponder their effects.

Yet by far the most salient fact about the relativizing of the mediations that are conflated or simulated within them is the double-ply (even when not literally superimposed) consciousness of media history that animates them separately and correlates them in museum consideration. If for Jameson the faux utopianism of installation "space"—as a topology supposedly escaped from commerce and utility—was thus radically time-suspended and ahistorical, instead the works that preoccupy us in this book (and the longer heritage of conceptualism into which they tap: Duchamp to Broodthaers) return to one defining line of history through the filters and baffles of their own transmediation. And this embedded media-history has the bracing effect of turning them not inward upon a sudden new cult of mixed-media specificities, in some revisionary aesthetic of amalgamation, but outward to a thoroughly mediatized social sphere in vigilance and critique. It turns them to history itself, mediated as well as narrowly medial. Until history catches up with them, in a work soon before us, through the accidental "aesthetic" record of the 9/11 attacks in the digital chronophotography of Wolfgang Staehle. At which point transmedial irony must recalibrate again for a newer age yet in which, to put it baldly, and especially in the ensuing satellite- and drone-guided response to that 9/11 terrorism, the specular has in its own right become weaponized.[7]

This aside, the "relativizing" of the aesthetic in transmedial work isn't a leveling of means but precisely a resistance to it—and on several divergent but interrelated fronts. In the threefold subdivisions of Scene One, we tracked the routes by which hyperrealism, with indexical registration exaggerated in the direction of photographic automaticity even under the banner of the painstaking, could lead us (in an opposite but cognate direction) to a fuller media-historical understanding of very different works. These include experiments in the retinal underlay—rather than technopictorial overlay—of the hyporeal composite (e.g., Fontcuberta) as well as of the derealized illusion (e.g., Sietsema): works we came to understand as comparably epistemographic. By a comparable triad in the pacing of the coming Scene, a sense of phenomenological reduction in the flattened "pictureplaning" (chapter 4) of experimental cinema and videography, brought into comparison with the "lightshown" abstractions of the most rarefied sculptors of motorized luminescence (chapter 5), can do more than set up certain polarized terms at far ends of a putative single spectrum. They can, in addition (chapter 6), work to anchor an appreciation of the irreverent and intractable "filmedivision" (elision/ liaison again in this terminology) associated, for instance, with the arcane numerical parsings of optic planes that characterize the "cinema" works of conceptualist forebear Marcel Broodthaers—as well as the counter-narrative deviances of his inheritors.

So that, yet again, one benefits from standing back—and off a bit to the side, to get a better angle of vantage on these matters. With transmedial work implicitly issuing in a new aesthetic epoch of "the perceptual" long after high modernism, even Jameson's broad trajectory can, that is, be enlarged upon. In a fully dialectical understanding of the history of visual practice, we move from the ancient iconicity (and mystified "presence") of the sacred symbol or icon through the rule of secular representation (mimesis whether of scene or, later, of sight)—including the rise of impressionism—down through the touted presence of application itself (surface treatment) in postwar modernism. Where the ancient image once embodied the "transcendental" thing, under the constraints of modernism it does so in a sense again: but instancing, this time, not the enculted and all-capacitating divine incarnation but the medium per se in its immanence. The Greenbergian viewer sought to find herself in the very "presence" of painting, not the painting of a space or bodily presence.

In response to this credo of purist cultivation, in a further backlash or counterswing beyond its mockery in Pop art, the discursivities of Conceptual art tried breaking from this circle of medial valorization into what we've seen as a different kind of abstraction—or its materialist opposite. There was, on the one hand, the philosophic or metalinguistic move: Kosuth's *Art as Idea as Idea* series. And in sculpture, on the other, there was the objectivizing move: the overthrow of medium specificity by the "specific objects" (Donald Judd's phrase) of minimalism. Since then, in the work of Conceptualism 2.0, the recurrent burden is, as repeatedly stressed, to configure a *specifying* structure, its material form often losing distinction in the transecting media it both discriminates and blends. In the full dialectical swing of the modernist aftermath that one might therefore extrapolate from Jameson, a former aesthetic touchstone (in literature as well as plastic art) that had mutated from the visual to the retinal in the run-up to impressionism, and had thence been detached into a reification of the separably "perceptual," has returned—in the second phase of its conceptualist chastening, after a first rinsing clean of strictly visual allure—as a newly *perceptualist* vehicle of ideation and irony.

One immediate question about transmedial works understood in this way, of course, and not in sum here but in resumption: why now? Or in light of Jameson: why this difference since he wrote? How has computer electronics, even from (or beyond) the periphery of certain works, tended to rewire the media field in which they operate? Caught up in the rapid if indeterminable *entr'acte* between postmodernism and its own indistinct conceptual posterities, history doesn't collapse into representation in the works under study—and often under self-scrutiny. Rather, they offer (or say slowly divulge) certain oblique metahistories of representation in their own right, and of imaging more broadly, and hence of mediation: verbal as well as visual—and sometimes verbal in its double valence (ironized in the coming example) as audiovisual. As it happens, when that work-in-progress essay mentioned above—in extension of my interest in the transmateriality of the book object as both paper base and print surface—was hosted by the Yale Center for the History of the Book, my seminar coincided, sheerly by accident, with an extensive show of conceptual bookworks called "Odd Volumes" at the Yale Art Gallery, including one among several pieces new to me. And one, in particular, by Brooklyn artist John Roach, whose auto-archaeology and artificial motion capture gets us close to where Scene Two needs next to go.

Roach's blatant and crowded "mixed-media" format becomes at once, on audiovisual engagement by the museum goer, a satiric transmedium: "Suitcase, security camera, microphone, motor, fans, motion sensor, monitor, and found book." Suitcase and all, it was a case, as the curators' wall plaque crisply had it, of "alienated reading." In the Fluxus-like open metallic luggage of its primary platform are mounted by turns Edgar Allan Poe's *Poetry and Prose* and Mark Twain's travelogue *Life on the Mississippi*. (It was Poe on display when I saw the piece.) But the parodic and indeed alienating upgrade of the codex in normal transmission—via electric motors through electronic sensors to video relay—prevents any subvocal access to the densely phonetic verse and prose of Poe's syllables even as the suitcase may seem to mock, in alternate presentation, the imaginary transport of prevented travel reading with the Twain. How prevented? That's the initial irony: right from the would-be reader's first move. A surveillance unit activates the suitcase mechanism when the curious viewer/reader approaches (too closely) to the book, distancing the reading option both as to physical proximity (the clunky manifold apparatus keeping the eye at arm's length, and thus decipherment at bay) and in a further cross-purposed remediation. This happens when the four electronically triggered fans blow over one page after another at arbitrary and inconvenient speeds even as, en route, the page's minor buckling and rippling motion is transferred to a small video screen on which it is barely possible to make out the gist of a passage in the rustle of its surface.

All the while, since there is no sustained reading other than skimming to be had, the only sound made (let alone internally generated) by this assemblage is amplified by small speakers pretending no access whatsoever to the phonetics of literary texture and its textaural effects but only to the puny hum of the instrumental fans under the title *Pageturner*. Already in 1997, then, a decade before Kindle was introduced, the e-texting of literary writing is debunked, or at least exposed in its dematerialization of the book object as imprint platform, when cumbersomely retrofitted in this way to classics of the American canon—and codex. By contrast with any standard motion-picture "adaptation" of the book form, motion here impedes capture as serial text. Many other comparable oddities follow in

Scene Two in this estranging kinetic vein, bent (inward) upon their own conflationary and inbred *mediarchaeology* (from here out, indeed: a seven- rather than eight-syllabled concept).

But what if, in equally conceptual but strictly photographic work locating us still within the formal perimeters of Scene One, the ironized textual page never moved, but was simply laminated with more of the same—until the image constituted a cursory reading of an entire volume? Digital palimpsests by London conceptual photographer Idris Khan rise to illustrate.[8] And, to pose a further move in this direction, and toward Scene Two, what about extending this compressive logic to photography's derivative medium in film? After having given a treatment similar to Khan's photo-"readings" to a volume of *Wuthering Heights* so that its separately overprinted lines become all dark streaks (of erotic blindness and fury like the novel's tumultuous content?), San Francisco artist Jim Campbell, in lightbox display, overprints every frame of Alfred's Hitchcock's *Psycho* in an "averaging" chiaroscuro blur leaving only incidental objects from a single *mise en scène* visible at the far spectral periphery (teapot left, lamp and phone right). The overall backlit effect can't help but evoke the kind of ghostly radiographic image necessary, for instance, in less necrophiliac circumstances than those of Hitchcock's plot, to make visible a human skull beneath the flesh.

[cine::graphy]

In thus inverting the logic of Douglas Gordon's *24 Hour Psycho* (1993), which slows each frame to a motion-retardant two seconds, the instantaneity of Campbell's appropriation, *Psycho 2000*—alternately called *Accumulating Psycho* in its "illuminated averaging" when shown at something more like theater-screen scale—goes equally to remind us, here under comparable transmedial duress, of that generative combine of framed image and motor series at the very basis of cinema as its own kind of "mixed" technological phenomenon. Further transmedial interventions at this techno-historical interface can seem powerfully inviting. So, then, what if—fusing the overprinting of words and images—an equally immobile and ironized volume of text, literary rather than film text, was arranged so that its very lineation, in drastic miniature, served to evoke the striations of video broadcast from within a layered history of video's own predecessor in the photocellular intermittencies of the film strip? What kind of triplex image would thereby be subject to historical "frame-up"?

To this query, one still-image artist, a metaphotographer of sorts, gives us a full theoretical answer by example. But in an effect that, to become *instance*, needs to be contextualized in the broader sweep of his career experiments, which are even more strenuously directed at the switch point between photography and film—and more stringently transmedial as a result. Widely noted by French image theorists and film philosophers, the research-intensive work of Éric Rondepierre consistently limns such differences (between "image" and "film," "frame" and "motion") as his own version of epistemography. He does so by arresting the very transit from cellular photogram to cinematographed space. Guiding our move from "Image Frame/s" to "Motion Capture/s" as the exemplary transmedium scenes of Conceptualism 2.0, Rondepierre can be compared, not just with the *Psycho* revisionists, but with two very different artists also experimenting, one might say, at the *inner limit of cinema*. Working in the opposite direction, from photos toward film, the British artist John Stezaker has recently turned from photocollage to photomontage, with results we will shortly examine. And, in a more complex layering of medial surfaces, a younger American artist, Matt Saunders, returns through cinema to photography by the route of their pictorial predecessor in painterly facture.

We've looked closely at Fontcuberta's "photograms" in the original sense of cameraless imprints, both his "palimpsests" and "frottograms." Entertaining a related transmedial divide, and gravitating, like Fontcuberta's work elsewhere, to Antonioni's legendary meditation on photographic process, Saunders's *Blow Up #5* (2013) typifies his own recent cameraless graphics in a painstaking hybrid mode. Often based on cinema stills or lobby cards, he draws or paints on transparent mylar, as if it were film stock, rendering the imagined negative image of a single cinematic frame. Then, either by direct contact print or by enlarger, his work in the darkroom generates an uncanny positive: the automatic register of an only approximate image never really there before (or in) a camera to begin with. This is the revisionary keenness of his method: an art-historical rather than just optical mode of reversal by which figure and ground remain in a fresh and unprecedented tension. And there is a more specific art-historical issue under negotiation as well. Seen against the Duchampian tradition of aesthetic work as its own "deskilled" *art concept*—thesis more than praxis, theoretically reductive as often as materially productive—here, rather, is a labor-intensive version of *concept art*. Far from the found object conceptually reframed in early minimalist gestures of appropriation, Saunders's work, as work, involves the found image skillfully unmade and artisanally reconceived.

Under a loose 2.0 umbrella of demediation and remediation, psyche intersects techne in Saunders's craft as if by *inhabiting the automatism* in the very paradox of hand-made photographics. He doesn't take photographs; like Sietsema, he makes them—but in a more elemental way yet. In a calculated retraining of the eye-hand circuit, the hyporealm of the photo negative must be optically schematized in the mind's eye as the underlay of the new imprint—imagined rather than processed, imagined *as* process—before being inverted again, in the darkroom, to its phantom double in light-traced painterly shadows. In a world where machines themselves now paint, where computers are their own photoshop, Saunders reverts to an understanding of media on his own transverse terms: by the oblique venture of painting the photomechanical. In this return from pictorial effect to technical cause, he is, one might want to say, more realistic than the photorealists. He pictures exactly the moment where photography veers, by structural negation, from the the very act of painting that now returns to inscribe such a point of departure, such an ulterior or hyporeal stratum of manifestation. Similar procedures "animate" his short videos as well, where the steady stream of the filmic chain must be patiently (re)made by hand: decoupage becoming its own painterly montage. Criss-crossing three pictorial media, then, Saunders occupies the neo-Duchampian *inframince* between each in turn, their own artificially restaged "entre'acte."

Compare this to Stezaker's paracinema. In reshooting his collection of postcards depicting, for example, the central naves of various cathedrals at the traditional twenty-four (but here wholly discontinuous) frames per second, Stezaker's filmwork (under an "averaging" singular title like *Cathedral* [2013]) gives us the strange feel of time-lapse church history: an archeotexture, so to speak. Similarly, by an equally formative implosion, the racing overlay of group portraiture in the re-edited film stills of *Crowd* (2013) crowds out all ocular clarity in a massing of form alone. And his images in *Blind* (2013) do just *that*—move to occlude all coherence of visual recognition in the edited flipbook of film stills—by the inflicted kinesis of their image barrage. In their presentation as HD video, these "infinite loops" again suggest, in a new way, the logic of Gordon's *24 Hour Psycho* turned inside out: a 24-fps retinal or synaptic psychosis. Sometimes, however, these works achieve a quite pointed mediarchaeology. In reshooting, for instance, decades of equine photographs from a horse-breeding magazine in their standardized profile format, Stezaker achieves a blur of differential vision that can't help but call up the prehistory of cinema in Eadweard Muybridge's chronophotographs of horses in motion—this time shuddering in place rather than running, an oscillation rather than a gallop. Nonetheless, just as in standard-issue (photogram-tissued) cinema, the seeming movement—rather than being parsed and analyzed—is refabricated: an artifice of activity rather than a direct transcript.

This, too, is the level at which Rondepierre's interceptions of the film strip intercede in the motion effect in order to seize it (up) from within, always stopping just this side of the present book's own turn, in the ordinary sense, to "motion capture" in Scene Two. For three decades, Rondepierre's conceptual brinksmanship has found him poised on the cusp between photography and film. Call him a "cinephotographer," or instead a "cinegrapher," his manipulations directed increasingly at the sense of a once conjoint and privileged image regime suddenly outmoded, as if almost overnight, by digital record and projection. Time and again, in the arrest of screen time, his detached pictograms exert consistent if varied pressure on the liminal switch between image and its serial machination. In this, his orientation is resolutely transmedium even while his materials remain fixedly fixed frame—however much overlain and cross-grained at the same time with those recalcitrant traces of motion, clutched momentum, and fissured sequence to which the keen blink of his eye gravitates.[9] For Rondepierre is a photographic printmaker preoccupied with the interstitial force of the cinematic "photogram" (the most precise term for the photo cell on a film strip) both in its isolation from a projected frame stream and in its obsolescence within the newer protocols of digital transfer and transmit.

Until these recent experiments in the digital recalibration of a photogrammic logic, however, his has been work well characterized by Philippe Dubois as "more than photography and less than film," the cancelation of each in the balked transit from one to the other.[10] In our vocabulary: a transmedium reframe; in Dubois' terms, "an axis or fold" between ocular regimes, "the precise crossing" of an inbuilt serial juncture that amounts to the "razor's edge" between media, though only, one might add, because there is no visible edge or cut incurred in the actual projection process. To recover the photogrammic trace as something between object and structure, now depurposed, makes work of this kind, for Dubois, like that of "an archeologist after a long excavation revealing what until then had belonged to the unknown," adding: "Éric Rondepierre's dig is cinema." Writing in the early 1990s, as filmic cinema was confronting the first broad incursions of a digital alternative, Dubois has this just right.[11] And it is the artist's more recent move into the 2.0 orbit that continues, for us, his evolving mediarchaeology.

On the way to these latest electronic experiments, the most ambitious of his transmedial gestures, closest in complexity to the photo/film and paint/imprint shifts of Saunders's interface works, are Rondepierre's disruptive captures, a decade back, from old-fashioned banner-flashing film trailers of the 1940s and 1950s for his *Annonces* series ("Ads," or in English, more euphemistically, "previews"). These involve rapid overlays of italicized and exclamation-pointed hyperbole sometimes intruding on the illustrative integrity of the advertised narrative sample, slicing open a star face, for instance, with a serrated edge of transitional typeface. In this way, it as if a defacilitated cinematic vision has again been made to render optic testimony—beneath advertised spectacle—to the pre- or proto-visuality it is inevitably built upon. And to which, inadvertently, it here adverts, indeed reverts. With the photogram's occluded operations suddenly made legible by an actual imposition of text, however fractured or blurred, Rondepierre then submits this sprocket-slipped disclosure to a further chain of distancing preservation. He first reduces the photo again to a transparency, projects it as a slide onto a crinkled paper surface to add a new layer of roughened and denaturing texture, depicts anew what he has anomalously seen in acrylic paint, rephotographs it, and, in what is no doubt a further allegorical move, ultimately destroys the painting—that belated trace of origination—on which the new photogrammic simulation, the virtually trompe-l'oeil photoprint, is based.

To give an example whose titular occlusion of script is in itself telling, one of the frame-grabbed, slide-projected, repainted, then rephotographed *Annonces* watches askew the Hollywood musical *Show Boat* announcing itself (showing itself forth) in a kind of amorphous, unborn blob of script slammed over, in an arrested superimposition, a shot of the same pleasure boat it thereby fails to image as well as name. Two levels of representation, two entire modalities, are submitted to transmedium reduction in such a work—and three times over, in the transit from photogram to slide to painting to print. The reduction is figured in this case, and with prototypical illegibility, as the emergent murk of interstitial text lost somewhere between an aborted and an only still embryonic gesture of cross-medial signification. And in this case, too, as in the others, Rondepierre does (and undoes) all this as if to evoke, by constitutive revocation, exactly the absence—rendered, again, in a kind of optic parable—not just of each photogram from the manifested strip but of all *mise en scène*, all recorded space (here by proxy in the destroyed painting), from the scene of projection. In this as well as his other works of motor, or later electronically mobile, registration in arrest, Rondepierre's transitional place between this book's defining Scenes has precisely to do with his favored betweenness.

As entr'actions in their own right, his *cinegraphs*, for want of a better term, repeatedly obtrude at just the changeover of frames that generates the look of change-over-time on screen. As previews writ little, there is too much pre-viewing of the next photogram; as trailers, these intercepted moments trail their own frame-advance process behind them in an encroaching micro-second delay. They thereby refuse, if only to highlight, the orderly sprocket traction that alone brings film before us as seemingly filmed action. In so doing, they spell out, in the log-jam of image and text, film's essential *[cine::ecriture]*.

Years after his first ventures in this line of snagged frame-line aggregation, Rondepierre has come to bear down on the serial strip in a new way, in the very form of its remediation. Rather than locking down on the piece-meal digital break-ups of DVD pixel defaults, however, he swoops in to study the more recent image splotchings of DSL (the "Digital Subscriber Line" format) in "live"-time film delivery. Here the momentarily roiled and smeared webstream is captured in instances of accidental disintegration by simple keyboard-activated screen shots, even as such residues of coherent picture are then delivered to the gallery wall as luminous and weirdly, sometimes gruesomely, beautiful high-definition archival prints. Chosen from classic films by Hitchcock and others, including *Marnie* (fig. 5), the images seem bleeding to death as we watch, film history included—with only still photography (albeit now routinely computer-facilitated) arrived from the deeper past to rescue them for aesthetic notice. Rondepierre's is a uniquely plangent form of avant-garde "glitch art." Out of degradation, the chance for an older order of contemplation. On view is something like a rearguard action—though decisively postfilmic—against the steady, mostly coherent, but ultimately ungovernable flux of the digital pulse in this latest delivery format.

Still engaging directly with the divided photostrip of the earlier filmic cinema, Rondepierre's most emblematic works of *[cine::ecriture]* remain those in a series from 1999–2002 called *Loupe/Dormeurs* (*Loop/Sleepers*). These are palimpsests that reinsert the discretely recorded film scroll into the longer history of communication technology, including the reign of the codex itself and its alternate (and almost equally dated) transmissive means in photochemical imprint. In these complicated, cryptic images, under the otherwise obscure title of numbered *Livres* (or "books"), Rondepierre may be thought quite directly to superimpose the historical implosion of one cultural regime (and imprint technology) upon the other, each—prose text and image text alike—impeded from full registration by the intersecting pressure of its fragile and beleaguered counterpart.

This explicitly "textualized" transmediation is accomplished by forging—indeed forcing—an association between the artist's typescript novel about filmic addiction called *Sleepers* (as yet unpublished; appearing from Seuil in 2005 under the title *La Nuit Cinema* [*Cinema Night*]) and the photo-images that might separately arrest and catalogue its moments. Hence two different kinds of highly provisional continuity: word sequence and image sample.

This conceptual link can only be realized—by an extreme transmediation, illegible except in drastic magnification—when Rondepierre photographs (with a mouth-held time-release switch) his hand-held magnifying-glass in scrutiny of certain photogram pairs or triplets from classic films. They are shot ad hoc against the out-of-focus background of another indiscernible scene, often with a woman's image dimly glimpsed, dressed or naked—and all of it related to events in the novel. But then, in a superimposed laboratory effect "visible," one might say, but not discernible, all of it is further transformed—or, better, trans-muted ("digitally half-toned," as the artist puts it)—by the overlay of softening horizontal lineations. These turn out, on explanation and closer inspection—if noticed at all in the first place as other than a function of focus and definition—to be so far from fine-grained video striations, for instance, that they are in fact the miniaturized overlain lines of an illegibly microscopic text, 156,000 characters in all, of none other than the artist's unpublished novel. For the whole typescript narrative is implausibly compressed into single hypersaturated frames: at that point the novel's only "printing," a text thus still struggling, disruptively, to make its mark by way of claiming any one image as its synecdoche.[12] Yet again, as with Rondepierre's later digital grabs as well, though more visibly here in these translucent laminations, the seized interface between image frames marks the systemic sighting (and citation) of a transmedial faceoff between entire perceptual regimes across the whole history of imprint matter.

In contrast to these sedimented photo-livres of compacted textual grammar and photogrammic "excerpts," however, the accidental death of the buffered image in DSL technology is a function of aleatory retinal diffusion, not intrinsic sequential occlusion. With these more recent studies, it is clear that Rondepierre's career-long work in the still image has survived a modular or incremental cinema to stand watch over the bewitching glitches of the new-media stream. Such is the mediarchaelogical long view of his projects in the increments of cinema's projectible image, gravitating as they do so consistently to optical dysfunction: to abrasion, erosion, asynchrony, failed focus, digital default, an obstreperous "persistence of vision" from frame to frame, and finally to the turbid flow of digital overload. In this way does his cryptic and often scissored metahistory of the screen medium involve the story of its material base—as told from the vantage of its lapses, its inbuilt limits, even its technical supplantation.

Image/frame//motion/capture, then. Backwards and forwards. That's the pivot of our transition here. From postcards to reeling montage strip in Stezaker. From filmic frame through painting to secondary photographic iteration in Saunders. And in work begun in the same year by Rondepierre, from strip to eerie composite image in a new move from montage to collage—with motion capture now the structuring absence of a fixed hyperframe. This shift is transacted in a series called *Background*, with both temporal and spatial coordinates insinuated. In these works the artist excerpts famous cinema footage, Hitchcock predominantly, in order to reassemble an unprecedented image of its diegetic space. He achieves this devious feat in extra-widescreen vistas that use digital technique (paratext once more to the rescue) to dovetail together each lateral segment of an indoor set without, so to say, its scene. As piecemeal bands or slats of unobstructed décor seamlessly fused together by digital editing, so we read, and thus manifested for the first time under a steadying gaze, these are the almost subliminally registered elements, and increments, of set designs. They are to be disclosed only in separate moments across the whole length (and width) of projection—and between the blockings of plot, so to speak—when not otherwise masked by characters occupying the foreground of our notice. What we get is the reinstated premise, and promise—because the suddenly unoccupied literal premises—of narrative space: the diegetic condition of possibility for so much screen action in the set per se. Such is the profilmic space, the newly coherent *mise en scène*, that is typically hidden in plain sight, as it were, by the narrative activity of bodies in motion within and across it.

On the way now, in Scene Two, from filmic motion variously suspended (whether of frames or of pictured bodies) to actual time-based imaging, one technological fact above all is crucial to stress about these *Background* "reconstructions." Unlike in other forms of computerized image-making that photo-shop human figures *out* of found-footage video presentations, for instance, or replace them by alternate digital insets, Rondepierre pays his usual respect to the photogram's chemical index. Nothing is digitally "tricked" here in these *Background* works, just "edited" together from one spatial hiatus after another in the horizontal progress of narrative and its laterally moving bodies. In the photographer's favored selection from Hitchcock, these sets include, for instance, the empty apartment in *Rope*, the unpeopled kitchen in *The Birds*, and, most suggestive, the suddenly unoccupied apartment in *Rear Window*, fully spread out before us in a pan-compressing width that nevertheless extends beyond any one VistaVision frame—and this time with no one looking back at us, like Hitchcock's hero, through his own telephoto lens. In such uncanny works, in their rendering of narrativized domestic space as itself *unheimlich*, the inherent "blinds spots" of backdrop constituted by the motions and gestures of screen drama have been horizontally deveiled all in one composite and impossible moment

No widescreen imaging could be farther in this regard from Rondepierre's frame-enhanced "interiors" than the resuscitated Swiss panoramas, in allusion to a longstanding national(ist) tradition of Romantic self-imaging, fabricated by Jules Spinatsch out of discrepant surveillance footage of exterior sites at the 2003 Davos economic summit.[13] In his work, electronic monitoring is neutered in its policing role, returned ironically to the now-pixelated mock-grandeur of historical spectacle and ceremony against the traditional backdrop of populated mountain valleys and their natural plateaus. In this respect, his wide-frame composites recall the vast pixelated stills of Thomas Ruff and their transmitted images of captured violence rather than securitized space.

And yet there is an element of invaded (even as invented) privacy even in Rondepierre's *Background* suite as well. We seem, for instance, to be caught in the act of spying through Hitchcock's rear window—along a perversely reversed axis—on a space never licensed as ours for wholesale perception. In any case, where Spinatsch's openly collaged panoramas overleap cinema in his tactical reversion from hidden digital camera to wide-frame composite representation, Rondepierre lingers there with the older form of projection instead, though now reinscribed transmedium by computerized editing and touch-up. For these latest works of a digitally implemented Conceptualism 2.0 are, in their nonetheless retro orientation, seen filling in the gaps of décor amid the forefronted distractions of onetime plot—and thus (with a wholly camouflaged pastiche) reducing movies to unoccupied stage sets in an invested theater of the imaginary. It might be said that Rondepierre installs here an elusive continuity editing *within frame* via the horizontal quilt of digital stitchery and its credible spread of inhabitable space. So it is that a single archive addict and laboratory practitioner—moving from photogram studies to post-DVD image delivery—has run the gamut (and the unforgiving historical gauntlet) between the first phase of a medium-chastening retinal minimalism and the new investigations of Conceptualism 2.0.

Rondepierre's latest work on the phenomenological contours of an outmoded filmic cinema thus returns by way of invisible computer facilitations to a predigital moment of aberrant and unnerving visualization—and to its previously unexamined (because never so fully disclosed) allure as a continuous world elsewhere. For our further purposes, too, it is no unhappy accident that this *Background* series is begun the year after Michael Haneke's film *Amour* builds toward its own transmedial implosion in the contrast between a grievously occupied, and then a precipitously emptied, *mise en scène*. But we're not there yet. As much as with the work of a cerebral cinegraphic researcher like Rondepierre, the screen imagings of experimental filmmakers and moving-image video artists also help pave the way by expanding our sense of the transmedial path.

Motion Captures

CHAPTER FOUR: *Pictureplaning*

Sometimes the moving image makes plain only the moving of image planes, not a motion separate from their sequencing. For pursuing the implications of this, we have tools at hand by now. Evidence has repeatedly shown—through whatever degree of constructive obscurity in the works reviewed—how it is that the term "transmedium," in its conceptual grammar, is less a noun for some "substantive" formation than a manner of seeing, more adverbial in its stress on the *how* of perception than categorical in determination of the *what*. And sometimes, in pursuit of a given work's operations, a way not just to see but to look again, harder. And often backwards at that, to precedence and obsolescence in a mix—an inmix—of sedimentation, tension, contest. In the projections ahead, this involves, to speak in optic metaphor, an internal shift of focus within an ongoing field of effect: a scrutiny moving back and forth from what is generated or projected for display to what is injected to produce it (as often explained by an accompanying textual gloss).

If normal film work simulates the world's movement in a secondary, and mostly ignored, motor sequence of its own, the moving images to be sampled here—experiments in the very transit of image, or sometimes of light alone—often incur the apparent trapping or gapping of serial picturing in its own stalled frame. So that here too, as in Scene One, whatever the relation of these time-based displays may be to the mediatic networks of cultural production at large, what ultimately emerges—if only from scrutiny and rumination—is that their time frames and their resulting media inferences, however conflicted, remain in the last analysis internal, hermetic, closed-circuited, self-regulatory. And again self-performing: the medial shown forth as mediacentric. In this respect, such "motion capture" is likely to expose its own constituted movement for just what it is: either the high-speed planing-past of rushed frames in film's cellular modularity or, more recently, its planar generation as picture by a many-times-faster pixel sequencing across an imperceptibly gridded rectangle.

Under transmedial inference, that is, or sometimes actual interference, the surface of picturing—the so-called screen frame, now projected, now electronically backlit, now celluloid, now digital—is confessed as either more than the planar surface that meets the eye (many more like it in an unperceived cumulative run of displacements) or much less (mere distributed blips). In either case, an evanescent support is submitted to conceptualization rather than given over to spectacle. Pictureplaning, then: not the fetish of planarity under the weight of high modernism, but instead, whether with the race of transparent rectangles or the spray of coordinated pixels, the uncertain determination of picture (as representation) versus plane (as material increment). A return to this issue in "Endscape," in the case of mainstream narrative filmmaking, will again invite that inherent divisibility of idiom pursued in this chapter, where image and its delimitation interpenetrate each other in reception at the slippery interface of picture/plane.

At this point, as regards surface, planarity, and lateral displacement, even exceptions can help orient us. Not all moving-picture surfaces are flat. Indeed, curvature itself can become part of the mimesis, the anthropomorphized form. One artist seems inclined to show this by way of an implicit media-historical trajectory. Before there were *media* plural in our sense, there was one medium or another, vehicular. Air was a medium for speech, light for sight, water for transport, a human go-between for messages, and so forth. Then came the expressive and technical senses of media. A wry video installation by Tony Oursler, one in particular, operates on the eye as if it were recalling this transitional history by projecting itself, in effect, across these differing measures of going-between, of transmission. I had often before seen Oursler's video loops thrown in gallery space onto his signature white fabric ovoids: his talking eggheads, like madcap decapitated versions of Hans Bellmer dolls. But *Pressure Blue/Green* (1996), which I discovered at the Des Moines Art Center only as I was finishing this chapter, struck me with new conceptual force. One of his elliptical 3-D forms, in durable ceramic this time, is permanently dunked in an elongated vitrine—converted, in this case, to a water tank. The rounded surface of this squashed sphere receives the video image of Oursler's own features— bifurcated between the apparent green-about-the-gills and the blue-in- the-face tropes of the eponymous color scale. This audiovisual "portrait" is straining with closed lips and swallowed groans in the hopeless need to draw breath in this endless loop of drowned-out speech. Unlike Oursler's freestanding *humanovoids*, this time the "screened" image is diffused and refracted by the liquid it traverses on the way to the anamorphic shape of its reception, looking strangely more natural and cinematic as a result, more supple and "realistic" in its pulsations. Say, more fluid. As enhanced by this new elasticity and diffraction, it is hard not to think of this assemblage as installing something like a transmedial allegory of a certain kind of artist always lost in transit—immersed and submerged in his own process—across the interpenetrating mediums (here light and water, sound video and sculpture) of any expressive effort. This rounded aquatic mask as persona—this self-portrait on a sunken convex arc—is only, of course, a quirky (if elucidating) diversion from the norm of the moving image in strict 2-D and rectilinear projection. But such screenings can have their own conception-prodding oddities as well.

[picture::plane]

So far, Scene One has featured the space of concrete display in contemporary gallery settings, from wall to plinth to freestanding sculpture in 3-D digital build-up, where each designated *objet* in turn opens a layered interspace within its own registers of mediation—rather than just in cross-comparisons with other integral objects under the same roof of exhibition. This, we know, has involved a *systemic compact* (both senses: compression and contract) as well as a media-systematic network. Moreover, as we will find from here out, to have viewed such composite works transmedium is a lesson, a conceptual regimen, readily transferred to their motorized counterparts in works of projection and kinetic display, from slide sequences to film reels to digital monitors. Under scrutiny in such works is a scene of metacinema (or, alternately, an involute videography) whose considered reception—whose transmedium vantage—requires the decipherment of more than a surface glance can easily take in. Along with the frequent magnifying lenses of our adjusted "reading" glasses in the scrutiny of such image systems, attention also necessitates certain calibrated conceptual viewfinders gauged to the ironic counterplay, within given works, between both evoked and revoked media determinations and their inscribed specular histories. These are histories often called out by being caught up short, their present operations thrown for a loop not engineered by the mere mechanism itself.

Yes, "a decipherment of more than a surface glance can easily take in." But, more important, a discernment of the *whereby* before that *what more*. This is a pattern we are by now well familiar with—in many of its varied *de*familiarizations. Transmedium work repeatedly entails, brings in train, a "commentary" that is pre-interpretive, explanatory even before explicatory, though often verging on hermeneutic in its own right. This tendency of conceptualist obliquity is very different from Niklas Luhmann's point that without language, there would be no art.[1] For him, this is because without language there would be no abstract model of communication that the achievements of art, without direct "message," find ways of creatively approximating. But an early leaning of Conceptual art—of a certain alphabetic stripe in the mode of wordworks—tended to expose instead, as we know, something at times like the institutional message behind all art. It did so through the frequent regurgitation of the very expository terms that, on Luhmann's model, the visual artifact would ordinarily be thought to rework or transcend. Elsewhere, such conceptual practice had a way of witnessing to literacy per se in deliberately impeded form: reduced, for instance, to blurred visuality in Mel Bochner's use of graph paper, though containing no "graphic" image besides text, simply to write out the eponymous LANGUAGE IS NOT TRANSPARENT (1969) in sequential overlays of progressive murk.

In the mode of Conceptualism 2.0, transmedium projects can be thought to extend this general tendency by requiring, nonetheless, despite their inevitable opacity, some such words in advance of any wrestle with the image that accompanies—and concretizes—them. Unlike the wordworks of a Joseph Kosuth or a Lawrence Weiner or a Robert Barry, including prominently Bochner's own, wording of this later paratextual sort isn't part of the art, but only of its orientation—or of us to it. Words don't achieve the effect at issue; rather, they simply make it possible to receive it. Yet that burden of ancillary but essential reading does leak back into moments of viewing to inflect our very sense of understanding as falling within an insinuated discursive frame. And I use the term "frame" advisedly. When American artist Byron Clercx pulps books and then carves them into an empty picture frame—calling up the not strictly legible but nonetheless compressed discursive armature or brace of all aesthetic perception—this is as much a theoretical work of art-history as in the more overt visual pun when the same artist reshapes crushed art-theoretical treatises into an axe handle (with affixed steel blade) under the title *Axiom* (1993).

And there are many subtler such hatchet jobs, as we've noted, where the art-historical as well as strictly perceptual nature of the works are brought to our attention not from defaced word surfaces within them but from explanatory notes alongside. We regularly need to *read up* before we can really *look into*, let alone *see*. We need to have spelled out for us, say, how that grainy photoprint (actually the granular aggregate of thousands of Web image searches) derives from the bilingual spelling out of *foto* and *photo*; and then, by association, need to consider the multiple discourses of the indexical image in transnational culture. We need, elsewhere, to have it spelled out for us that the seemingly contingent newsprint laid down to catch dripping paint is actually the hand-inked text of the artist's own equivocal newspaper review—and, further, that it is executed on the invisible backside, turned forever to the wall, of a ransacked art print. Even when there is nothing linguistic associated with the image, sometimes such gallery or catalog paratexts are the only reliable "optic" we have in taking a revisionary view of the thing before us. At all such moments, it is only through transmedial orientations of this sort that understanding and vision coincide in that frequent double sense of "Oh, *I see.*"

If this sensory equivalent of "Oh, I get it" depends on up-front discursive supplements in the case of certain fixed-frame obscurities we've come upon so far, so too when the image moves, but not quite accountably, across our field of view. In these coming works, anything like the verisimilitude of mainstream cinema is wholly foregone, so that they compare most closely not to the exacting hyperrealm of Scene One but to its hypo- or de-realized counterparts, whether electronic composites or minimalist executions. One recalls here those works, like Fontcuberta's Googlegrams, that remain "unreadable" in their superficially rough resolution until viewing is directed to their undertext, in his case to the amassing of separate downloaded "thumbs." As noticed at length, and by contrast, photorealism (otherwise and more recently known as hyperrealism) may show you what looks, as painting, too good to be true—and may thus deliberately evoke automatism rather than handicraft. But the moving-image sequences that await us, like the hyporeal of wall art, operate by withdrawing to varying degrees from coherent representation altogether. Even as they may at times be photographic in their own right, in the form of slide transparencies or celluloid strips, they call up a different stratum of transmedial notice from the implicature of photography and pigment in photorealism. Whereas such "hyper" production speaks mostly for itself, these films join the main weight of evidence in chapters 2 and 3 by requiring a prompt text before one can begin to "visualize" what they are actually *after* in the unrolling track of what they present. Again, a good deal of telling may need to be dealt out along with the show—and some history of cinema taken on board, if mostly for granted.

Lights, camera, action!—and, in 1895, a new medium was born, one incidentally appealing (as we've recently seen) to the reborn Count Dracula a year later in their coterminous London debuts. The motion picture, of course, is a form of kinetic mediation inherited half a century later by video, then screened and streamed since by computerization. But this is a mechanized motion not left to breathe freely in the composite experimental works to which we now turn—in their churning rather than mere framing of the image. For these are projections in which motion can seem either congested beyond recognition as picture or openly nonrepresentational altogether. Light, image, often camera (these we've pursued in Scene One)—and now action, sonic at times as well as optic. So the "scene" of investigation necessarily changes. In the dance, flicker, and skid of the visible—rather than its affixed surface, whether planar or sculptural—the staging is more choreogrammic, as it were, than strictly pictographic. Motion is captured, not just image. But this involves no mere genre distinction among art practices. Not only can each operation as such—moving and even still image (the latter itself composited)—be registered transmedium, or in other words transmedially, but the very difference between fixed and flickered image may, sometimes slammed together in lamination, address common preoccupations in a single artist's work rather than just across a populated array of contemporary visual enterprise. However layered their makeup, experiments of this sort in the vexed recognition of surface versus image—the former being material or not, anything from etched to projected—operate within the broadened field of self-pictured planarity.

This is where transparency assumes no premium; where surface need yield to no persuasive illusionistic depth; where the plane of medial interface is all. So we'll eventually move in discussion, building as Sietsema does on his numerous trompe l'oeil executions—in their inverted lure to traditional credulity despite their almost comic lack of thrall—to his equally "derealist" and nonimmersive film work. Operating across so many ironic registers at once, rather than closing on a single reductionist trope as do his minimalist and dizzyingly stinted paintings and drawings, his "brainiac" films can then be seen, in their own kind of comparable epistemographic irony, as a trumping of the eye by the parsimonious moving image. But this means that on the way back to that MCA retrospective in Chicago for a considered look at Sietsema's moving-image experiments, we are advised to turn first to other artists, less obscure and rarefied in their motion work, who install similar crossover interfaces between fixed optic frames and the serial planarity of moving images. Explored in these works is the image's sequencing, overlay, or arbitrary shuffling apart from full cinematic mobilization: in other words, the image's pictureplaning per se rather than anything like its orchestrated representational spectacle.

[figure::horizon]

With a more focal center of gravity in photomechanical assemblage—but still veering between, or overlaying, separate media determinations in his time-based work—there are the career-long experiments in "para-photography," as he called it, of Robert Heinecken, as assembled in a posthumous retrospective at MoMA in 2014. In one work, oversized foot-square photo enlargements, printed as transparencies, and marked as "Kodak safety film," simulate separate images of discrepant female body parts frame-advanced on a numbered photographic roll—not just para-photography, then, but proto-cinema as well. The piecemeal array is stretched horizontally like a reclining nude but produces instead, under the title *Figure/Horizon*, a kind of abstract vanishing point of desire, fueled by image in general—the image *system*, as it were—more than by any one coherent picture of its sexualized object. The title's slash might well have been used instead to indicate the work's dissevered Strip/Tease.

Heinecken's frequent impulse to comment on the erotics of the specular itself, apart from its content, is even more apparent in an actual moving-image equivalent from his work—in the form of an ironic video installation from 1970 called *TV/Time Environment*. There, the para-photographer has simulated, via minimal furnishing, a modest middle-class living room with an old-fashioned small-screen TV set running on a video loop of separate broadcast excerpts visible only through the torso and crotch of a female nude transparency plastered over the "home screen": TV's cathode fixation as its own kind of addictive erotomania—where the "horizon" of every image is the "figure" of unquenchable desire, serial, culturally saturated, but never satiating.

In contrast, *Surrealism on TV*, from 1986, offers a kind of reverse companion piece. It deploys, by a salient transmediation, the low-resolution grain resulting from photos of separate broadcast images on a TV screen—long before screen-shot computer technology. These are photos arbitrarily reconfigured in a nonrepeating series of three slide projections: a motorized version of that of arbitrary optic seriality, sans video motion, seen in *Figure/Horizon*. Each work seems operating in the spirit of Surrealism's "exquisite corpse" (with its folded experiments in noncontinuous representation by different artists' hands). Heinecken's *Surrealism on TV*, of course, is a thirty-some-year-old work rendered all the more fully mediarchaeological, in its play between moved still and stilled movement, when seen at the MoMA retrospective in light of the double outdating of both cathode TV and the traditional slide projector. It thus takes its belated and unwitting place in the company of an installation like Simon Denny's for the 2013 Venice Biennale, a punning assemblage called *Analogue Broadcasting Hardware Compression*. Huge images of the bulking broadcast apparatus in the studios of old-fashioned TV transmission are digitally photo-printed onto the equally superseded surface of stretched canvas on two sides of a dead-ended pathway—or lightless tunnel—lined with increasingly smashed and trash-compacted curved-screen TV monitors, sacrificed in punning deference to the new digital "compression" and its finer representational fidelities.

[flat::screening]

In the same months as Heinecken's career retrospective, the instead forward-looking Whitney Biennial gave over a whole wall to a palimpsest comparable to Heinecken's staged TV room in its transmedial mode of photo/video overlay. But instead of an optic competition between photo-static nudity and image flow, in this case we find a not-unrelated overlap of painting upon video. At the same time, the high-modernist Greenbergian shibboleth of flatness finds a new form in Ken Okiishi's *gesture/data* (2013)—and a new format of verticality, to boot—as five Samsung monitors are turned on end and wall-mounted, as if in portrait format. On each (fig. 6) appear a few broad strokes in varying acrylic pigment—somewhere between vandalism and gesturalism. Behind these swaths of color, one can make out a discontinuous montage of old low-resolution TV shows in VHS capture alternating with more recent HDTV images—as if this were the recorded result of uninterrupted dial-spinning not just across channels but across whole media time frames in technological evolution. As these clips tease the eye through the only partially occluding chromatic smear, they throw the supervening paint strokes into a kind of conceptual, if not entirely retinal, demotion. The viewer is confronted not just with some history of screen technology eclipsing painting in two stages as the postmodern form par excellence—that would be too easy—but rather with a palimpsest of channel-surfed surfaces that put graphic flatness and cinematography's evocation of depth into an unstable transmedial contrast. The painted stroke dissipates slightly into a vaguely encroaching thing within the picture, while, partially blocked by it, the picture loses some of that phenomenological depth to which, even in low resolution, it would ordinarily lay claim. In its variant on the logic of painted transparency in the mirror work of Bertrand Lavier, the effect is, one might say, to deanimate both the lateral thrust of the pigment strokes and the moving bodies fighting through it. Prepared by such explicit overlays of gesture and technology, painting and electronic trace, as well as by the medial laminations of Heinecken's practice, we are ready now for the mental and retinal calisthenics of Paul Sietsema's film work.

[de::scription]

In the intentionally dated avant-garde medium of 16mm film, availing itself of no video transfer, Paul Sietsema's moving image venture, especially in the 2013 film *At the Hour of Tea*, is not overlain in the mode of Okiishi's so much as undercut in its optic invitation: an invitation to see what we are never shown, and thus instead to *visualize*. Such a projection might be classed simply as an instance of "gallery film," for museum purchase and display, if it were not so explicitly transmedial in its withholding of image within a discursive (in fact typographic) continuum. The film lasts long enough to describe and analyze a painting never revealed to us. Its strange conceptual process needs, therefore, just the explanation that the film only implicitly provides. The sixteen minutes of *At the Hour of Tea* honor the materialist tradition of 16mm work—with its typical emphasis on the low-fidelity resolution of the strip itself rather than on the representational image generated—in part by exposing a streak of damage down the right side of almost every frame, an effect in itself reminiscent of early conceptual projection in the vein of exposed material vulnerability rather than world-making (as well as of the abraded surface of Ruscha's celluloid renderings).[2]

Sietsema's is a film that montages together a surface full of collectibles, antique time-pieces prominent among them, within the antique art medium of 16mm celluloid. These relics include an old-fashioned desktop calendar whose pages (one per day) are not turned, but rather intermittently lap-dissolved, so as to log the timeline of the film's own dates of recording. Again, the conflation in Sietsema of production and image, cause and effect: time passing as calendrical synecdoche for the editing that indexes it apart from any portrayed event. And two further synecdoches for sequential recording emerge from within the frame: an obsolete manual typewriter, and, in no direct relation of source to result (no keyboard action visible), a text arriving in time-lapse typeface on separate sheets of formal notepaper. These are inscriptions that disappear, in the subsequent jump-cut editing of the strip, into black-bordered envelopes, disappearing in their turn as if for a funeral of their own material format as well as the forever absented topic of their prose. For what they spell out, though never by name, is the drily expert ekphrastic analysis, in the mode of precinematic imprint (or, in other words, sheer textual account), of an easel painting that remains always off-screen, unseen in its very appreciation. In their transmedial communication across the superannuated media of typescript and photochemical mechanism together, these parodic "text messages" thus offer a description of the even more dated modality of classical rendering in paint, which Sietsema's other canvases have both mastered and inverted in his sardonic trompe l'oeil executions.

In its heyday, heroic painting tended to heroize the painter's craft itself, but in this case, via serial text, we have the conjuration of a never-seen equestrian painting in a quintessential academic mode, subjected in turn to a uniquely academic and finally denaturing analysis—with compositional geometry, optic vectors, and structural balance delectated upon in a way that nonetheless falls short even of a satisfying "word picture." But the larger point would seem to be that of framing itself. The rectangular viewing field once monopolized by painting—before ceding ground to photography and then being displaced by the moving frame as well as moving image field of cinematography—reverts here to the fixed-frame view (within the black-bordered rectangular typed texts) of a strictly verbal representation of the painting's previously privileged "dynamics" in absentia. The transmediality of all this is no less potent by operating under bland, blank negation. Given the fixed frame's still life of antique time pieces in a motorized projection, but with no mounted horseman to be seen on the loquaciously analyzed canvas, certainly both the movement-image and the time-image of Gilles Deleuze's philosophical film theory appear under erasure, or at least suspension, by serialized verbal (rather than visual) imprint.[3] In the minimal planar increments of Sietsema's barely moving picture, this intensive stress on the unseen, in its ratio of words to exiled image, turns the very medium of spectacle to a serial effacement of its own linguistically imprinted reference: a picturation swallowed in both machinic and discursive process as a serial *pictur/e/rasure*. And this with another irony in tow. The laborious paratextual comment often necessary to pinpoint the material and thematic ironies of Sietsema's imaging is here, from inside his own film, squandered on a work so subordinate to discourse that it goes altogether unseen.

This is where the debt to Hollis Frampton's transmedial landmark, *Nostalgia* (1971), is most obvious. Frampton's is a film where images in patient slow series are deferred from any convenient mental capture on the viewer's part through an ongoing mismatch of voice and image track. Hearing about the image without being able to see it yet, and then trying to concentrate on a description of the next one with the previously reported photo finally in view: that's the cognitive (turned conceptual) test of Frampton's irony. This philosophical comedy sustains the dilatory shunt of separate photographs and, one after the other, their eventual ignition—when supported too long, that is, on their makeshift platform: not projector and arc light but, in Frampton's case, another and less technical apparatus, a simple hot plate, which gradually brands each photo with a labyrinthine singe before shriveling it to ash. This all takes place in Frampton's serial send-up of synchronized sound film, as we are repeatedly hearing about the next photo in quasi-photogrammic line—and too soon, therefore, to match description with picture in the result. Anything conceptualized as the eponymous "nostalgia" is travestied by Frampton at the materialist level of metacinematic passing, just as it would be for Sietsema at the level of outmoded media and its themes, including in his case horseback portraiture of any stamp or conviction.

But a central difference remains between the two films. Frampton's voiceover ekphrasis turns upon what we do in fact come eventually to see, but always too late for match-up with its anticipatory prose—as if the calibration were straining, beyond cognitive bounds, the inherent limits of cinema's foundational "persistence of vision." Sequence, out of sync, becomes in *Nostalgia* all titular loss and artificial reconstruction, the image gone missing—rather than generated—between retention and protension in the viewer's mind and mind's eye. By contrast, the drastic ekphrasis of Sietsema's film never gives us, never yields up, any trace of the image it analyzes—as if the painting's own description disqualifies it from contemporary notice, subsumes its realist classicism to subsequent art procedures so fully as to efface it. But the irony is double, circular. Certainly the equestrian image's contrived dynamism, so patiently discerned, is lost to the moving media that have so thoroughly marginalized any canvas "scenario" as reigning visual aesthetic. Yet this happens now, in the case of Sietsema's conceptualist reduction, in a filmic medium far less dynamic (and dramatic) in its present minimalist deployment than classic painting, especially as the latter is structurally decoded and kinetically understood by these veritable typescript subtitles to the unseen.[4]

The deepest transmedial grip of Sietsema's several initiatives comes clear, then, only when one begins to intuit in them one overarching project. It isn't easy, isn't meant to be—is certainly not designed to ease us into meaning. What is solicited, instead, is an effort of balked observation—and interpretive will—in order to bring his 16mm films, for all their minimal trick effects, together with his minimalist trompe l'oeils, and the latter together with their own commandeered backsides (those found and vandalized junk-shop canvases) in the appropriated and more routine illusory optics of hackwork reproduction. The films never look like other than what they are, conceptual exercises in a grainy, dated medium. The canvases always look like something other than standard representational painting or drawing. The transmedial charge, and discharge, comes between these separate modes as well as within each. This happens only as we move to rethink film itself in line with the art-historical evolution of realist painting as well as automatic imprint, even while across the gallery we are fooled by the same artist's reduced versions of hyperrealism into thinking of his wall works either as automatic imprints (the faux negatives in oil, the weathered boat drawing) or as slapdash collage (the figure/ground newsprint framing). Faced with either made or filmed images in Sietsema's catalog, we are likely to encounter less a freestanding artifact, internally coherent, than a foregrounded interface: now of the handmade image with photography or newsprint, now of motion picturing with some heroic pictorialism cemented in unseen oil. And so forth—on into the hinterland of representation and the inner arcanum of craft.

[empiri::schism]

In their break from any purist doxa of high modernism, these works of Sietsema's are so diverse that they're hard to register together, let alone at once. Yet there is no dispersion of focus in the multifariousness of method. They are all very much of a piece in rethinking what it is that makes a piece of art—and signals it as, first of all, a piece of work. "I am interested in what it means to make something today," says Sietsema in the flyer for his retrospective exhibition. And, one might add—to emphasize the conceptualist motive across his motifs: what it means to make meaning with a thing. We have seen in chapter 3 how the trompe l'oeil stress in his paintings and drawings, a conceptual romp more than a bedazzlement, inverts the classic scenographism of the mode. Rather than smiting us with a real space beyond any brushwork, it returns us to brushes and work space. Rather than fleeing all trace of the studio, it often deposits only its traces and leavings. In this sense the trompe itself is only the halfway house of its conceptual agenda. A similar logic organizes his abstract film about the modernist *Empire* (so-called) of Clement Greenberg—where a process of quirky abstraction inhabits the cult(ivated) scene of an earlier and reigning ideology of abstraction. Sietsema achieves this by filming through different filters, in demystifying invasive close-ups, a clunky cardboard mock-up based on a *Vogue* photograph of the modernist guru's art-laden Manhattan apartment (more in a moment). So, too, in Sietsema's splat paintings, is the fetish of medium specificity turned almost physically inside out.

In this artist's low-key ramping-down of the trompe l'oeil gambit, one destiny of all painting—the frame of display as the afterlife of its labor—is reduced in many of his wall works to a mere aftermath in the spillage and discards of the studio: not as found and appropriated residuals, but rather as sedulously reconfigured ones. The opposite of abstraction, this is a simulation of the abjectly concrete. Impressionism, cubism, surrealism, abstract expressionism: all give way here to a nugatory realism of the scene of making rather than the making of a scene—or even the veiling of a plane. Instead of opening rectangular portals on a world of representation beyond the site of production—and very much instead of foreclosing picture in a modernist celebration of tincture, some detached rapture of form, color, and surface—Sietsema's depictions return, at arresting right angles as it were, from gallery to workbench in the paradox of a new illusionist candor, whose exacting and considerable wit is as dry as his portrayed waste matter still looks wet from its own contingencies in the studio. No concept is pictured, just picturing reconceptualized—and often caught on the cusp not just between craft and accident but between the separate mechanisms of photography and drawing. These aren't visualized ideas that get to you. That's what's so radically *trans*medial about them. They are images slung between competing recognitions, deferred and reversed, derealized, images that *get you thinking* visually.

And the films do this as well, and all the more so by subtracting from the projected track any of film's normal scenic interest—or, in the case of *Empire*, simulating it as sheer setting without scenario: the cardboard fortress of an entrenched but fragile agenda. This travesty, as it were, of Greenbergian "space" stands as the deskilled but kinetic counterpart to Thomas Demand's painstaking sculptural reconstructions of photographed sites for hyperdefined rephotographing, but with a further art-historical torque in Sietsema's case. To take a two-dimensional photograph of Greenberg's domestic gallery, an apartment hung with iconic works of abstract expressionism, lift it from a popular and "trend-setting" magazine, and then remake the space and its signature framed works in crude mock-up for examination by a film camera: this is to ramify flatness beyond fetish to a kind of farcical shuffle of planarities, one whose dollhouse sculptural architectonics are asked to transmediate between film frame and painting frame across a cartoonish send-up of both inhabited space and the modernist iconology of surface. In this re-troped *Empire* of pure form over image via the optic discourse of the film's own simulated 3-D space, that Greenbergian sanctum sanctorum, in its dummied-up representation, is manifestly a send-up rather than a testament. Similarly, in *At the Hour of Tea*, to effort to recover, via a satirized typewritten ekphrasis, the time-based nature of verbal description rather than visual exhibition, and align it with the temporal calibrations of a frame-advance medium, is to triangulate representational discourse with both static and kinetic display around the groundless basis of each.

One senses a deep optical pleonasm at the core of Sietsema's production—as if it were pressing fundamentally rhetorical, if still foundational, questions. In this latter day of image culture—his "makings" may seem collectively to ask—what two-dimensional images *don't* bring photography, drawing, painting, and film to mind together, each free-loading on the others' premises and history? More to the point yet, why not accord fresh confessional weight to the very fact of *studio* paintings or *brush* paintings? Sietsema's effort is only, in quasi-grammatical terms, to transfer those epithets, those modifiers or descriptors, up from ground to figure—so that the *look* of the studio and of the brush, and in turn of the camera, even before the *work* of the same studio and brush and camera, are made to enter upon such an inferential and transmedial zone of contemplation. And so it is that the spooled materiality of film, whatever image protocols of the past it would seem to occlude or preclude, is shown to confess—projected to confess—its own debt to the geometries of painting and the seriality of typescript. Art is in part about rendering, storage, and communication, if it is about anything. Often in Sietsema's work, it is about *only* this: a semiotic burden unflappably stripped of any relaxed distractions. In the grip of his exacting technique, this is its own surprise. And more: its own brief, a tacit argument under submission to us while we look. As usual, in reduction begins redefinition. With *Empire* or *At the Hour of Tea*, celluloid is what the medium *is*; transmediation is what it *does*. To watch it in action is to traverse its inmixed terms. To probe them is to engage with the work's own mediarchaeology.

[effect::cause]

Another artist fully as "brainiac" as the supposedly marginalized Sietsema, Turner Prize–winning Simon Starling is equally committed to working across the borders of still and moving imagery—and with at least as involuted a conceptual agenda. So involuted, in fact, that it is characterized by one commentator as a tail-swallowing "ouroboros" effect in various photographic instances and full-scale installations.[5] We can readily specify this apt suggestion first with a photographic sequence of such autotelic ingest-stations (five widely spaced prints in all—works feeding on their own material base, as if consuming their referent in the process) before turning to a metamedial work in the all but redundant projection of celluloid motion itself on film, yet with a transhistorical twist organizing its looped plastic imagery. These typifying conceptualizations appeared together in a 2014 mid-career retrospective of Starling's work at Chicago's MCA (a year after Sietsema's show) under the double-edged title "Metamorphology," evoking both a metacommentary on form per se and an ontology of metamorphosis—or, in other words, at once an unchecked reflexivity and a transmedium alchemy.

First the self-feeding photographs, then the mechanically fed filmic strip. In a series of five large-format prints from 2005 called *One Ton II*, hand-processed in a platinum/palladium emulsion, the glinting, richly toned images exhaust—as explanation has it (without which, nothing)—the miniscule amounts of platinum extracted from a ton of ore at the vast mining site they picture, with its gutted and grotesquely unphotogenic pit replicated identically across the five framed high-gloss prints. Trenched out by the Anglo American Platinum Corporation in South Africa, this is a desolate gouged terrain having lost all contours as a natural landscape and thus serving to italicize, when treated in high-definition print form, the extravagant ratios of extraction and devastation that result. With mined cause manifested as bleak effect, the vicious circle of this environmental predation has passed through image without making it to any retinal payoff beyond its own satiric transmedial minerality. Evoking under aesthetic erasure—and wasted expenditure—the platinum-print glories of late Victorian photography (exhibited shortly after, by coincidence, at a 2014 exhibition at the National Gallery in DC), these preservation prints have a way of suggesting the museum itself as the structural opposite of a mine: repository over against scoured pit. Yet in Sietsema's case, with his premium "archival prints," the aesthetic dossier is compromised and poisoned by its own exorbitant material economy.

Art history and material history often coincide in such transmedial exactions of Conceptual art. Whereas Starling works literally from the ground up, to quantify the amount of dug earth necessary to picture itself in an amalgam of its own embedded mineral basis, the Cuban artist Renier Leyva Novo, in work of a decade later that one might well imagine influenced by Starling, introduces electronic transmediation into a related idea of textual and painterly, rather than photographic, reductionism. Using software designed to measure the amount of ink expended per scanned page, Novo portions out the radical manifestos of twentieth-century politics, from Lenin through Hitler to Mao and Gaddafi, according to the amount of fluid entailed in their drafting—the ink spilled, rather than blood—and displays it invisibly in proportionately scaled opaque ink bottles. In an installation project called *The Weight of History* (2014), sampled under the title *Five Nights* at the Hirshhorn in 2016, he then transfers just those appropriate amounts of black to "monochromes" on the gallery wall, thus pitting the aesthetic defiances of modern art against the violent calls to arms marking the same century. Not just from "weight" to rectangular volume but, before that, from text to computer calculation, and then from polemical script to compressed and nonrepresentational image: the leaps of transmediation are multiplied in an imploded logic of communication.

Other photographic reductions by Starling operate—self-circulate—in the same vein, and shed light in the process on the related transmedial photographics (or photo-aesthetics, even photo-ethics) just considered— as well as on the time-based work of his to which we are soon to turn. His otherwise old-fashioned slide-projection piece *Inventar-Nr. 8573 (Man Ray)*, *4m-400nm* (2006) appropriates a 1930s Man Ray photograph for a "closer look" that in fact surrenders all "view" to raw magnification—pointillism gone mad, until just the molecular shapes of the original photo-emulsion are visible. In this very different kind of "mining," burrowing into the constituents of the image surface itself, no visual data remain but those of the recording act in its chemical substrate. Elsewhere, too, the ouroboros continues to bore deep in Starling's "research."[6]

Though new terms keep getting summoned in this way by each instance of such conceptual photography—such epistemography—in various works by contemporary artists, the viewer is nonetheless encouraged eventually to generalize. In Starling's case, mediation redoubled by such materialist reductions is, one recognizes, its own kind of transmediation. Where both Fontcuberta and Rondepierre, for instance, operate between surface and hyporealm at the level of the immanent image, Starling's negotiations can be seen to open a further invisible space within (or across) mediation: between apparent material process and raw matter itself, undoing any coherence in the idea of medium per se, medium perceived. His work intrudes between ingredient and optical gradient: now between rephotographed chemical minims (in molecular substructure) and their place at the basis of appropriated photographs, now between platinum extraction and its chemical compounding for art prints. And in that last particular transmedial loop, his "exposed" mining practices connect with the "rare earth" materials tacit in the ersatz video landscapes of Mark Tribe's high-gloss videogame frame grabs, yet another mode of ouroboros irony. In interviews, Starling's own word for this tail-swallowing circularity of conception is "collapse"—especially of time and space across media and materialities.[7]

[computer::generated]

Or call it synchronic media archaeology. In any case, the nature of this closed transmedial circuit in Starling's practice is no doubt clearest in the formal patterning and motorized spin of his "film" work. In another evident materialist "collapse," for instance, a 2009 installation returns the remote wireless connectivity of our latest communications procedures to the dawn of computerization itself. Here, at the height of our Second Media Age, is a quintessential experiment from the ranks of Conceptualism 2.0. Starling has executed what amounts almost to a visual pun on "computer modeling." He has, that is, reconstituted by digital simulation (one step short of digital printing) the very first programmable computer, the Z1 from 1936, with its key-punched bites originally taken out of standard 35mm film strips as the most convenient feeder material (and totaling in its first version only 172 bytes of memory). The ratio-format of the installation's parenthetical title suggests the scalar leap of its evolutionary irony. For *D1 - Z1 (22,686,575:1)* is a thirty-second sound film made by recording, at one celluloid remove from his electronic construct, the digitized image model—with its multi-millionfold data input—of this original and primitive binary apparatus.

The effect makes the head spin along with the gears of its cumbersome projection from yesteryear. Following are some clarifying snippets from the accompanying description of Starling's multiple-loop projector and the virtual reality of its beamed image, each of equal weight in the metahistorical conjuncture he has arranged: "The footage for *D1 - Z1 (22,686,575:1)* was generated using state-of-the-art computer animation technology including surface-rendering programs developed in Berlin." The technical fabrication thus returns in this sense to the home base of its German inventor. And that's only part of its conceptual circuit—or double helix: "Generating this simple 30 second long animation sequence, depicting the punched film reader (a tiny part of the vast machine), required 3,992,837,240 bytes of information— over 22 million times the memory of the Z1." Finally: "This computer-generated, 'virtual' reconstruction was then transferred onto traditional 35mm film stock ["traditional" in the negative sense of electronically obsolesced] and exhibited on another piece of mid-century German technology—a Dresden D1 projector." Cause and effect indeed swallow their own shared tail in this half-minute, half-century circuit. Through the auspices of a lumbering and outmoded apparatus with over half a dozen vertical film loops snaking their way up and down on the outside, rather than interior, of its mechanism, interwar film procedure is figuratively *laid bare* in the act of projecting (both senses) the very digital technology that has in every sense outstripped its material—and even at times indexical—base in the new circuit of computerized production and digital distribution.

But here this process of a played-out material substrate, under Starling's conceptual pressure, takes place with full transmedial irony. Film goes through its motions in an overexplicit and estranging simulation of cinema's own eventual successor in nonindexical record, limited at first to computational tracing and machinic tabulation. Where the depurposed film strip, exiled (only temporarily at that historical point) from its photographic or cinematic use, was once tactically commandeered as the material support of wholly binary operations, it is now the case that advanced binary operations are more typically the digital basis of both still and cinematic imaging—as well as, of course, of all other electronically processed data. The gallery result in Starling's mediacentric (if, this time, not vicious) circle comes to the screen as a twofold transmediation—and its tacit allegory: the filmic transfer of a CGI rendering of film stock's former ancillary sacrifice (but eventual total surrender) to the cogwheels of computation rather than the gears of projected transparencies.

Repeatedly in works of Conceptualism 2.0, we find that only with a practice so little brisk in its wit as that which Sietsema and Starling push to a limit—so patient, layered, impacted, and far from obvious in its constitution—can a perspective be gained sufficient to render the transmedial give-and-take as urgent as it is often initially obscure. And then available only, at that, when coached by discourse. In Conceptualism 2.0, as often noted so far, the discursive burden of early Conceptual art has evolved exponentially. But it is typically detached from the image plane, still or moving, and now sidelined to one or another mode of linear text accompanying these new versions of optical reduction—and, more important, technical *induction*. As pointed up by the supplementary labors of curatorial exposition, we've seen the results time and again. In the engaged "reading" of such works, in sync with their accompanying explication, the viewer regularly encounters no less than a *retinal essayism* in fixed or moving form—and, more and more often, too, an inbred archaeology of emergent platformatics. So the point is worth stressing again: where the commercial skeuomorph freezes some aspect of the technological past as the icon of its own repurposing, the transmedial object, instead, is more likely to reactivate the retro, if only to restore such mediation to a performance of its own endangered or defunct status. And to do so in ways that turn its very exposition, its gallery exhibition, in part expository.

A quite different work in Starling's itinerary makes a quite similar point. Appearing in more than one iteration for separate international venues, this piece involves a 35mm film variously configured in installation space alongside supplemental objectifications of its theme in a cryptic sculpture. The film on its own is indeed just the exception to Starling's typical laconic mediality that the word "theme" might suggest. For this is a documentary "narrative" in which one specialized prehistory of filmic cinema (the use of moving-image cameras for astronomical research) is "telescoped" and overvoiced onto the image of the medium's already antiquarian operations on the editing table—while Starling's footage (rather than video capture) of the so-called transit of Venus is readied for projection. The work thus carries with it, for once, its own oral discourse, rather than necessitating an explanatory supplement. And it is actively—or at least structurally— transmedial only when, as with its 2015 projection in Vienna's mumok (Museum of Modern Art), it plays alongside a "sculptural" adjunct of Starling's own cryptic devising: two facing telescopic mirrors on eye-level stanchions arranged so that viewers, positioned one at a time between them at the proper self-adjusted angle, can note, superimposed in black circles on their anamorphic surfaces, the serial stages of planetary motion in the Venusian "transit." This is the rare astronomical phenomenon whose moving-image record Starling has also undertaken from separate camera emplacements at outposts in Tahiti and Honolulu.

Running alongside this bipartite mirror sculpture, then, the accompanying film tells the fuller story—and narrates it as part of a larger story yet. It does so in the very form of staging the story's medial finale from within the postmodern foreclosure of an entire visual technology. Only the film's own media historicism can prepare the way for this impasse. For Starling's footage narrates the history of astronomical optics as if this were not just inextricable from, but equivalent to, any digest of photographic and film history at large. Jules Janssen's chronophotographic "gun"—a rifle-like telescopic apparatus used to mask the blur of sunlight from the shifting disk of Venus's passage in the work of its recording lens—is as important here as are optical toys, magic lanterns, or the frame analyses of Eadweard Muybridge or Étienne-Jules Marey in the preconditioning of cinema's advent. This is media archaeology at the end of its evolutionary curve, however. The huge close-ups of the editing table, the slicing and splicing of film frames behind the spoken narrative, find their true context in the film's dead-ended historical prognostication. After more than a century of such planetary filming, the photographic efforts preceding it, and the ocular experiments before them, Starling's overriding point is that when the next transit of Venus occurs in 2017 (and then not for another century after that), there will certainly be no film made of it, just any number of digital records.[8] The pictureplaning of discrete serial frames will be a thing of the past, with nothing resembling a cosmic cyclicity to bring it back. Here, then, with his present medium's spooling loops and their hard-earned precision timing in extreme close-up, and whether as science or as art, is photochemistry's last go-round. Analog's last stand.

[epitaph::ography]

Among such anachronisms in an age of post-photographic projection: gallery film itself, whose typical current display—whether entailing an actual screening or not, sometimes just the projector noisily overstaying its cultural welcome—has the frequent aura of a last rite. Indeed, Starling's *cine-clips* of Venus in transit are there, as we've seen, to mark more than one *eclipse*: not just a very partial darkening of the sun but the outmoding of its actual medium of record by new forms of digital inscription. An ocean away from the "Present of the Modern" exhibit in Vienna, in a context exclusively film-historical at MASS MoCA, Starling's metacommentary on this celluloid-tracked astral transit—in the light, literal as well as figurative, of ongoing technological transitions—was screened as part of the museum's anatomy of a lapsed filmic century. Starling's photochemical elegy was in this case reconfigured for display under the title *Black Drop*—with its play on historical backdrop, one assumes, as well as its metaphoric name for the sequentially positioned silhouette of Venus arcing in the manner of a black circular photogram across the sun's aperture-like backlight. The "transit" film is accompanied this time, not by the paired mirrors, but by a wall-mounted piece in which Starling puts under glass, like a solemnly framed museum masterwork, a few arbitrary folds and loops of exposed celluloid—as if on the drying racks of a once-functional technology. Framed there is an inference that the accompanying and self-consciously dated film projection—with its own "ouroboros" turn in the editing table's visibly looped feeds—serves laconically to italicize, with celluloid still in operation at once by lingering exception and by overt medial vestige.

Starling's tandem reflexive commentaries at MASS MoCA—film in projection versus film under archival glass, left out to dry by history itself—are joined in that group show by other 35mm and 16mm projections, some with no image at all except what the projector's beam might cast by way of wavering blur from the racing blank strip. Figured in this way is the translucent "shadow" of a medium's whole foregone conclusion (both senses), an irony hardest to miss in several works there by Italian artist Rosa Barba. In one of these, as just evoked, a projector casts on the wall only the murky band of unprocessed coiled celluloid looped in front of its beam. In another and more arresting piece by Barba, called *Stating the Real Sublime* (2009)—as if in its muteness it could do anything more than instate (or instantiate) it—multiple loops of blank celluloid seem, even in motion, sufficient to keep suspended from the ceiling the lumbering mechanism of their own visual irrelevance: the iconic movie projector itself left hanging in its own abandonment. Akin here again to the transmedial ouroboros of Starling's work elsewhere, Barba also installs the loop projection of a circular race track in the California desert, filmed from a wheeling helicopter. The track is presently untrafficked, disused, appearing under the media-historical as well as topographic title *The Long Road* (2010). By sheer association, and despite the unseen propellors of the helicopter's own rotary motion, a further use of circularity seems presently deserted in the obsolescence of the film reel.

This whole quintessentially "retrospective" exhibition at MASS MoCA bears the collective title "Dying of the Light: Cinema as Medium and Metaphor"—in allusion to Dylan Thomas, with his call to "rage against" that death. Instead of either rage or acquiescence, these works tend to stage their own anachronism in gestures more sardonic than polemical. Lament is checked, or perhaps truer to say sublimated, by the ingenuities of a recognized passing. And in their concentrated sense of antiquation, the projector installations yield up terms for automated motion capture—for the whole cinematic mirage and its constitution—that are elsewhere central to more deliberately transmedial works, sometimes by the same artists. Alongside Starling's docudrama of "eclipse" (astronomically partial, archaeologically final) and Barba's almost melodramatic ironies, there are pieces gathered as well from Matthew Cunningham, Tacita Dean, Rodney Graham, and Lisa Oppenheim. In all of them, that long and richly traversed filmic "road" we know as institutional cinema over the course of the celluloid century, in its technological derivation from the same rotary mechanics that led, for instance, to and beyond the possibility of such a helicopter overview as screened by Barba, has reached its evolutionary dead end in digitization.[9] And the MASS MoCA show is by no means a standalone venture. So much of the (passing) moment, so timely—so technologically obvious if no longer urgent, yet still plangent—is this kind of specialized thematic exhibition that, during the run of "Dying of the Light," there was an extensive and comparable installation at the Camden Arts Center in London by Portuguese artists João Maria Gusmão and Pedro Paiva. Like the proliferation of projectors in the former factory space of MASS MoCA (industrial aftermath twice over), this London project filled three galleries with over two dozen whirring 16mm projectors generating the chugging sound of an obsolete image factory operating in a last burst of frenetic and self-exhausting overdrive.[10]

[photo::auratic]

A digital trace or impression may still loosely be called a photograph—rather than an electrograph, for instance. But a cinema without separate photograms is no longer in any sense filmic, as an art like Éric Rondepierre's is sustained to insist. In the "pictureplaning" of the cinema screen, it's hard to say what is lost to our sense of the screen frame without its cognate planarity (and independently coherent pictures) in the frames of the strip; hard to say—and for the most part impossible to notice. But equally hard to deny. And equally tempting for postfilmic art to call out—if not quite back—in its transmedial, and thus perforce mediarchaeological, play between indexical formats.

Mounted on the assumption, and mounting evidence for it, of an altogether superseded filmic cinema, those 2014–2015 shows in the United States and the United Kingdom receive what amounts to their dual catalog overview in a book that went to press well in advance of either curation: a scholarly monograph by Erika Balsom containing a chapter on the distinctly elegiac register of recent gallery film and thus perfectly at home in Amsterdam University Press's "Cinema in Transition" series—with the volume's own specific title aimed at the multiple and sometimes troubled cusp of one such transition: *Exhibiting Cinema in Contemporary Art*.[11] After the early heyday of minimalist video in museum display, Balsom tracks the gradual return of cinematic elements (like spectacle, scale, and narrative)—distinctive features of the feature film—into video display, as capped more recently yet by the prominence of the dated rotary apparatus itself (rather than just the "gallery film") introduced into the realm of aesthetic as well as historical display in both white cube and black box installations. The exhibition space for this antiquated medium is thus more a reliquary than a showcase. Archaeologically grasped, filmic projection has found its apt last home: what might be called its cinemausoleum.[12] Balsom's emphasis could in fact be figured this way: only with the rapid digital eclipse of cinema is the glare of its waning hegemony sufficiently reduced to allow for its clear sighting as social form. Or, to borrow Raymond Williams's famous triadic terms for cultural transition, only when thrown into shadow by the "emergent" can the "residual" elucidate its nature as former "dominant."

Balsom's interests revolve around how filmic cinema, as a suddenly vestigial image system, is redefined by gallery installation; mine, around how transmedial projections in similar exhibition spaces (no longer quite cinema at all, nor quite film, like Starling's thirty-second CGI epic of celluloid as substrate for the first computer) help redefine, under the category of mediation, the work of other and diverse materialities—and their transfusions—in gallery display.[13] No need for sharp demarcations between the arguments here, just clear ones. The works Scene Two will continue to take up are kinetic operations that parse and redistribute the ratios of movement and image in projection practice, and otherwise jettison the production of spectacle in favor of investigated process. This is how they speak across their own cross-conditioned technology to the formal ramifications not only of experimental (or for that matter "senescent") projection but of medial assumptions at large. Transmedial kinesis in gallery manifestation—the moving picture as a *[photo::filmic]* effect, when isolated as such for exhibit in its status as celluloid-based and machine-tooled—can gloss in this way, within the purview of Conceptualism 2.0, the different work of sculpture, drawing, and painting, including their own medial impurities, as much as it may reflect on itself in any privileging (or funereal) way.

Yet none of this, however insisted upon, detracts in the least from what Balsom is after—and accomplishes. Building on Rosalind Krauss's claims for contemporary art in a "post-medium condition," to be pursued on Krauss's own terms in our coming discussion, Balsom signs on to this overthrow of a "specificity" aesthetic while insisting nonetheless on a "dialectical" relationship between certain postmedial gestures and all those previous differences leveled by universal digitation. She does so in an effort at "demonstrating how it is precisely in tandem with an anxiety over the limits of a medium that one finds articulations of its specificity" (69). Emphasis in Balsom's chapter, then, falls on the historical limits of a superseded medium staged in isolation as a kind of cathartic obsolescence, whereas other works of liminal adjudication build a concentrated force field of oscillating limits into their own transmedial process. The film screenings she takes up, or sometimes just antiquated projector installations, are located conceptually, as she stresses more than once, *between* a previous regime of distilled "specificity" (in the sense of modernist formal purity) and the computerized leveling of all platforms in a binarized uniformity of encoded storage and access. The works we're exploring—including some by the same artists who provide her with illustrations—locate that volatile "between" within their own cross-specifications. Gallery film for Balsom falls, rather than oscillates, somewhere between the cracks of medium salience versus medial sameness, uniqueness and "convergence"—the fading medium sacrificed in this way to its fullest retroactive estimation. Instead, in a transmedial sense of these practices, the use of—or allusion to—film process in conceptualist gallery forms operates as an analytic of present aesthetic force or irony.[14] Even in Rondepierre, for instance, the photogrammic capture looks out to other modes of inscription and framing—textual, televisual, painterly—as well as looking back to the track.

The relation of Balsom's chapter on a dead-ended filmic projection to our ongoing evidence is, ultimately, not so much complementary as chiastic. What Balsom sees the museum doing for film, we can see film doing for the museum. In her argument, definition is bred of the intrinsically obsolete: call it an *obsolessence*. In mine, that mode of definition fans wide across many divergent aesthetic materialities. Estranged from cultural centrality, the vestige helps explicate other related decenterings. In the fading away of cinema's "plastic art," with the loss of celluloid projection's unique grain, luminescence, and pulsation, that very passing can itself stand forth, for works other than celluloid projections, in a tacit clarification of material immanence and its often-hybrid fashioning: exactly the generative interfaces that transmedial work typically layers, remixes, cross-questions, or undoes. When culturally dethroned by having its apparatus set on a gallery pedestal, antiqued by this mode of mostly *self*-exhibition, what celluloid film thus achieves by contrast with its former communal function, its lapsed context as popular medium, is what other and more internally complex transmediations can work to achieve, by conceptual inference, in their own internalized formal tensions and dispersed purities. In many of these we sense again, as proposed early on, a case of art at large understood as the temporary depurposing of the world by its contemplated image.

With Balsam's emphasis on the "cultural vernacular" of cinema as a "social institution" (112–13), another methodological sticking-point emerges. Regarding film's residual exhibition, the prevailing "media studies" question would remain *who* or *what* a given (i.e., socially received) mode of signaling is thought to communicate *with*. But another question cuts across this endemic emphasis when confronted by many works of Conceptualism 2.0. And that is this: *how*—by what material means—may a specific transmedium juncture or interface be recognized to unsettle any normative or programmed reception in cases where messaging (or socially framed communication) must first turn back on itself to query, across an inbuilt material gap, its own con-foundation? Or ask it this way: what is the relation, even by the same name, of the composite "media studies" performed by specific works—within their ad hoc transmedial laboratories—to institutional Media Studies at large (differently pluralized, within a broader-gauge comparative spectrum)? This question all by itself, it should be clear, poses a certain resistance—behind which much of our evidence stands arrayed and committed. Evidence whose elicited leading question is this instead: with *what*, rather than with *whom*, does mediation do its communicating? Again the technical question: *how*?

Instead of throwing out the medium with the cultist discourse of specificity in which it was once canonically bathed, transmedium objects are understood here to respect (by respecifying) their own interpenetrating modalities. In contrast, when too much insistence is placed on the exclusive criteria of social interaction—as one might have suspected from the "contextualist" definitions of Dworkin and Foster considered early on, if it were not for the ensuing materialist grip of their exemplification—the reigning methods of media analysis can too soon forget that there is any demonstrable (or operable) medium there, by way of material conveyance, to begin with. Though Balsom's work is also, like that of those previous media theorists just recalled, far from falling into such indifference, such suspended differentiation, still the general field of her disciplinary allegiance is less inclined than it might be toward that moment in certain works—moment in the fulcral sense: conceptual pivot, a switchpoint in the realm of tangible and often technological support—where material specification must precede cultural or communal orientation. Hence, of course, the motive for a book like this.

Beyond the cinematic breakpoint wrought by digitization, we have been concerned with the way film's relation to other functional visual tracing and its kinetic manifestations holds open a transmedial model for a whole range of quite different image "research" in museum space. At this horizon, the category of Conceptualism 2.0 is found to exceed questions of superannuation per se even when sprung from them. Or put it that the "dialectic" of medial estimation rather than essence won from ruin in the works at MASS MoCA's "Dying of the Light" show, for instance, as in the larger number of kindred works surveyed in Balsom's chapter, is an analytic process internalized—in more concerted transmedium work—as the enacted (rather than implied) dialectic of cross-specification. Partly by conceptual proximity and free(d) association, this takes place—by various displacements and transpositions—in many other gallery works aside from (and alongside) film. These are works, as we know, that grow integrated only in regard to their own impurities and counterpulls: works transmedial at base, cross-purposed in their material support, differential at root rather than merely triggering in context certain valedictory differentiations. In this respect they are like film itself, film in its transmedial sequencing between photography and projection—as an artist like Rondepierre has made it a career's mission to apprehend.

[stop::watching]

As one might expect, it is precisely in the nature of the transmedial experiments of recent art production, in the very texture of their conceptual resistance to a cult of the image, that the history of photography and film—in relation to the gallery prestige of painting—would be cycled through a binary technology subsequent to them all and directly ousting the last from anything like its unique cultural prominence. Yet this happens only, at times, by rehearsing painting's own transmedial dialectics in evolution: this, for instance, when Wolfgang Staehle hangs a computer monitor on a museum wall in place of the landscape genre whose very history, as we'll see, it implicitly visualizes in review. Elsewhere in Staehle's webworked ironies, a similar mediarchaeological effect carries with it a more specific avant-garde history as well. Decades before Sietsema's cardboard-allegorized *Empire* there was Andy Warhol's *Empire* in 1964, about another kind of modern monument besides the later paper-thin edifice of Greenbergian aesthetics in Sietsema's satire by that name. This amounted, in Warhol, and as if in allusion to Fellini's title from the year before, to no less than 8½ slow-motion hours of a fixed-camera film, in the requisite 16mm of experimental practice, portraying only the drama of urban spectacle itself, shorn of action or actors. An icon in situ, the Empire State Building is offered up in its fixed frame of metropolitan reference under a monocular gaze—and all before the subsequent presumption of surveillance cameras at closer range. Then, too, that last proviso (that "before") is more than a merely historical distinction. It is an art-historical one. For the Net.art version of this fixated record arrived exactly four decades later, in 2004, with Staehle's *Empire 24/7*. Here a round-the-clock webcam stream, in the digital mode of an electronic sentry—from a tripod's long-distance vantage—is fed directly into his gallerist's video screen, where the now global empire of electronics seems part of the title's encompassing reach. This would constitute a new media procedure in a quite direct, if artless (though, with Warhol in mind, intertextual), sense if it were not for the extra feature Staehle has made typical of his video feeds. His images aren't continuous, it turns out, but frozen briefly in place every four to eight seconds, depending on the work; as distinct from Warhol's slow-mo deceleration, what one sees in Staehle is a real-time but stop-action (photographic cum videographic) rendering of digital "slides"—step-time video, as it were—rather than the indexical continuity of experienced duration.

This is where the transmedial edge of Staehle's work sets in. I first saw a piece of his in the Baltimore Museum of Art, displayed next to the reproduction of a Hudson River School painting that was hung elsewhere in their permanent collection. The wall placard: "*Eastpoint Sept 14 2004* (2004–6), unique composite of 8,189 digital photographs, in a 24-hour cycle." A far cry from such straightforward medium designation as "ink on paper" or "chromogenic print on aluminum." In fact (which means as one reads further in the explanatory copy), this is a tripod-mounted camera piece shot from a hillside above the Hudson, originally beamed in real-time to a downstate New York City gallery, but now in a video loop synchronized with the Baltimore museum's own clock time, its frame captures configured, in this case, at eight-second intervals. By this effect, we are reminded of how the very locus of art is, for the first time, capable of telepresence and extreme spatial displacement. In one sense, of course, the art of painting could always take an image of the Hudson River anywhere it was to be displayed. In another sense altogether, transmission can now, only now, take anyone to a temporal experience of the river—and thus to the source of the image's own execution, its real-time video streaming, so to say, in a channel of art's own. Moreover, given the transmedial museum context, it is all the clearer how Staehle's digital videograms—his light-sensitive indexical traces—intercept the tradition of realist painting by turning the privileged moment of recreated epitome into the time-based dissection of change.

But the transmedial effect is more complex than that—as is, moreover, the art-historical effect as well. The myriad adjustments of leaf movement or reflective ripple across the river setting are at first easy to mistake for the unsteady glitches of pixelation in the HD image plane. But the longer one looks, the longer grows the media-evolutionary view. On evocation's way back to the mid-nineteenth-century landscape in oil, Staehle's video may seem passing, in self-conscious review, through impressionism and pointillism both—and particularly in their tacit reaction to the automated record of photography. By a second-order extrapolation from their break-through techniques, however, the "landscape treatment" is now actually *computerized* to transmit (rather than merely simulate) the kinetic shimmer and blur not just of eyed motion but of retinal uptake more generally—and more pointedly, too, as if by further allusion. For even in the earlier stages of that nineteenth-century "perceptualist" movement, artists like Monet were interested in the virtual time-lapse treatment of a *plein air* scene across different canvases in a daily or seasonal cycle. More explicitly yet, of course, Staehle's work also passes through an exaggerated version of the very cinematic flicker of frame-line paced seriality ("8,189 digital photographs") that was historically overcome by both analog and digital video. There is no facile "convergence" here in this "new media" work, but rather an internal divergence in the form of analytic breakdown, with previous retinal premises (medium specificities) under evolutionary review.

Certainly the art-historical suggestions, stretching even beyond impressionist perceptualism into a default cubism, seem confirmed by a further familiarity with Staehle's practice. For in other of his video tableaux, especially his cityscapes of Manhattan under a volatile sky—digitally captured from across the Hudson in the New Jersey docks—the rectangulated cascade of changing light and shadow showering down on the right-angled facets and caverns of the skyline, given the several-second intervals of the videogrammic sampling, jump from frame to intermittent frame with the abruptness of a signal break-up: a volatile checkerboard of digital (second-order) rather than architectonic collapse. But not second-order for long enough. It is true that in the noncatastrophic phase (and intent) of this work, we find the dimensionalities of urban modernism stuttering into bitmap-like (dis)array. The logic is almost fractalized: jittery architectural rectangles magnifying the unseen shifts of the pixel grid in a transmediation between the pictorial and the technological, even as the result turns an iconic geometric skyline into the cubist rendering of itself in dovetailed and pseudo-kinetic pictureplaning. But this almost balletic breakup effect, clocked in at four seconds apart in these works, becomes almost unwatchable as, in one of the series' 24/7 transmissions—from mid-morning on the eleventh of September, 2001—Staehle's intrinsic calibrations allowed that same four-second ellipsis to bring the first of the two hijacked planes, from an initially ambiguous distance, slamming into the side of the first World Trade Center Tower. The empire of the computerized eye had become a surveillance monitor after the fact—too late for intervention, able only to mark, by elided trace, the elapsed vector of disaster.

But short of this cataclysm, or the cubist jitters of the earlier skyline works—with one shadow-framed luminous concrete rectangle abutting another in variant angulation—the full diurnal round of the *Eastpoint* video at Baltimore mines something further, and farther back, in media history. Long before digital video, with the potential surface manifestations of its pixel composite, the fixed-frame view of this neo–Hudson Valley "canvas" (or say its sampling by electronic canvass) evokes early cinema's own initial wonderwork. Such is the prenarrative marvel of motion itself, change per se, with all the induced serial similitude—despite intermittence—of felt duration that it generates. No one insists on this artifice, and its ocular overcoming, more explicitly than French filmmaker and theorist Jean Epstein. His book *Intelligence of a Machine* (1946; translated 2014) is willing to cede everything to the reel's rotary mechanism and its spooled strip with no attempt to mystify projection's seeming continuity—and yet without any loss of cinematographic privilege, any surrendering of film's "genius," in its new philosophical mode of epistemology.[15] This is precisely because, in its precision timing, the fabricated continuity, the sheerly *constructed* duration, of the film image speaks truth to power—or, in other words, speaks back to visibility's own typical sway over our falsified perception. It does so by reminding us of the continuously suppressed and elided blanks in even our everyday ocular and synaptic uptake—and not just this, but also the physical world's own scientifically parsed discontinuities within the no longer settled *a prioris* of space, time, and matter.

In a metaphor that might appear to anticipate the digital composite as well, Epstein sees film as a sequential "mosaic" rather than a holistic screen manifestation. Any sense of continuity is not in the flickering visual object that reaches the screen but is instructively subjective instead: "Outside the viewing subject there is no movement, no flux, no life in the mosaics of light and shadow that the screen always displays as stills"—"stills" that, of course, appear to us only as they are vanished into action, their separate image cells sprocketed past the aperture.[16] Epstein verges here on a point he doesn't quite make: that the mosaic model applies not just to the variegated (chiaroscuro) pattern of the fixed frame but to its own sequencing with the next in line—as if to say that "tile" after racing "tile" in the aggregate image of motion defines the linear mosaic of a vertical strip. In any case, when Staehle allows us momentarily to "misread" the rippling pulsation of his streamed or looped digital image of the Hudson Valley as a flaw in the representational transmit rather than the confessed economy of its deliberate piecemeal continuity—that is to say, its spaced-out, quasi-cinematographic digital sampling—he is returning to the first ruse of the moving image in the previous century's art of machinic animation. There, all continuous process, all gesture, all motion, is, according to Epstein at the close of his short treatise, a "special effect" (104). But that scarcely diminishes its mimesis, Epstein would insist, since reality as we know it—or at least as we perceive it—is a similarly subjective construct of intermittent matter, energy, and signal.

Same as well, Staehle might argue, with his "live-feed" from up the Hudson. It's more like actually being there than you thought. The eye, too, not just the digital camera, works by electric impulse and pixelation no less than does his video transmission. Here, in this new electronic picture-planing, is the world's very presence under transmedial investigation by a technique operating somewhere between photographic slice and cinematic slide. And if all film images on screen are manifested as a spatial mosaic generated by a more strictly rectilinear and serial one, so too with the invisible pixel array of the digital image, whether or not its constituents are visibly fractalized in that sort of manifest quilt of rectangular jigsaw chips that Staehle's sun-sliced Manhattan skylines conjure up. Yet Epstein's cinematic emphasis remains. And it is just this that our sixth chapter on the interstitial "filmedivision" of the projected strip will track back to earlier conceptualist experiments before, and then resumed by, the 2.0 moment.

[color::ration]

As important as it is to see the links of artists as different as Sietsema (via Frampton so far, Broodthaers pending) and Staehle (via Warhol) to the 16mm avant-garde of a previous cinema century, or of Starling to a nonphotographic use of the celluloid substrate in early computerization, another alignment is equally crucial. In sensing the widespread transmedial checkpoints of such allusive form, one finds work like Sietsema's responding, at least tacitly, to the more overt medial undoing (rather than simply cinematographic undercutting) of filmic projection by the same newer technologies that might otherwise remediate it—even for museum distribution as a DVD. This is to say that the washed-out palette of Sietsema's all but black-and-white screen in *At the Hour of Tea*—centered on an ekphrasis spewing out quasi-filmic intertitles for an image (an imagined painting) never framed for us—still bears comparison (in its evasion of the original picture by alternate mediation) with other contemporary work in a computerized vein of distanced immediacy. This includes a DVD installation by digital provocateur Cory Arcangel that reduces narrative cinema—by the computerized "slit-scan" process—to something approximating a color field painting in gradually moving vertical bands. Here is an abstract schema that rations out a narrative's chromatic spectrum—and in the process denaturalizes it through such electronic rationalization—by preventing all photographic vestiges of any recognized scene in a digitally remastered 35mm film named for coloration itself.

As no more than partially sampled on any one visit to the Tate Modern, this work takes an entire month of running time to screen a Hollywood DVD: to "screen out" its images, that is, in favor of their digital constituents, line by laser-read line of chromatic data traced by computerized scan. The original film is thus unraveled full screen (as a distended vertical curtain of striated coloration) over a full-length and real-time soundtrack, many times rerun—a track with which the work's optical tracings can never catch up, let alone realistically match up. On display is a case of slow motion so drastic that there is no visual action left, just optical activity hovering between narrative (still audible) and its artificially extruded retinal substrate.

The "found" film in question, though no longer in view: Dennis Hopper's 1988 police procedural *Colors*, the title initially suggestive of the LA-based plot's racial crises for the dubious men in blue. Arcangel's software proceduralism, with its analytic reduction from DVD to dilatory pixel scan, builds to a lurking grammatical pun like the famous Hitchcock promo tagline "*The Birds* is Coming." The tacit question and answer: "You want to see *Colors*? Here they are." No cinematic medium left, just its split-second analysis in transfer to an underlying stratum of coded generation. Transmedial as it is, probing the space between narrative imagery electronically transcribed and its gradient digital inscriptions, this work burrows beneath anything advocated by formalism's "baring the device." In this case there is no sparing of the artifact at all, no informed reconstitution of its structured nature. There is only the technological comedy of loss—and of course the art-historical irony by which Arcangel's work bridges the likes of Gene Davis's vertical stripe paintings from the 1960s and 1970s as polychrome studies and Gerhard Richter's 2011 computer scanning of his own abstract canvases to generate lineated horizontal arrays in photographic transfer.[17] Between a postwar refusal of expressionist gesture and a contemporary embrace of computer analysis in wall art, Arcangel has also, in effect, parodied another privileged mainstay of experimental work, the gallery film, by rendering entirely abstract nothing more than a routine Hollywood genre picture.

At the same time, and over the span of their quite different temporalities, his distensions of chromatic data are the suggestive complement to Staehle's elliptical samplings, each opening a space in the fabric of continuity for its exposed ocular fabrications. Then, too, the fact that the obvious contrast between Arcangel and a nonelectronic artist like Sietsema couldn't be stronger only makes the grounds of comparison seem more pervasive—as in fact, in the broader cultural context of our contemporary technosphere, they are. The markedly dated apparatus of "silent" projection, in all its unmasked distracting noise (Sietsema), and a high-tech evisceration of our latest audiovisual delivery system: these are two sides of the same coin, a coin removed from mass circulation by polar approaches that speak distantly to each other across the investigations of Conceptualism 2.0.

[kineto::grams]

We move forward now to another artist who is currently working in the time-based ironies of syncopated optics—and these related in their way to the timepiece still-life settings of Sietsema's eponymously temporalized but indecisive *Hour*. The framed temporal calibration of each artist's chosen medium has its own historical time frame as well—though more obvious in the coming instance than in Sietsema's play between cinematography and painting. For in aesthetic chronology, as we've seen, the transmedial is always transhistorical, and sometimes pointedly so. If the yoked media are close enough in technological time to be credibly bridged in a synchronic rehearsal, one medium always bears some historical relation to its counterweight, whether as its predecessor, successor, competitor—or even all three together at a recovered moment of contested transition. In the explorations of one among several new media artists, German-born, Glasgow-based Torsten Lauschmann, this emphasis is made central. In his most arresting conceptual pieces, each with its own intense visual fascination, Lauschmann operates at the crossing of modernity's second great fault line in media obsolescence—the ascent of the computerized picture—by referring it back to those animation effects in photomechanical experiment that turned picture into movie at media culture's earlier epochal watershed.

Two signal works of Lauschmann's relate the digital to earlier logistics of calibrated temporality in mechanical imaging, as well as to the general machinic function of synchronized gears.[18] In this respect, we again recognize how, with certain artists, it is not just that some works are in themselves insistently transmedial, but that entire oeuvres can be historically situated in this way to review the interplay of optical forces in an inherited evolutionary lineage—and its calculated throwbacks. The archetype of human temporality itself, once mechanically geared in its measurements, now binarized, is manifested by Lauschmann in the auto-archaeology of conceptual legerdemain. One of the two works in question digitizes the prephotographic optical toy called the thaumatrope, often seen as a hand-held and therefore pre-automatic forerunner of filmic motion, and thus overleaps a lineage to its point of origin. The other optical gambit on Lauschmann's part, in the manner of incremental temporality, reinserts analog mechanics (in the form of bodily performance) into the frame-advance simulation of a digital time piece.

Though from different conceptual angles, both works are optical retrogressions that send the electronic automaticities of the present back to their technological prehistory: in other words, back to what—in one black-box video show—Lauschmann calls the "Dark Ages" of mediation. To begin with, a decisive contemporary axiom is turned to reflexive praxis in Lauschmann's montage troping of the thaumatrope. By the tenets of our latest technology, the moving image no longer needs spooling any more than does a clock need winding. Rotation has been supplanted by mere differential iteration. The hand-held binary synthesis of the thaumatrope can now be facilitated, therefore, not by twine and disk, flipping two pictures fast enough to fuse them into one, but by computer chip in the most routine processes of digital animation. That's the one work: a study in duration's piecemeal construction. The other follows suit. Like the sundial as index before it, the clock face has here given way to the binary indication of its on/off backlit increments in the combinatory of high-tech numeric forms. Yet, as we are to see, what has given way is often given back with a vengeance by Lauschmann—returned, so to say, archaeographically.

What I'm singling out from Lauschmann's prolific gallery ventures, then, are in effect two video "movies": one a two-minute loop of telescoped photomechanical history, one a twenty-four-hour loop that "handmakes"—painstakingly and high-handedly—the rectangular time grid of a digital clock array. In taking up the "short subject" first, we note how 2009's *Thaumatrop* [German spelling], *Bird in a Cage, No. 1*, reverts to the prehistory of cinema in optical toys (often called "philosophical toys") by playing on longstanding debates about "persistence of vision" so as to reverse-engineer a thaumatrope by a gesture of digital editing performed upon intervening cinematic imagery. This resulting trimedial gesture amounts to a two-minute abstract for many lines of thought in mediarchaeology. Archival footage of an edited rather than fixed-frame *actualité* shows the carnivalesque spectacle of a woman knife-thrower and her "assistant," a young girl at the receiving end of the flung blades. It is a document suturing us in by a uniquely unnerving reciprocal displacement between a shot of the thrown knife, then of the near-missed girl, then of the thrower again, then of the blade's penetration alongside the body— back and forth repeatedly—but sped up by Lauschmann's digital editing in a pace ultimately so accelerated that the two faces and torsos blur into a composite female image as if some jumpy (nervous? hysterical?) attempt at a stable portrait.

Writes one critic with a common and here forgivable idiomatic solecism, deviating from the formulaic "one and the same," the female faces are rendered "on either side of a computer-generated image of a disc" so as to become "as it spins" no less than "one *in the same* image" (my emphasis on the vernacular slip)—a phrasing that evokes something of the reciprocal incursion, rather than true fusion, induced by editing in this case.[19] The use of the filmic footage to begin with, let alone the further elisions in the shot/countershot tempo of filmic editing, is what marks this particular

Bird in a Cage as so radically different from its namesake pre-Victorian toy in the typical recto/verso—or rectoverse—picturing. In the process, no experiment, no archival "research"-in-action, could approximate more suggestively—as prefigured by that truly "philosophical toy"—Epstein's sense of cinema as a testament, beyond its own illusory projections, to ocular discontinuity at large.

For all this, the classic prototype of the thaumatrope—bird-and-cage turned to bird-in-cage (bird 'n' cage to bird 'n cage; one and the same to "one in the same")—remains a curiously antithetical precursor to cinema, at least in its particular scenario of entrapment. In this deceptive exchange of figure/g(o)round, what the bird on one side of a disk, the empty cage on the other, spin into view—with no need to mask what amounts to its only paper-thin frameline—is not a motion picture, but rather an immobility effect. Such is this one example's peculiar dialectic of arrest rather than impetus. But when the allusive name *Bird in a Cage* is retained by Lauschmann for his videography of a derivative but pictorially unrelated sideshow event, it may also remind us that the sometimes static image on the cinema screen, even if only ten seconds worth of stillness, results from 240 alternations en route. And of further note for the history of vision and the archaeology of motion capture, Lauschmann recovers here, by electronic simulation, an early case of the image per se apart from any single picture: an image retinal not material, *realized* rather than "real."[20] Virtual. From this point forward in the techne of vision, all that would be necessary for cinema's fuller anticipation by machinic imaging—and even before photography arrived to contribute to the thaumatropic game—was somehow to displace (or "superimpose") more than one image in a row—as in the multiple spinning images and slotted views of the phenakistoscope. All one needs do, that is, is to make the cage repeat itself while alternating "within it" different rather than more-of-the-same bird forms—in various positions of inferred motion—and the suddenly shifted angles of wing span would read as an actual flapping. Cinema born on the wing.

From this perspective, in further contemplating the media history thrown into reverse gear by the *concept* behind Lauschmann's *percept*, other technological and metahistorical inferences begin to unfold and jostle each other. What is the pertinent relation of the digital similitude of a spinning disk that we're watching (variant of the simplest desktop picture tools in the computer era) to its intertext in the actual thaumatrope? And what does this rapid alternation of the digitally generated rather than hand-fabricated toying with picture planes—this reversible pictureplaning—have to remind us about digitization all told? For one thing, the process once undergone by motion in the ordinary toyshop predecessor of cinema's superimposed rather than moving image—in order, in the former case, to laminate two views into pictorial stasis—finds itself, in a roundabout way, repeated in the constitutive operation of the digital image all told. For computerization generates an image, not a picture. We know—without actually recognizing it optically—how everything depends, not on a spooling multitude of discrete photograms, but rather on the many pixels necessary not only to animate an image but even to hold a "single" picture in place. Such is the composite figment reconstructed as it is (say, from microsecond to microsecond) by computerized signal traces. Here is where Lauschmann's video work on prefilmic illusionism in regard to the pending regime of cinema—with found footage returned by editing to its predecessor in an exchange of single photo cells rather than sustained countershots, and thereby recalling optical illusions available to alternating pictograms in its hand-spun precursor—is at the same time *recalled to its future* in the computer lab. The *optical allusion* effected by his piece is thus reciprocal—and in the process transhistorical, again, as well as unremittingly transmedial.

A similar technohistorical as well as transmedial loop—we momentarily step aside from Lauschmann to note—underlies the rotational circularity announced by the wordplay of its title in Rodney Graham's 2001 installation work, *Phonokinetoscope*, as derived from Edison's kinetophonograph via precisely the Victorian phenakistoscope recalled above: that optical toy on a revolving platform whose animation effect can begin and stop anywhere at will. In the original device, with which Muybridge among others experimented, optical slits between serial animations on a circular disk allow the staggered pictures to be viewed in a mirror rotation, almost as if the eye-line slots were the exact optical inverse of the black bars between photograms in the successor medium of cinema—as anticipated as well, in Lauschmann's piece, by the vanishing edge of transition (what Dworkin again, after Duchamp, would call the *inframince* switch) between alternating spun planes of the two-sided image. Graham notches up the arbitrary and serial nature of this motion effect in a work not of silent mirage but of actual "sound cinema." For by grafting the phono- to the visual pheno-menon in the Edisonian mode, Graham's transmedial loop wires a 16mm film of him cycling through Berlin's Tiergarten on LSD to another wheeled mechanism, an equally dated phonographic turntable. He then turns the tables on the optical rapport of normative transmedial display in this regard by having viewers start the visual loop whenever (and wherever) the needle is placed by them on the vinyl disc of a therefore always-out-of-sync sound/image conflation.[21]

With the media-historical touchstones of the thaumatrope and the phenakistoscope in our sights, the conceptual logic of such work in motion capture's time-based projection asks comparison with the more extreme reduction of another optical toy—the spun drum of the slotted zoetrope (the "life-turner")—when parsed out as single serial images, with these in turn reduced from photographs (or, before that medium, drawings) ranged on the inside of the drum to the now detached cameraless images of preprint optical "photograms" (the other and original sense of that eventual cinematic term). This happens in a 2013 work by Liz Deschenes displayed the next year in the timely "What Is a Photograph?" show at the International Center for Photography: an exhibit deliberately poised to address the overshadowing of the print picture by the billions of electronic images now in electronic circulation.

In light of this backlit deluge, and thus assuming its place in a 2.0 conceptualist aesthetic, Deschenes' innovation mounts a double outmoding. Instead of the once-slotted views of bodily stances turned to gestures and movements by the rotated cylinder of the precinematic mechanism, her polyptich, titled *Zoetrope #1–#13*, all but entirely flattens out the mechanism's principle of intermittence by lining up narrow cameraless photograms of about four feet in height displayed on slightly curved backings along a wide gallery wall, with each shadowy image just minimally different from its neighbor in the spatial disposition of its traced abstract shape. What remains as a kinetic ocular potential, therefore, is only a latent perceptual transition spurred by the viewer in moving past the sequence. Anomalous in the chapter on motion capture—because performing the immediate breakdown (both senses) of its kinetic syntax—what is here derived from the spun flickers of pictureplaning in a premotor apparatus are the curved picture planes of wall art in a premechanical "photogrammar." In this manifestly transmedial installation, not only does the concept at work dismantle the named Victorian mechanism but it deconstructs the destiny of two related media at the same time, photography and cinema. The former is returned to origins in chemically affixed light traces before the invention of the photo negative and the daguerreotype, and the latter is denied the differential play of those "photograms" (in the newer sense) that spool, rather than spin, past on the projected strip of that cinematic technology descended from the zoetrope. The disembodied streaming of images yet again, in certain gestures of mediarchaeological thinking, throws us back—in complex patterns of displacement—on the predigital materiality of the picture plane.

[digit::timed]

Returning to calibrated temporal media, one notes that a comparable ironic "nostalgia" to what we saw in Lauschmann's protofilmic *Thaumatrop*, as well as in Graham's technological interplays of medial valediction, also permeates Lauschmann's *Digital Clock (Growing Zeros)* from 2010. This is a work that stages as its eccentric—and temporally decentered—sculptural performance piece the additive and subtractive graphics of the digital on/ off rather than tick/tock. At rapid play in this video are the subnumeric composite shapes (those tiny elongated trapezoidal increments) that come and go and meet and separate in the formation of the digital clock face (in LCD materialization), where even the zero of the decimal system has to be "grown" from a blank background, a "figure" multiple, geometric, in flux. But in this case shuffled by hand. Six variable pieces for the 0, five for the three-pronged 3, and so forth, all seven for the vertically overlapping squares of the 8. The disengaged elongated modules of each nonintegral graphic integer are represented by dark brown pieces nearly invisible against the slotted black background that awaits them—as well as against (when "engaged") their bright-red (as if backlit) hyperlegible counterparts. All this takes place, though in far from familiar fashion, across the adjacent three panels requisite for digital enumeration: dark and light, on and off and on again, but here with the artist's hands and forearms coming in and out of separate decimal sectors. Seconds, minutes, hours, are "clocked in"—often with the rapid-fire precision, and then some, of a card shark finessing a deal. No other hand, hour or minute, and no circular clock face for it to sweep: just the manically hands-on paradigital engineering of the mutating display in this frenetic twist on the piecing-out of time. Our long acclimation to strictly numeric rather than rotary time-keeping, by now so fully naturalized as to bear no nostalgia for the epoch of sun dials, is not facilitated but estranged here by an evoked archetypal cliché like "the hands of time." Seldom is the concept of reverse skeuomorphism, with no paratext needed this time to call it out, more unmistakably called up. Nor could a motion-capture aesthetic be imagined any more directly, if parodically, to return us from a Deleuzian placeless duration in the time-image to the almost slapstick action-image (the body in motion) that temporal measurement ordinarily abstracts.

With this time-based performance of time itself in action, there is no vestigial analog process in some inching forward of the analyzed moment, but simply the toggling on or off in mathematized sequence of the timepiece as kinetic puzzle piece. Manually rather than digitally, in Lauschmann's clock-quirk mock-up, the body is returned to labor time, slowly in the hours column, with manageable dexterity in the minutes, and with time-lapse rapidity in the third (rightmost) panel of this electronic triptych. It is there that the enumerated seconds, especially at the far right of their per-second transformation from 1 to 10, often require several internal moves per instant of the oblong half-strokes of red display—or their drowning out by brown counterparts. All this is dizzily reconfigured at an expressly superhuman speed, so that only a latent pun on hyperkinetic "prestidigitation" is sensed to control the assemblage and breakdown of these thin rectangular girders of enumeration: these drastically literalized and synecdochic *time pieces*. Call it a performance sculpture on the assembly line of time itself, with machine-made increments dispensed in an unmachinated piecing together that then elides the real time of its labor with special effects of tempo to emerge again, in gallery projection, within a typical cycle of diurnal recurrence. Or see it this way: between the competing media of simulated digital array and simulated real-time assemblage, the apparition of a twenty-four-hour live-time projection is materialized as a transmedial compromise—or, more precisely again, dialectic—between filmed but doctored pantomime and digital abstraction.

In this sense, *Digital Clock* (*Growing Zeros*) isolates even the negative placeholders (in disappearing dark brown) and renders them cumulative, along with the numeric aggregates in red, as the video loop whips by. In broader mediarchaeological terms, it is a kind of stop-action animation without the usually disguised hiatus requiring the puppeteer's hand. At several levels, then, Lauschmann's video unsettles the very idea of continuity, all under the codified span of uninterrupted duration. By contrast, the archival footage recycled by the thaumatropism, as it were, of *Bird in a Cage, No. 1* undoes an illusory photomechanical continuity, between both frames on the found strip and camera positions, and does this undoing at the level of substrate and editing both. The result is to implode the thrust-counterthrust suture of the knife-throwing docudrama and reduce subject and object to the same flickering figuration that each in fact separately is. In the complementary relation between these two time-based works of metatemporality by the same artist, the one, *Digital Clock*, parses the "image" of temporal transition (as mutation) into the synchronized real time (in tampered version) of its instrumental indicators on a pantomimed digital display; the other parses the filmic frame line into its throwback modularity in the optical toy. In sum, each transmediates the new, through the old, into its own kind of temporal (as well as historical) "display"—and displacement.

[time::pieced]

Whereas Sietsema's *Hour*, replete with its still-life array of various antique watch faces and fobs, reels past in its quarter hour of footage so that the immanent medium of celluloid surrenders its capacities as pictorial record to a generalized transmedial inscription, Lauschmann's works divide up this terrain of duration in equally disorienting ways. In *Digital Clock (Growing Zeroes)*, electronic calibration has reverted to the punning "hands" it has deliberately outmoded. Two mechanisms, therefore, in analytic suspension: one movie (Sietsema's) not doing the picturing it only spells out, one visualization (Lauschmann's) not telling its engineered time except by laborious enactment. And in Lauschmann's complementary reversion, capturing the urge to image rather than its squandered opportunity (as in Sietsema), the digital loops of his thaumatrope redux simulate the origins of cinema from a transmedial appropriation of its own unsophisticated found footage, even while further backdating the narrative vestige to its own optical foundation.

It's easier than ever, with this last conceptualist "trope," to see why those optical gadgets of the early Victorians were often called philosophical toys. In their rotation lay their very meditation on the physics, and hallucinatory metaphysics, of the image. In the hands of a transmedial artist like Lauschmann—or say, rather, in the digital approximation of the plaything's onetime bodily manipulation—his variant becomes no less than a Conceptual toy. For Lauschmann's transmedial return of the cinematic spool to the narrowed binary of the single disk reverses the gradualism of the filmic (serial) photogram and reduces it to a primary dualism across an almost emblematic cut on the knife slice: the thrown blade as the reverse vector of a severed and sutured continuity that gives us effect to cause in a shot/countershot pattern of fling and incision. The reflexivity is indeed all but rending. Across the risked stabbing or laceration of the young female operative, we sense the foregrounded scissoring of the strip in its rudimentary montage. And across this second-phase narrative innovation in the fixed-frame screen scenario, cinema reverts from the cut-on-action to the prehistory of all such disjunction in the recto/verso spin.

When in this way the retroping of the thaumatrope undoes its otherwise evoked historical eventuation in film—as a continuous (though materially intermittent) optic—and severs it into a binary toggle of here and gone, on and off, she and her, s/h/e/r in sheared collision, it is thus just t/here that a passing claim of media theorist Friedrich Kittler—typically tendentious and suggestive—comes to mind. As always under the telos of the numeric and computational in his thinking, even the predigital cinematic strip is fundamentally understood by him to be binary rather than analog in determination. He finds digitization not just the eclipsing destiny but the underlying model of a discourse network of representational practice that comes to one plateau of fruition in moving-image cinema, but that is traceable all the way back to the print array of exchangeable blanks and letters in Gutenberg-era reproduction and in the graphic grids of optic activation in the roughly simultaneous rise of perspective painting in the Renaissance. On this understanding, Kittler stresses in the case of cinema not the serial indexicality but rather the on/off alternation of the strip across its speeding frame lines. For this involves the inbuilt bars, so to speak, to its own cellular advance: the very blackout between photogrammic flashes—glimpses limping instantaneously in and out of view—across the occluding ridge (turned subliminal bridge) between exposures.[22] As Rondepierre exposes in his attempt to arrest just this process in photogrammic excisions, projection has no "support" any more stable than the algorithmic—and algorhythmic—flux of mere binary switchpoints in a subsequent medium, with cinema's filmic substrate submitted to rapid visual conflation across its own structuring syncopes. Such for Kittler is the inherent structural intermittence, the binarist dichotomy, that would situate film's transitional place between the first "wonder-turners," like the thaumatrope, and the now-ubiquitous permutation of the binary on/off behind every offered screen image—let alone behind, and beneath, the vaster range of computational devices for which the digital picture, even in visual art, is often just a stand-in: flashpoint for the totally mediatized environment of the contemporary technosphere.

And so it would seem for Lauschmann, too—whose experiments might be thought similarly to rewrite media history in light of the digital. In the case of *Thaumatrop*, what its recycled digital edit may ultimately evoke, from the very bowels of computer manipulation, begins only by pressing cinema back from its constitutive differentials—both of separate bodies and serialized gesture—to a false synthesis in default of steady focus: a fluttering superimposition of the two female faces too opaque for the gestalt of coherence. What results is the pulsional misfit of two separate pictures on the verge of being melted into each other and remolded as one virtual image. In effect, Lauschmann's intervention—with digital sampling rather than scissors—has reverted to the prehistory of photogrammic animation to produce, avant la lettre, nothing less than a speeding digital morph: a virtuality in this case not just blatantly transformative but dramatically—or let's say openly—transmedial. As such, and in terms all its own, it answers to Starling's work in "metamorphology."

Here, then, is one fate of the picture plane under conceptualist pressure—and in archaeological recess. The subtracted equestrian portrait in Sietsema's *Hour*—whose verbal analysis alone comes under the lens, never whose painted surface—represents another aspect of this fate (in the form of a missing interface). So it is that the anomalous fixed image that conceptual filmmaking or videography either locks down on by elision or animates by foregrounded alteration serves to compress a more encompassing agenda of optic estrangement. Examples could scarcely be more different in making this same point. When the serial picture-planarity that *is* cinema is found giving way from within—trans-medium—to image surfaces preceding cinema (the equestrian painting, the complementary inversions of the photographic thaumatrope, the slitlike panels of the zoetrope, and so on), conceptual mediation plies its layered, multi-ply trade so as to precipitate its deliberate(d) triple-take: that recurrent dialectical counterpull—and attempted resolution—between operative terms not set in place but kept in elusive play. Then, too, as we'll see in the next chapter of this moving-image Scene, there are many other ways as well of subtracting image from projection or reducing it to pure traced draughts of light.

In approaching such evanescent imaging, work as theoretically charged as Lauschmann's, and especially as abstract and cerebral in its theoretical resonance as Sietsema's and Starling's, serves to reopen certain key texts of art theory for us. By the title and subtitle, respectively, of important studies by Rosalind Krauss and later, in her mentioned debt, Craig Dworkin, we are directed, so we've noted, both to the state of "no medium" in certain hyperminimalist gestures and to the broader category of the "post-medium condition," with Krauss admitting at the start (in a spirit quite the reverse of my own agenda) that she would have preferred at first just scoring through the term "medium" altogether so as to eliminate its ideological and discursive overtones from her investigation. Nonetheless, and leading up to the work convened in the present study as 2.0, the earlier line of Conceptual art she isolates—in its rejection of medium specificity as an aesthetic standard—locates exactly the "condition" of aesthetic experiments that have succeeded in the wake of that dominant modernist ideology. Experiments not "post," I would argue, but contrapuntal. These are works, often polemically so, of no one or predetermined medium in particular, sometimes (Dworkin's point) in "no medium" (or no recognized one) at all. Yet the long line of such production includes practices transpiring across—and sometimes quite "specifically" at that—the staged space between adjacent or discrepant media. These last ventures, of course, center our attention in this study—even from their frequent sense of an empty center of medial gravity.

This transmedial awareness, as we know, has to do not with what one can *say about* an art work in estimation, let alone celebration, of its eschewed purity, its overt hybridity. What this frame of response highlights, instead, is what one can *see about* the work to begin with (or sometimes not, in its occulted production). The first response is one of *discernment* in the nonevaluative sense: a determined sifting through of perception, often coached by supplementary discourse. Usually, in such works, two separately detectable media conflate across an uncertain substrate or support so as to debate each other's priority or collaborate over a shared platform or process. And sometimes it's more than two, as in the forthcoming "light sculpture" (or "solid light films") of Anthony McCall, even though that plastic designation may seem to indicate a mere double (and oxymoronic) modality. But such a categorization hasn't taken into account, as chapter 5 will soon do, the work's intentional aspect as, at one and the same time, experimental cinema, abstract sculpture, and drawing ("animation").

In our familiar typographic buckling, to speak of *[light::sculpture]* or *[light::drawing]* would be to understand light as a medium (the medium, say, of sight itself). But with McCall's work in the offing, the already threefold basis of "film" as medium of rechanneled light (machinic, plastic, imagistic) is directly instructive: film understood in its hyphenated photo-chemical and then photo-mechanical projection as a throwing of preinscribed brightness and shadow. Where medial consensus is hard to come by. Are single transparent photograms in a differential strip the medium of David Lean's *Lawrence of Arabia*? Or just its material support? And then only, perhaps, when threaded through the machine? Is 70mm projection (in the extended sense of "the apparatus") that epic's real medium (filtered light this time)? Or, as Stanley Cavell would say in a phenomenological vein, is the medium of this and any film to be understood as a succession of automatic world pictures as received by the eye?

To further mince distinctions, does the medium change when one moves from roadshow to general release, from 70mm to 35mm? Or to digital transfer? And does such a "cinematic artifact" as the photochemical

Lawrence lay claim to the same medium to begin with, even in first-release theatrical exhibition, as the mostly digitally generated 3-D *Avatar* (James Cameron, 2009) four decades later? And what is the medium of *Interstellar* (Christopher Nolan, 2014) when seen in multiplex digital projection versus the "image-maximization" of IMAX, and the difference then again between digital IMAX and the vestigial (though still cinephiliac) 70mm incarnation available only in selected theaters? Whether regarded as issues of different media (filmic versus digital cinema), or as the difference between a medium (moving pictures) and its material conveyance, these queries may seem dismissible in the grips of screen experience, but they are far from trivial. Translated to more unexpected installation pieces, as for instance the minimalist cinema of McCall's gallery projections, they certainly aren't questions decided in advance by a transmedial work; they are distinctions, or say "conditions," worked at by it.

[cinemato::graphics]

A grandstand anomaly helps secure the rule of "impurity" in this regard. As it happens, a "post-medium" version (one might say) of the film *Lawrence of Arabia*, beyond any pertinent deliberations about its celluloid essence (and its plastic or digital transfer), is rendered with deadpan bravura by the British Conceptual and "text" artist Fiona Banner. For her nonpictorial version of David Lean's screen narrative, the broad upright rectangle is the only retained condition of display. This occurs in a transliteration, let us say, of the film's shot plan and dialogue into a printed narrative scroll of roughly the same dimensions, or at least ratio, as a widescreen optical performance of the film, letting us see *The Desert* (her 1994 title) of its setting—"a great moment," as she puts it laconically, "in the history of wideness"—only by a reading of its widespread vistas in the broad horizonless granulations of typescript, not sand.[23]

"No medium" there at all, perhaps, in regard to the epic film as film—except of course by dint of the "post-medial condition" of aesthetic production in conceptual text art (language the "overstretched" means of evocation), emerging in this case as a transmedial irony about verbal rather than visual discourse and their divergent material supports. For this is a divergence articulated here from within the common denominator of a scale-adjusted two-dimensional rectangular format, yet with the means transformed from automatic index to lexical presentation, from filming to cinemato-graphism—and the latter, at that, as little more than the index of an artist's labor in the veritable remake, word by impressed word, of a landmark (and now simply re-marked) film experience.

Post- or non-, aftermath or cancellation, call it what you will: what's missing in Banner's *Lawrence* seems punned on by title in the deserted imagery of this double *Desert*. One brunt of this transmedial irony, in the mode of Conceptualism 2.0—with the artist's tongue-in-cheek delectation of "wideneness" per se—must be meant to score against the fetish of flatness in earlier abstract modernism. Beyond this, however, the room-wide scroll by the artist named Banner (nomen est omen?) is so much something held *between* media that the optical scale of the screen-like format makes sheer reading almost impossible; one loses one's way in the tightly spaced vertical enjambment from line to madly elongated line. The typographic discourse is all but pulverized in its continuity like the shifting drifts and ripples of desert surface. Certainly at a glance, and even to the committed eye, the work reduces after all to a transmedial vista rather than a functional inscription: an exacerbated ekphrasis turning text itself into an ordeal of passage.

To "translate" film exhibition to gallery "exhibit" (Balsom again) is one thing. To textualize the world's once-largest film format on the topic of one of the world's largest geographic spaces by evoking the former's scale and image ratio for similar gallery display—though not its spec(tac)ular duration—is quite another. The time of epic viewing, condensed into a single oversized frame, is then precipitated out again in the frustrated duration of serial reading, with the immaculate flicker fusion of the frame line replaced by the frustrating disjunctures of hypertrophic lineation. The year 1995 was scarcely too soon to involve this image in a mode of mourning for the whole medium of film. This aside, Banner's quasi-canvas gallery expanse as a textualized cinematic display serves not just to equivocate, but to accentuate, the crucial plat-formatic basis (and difference) of the narrative manifestations in play. If her outsize presentation were made and mounted today—especially if executed as a moving LED display rather than a textual imprint, or all the more so if taking shape as a crammed rectangle of algorithmic code, like an reverse-engineered DVD—it would be seen/read as a parodic send-up of "convergence culture," where all media manifestations are digitally encrypted and binarist at base. Short of this, when media could still make their separate claims on the ironist's eye, no second-wave Conceptual art could be more medium-specifying (though not singular, precisely not) in the cross-bred estrangements of its letteral representation than Banner's evacuation of image and sound together from a widescreen audiovisual event while still retaining its graphic format—as if in the fossil form of its own petrified theatricality.

However many such platform crossings seem in play in other (less text-driven) transmedial works, the challenge, as we've found, isn't to sort and categorize. Rather, it is to recognize each medial source from within the new resources of the work's combinatory (even when subtractive) effect. And then to contextualize it, where invited, within the latent technoparameters of Conceptualism 2.0. Long after the commercial viability of its evoked medium, Banner's *Desert* conjures in wry homage, as well as with a visually unslaked thirst, not just the wideness but the high-definition of 70mm cinema. It does so in stretching out at galling and nearly illegible syntactic width what amounts to the belated, reductive, strictly scriptive story-boarding of the film's own vertical spooling past the aperture. To sense digital projection, rather than the plastic materiality of film, looming beyond the far horizon of this conceptual "vista" would only compound the sense of a toppled regime of mediation. Such is also latently the case, as follows, with works of electronically sourced "cinema" whose minimalist *light shows*, so far from spectacle as to invoke pure specularity, seem configured to reduce pictureplaning—all picture planarity—to nothing but a surface for the *showing forth of light's own beamed effect*: its effect not in pictorial image but in sheer visibility.

CHAPTER FIVE: *Lightshown*

IN OUR LOOKING BACK ON CERTAIN WORKS INVESTIGATED IN THE LAST CHAPTER, AS PRODDED by their own medial interrogations, an extra question takes shape. Beyond the missing central picture, for instance, in Sietsema's cryptic moving picture (*At the Hour of Tea*), if there is such a further thing as cinema without image altogether in Banner, what about cinema as a writing in light without rendered event (even in words), cinema as sheer drawing without picture? That is Anthony McCall's question—and his answer at once—in his "solid light films." When also understood as "sculpture," they must further be rethought, transmedium, as the shaping not just of immaterial light but, more powerfully yet, as the sculpting of a gallery's own ambient space with a chiseling keenness of illumination: a veritable cutting edge in the concept of projection itself. Indeed, a critic skeptical, in general, about such bleeds between installation work and its institutional and architectural environs, yet who singles out McCall's ventures for their genuine social dimension, is notably instructive about such commingled parameters in other overlapping spheres of image-making. Hal Foster's polemical survey of these issues should therefore help orient us as we come upon—reversing Banner's conceptualist subtractions—the actual optic projection (but entirely absent narrative) of McCall's "films." These are visual systems etched (that is, both drawn and sculpted) across the space not of image but of attention itself—as is the case, to be taken up before them, with the more structurally enfolded (gallery-built) lightworks of James Turrell, each artist mobilizing related archetypes (as well as architectonics) of visibility in action.

[light::works]

Art as architecture; art inside architecture; architecture as art; architecture as image; structure turned virtual: a sliding and suspect scale, according (in his own different terms) to Foster's pointedly critical study.[1] Add: light as medium; light as object. Or otherwise: architectural lighting versus light sculpture. Apart from the signature minimalism of Dan Flavin, with his direct lifting of industrial fixtures for abstract patterning and reflection as well as for chromatic variation, this chapter will be putting into contrast two other light artists—working by projection or reflection, rather than sheer exposed fluorescence—who distort or reconfigure display space in ways that bear comparison within, or against, what Foster sees as a dominant aesthetic of the virtual in the new "international style" of "light architecture," with its late-capitalist premium on functional transparency (a metaphoric smokescreen in itself) and deceptively weightless facades. This is the global tendency toward a rejection of structural candor in favor of a sheathing translucency and blur: offering luminous aura rather than revealed function, spectacle rather than engineering. Such is the frayed border between form and image that Foster has diagnosed at length in *The Art-Architecture Complex* (2013)—as built upon his definition of "mediums" we began by considering—and where the third noun of his title suggests not just a spatial manifold but a cultural syndrome.

James Turrell's work is only briefly discussed by Foster, whereas Anthony McCall's is given a chapter of its own without cross-reference to the other light artist. Tacit comparisons do surface, however, from what Foster later has to say about Turrell, who also began, like McCall, in the mode of quasi-cinematic museum projection. One of Turrell's best-known early works involves the beaming of a simple square of light into a gallery corner so that, as one confronts it from different angles, it produces the illusion of a Necker Cube hugging the angled walls in thrust and regress at once (or by turns). Most of Turrell's later work is not illusionist in this same arresting way. Rather, it bemuses rather than wholly fools the eye, offering a local puzzle more than a ruse. Its effects remain sensuous first of all, sensory rather than cognitive. This is confirmed by his own insistence in refusing to identify these works as "literalist" (minimalist) and self-contained.[2]

But a word more, first, about this chapter on "lightshown" aesthetic phenomena—and, in effect, their transmedial manifestations—within the triptych of considerations developing in Scene Two. Situated between the picture-plane manipulations just considered and the further concerns with filmic (and even digital) segmentation ("Filmedivision") on the third front of our inquiry, the current discussion might seem delayed or out of place in its retreat, even within a time-based aesthetic, from the complications of "motion capture" to the unflinchingly distilled and "reductive" question of projection per se, cinema degree zero. Might seem so, if it were not soon to become clear that the effects summoned here are bent precisely on deepening our foundational sense of visibility in time-based projection—and can thus serve to anchor more firmly what we've just seen in a fuller preparation for what's coming, not least with regard to the art-historical trajectory of experimental cinema on which the previous pictureplanings have so knowingly built. In short: what is foundational need not come first, but can be placed in explication more as pivotal than as preliminary.

Certainly this is the case when even light in its own right can be construed transmedially, as in a sense not only for McCall but for some notable works of Turrell as well. About the latter's installations in general, in the artist's words still: "There is no 'object' because perception itself is the object" (209)—a usage such as one would deploy in saying "the object of my art is perception." These works are seen to be entirely about the condition of their own viewing, but only by way of an oblique duping of the eye, a subtle ambivalence concerning surface itself—or as Foster puts it, a process of turning phenomenology faux. And yet there is a material substrate in this mysterious "objectification" of light that is part of the lure, the tease, the eventual release to pure viewing in Turrell's work—or, in other words, an enigmatic sense of procedure that keeps the operations of the medium both from view and in mind. To begin with, what can only be called a sculpting of the gallery wall is often involved: a carved recess necessary in order to trigger the luminescent bas relief of shaped—and sometimes moving (if only flickering) light. This is never more obvious, complicated, or indirect than in Turrell's "Magnetron" series, nor perhaps ever more open to Foster's potential critique, since the play of "virtuality" borders almost on trompe l'oeil. Despite the light sculptor's avowed purposes, there lurks a certain complicity between Turrell's introspective agenda and the luminescent contemporary façades of the new International Style from Times Square to Potsdamer Platz—even when his lightworks are meant instead as prompts to contemplation rather than as sheer exhibition pieces, perceptually revelatory rather than just showy.

It is in this respect, then, that the "Magnetron" works offer a particularly tricky instance of the optical distortions and connivances of Turrell's recurrent effects. In the 2013 retrospective at LACMA running concurrently with a highly touted Guggenheim show, one work especially seems to assert an implicit hybridizing equation: minimalist sculptural effect (wall cut) + cathode video = electronic light sculpture. In sensory effect: a transmedial mirage. It happens this way, as one has to discover (yet again) by reading about it, unpacking its ocular conundrum by the patient discursive revelation of its explicated procedure in catalog copy. A TV monitor is hidden "off frame" behind a gallery wall that has been "defaced" by a cutout, to be approached at the end of a narrow corridor where two flanking incandescent spots throw their beams needlessly against the side walls—as if merely to distinguish that kind of routine gallery lighting from the pulsing glow beyond and between them. This glimmering lozenge of a hole—which, until stared at up close, looks like a beaming surface of transmission—resembles at first nothing so much as an embedded monitor in standard museum installation, a TV set fixed from behind to the wall's surface. A distant contrast comes to mind. Whereas the vertical rivulets of a slit-scan chromatic tracing in Arcanagel's *Colors* recall, for Dworkin, the "no medium" of mere "test patterns" from predigital TV, in Turrell's recessed cathode glow the less-defined image appears more like the aimless ocular static of a channel lost to content from beyond the broadcast band, where retinal noise can never recoup itself as signal.[3] Yet, wrong so far. This is not a TV image at all, but merely the image of a TV, derived at one remove, in reflection, from an invisible set located somewhere below the opening in the wall—with simulated effect (via framed shimmer) thus being taken for its own hidden cause.

Described to this point, in other words, is only the first feint in a developing irony of ambience, since the apparent video interface must eventually come to be seen (one guesses at this, on gradual approach, almost before one recognizes it for sure) as just a sawed-out aperture shaped like the rounded-off rectangle of a once-standard TV screen. Depth reads, at first, as plane, 3-D as 2-D manifestation. Certainly the initially supposed "medium" is no medium at all, just the hollowed frame for another not unlike it in the mere play of light. For the actual TV, sequestered (on the floor?) beyond our sight, its images never seen directly, instead throws the variant abstract hues of its silent playback on a second white wall behind the cut-out. It is as if the cathode-ray image has returned across the evolution of moving-image technology from electronic broadcast to cinematic projection, but its beam radiating now by indirection—by sheer reflection rather than direct transmit—only with the indistinct glimmer of oscillating color tones. Providing a useless flicker, as if dialed up by accident from the optic limbo beyond commercial TV's active station roster, it appears as a default to pure medium without message. And in this telescoping of optic planes, the carved aperture becomes yet another inverted (and here imploded) skeuomorph: the iconic shape of the TV screen as access-granting emblem to none other than its own now-disembodied video "image" (hence simulacrum) in afterglow.

With these "Magnetron" works, burying their pertinent source within a derivative pulsating glow, we have here the spectacle of spectation itself, not just "perception." The fact that these light sculptures actually sculpt the gallery wall, rather than stand free from their architectonic support, might well in itself link them indirectly to the questionable end of the spectrum in Foster's critique of the art-architecture complex. Certainly their commercial installation, across town and well before this LA museum show (their commission for the once uber-chic Mondrian Hotel in West Hollywood, one in front of the elevator on every floor, each secreting a different TV network's typical color palette) puts them squarely in the precincts of illusionist architectural décor, of spatial "atmosphere" and its virtualities, of design rather than art—and this in a hotel whose red carpet thrown out to guests is only the overhead digital projection of a Persian rug on the lobby's uncovered floor.

How long can Anthony McCall's mesmerizing overhead projections hold out against co-optation by the branded cachet of upscale lobby décor? It's the kind of question Foster might well have floated. But he is concerned instead with the very different effect McCall's work has in its present museum form, and on this score the comparison with Turrell remains latent in his commentary but no less definitive. Faux phenomenology in Turrell, a mystification of perception given over to the time of immersion, is contrasted with the temporal openness of McCall's work, which discloses its own workings over time (if only, again, with the help of paratextual information). One might well want to say, and in precisely Foster's terms, that where Turrell equivocates the wall, the spatial plane, turning the white cube into one large light fixture, McCall transfigures the equally canonical black box (even when at industrial train-station scale) into a theater for weightless tents of light. Neither are trompe l'oeil artists exactly. Their works (even Turrell's at his most elusive, as in his redoubled televisuality) are not primarily staged to fool the eye with an alternative version (and vision) of a thing not there. They merely (because never simply) make the thing that is there, the vertical pool or rotary shaft of light respectively, hard to reckon—mostly at first glance in McCall's case, though, while more resolutely in Turrell's. Discourse, including criticism like Foster's, certainly helps in any such reckoning, both in acquainting oneself with the process and in taking stock of what it implies for a contemporary art space. With work like this, in short, aesthetic configurations of the ocular body begin with simply figuring out what it is your corporeal eyes have encountered.

Beyond his exemplarity for Foster, then, there is McCall's more particular fit with the moving-image phase of the present study. His is a case of Conceptualism 2.0 not because of the turn to digital projection after his much earlier 16mm work, but rather because, in the process of this transition, his paracinema—as metacinema—has recovered (as we are to see) something in the earlier filmic arsenal of screen editing (in particular, a prewar fondess for the "wipe")—and thus has deepened the transmedial tunnel vision implicit in his rotating cones or optic funnels. Whereas Turrell rejects the term "conceptualism" as well as "minimalism" to describe what he insists is the pure perceptualism of his glowworks, the difference in the *[light::shows]*, as it were, of the two artists might be articulated as that between light shown off for its own engulfing aura and light that shows forth the body's own contribution, in the person of the moving viewer, to its effects. Perceptualism, rendered more somatic than strictly ocular, and thus turned minimally interactive, in turn activates its own concept of participant spectatorship. We've yet to see how exactly this comes about—as one moves about under such digitally calibrated showerheads of light—but this very encounter takes us directly to the concept behind the percept.

It leads us directly, that is, to a further distinction that sets these installation displays, Turrell's as well as McCall's, into relief along the lines of their own comparable derivation from cathode aura and cinematic beam. For what is obliquely transmedial about the works of Turrell in one case and of McCall in general principle (respectively tele-visual and cine-matic) comes through by contrast with light-art installations that abstract their own medium of vision without cross-reference to any material substrate or even technological process. In 2014, for instance, at the David Zwirner Gallery in New York, light artist Doug Wheeler, long associated with the LA "Light and Space" movement, installs the deliberate conflation of those two programmatic *a prioris* in a semispherical zone of gleaming indeterminacy, its horizon ambiguously discerned just beyond the edge of the exhibition's slightly curved floor. This whole space of immersive spectation effects a spooky englobement by lambency per se, identified as "*LC 71 NY DZ 13 DW* (2013), reinforced fiberglass, flat white titanium dioxide latex, LED light, and DMX control, 771 × 811 3/8 × 219 in (1958.3 × 2060.9 × 556.3 cm.)." One enters here a ballroom-scaled zone of enwombing glow whose despatialized medium of light effaces all sure sense of form or border. In this respect, Wheeler's architectonic but diffusive tour de force is related, almost by way of inversion, to a black box–style installation by another artist of embedded luminescence: the centrally unlit, curve-floored, light-rimmed environments constructed under the title *Contact* by Olafur Eliasson for his inaugural exhibition at the Louis Vuitton Center in Paris later that same year. It is by contrast with this space-defining apparition of light in Eliasson's case—and by way of effecting a more intimate "contact" yet with the installation viewer—that the space-penetrating compass-sweeps of McCall's projections do their "inscriptive" rather than merely delimiting work.

[drawing::space]

Once we recognize roughly what is being done to darkness by McCall's rotary motions, questions have only begun. What affect arises in these environments when, in descent from an embedded overhead source, a searing blade of light makes visible, borrowing Faulkner's famous baroque epithet, the "mote-palpitant" space of a thick-aired gallery misted by benign dust particles?[4] Each viewer comes fresh to this self-spectacle: this spectacle of illumination itself—and then of the selves, merely as bodies, that intersect it, the viewer's own in good time. So there I was, in the spring of 2012, moving among and through the angled beams in their grand Berlin installation. In the huge central hall, the former terminal waiting room at the Hamburger-Bahnhof Museum, a gargantuan cave loomed: not so much shrouded in darkness, as the saying goes, but punctuated by conical shrouds or sheathes of piercing light produced by digital beams that seemed to have penetrated the space through pinprick openings above (no real ceiling visible, nor projectors either [fig. 7]). These descending slices of light come clear, on further encounter and contemplation, with a low-keyed conceptual brilliance as well as an obvious specular bravura.

As aesthetic "objects," these "solid light films" generate, each in its own wheeling arc, five widening linear scrims of muted white radiance, their medium (at first glance) being projection itself rather than—as in standard cinema—the thrown field of shape and tincture and implicit depth. In separating projection in this way from the necessity of secondary image, and by turning the beam itself into a sculptoid form, McCall has, in Foster's way of putting it, recovered from the screens and masks of "repro-duction" the very basis of cinema's optical production. In accomplishing this, the black box has gone virtually borderless in its encaverned darkness, the only shape being the angled slant of light, barely moving across the floor—and the spectators it intersects as they cross paths with its resultant luminescent curvature. With five such conical icons of abstracted visibility installed across the gallery in five-minute loops each, *Five Minutes of Pure Sculpture* (2012) is at least as much like a slow-motion *ballet* of light—or, returning to sculptural terms, a cluster of glowing mobiles rather than stabiles. For these are sheer—and shear—incandescent canopies still being built up (even as simultaneously dismantled) near, around, and above us as they are hewn out from darkness and thick air—all in the process, one comes to see, of delineating shifting patterns on the black floor.

If these are "films," of "solid light" or otherwise, they are also—before sculpture, yet at one with it—immaterial drawing. Not quite animation: just the drawing out of drawing itself, drawn forward with no representation formed, no motion conjured other than lineation itself in process. Towering conical havens at a distance, from within or alongside their curtains of light they become cursive horizontal gestures on the ground plane beneath, where the beam inches forward in curvilinear tracks of weightless white monochrome—as if, by radical synecdoche, to refigure the nature of their optic source in the manifested wave motion of contoured light. Between digital projection and surface contact, then, as between sculptural form and drawn horizontal trace, the beam emerges as both technical support and intangible monument: light as material cause to its own isolated aesthetic effect in this trimedial encounter with the participant's moving body as the spectator crosses in contemplation the vertically intersected space. Film, drawing, sculpture. Film drawing sculpture. And drawing the reader into its patterned form.

Moreover, in a side gallery at the Berlin installation—adjacent to the dazzle and initial mystery of these overhead projections—there was one revealing horizontal anomaly (and genealogical throwback) that can help bring out the logic and the evolution of its perpendicular counterparts. It seemed set aside to set off the rest. When beamed sideways against a black wall, and in a conical swath of narrower radius—a geometrical zone that must be vertically intercepted rather than fully occupied by the spectator's body—the paracinematic basis of McCall's work comes all the more immediately into view. In the horizontal alignment of this digital projection, McCall's installation harks back to his own earliest work in this luminous vein, four decades before the Bahnhof show. These earlier "films" of his appeared during the heyday of materialist counter-cinema, including its "flicker films" of sheer pulsing light. Even the title of the new exhibition, *Five Minutes of Pure Sculpture*, is meant to leave "nested within it"—as McCall puts it in an elucidating lecture available on the

Web—a marked allusion to Henri Chomette's *Cinq Minutes de Cinéma Pur* from 1926, an early venture in exactly that flaunted material specificity of high modernism that, even after the decline of Pop and early Conceptual art, still had a way of preoccupying artists well into the 1970s (if often in resistance to its institutionalization).[5]

One might, however, think at first that these laser-like beams of digital projection in McCall's post-2000 work are in fact less "pure" a source of cinematic sculpture (or, again "solid light films") than his original 1974 installation. For one thing, they are not film at all, technically speaking, whatever they may do from within "cinema" to alter the relation of motorized image to participatory spectation. To say so bears explanation, and precisely as it returns us to the materialist and antinarrative avant-garde of McCall's origin (where his representational resistances will be seen making common cause, in the next chapter, with conceptualist forebear and transmedial innovator Marcel Broodthaers in his own anti-cinema).

In McCall's current work, the electronic supplanting of film—from within the cinematic rudiment of projection (now digital rather than photochemical)—involves the overhead light source slowly stretching out, etching out, its curvilinear stroke along an assigned "footprint" surface beneath the "body" of the cone (McCall's terms for this dual functioning). The floor becomes the new ground—which is to say the receptor or support—for the angled vertical "screens" sliced like partitions from misted space. What ordinarily needs a surface for manifestation (cinema) has become a slanted translucent surface all its own. Yet this whole process of illumination, three decades after the photogrammic projection of McCall's *Line Describing a Cone* (1974), no longer passes through celluloid in the form as a visual slice through exposed blackness.

By the time that 1974 piece was acquired by the Tate in 2005, McCall was already well launched on his series of digital updates. In its original function as a minimalist animated film, however, the slowly drawn circle of *Line Describing*, its belted ribbon of incremental advance cinched tight on the sprocket-pulled spool, was inched forward one nudge at a time through the increments of its stop-frame animation. Such work might almost have invoked, in some distant media-historical sense, the rapid music-hall cartoonists who provided some of the brief attractions in the anthology films made for the first London screening of the new Animatograph (one of cinema's early British trademarks).[6] But McCall's is no performance piece. It doesn't show us the act of drawing, only the coming to be of the drawn: only cinema as itself an animation effect.

In the minimalism of its simple circular line, this is cinema less as representation than as sheer thrown light. The titular cone is not submitted to depiction; it is only "described," as indicated by title, in the specialized sense of geometry. Its manifestation is sketched between mechanism and screen only by an inevitable angle of deflection from what amounts to an unseen horizontal apex inside the apparatus and its arc-light. The projection issues by passing through an optically seared photochemical print as a slowly closing circle half an hour in the making. To cast it in a laminated phrasal overlap, here is *cinema as (well as) drawing* on its immediate way, in a further genealogical irony, to that "sculpture-in-motion" by which Vachel Lindsay famously characterized silent film.[7] But this time there are no bodies wonderfully moving, just the mobilization of light itself to which all figuration has been geometrically reduced. Call it, again, cinema degree zero, where (in Foster's broad terms) reproduction cedes instead to disclosed production.

The context was well prepared by the art of *Line*'s day. A few years before McCall's installation, a 1968 lecture by Hollis Frampton—given as a performance piece in a darkened theater at Hunter College—stressed a fundamental point, in its absence, about the projector's beam. For Frampton, the defining basis—not some Greenbergian essence—of cinema is "a rectangle of white light."[8] But that radiant flatness is precisely what must be overcome, not fetishized, even while honored—and honed into image. Everything else we think we see is blockage and subtraction. "We can never see more within our rectangle, only *less*"—as results precisely from the original exposure on celluloid of spaces and bodies that occlude the burn of pure light on the vulnerability of chemically treated plastic.[9] And when that lessening, that partially interrupted beam, that masking or occlusion, lets only a pencil-thin line of light through, it may seem to be returning, photo-frame by photo-frame, to the legendary "pencil of nature" in Henry Fox Talbot's original nineteenth-century sense of the automatic image, there at the dawn of modern visual media. If so, the collective venture of 1970s materialist cinema had found in *Line Describing a Cone* yet another way of disclosing film's own plastic basis, even as that transmedial act of cinematic drawing registered the temporal accretion of the strip's incremental image over the course of viewer duration. But three decades later, without the film stock actually passing through the projector any longer, what we have with the digitized light source in McCall's newer work is the generation of a cinematic line without the serial strip and its filmic frame lines.

In McCall's revamped digital projections, one may say that the cinematic condition, no longer filmic at all, is the sole point of reference and departure. But in new ways now—and at right angles to its theatrical or auditorium norm. When, after a twenty-year sabbatical from art making, McCall returns in a new century to the enterprise of his "solid light films," he points to two main developments—one technical, one conceptual— that spurred his fresh initiative. One would seem almost anti-cinematic: the shift to radiant light as a vertical cascade, rather than horizontal throw, an effect made possible by compact, lightweight, and highly portable elec- tronic (replacing electrical) projectors. He is thus able, as it were, to step off a floor space with a digitally generated—and entirely silent—footprint as well as traverse a vertical screen. As if in compensation, however, the other new impetus is more deeply cinematic than even in his early film work. His recent digital projections entail the new possibility of expanding the simple time-based and protocinematic element of duration (as the line grows and curves) with elements of editing facilitated by computerization: what we might call "seen change" rather than scene change. The elisions of the image plane involved are neither readily visible in person (only their results showing forth) nor easy to describe. But they are his work's new transmedial impetus, caught between a vestige of narrative editing and the installation of sheer light.

[cine::ellipsis]

In this way has the cinema he once "minimized" in the 1970s served up to McCall's art a residual possibility from its fuller reservoir of technique: a once-laboratory editing option (now achieved by computer console) not previously involved in his step-frame animations. Without abandoning the moving image's status as drawing platform—planar, abstract, rath- er than a photomechanical projection of recorded bodies and things in space—McCall has explained how he found a means for tapping into the medial options of the cinematic apparatus, or, say, the cinematic mani- fold, even more than before. This involves his recourse to one particular cinematographic device known as the "wipe": that rhetorically dated me- chanical, and now digital, manipulation for laterally disappearing one image slowly enough (though without dissolve)—edging it horizontally out of frame—so as to make visible in progress the arrival of the next. It is like a sliding lateral ellipsis…its wiping-away offering, from one point to the next, a kind of *eye/swipe*.

And so it is with those new overhead projections of McCall's: where a slowly "moving image" on the floor encroaches upon, transforms, swallows, and reissues a tandem form in a continuous digital cycle. This is at its most complicated in McCall's application when—as if in yet another punning optical allusion so common in transmedial works—this elliptical technique is tested on the geometric lozenge of an actual ellipse. Perceptible but indiscernible even in person, the wipe provides here what one wants to call the cinematographic unconscious of his traced beams. Unlike *Line Describing a Cone*, there is no way fully to "describe it," but the very effort of evocation feels itself conceptual. In one of his projections, for instance, the wipe transpires when a slightly flattened circle or ellipse (an off-angle reminiscence of the cumulative circle in *Line Describing a Cone*) yields place, in almost infinitesimal measure, to an impinging wave pattern in the same floor projection (his Web lecture in illustration being the needed paratext for recognizing this effect in its technical explanation). Such applications of the wipe are thus slowed to an almost imperceptibly gradual shape-shift and mutation beneath the very cones whose draped light they renovate from moment to moment, suggesting from a distance the perspective one might get if a sculpted and irregularly surfaced vase of light were slowly rotated, upside down, until the whole curvature had passed in review—only, with patience, to come round again. All this, in McCall's installations, is only to be noticed in respect to its elliptical floor drawing when one has stepped closer to, or entered upon, its "described" conical elevations: dropped approximately thirty feet from the ceiling to generate the "footprint" that itself anchors their tapered "volume" (McCall's terms again).

Within these hazed and hollow vertical cascades of his latest "site sculpture," so to say, in their attenuated adaptation of an initially "narrative" technique, it is thus the case that the "wipe"—whose sweeping away of one image by the next, shuffled in from behind it, is slowed here to the point of a lingering erosion—makes something unforeseen happen to seeing. These digitized and deeply nonrepresentational image tracks (and their projected traces) become, though less filmic, more cinematic after all in the very production—almost by way of an optic allegory—of a new media environment. They end up generating a spectatorial space more *immersive*, more incorporative, than any 2-D recessional mirage (or even 3-D simulation) of indexed action on the narrative screen. McCall's are moving images, though not pictures, you can really *get into*, animated drawings you can tenant rather than stare at, sculpture you can examine from the inside out. Their shimmering involutes are—in a whole new way—involving. Again, the recurrent formula: digital projection is what they are; cinematic transmediation is what they do. Or put it this way: cinema seen transmedium is what they accomplish.

[vision::cones]

In this digital refinement of McCall's conceptual program, we are both a far cry and a stone's throw from 1974. No longer, as in the 16mm film work *Line Describing a Cone*, is the basic medial function a curvilinear slit of permitted light inching forward through unexposed black in a photo-grammatic series so as to manifest itself as a lengthening screen curve and eventual circle. Instead, in these vertical works, the digital tracing of light turns the mist-laden black box into the translucent angles of various demarcated, though wholly porous, social enclosures, a forest of immaterial optic teepees, shapes exceeding even the 1974 work by open-ing (wide) the possibility not just of interaction with the light form but a complete occupation of it. Yet it remains the case that the horizontal works are quicker to expose another conceptual inversion at their very point of projection. Beginning in 1974 and renewed with *Between You and I, Horizontal* (2006), with its ungrammatical play, no doubt, on the "eye" as well as the subjective pronoun, these elongated fanned cantilevers of light have the rather stunning effect of evoking, in hyperbolic form, the very cone of vision that manifests them to us.[10]

Faced with McCall's own question regarding the staged evanescence of these installations—namely, "Where is the work?"—Foster rightly adds: "In effect this is also to ponder 'What is the Medium?'" (198). The start of Foster's answer—"film denatured, stripped bare"—might be complement-ed since, by Sean Cubitt, as "a practice of light."[11] To sum up McCall's ocular motive in Foster's words, there is no attempt "to deliver film into a stable state of autonomous purity but to place it in correspondence with various arts" (170). The aesthetic file stays open, the case unclosed. Moreover, it is not just the self-conscious and arresting transmediality of these works, but their human "interactivity," that can be said to recommend them as antidote to the faux phenomenology diagnosed by Forster in the global design environment. If McCall's intangible *objets* intersect and envelope me as I walk through and within their mutable parameters, then they have, as it were, left themselves behind, foregone their autonomy. They make me newly present to myself in their own light. In being slashed here by a line, wrapped there by a curve, I am made visible—both to myself and to others—as taking my place, my part, in the exhibition, not just taking up space in it. These works are thus more genuinely architectonic than many new buildings, shaped for the body not of the passerby but of the temporary mobile inhabitant. Beyond spectacle, they are pertinent environments of glow: the beam (of light) as structural girder. One might be tempted to say of McCall's recent works in digital projection that they are cinema without film. But the more one dwells on his own terms for these works, and for their photomechanical prototypes three decades back, the more one suspects that the continuing sense of their constitution as "solid light films" is not anachronistic at all, but figurative, almost punning. They are, in short, and in this sense have always been, *films of light*: their membranes offering gauzy integuments of misted visibility in the re-engineering of the cinematic apparatus as something like an architectonic lamp.

[apparatus::theory]

But that filminess doesn't make McCall's installations any less cinematic, or metacinematic, in their oblique technological intervention. In terms of that renowned flashpoint of so-called apparatus theory known as "suture," one might say that projection's "Absent One" at the focal point of reception, a center of ocularity regularly disappeared in the space not just between projection booth and screen but phenomenologically—reversibly—between a shot and its countershot (say, her facing him and his looking back at her), is in fact no longer absent. Viewing in McCall doesn't depend, as its technical requisite, on a forgetting of oneself *by way of* structural subtraction. Moving through the gallery, you are already *in the way* instead—and must let projection have its almost tangible way with you: not via narrative identification, but as object rather than subject in your furnishing forth of bodily surface and its curves.

As the current subheading would suggest in its characteristic two-way typography, McCall's sculptural mirages render interpenetrable the apparatus and the theory of haptic vision it engenders. The issue is, as always, a *transmergence* of means. With McCall's nonimaging lightshows, a sense of derivative 3-D articulation in the drawing of space (*[drawing::space]*), enhanced by the "wipe" device of gradual effacement (phonetically self-exampled as *[cine::ellipsis]*) turns visibility itself pyramidal and curved (*[vision::cones]*) in a construct of illumination itself that was bracketed off, from the first, into self-enaction as *[light::works]*. Such is the manipulation that works light so that luminosity per se is made over into a traversable space. In so much of this and related typography, modifiers (like medial attributes in this regard) are no sooner attached to their nouns, in specifying such transmediation, than they are rendered substantive objects of its transitive operation. Once again, each two-sided coinage rings its own changes on the very paradigm of interplay.

Yet beyond the art-historical lineage that McCall's long hiatus from the galleries helps delineate, and beyond the tactile sociality his work encourages (as singled out in Foster's account), broader questions remain about platform evolution that his mode of display makes salient: questions, again, of mediarchaeology. Under unexpected torque, the McLuhanesque model appears once more. According to this paradigm of normal media development, the form of a former medium reemerges as the content of the new—as for instance feature films, in rerun, crowding the roster of early TV broadcast. Apart from standard media genealogies, this is also the case with the auto-archaeology of conceptual practice, as when in McCall's work (in a kind of materialist devolution) the form of projection, thrown light per se, has reverted to its status as the artifact's exclusive content— so that the apparatus of cinephiliac identification or spectacle is replaced by the process of material, if weightless, encounter.

The inferred reflexive logic of McCall's practice might therefore run this way, beginning in the same period that saw the rise of an apparatus theory that can best measure his departure. Under avant-garde revision, the form of traditional cinema, in the electric projection of moving human images and scanned settings, became in the late 1960s and early 1970s the disclosure, and thus reenclosure, of its own serial materiality or flicker or sheer beam (Stan Brakhage, Tony Conrad, Frampton). This includes the abstemious content of McCall's own early experimental film work (being more than mere screen work): the isolation of light itself in linear projection, generating as content nothing but its own luminous trail, "describing" nothing but its own space of visibility in the newly traversable cone of reception extending forward from the screen. In this way the form of the old (optical projection itself, regardless of image)—in becoming the new reductionist content of screen presentation—was no longer actually contained by that screen at all. Then, two decades later, in the midst of a still-swelling digital deluge, McCall's art of the vertical electronic stream discovers something in the prehistory of electronic editing (the "wipe") that can be imported to inflect the seamless downpour of his cascades with the mysteries of the discontinuous.

Moreover, it is only a further ramification of the ambient interplay between viewer's body and such light sculpture that can best explain McCall's subsequent return to the realm of soundscape as well, where his earliest experimentation began. For sound is even more enveloping—more in some cases a conic envelope—than light. Or more at times a sheer "flood." As late as 2014, a never-exhibited piece by McCall, though conceived as early as 1972, was mounted at the Yale School of Art. In the artist's description, *Travelling Wave* is an installation that involves "a dense cloud of 'white noise' … repeatedly launched down an empty 60-foot-long gallery, creating a rolling, invisible sculpture." And in newer audiovisual work leading up to this recovered and finally debuted *sound mobile*, McCall collaborated in 2012 on *Leaving (with Four Half Turns)*. This is a version of one of his familiar horizontal projections involving a circle that is four times inscribed, then disappeared, by digital editing while accompanied live by David Grubbs in an original guitar composition that shifts gradually from acoustic to electronically amplified sound, its sonic scheme keyed to the screen's progressive graphic delineation and the repeated evanescence of its resultant sculptural cone.

[image::resonance]

This latter performance piece is still familiar ground in McCall, the "light-shown" space becoming what we might call acoustically materialized. But we can turn now to more radical work in the audiovisual register, far beyond anything resembling mere synesthesia—though equally participatory, and even "healing," in its appeal to embodiment. For since McCall's return to the digital scene, another artist also first coming to prominence in the late 1960s and early 1970s, but continuously active since, the German American painter, sculptor, and videographer Hans Breder, has also been freshly empowered (like McCall) by new electronic technology. Through its painstaking implementation, Breder has carried the question—the literal matter, or materialization—of the sound/image link (or call it, when phonetically merged as well, the *imagedsound* fusion) a good deal farther, and deeper, than McCall. Not incidentally the founder of the first Intermedia Arts program in the United States at the University of Iowa, Breder has lately pursued his time-based and cross-media investigations into a remarkable suite of video works (completed in 2015) called *Mindscape* (with relevant key signatures appended, like *E* or *F#*, for each installment). These extended transmedial fugues are associated, one by one, with the seven chakras, or nodes of bodily force, in the Hindu tradition—quite intimately, indeed viscerally, associated. This is a mystic intertext one needs to know in encountering these video works, not necessarily in order to feel the physiological link but to think through its process: paratext again as frame.

In this instance of a typical discursive backstory, the technology behind what one might call, beyond paradox, the *physiological affect* of this work can only emerge from exhibition notes. Yet in the manifest, indeed palpable, aesthetic charge of these pieces, beyond the technical expertise so disclosed, Breder's is more than a thought experiment, though no less. The audiovisual micropoetics of these works owes allegiance to the "cymatics" (from the Greek for "wave") of Swiss scientist Hans Jenny, with his experiments in the shaping and texturing force of sound waves as they redistribute particles on a surface (categorized under the general rubric of "modal phenomena"). But what Breder achieves, by putting image and sound—not separately but together, via digital feedback— under the delayed action of multifaceted subdivision is nothing less than a conversion of the cymatic into the somatic. The result is what analysis might best term transmodal.

Its complexity is all but unprecedented. Breder's computer work submits both ends of the "imagedsound" spectrum to micro-acoustic as well as micro-optic (microptic) analysis. A prolonged—drawn out, drawn harmonically thin but insistent—version of his own twelve-tone composition for piano, trombone, and Tibetan singing bowl is slowed so that the soundtrack registers, in dilated legato spans, the yawning and haunting space between notes. This tonal wavering is generatively linked (not exactly synced) with the complex set of digital filters applied to a video of one of Breder's own early choreographic pieces with mirrors and nude dancers, an indexical image long lost to the shimmering abstract patterns into which it has now been electronically dismantled, parsed, distilled—or, say, by which it has been entered and mined more deeply, in and between its pixelated grain. With the motion and palette of the screen image split, unfolded, and ramified again and again by digital transforms into a quasi-fractalized and vibrating mandala, these video works (intended for gallery projection) mutate before our eyes (and ears) according to the main harmonic "spine" of their attenuated and mesmerizing sound waves. When, in the process, and by comprehensive design, each separate work in the *Mindscape* series is targeted, in tantric fashion, to an area of the perceiver's body set into resonance with its emissions, the all but tactile pulse of the work has achieved its full reach. Transmediation becomes its own spur to meditation.

Sonic and optic frequencies do not, of course, match up with, but rather interanimate, each other in these tandem audioptic channelings, with both sustained transmissions—in their audiovisual transmediation—finding their multisensory sounding board in the recipient body. Breder's art flows in these works from the specular to the anatomical without passing through the haptic—except, of course, via the caress of tone, and hence by its resulting ability to *retune* the whole organic frame of our embodied attention. So it is that a work whose retinal surge begins in the mirrored body of a gestural performer (not usually visible onscreen except in the optic afterwaves of the choreographic motion) ends up finding its own newly orchestrated dance of hue and luminescence conveyed by sonic translation to the registers of the body (ours) after all. Certainly, the transfigurative image plane in these computerized works is more pulsional, more rhythmic, more in its own right harmonic, than much of the new digital work propagated under an "aesthetics of glitching" (to which one can, for instance, link Rondepierre's captured webcast jams). Nonetheless, the obvious platform of Breder's work in software manipulation is visibly contemporary with the "datamoshing" that otherwise results, in recent video practice, from the hacked and remastered compression algorithms of found image files—to the likes of which (based on his own previous art videos) Breder has not "added" sound so much as empowered it to take part in spurring, and at the same time reverbing with, the optic transforms in progress.[12]

For Breder, sound and image oscillate in an interrelationship that is "mimetic rather than symmetric," hence aesthetic rather than technical, with each sensory flow, sonic and optic, miming the distended vibratory continuities of the other. What we meet in these works, with a therapeutic upshot all their own, is something like the aesthetic equivalent of medical science's MRI: in this case, not magnetic resonance imaging but mesmerizing *image resonance* across an axis that opens each moment ("nowtime" being the original working title of these videos) to its internal flux and retentions—and opens the mind to the recuperative rhythms of this decelerated and resynthesized somatic pace. This is beyond the usual reach of Conceptual art, even cognitive art. Between its "now" and ours in felt response, Breder's inventions for eye and ear work to institute a visceral transmedium. Zones of the body, keyed to the chakras of sympathetic (anatomical) vibration, become in effect the echo chamber of Breder's digital remix. In McCall's work, we enter the space of projection. In Breder's, the audiovisual oscillation enters us.

Part of the medium-specification inherent in Breder's experiments, though hardly a matter of canonical "specificity," is indeed the manifestly digital editing that he, like McCall before him, exploits so notably—if along such a different path. In this respect, the vibratory particularity of Breder's *[image::resonance]* dialectic, his videophony, connects more obviously than might at first appear with the detached resonance of image per se—in resistance to the cinematic—that characterizes McCall's work. And this is where the "post-medium" axiom of Krauss's overview again claims attention, even if one would wish to insist in demurral, as do the constructs of many recent artists, that the parameters and demands of mediation survive the waning of a catch phrase like "specificity."

Be this as it may, in framing her sense of the widespread revisionary initiative of which McCall's early *cinematographs* (my term, not hers) were a part, and of the place of experimental film at large in the divestments of Greenbergian modernism, Krauss goes back to what she understands as a watershed post-medial moment in the early 1970s that one can also see pursued by Breder's founding ventures in intermedia pedagogy. For Krauss, the moment is marked most vehemently by the multifarious deconstruction of autonomous art forms (and formations) in both the installation and film work of the tireless provocateur Marcel Broodthaers. This investigative return on her part, this act of recovery, is in every way instructive. For our purposes, spurred by her account, a trans-medium (rather than post-medium) view of Broodthaers's wry twists on the museum aesthetic, as well as on the filmic support for cinematic exhibition, should serve further to elucidate a systemic paradigm for hybrid aesthetic modalities at large: one never more relentlessly or definitively pursued than in Broodthaers's own anomalous optical crossbreeds, where film, let alone image, divides peremptorily against itself—sectioned into static increment, all spectacle taken to task and to pieces at once.

When we review Broodthaers's innovations in these terms, his forerunner status is clear. He died in 1976, well before the electronic experiments to come. More should therefore be said, in the manner of historical generalization, about the differently representative careers of artists like Breder, McCall, and Rondepierre that outlast the analog era and thereby run the gamut from, respectively, early video art, experimental film, or celluloid frame extraction through to computer imaging (Breder's electronic kaleidoscopes), digital projection (McCall's "solid light films" in electronic iteration), and webcast default (Rondepierre's captured DSL implosions). The marked technical transitions of these artists are "representative" in regard, not least, to what we began by noting as the inclusion of Conceptualism 2.0 within a broader scope of transmedial investigations. With the work of these makers being cross-medial to begin with, whether in the play between performance and video projection, drawing and cinematography, or photogram and filmic sequence, their "research" has thus evolved into a 2.0 phase that sustains and elucidates early explorations on their part and that of others (and of Broodthaers most unflinchingly, as we're now to see) into not just comparative but interknit medial gestures—and their roughened, worried, and unstable interfaces.

CHAPTER SIX: *Filmedivision*

In DIVISION BEGINS ALL SCREEN VISION: ORIGINALLY SERIAL IN FILM, NOW PIXEL-LINEAR (indiscernibly pixelinear) in the lightning-fast checkerboard ignitions of digital imaging. It is within the framework of that former frame-advance apparatus that Rondepierre's photogram studies, for instance, pertinently refuse all continuity in the name of its filmic cells or modules. Conceptual cinema has its own way of proceeding along similar, strategically broken, lines. And Broodthaers, in this respect, is only one point of departure. What is brought forward by this former poet turned installation artist and filmmaker is above all a complex interplay between material surfaces and textual (including optical) platforms. Against the full historical and conceptual backdrop of Broodthaers's continuity-dismantling film work—as an outgrowth of his earlier installation practice—Rosalind Krauss's appreciation will help us see more clearly the Conceptual art lineage in motion picturing, rather than the picturing of motion, to which Broodthaers made such signal early contributions. As with Breder, too, and other artists in this time-based line of film or video experimentation, the "apparatus" is pried open to more than an apparitional technology.[1] In Broodthaers's deliberate impedance to all imagistic coherence, let alone spectacle, his anti-apparitional logic is first "on display" in the "Film Section" of a fabricated museum exhibit in which vision is rendered inseparable from the sectioned segments of "film/e/d/i/vision." Looking into the sectorings and crevices of his work is, therefore, a way of looking ahead to other conceptualist "media studies" directed not only at the photomechanical strip but at its superseded materiality in newer screen transmission.

Once the Belgian artist shifted from a career as surrealist poet to, first, a book sculptor (plaster-cast entomber of his own unsold verse volumes) and then a conceptualist gadfly at large, filmmaking included, Broodthaers's foundational contribution to postwar conceptualism is indeed most obvious with his installation effort in the "museumizing" of discrepant found objects.[2] These were appropriated under arbitrary conditions of display as cultural "illustrations"—or "figures" (figs.)—and thus served to convert an all but random cross-section of cultural material into image culture on the spot. Broodthaers accomplished this curatorial imposition not just by painting "fig." numbers on random things, recycled artifacts among them, but also on various sub-zones of a cinematic screen, arbitrarily singling out discrepant pockets of optic data from frame to frame. These counterintuitive categorizations were part of a 1971-72 installation, under the outré title *The Museum of Modern Art, Eagles Department, Film Section*. Ornithology and cinematography were lumped together within this bizarre new taxonomic dispensation—with overtones, no doubt, of the chemical taxidermy incident to each. After such a sectoring of the film frame into virtually synecdochic "illustrations" of some unspoken abstraction, Broodthaers's move to projected film itself seemed all but inevitable.[3] Before explicating his turn into that experimental screen montage that lends the title to her volume, *A Voyage on the North Sea*, Krauss gives considerable thought—and space—to his earlier ironic cataloguing of "museum" works. This is the practice that included, at the outer limits of his parodic taxonomy, that disruptive affixing of separate "fig." numbers to various sectors of a single screen—and hence to the beamed celluloid frames (as shots) that pass over it.

[fig::uration]

In "Film Section," his white "fig." indications on small black placards, ten in all, pepper the screen in an arbitrary coverage. Their numbers are called forth in projection by the play of light flickering within the width and height of the white reflective numerals—or disappeared into dark objects or shadows as the shot "scene" or snapshot changes from one discrepant locale or perspective to another in its disposition as a kind of mock travelogue of stock footage. This arbitrary parsing of the otherwise "unitary" screen vista operates to disintegrate the film "image"—in its absorbing and totalized display as function of narrative action or, at least, of human movement. Broodthaers's odd taxonomy of the screen plane zones it into the separate yet adjacent image-events that compose it, not from shot to shot but in its very array as a single thrown rectangle of light and shadow. He defies in this way the unifying gestalt of apparatus theory, with its immersive hold on the viewer, through a further reduction of filmic representation to its own layout of curatorial "details." The joke is to have turned a moving image into a schematic diagram of itself. It is as if the visually implied but retinally denied "mosaic" that, for Epstein, characterizes film—both as mottled single frame and as motorized composite—has been pinioned, subdivided, and tagged as such, flagged for arbitrary analysis rather than flashed by in passive review.

This photo/cinema interface, whose "figural" art is here lampooned by its abbreviated subsumption to an institutional metadiscourse of the captioned display, is certainly an aspect of Broodthaers's irony destined to return in his actual film (or photo-montage) work. It does so two years later, under the title *Voyage on the North Sea* (1974), for a nonnarrative sequencing whose shuffled fixity of image seems going nowhere—and slowly. It is among the treasure trove of early Conceptual art in the permanent collection of the Hamburger-Bahnhof, purring and spluttering away last time I was there, in its own introvert fashion, in a dedicated small cubicle almost all its own. Stopping short of any animation effect, the frame line of Broodthaers's montage alternates between photo images (lackluster seagoing shots) and nautical painting in a movement both forward in time and back upon itself in disjunctive spatial alternation. Filmic figuration lapses to individual "figs." of representation yet again—in another kind of museum-like taxonomy—but here, too, caught up at the same time in a transmedial anatomy. Where "figs." once spoiled the picture plane's assumed holistic index, now "pagination" does a similar divisive work. Broodthaers effects this by parceling out his footage in that *North Sea* "documentary" into sixteen separate "pages" (their indication inserted as intertitles) that alternate with photographs of boats at sea whose wave-lapped ambience seems almost to shimmer with motion from the sheer flicker-effect of the low-resolution spool. In punctual contrast to such full-frame indexical images, the effect of the paginal indications is at times to imply that the counterpointed full-frame drawings are themselves "figures" from some unseen illustrated volume, shown at times as magnified "details." And in the way these images *navigate* between medial assumptions, they suggest themselves as conceptual precedent for the drawing forward (stasis suggesting lurch) of the derealized photo of Paul Sietsema's *Boat Drawing*. Launched as well (like Sietsema's later drawn boat) from a minor adventure on the high seas, the foundational *Voyage* is a derealizing graphic venture, time-based here, into the near and far horizons of what the eye sees.

In this way each transmediated mode of presentation, painting and photography and the vestiges of codex textuality, linked by serial projection, serves to ward off the autonomous claims of the others. What we watch happening is a spun-out simile: a set of "figures" rectangular like the page, sequential like books and their "passages," indexical like photography, representational like painting. In the process, what such analogizing accomplishes in this *Voyage* is nothing less than a return journey across the very history of reproduction from Lumière through Niépce and Fox Talbot and on past Gutenberg back to Lascaux—or, in other words, from wheeling celluloid to photo frame to turning pages to moving brush or charcoal. But Krauss has something else in mind as well, or in view—a different medial reversion. For her, in the spluttering pace of this throwback silent film, this rudimentary serial collage, Broodthaers has in fact returned us to "the openness promised by early film, an openness woven into *the very mesh of the image*, as the flickering irresolution of the illusion of movement produced by the experience of sight itself as dilated: a phenomenological mixture of presence and absence, immediacy and distance" (emphasis added).[4] *Filmedivision*, by any other name: the weave of canvas transferred by magnification, in Krauss's metaphor, to the very trope of intermittence. In this, as well, Broodthaers's work is pitched in refusal of exactly that "special effect," that *enmeshed* and essential artifice, by which Epstein characterizes typical cinematic motion.

Not for Broodthaers, certainly, does film constitute "the redemption of physical reality." In line with Siegfried Kracauer's famous phrasing—a line of thought that includes André Bazin, Stanley Cavell, and Gilles Deleuze as well—one abiding view of cinema is that film's automatized "world view" restores experience to us in the form of *a* world, both bracketing all skepticism and thus training us in its overcoming. Such, then, within re-presentation, is one influential sense of cinema's redemption (recovery) in regard to the real. For Broodthaers, instead, the determinate gesture amounts not to the world's "redemption" by representation but to a trans-medial *prevention* of reality as image, let alone as object of epistemological faith. Broodthaers's work recalls us not to a seen reality but to the *real of the visible* in itself, the fact of vision, across screen or page: the very texture of optical (which may include verbal, but not here acoustical) apprehension.

One can readily extend Krauss's claims for a "flickering irresolution" retrieved by Broodthaers from early silent-screen projections, a kind of re-covered retinal innocence, to the broader inferences of his "film sectioning." It is as if—in the tacit exposure of early viewers to the traced exposure time of the photogram—the very idea of the image, in its vanishing retention from frame to frame, retains in turn for its audience, sustains and reinvigorates, a wide-eyed wonder not just at the apparatus all told but at the deeper mystery of vision itself, the data it elides, the continuities it both grasps and fashions. This is just the wonder—turned implicitly quizzical, then diagnostic, in Broodthaers's hands—that cinema introduced at a new level of automatism into human optics. Again: the invited unpacking of *filmedivision*, for which the museal "film section" in Broodthaers offers an early indirect clue.

Since chronophotography first—and then (though the differential measures were elided in projection) cinema—may be said to have *filmed divisions* in optical continuity that had gone previously unregistered by human vision itself (states or stages of change otherwise overlooked, over-run, by sheer looking), it was therefore the case that the new celluloid art, eventually standardized at twenty-four glimpses per second, was equally rooted, even while overriding it, in the motored increments of motion, cell by celluloid cell. Broodthaers moved to uproot these serial elements, as "figures" of sequence, so as to project instead, from within cinema, the rudiments of sequential imaging prolonged, abstracted, denatured: analyzed rather than reanimated. To put the itinerary of *Voyage* in terms developed in Scene One from still-image conceptual ventures, such refused illusionism—from within the potentially immersive virtuality of cinema in its normal thralls of representation, its hyper- or ultra-real power over the audiovisual sensorium, the apparitional force of its apparatus—is another plunge into the hyporeal of its modular constitution.

Again, one certainly sees what Krauss means, in her own terms, by "post-medium condition," even as early as her backcast to 1974. Yet to my eye, and in particular through her lens, *Voyage* appears as more like a reversion to conjoint medial rudiments (of spatialized temporality) than a journey beyond. As much about projected celluloid as it is about painted facture, it is also anchored in both rather than neither. In its short, slow montage of page-numbered photo frames and painted seascapes, the inference is cumulative—and quite fully triangulated. In the medial simplifications that the work contemplates and cross-stitches, the venture of *Voyage* is, as it were, all (rather than none) of the below: film and painting and paged sequencing together; cinema, slide show, catalog. If this is post-, it is also proto-medial, aimed back at the conditioning possibilities of screen motion as well as moving past them. The critical instinct to find in Broodthaers's experiments a defining link, in effect, between Duchamp's surrealist modernism and its legacy in Conceptual art is so far from overdone in Krauss that it is by now all but a consensus. I would simply add that the lineage is all the more flexible and suggestive as a tracked line of descent if seen as involving not so much a gauntlet (postmedial) thrown down to material specificity as a wrenching open—and wide—of the transmedial premise. If you cross-reference the outmoded often enough with itself, then new modalities, new mediations, come forth. We have been developing, of course, a fuller vocabulary for this cross-referential motive. Again, one can ratchet down a received terminology from the level of reception to that of construct or generation. Interfacial in this internally composite sense—or, in other words, arranging the face-off of divergent aesthetic or technical modalities—works of this multiple stamp explore the transmedial inner facets of the transmissive contact they arrange to fabricate.

This can happen no matter how contrived and counter-intuitive the fabrication. One might think of Broodthaers's own outré gesture as a mock-conciliation—a strained compensation for media progress—when he numbers a montage like a paginated book, familiarizing the new via the old. It is a process similar to that early conflation in chapter 1 between overlapped imprint modes—ink and celluloid—in *The End* lithographs by Ruscha and Pettibon, with their seized-up cinematic frame advance and interart captions. Hence, from there out, we have found the relation of the instrumental skeuomorph—with its visual emblematics of remediation—as an occasional oblique model for the transmedial vaunts and reversals of Conceptualism 2.0. (I think, most recently, of the reverse skeuomorph of Fiona Banner's hardback book cover: an actual bound volume whose very title, in parody of the codex simulations of website marketing, is embossed with "NO IMAGE AVAILABLE.") Such works may seem to intercept—and often upend—the commercialized evocations of skeuomorphic design in its standard work of conjoined nostalgia and normalization: as for instance, in adding to earlier examples, the pictured desktop "mailbox" or "envelope" with no box, no normal spatial volume at all, nothing to envelop (but only algorithmically to dispense). These are familiarizing gimmicks, safely embalming a new dispensation in an older mode. Transmedial art deacclimates by a similar logic, estranges the comfort zone that the skeuomorph is meant to secure—as when the "swipe to unlock" function becomes a formal life-size oil portrait of the licensed user in the work of Evan Roth, a striated black thumbprint no longer thumbnail in scale at all.

Where the skeuomorph retools and "humanizes" by optical allusion, cushioning the unfamiliar, other conceptual works, like those of Christiane Baumgartner, Paul Sietsema, and Simon Starling, contort their opposite disacclimating process from within. They go beyond any superficial reverse mode of mere defacilitation. Instead of TV aspiring to the graphic art that long preceded it—via some inner picture-framed titles, say, for an early broadcast show—the venerable art of the woodcut is made by Baumgartner to look like low-resolution TV. In Sietsema, as in Saunders by a further reversal, we find a manner of painting made to look like a photo negative, not only to suggest the obverse face, or procedural interface, of a lackluster photorealism but also to evoke—in a longer art-historical perspective—the mechanical imaging that once arrived to usurp painting's whole representational monopoly. And such effects can, as we know, involve—evolve—a more tortuous logic yet. Reading our way into certain works, we arrive at the in-joke that turns technological history inside out. Reversing the skeuomorphic template whereby a computer process simulates a precedent form by, for instance, the "scroll" function, Starling travels the path of planned obsolescence in reverse. Rather than his electronically generated thirty-second historical reconstruction being made to look like dated (digitally "antiqued") footage of the first creaky computer, he wields a more involuted mediarchaeology. His reverse his-torical "projection" simulates (by ambitiously rendered CGI) a germinal moment in the very technology that is to outstrip (twice over) the plas-tic basis of film's backdated rotary mechanics in the processing of both key-punched computational ciphers and projected images. In place of straightforward (however duplicitous or skeuomorphic) remediation, yet again an impacted transmediation. And we see the process compounded elsewhere when, for instance, the award-winning cover (designed by Sara Sauers) of Alexander Starre's 2015 book on *Metamedia*—with its emphasis on the way digital biblio-graphics can simulate older forms of typeface—is rendered (backwards to such effects) as if it had not yet left the design-er's electronic desktop, toolbars and crop-boxing still in progress. It is only later, of course, in distribution, that the text is rendered partially accessible—the digital confession once more reversed—by the typical curled-page curiosity of skeumorphic cliché in the look-"inside" trope of flat-screen Web marketing (image, reversing Banner, readily available). Until then, with Starre's actual cover, we've been teased by a commercial art version, one might say, of Starling's "metamorphology."

[type::ping]

One more unmistakable exemplum from the explicitly 2.0 end of the spec-trum involves an unblinkingly explicit version of sustained skeuomorphic imaging in a media-savvy conceptualist vein. Akram Zaatari's epistolary send-up, under the title *Tomorrow Everything Will Be Alright* (2010), has, in its time-based (and time-erased) video, already allowed one (technolog-ical) tomorrow to swallow up its in-frame apparatus. For what we see is a full-screen typewriter carriage digitally edited into a simulated exchange of rapid text-messages in transmit, "pinging" (the technical Internet term) back and forth—though silently—in the paradoxical closed circuit of real-time typescript. Zaatari's videography thus oversees (by keeping in view) a flurry of reciprocal "intimacies" between former gay lovers, feeling out the possibility of a reunion across the curved "scroll" of an outmoded IBM Selectric and its platen. Here is an apparatus whose eclipse by instantaneity is captured, in Zaatari's video montage, by classic cinematic (now digital) jump cuts between messages.

In this sense, the technohistorical interface is remarkably unstable. Despite the nostalgic typeface platform, the erotic communiqués are e-texted rather than typed, "sent" rather than mailed, emerging in an alternating rhythm from the rotated paper that therefore seems paradoxically (and anachronistically) wired rather than impressed. The edited supplanting of one keystroked utterance by the next in the rotary queue bears clear comparison with Sietsema's serially displaced visual descriptions on formal notepaper in *At the Hour of Tea*. In each case, the protocols of one medium are visibly outdistancing those of its predecessor: inscription overleapt by jump-cut projection. Yet this time, by a twofold reversion within Zaatari's updated digital video, we are returned from these evoked "instagraphs" of new media to the parallel datedness of carriage return and rotary frame-line editing. The same inherent filmic divisions beneath a reassembled continuity that are refused by Broodthaers's *Voyage* (and exposed by this very refusal) are recalled in Zaatari's video by a postcinematic—and transmedial—version of discrepant serial succession. And there is a further level of transmediation entailed in his work—in the form of communications archaeology, with its tacit overtones of telegraphy and teletype as well. This emerges when one of the exchanges in Zaatari's electro-epistolary sequence involves a refusal to answer a telephone that is said by the typescript to be ringing in the background—in hopes of a more "immediate" emotional appeal. Communications archaeology, yes—and interface allegory as well—for this video of lovelorn desire concerns a gap in human "communications" that no technology, however instantaneous, can bridge.

[spool::loops]

From this videography of transmedial address and appeal, we come round now to traditional film (together with its electronic DVD transfer) for a celluloid-tracked testament to an unraveling psyche and its libidinal exhaustion. In this "restaging" of the celluloid, then digital, imprint of a filmed stage play, none other than Beckett's *Krapp's Last Tape*, the transmedial interface operates across the recorded data of magnetic tape, celluloid trace, and digital remediation—all under the sign of media storage as cultural warehousing in museum space. What Hal Foster locates in the postindustrial complicities of the art-architecture complex can induce all the more potent an irony when the locus in question is an already abandoned and not yet repurposed museum, rather than a refurbed factory: a museum that becomes in its own right part of the display. Often enough, especially in works Jameson would identify with postmodernism's apolitical "utopian" drift toward the supposedly rejuvenative negativity of an escapist cultural "no-place," museal assemblages may seem "installed" (like most of those that precede us here) in the Deleuzian "any-space-whatever" of anonymous postmodern urbanism and its gallery annexes. But with his medium-elegiac film of *Krapp's Last Tape* and its accompanying digital transfer, Canadian film director Atom Egoyan is far more specific: housing this double "replay" of a staged *Tape*—with its titular medium a threaded and spun threnody for a life gone by—not in a traditional art venue, but in a defunct anthropological museum. The institutional context is thus hard to overlook for this failing specimen not just of homo sapiens but of two vestigial forms of wheel-based analog technology.

Some works, though not in any way site-specific, can seem in fact perfectly housed just where and when they belong, whether in their timeliness or even their belatedness. Such is the case, from February to March of 2002, with the projection of Egoyan's 2001 DVD transfer of his 35mm film version of Beckett's play (commissioned for initial television release) screened in the disused rooms of a defunct London gallery. The fitness of venue is not thematic alone, as we'll see, but more deeply medial. Written in the late 1950s, this play by Beckett, high watermark in the so-called Theater of the Absurd, can be thought to catch the turn, in theatrical as well as cultural history, from modernism to postmodernism. It can also be seen, in its function as a so-called psychological monodrama, to be giving way across its own duration to a now mostly vestigial and prosthetic humanism, where an old man's tape-recorded memory offers a machinic adjunct to the lived body: a proto-cyborgian consciousness under self-anatomy. If the title doesn't say it all, it does blazon the punning gist: the last excreta of involuted memory passing under stinging review in a recorded biographical voice. Here before us, all gone before and unwound in retrospect, is a life reeling past in the further metatheatrical demotion, for long stretches at a time, of the "live actor" to his prerecorded (younger) self, a subjectivity looped and duped by its own vanished technic double.

Beyond or beneath all this, at the level not of the drama but of its recorded screen capture by Egoyan, the audiovisual "play text"—seen first by the spectator in high-definition digital—is eventually manifest to us in cross-mediation with theater's own previous means of a paradoxical "live record," namely film itself (with its subsequent TV distribution). But such "canned theater"—as projected and viewed here at first only in its eventual digital transfer—needs no actual canister now, being no longer stored on a reeled transparent strip at all. Beckett's French title, *La Dernière Bande*, would evoke more directly the common spooled ribbon or "band" of audiotape and celluloid that is now "upgraded" to nondegradable (or at least differently vulnerable) high-definition digital. The recorded stagecraft thus passes before us in instantaneous bitmapped presentation rather than in the wheeling of a photogrammic strip: through compressed electronic files, that is, instead of a filing-by of discrete cellular images. In this relay of material supports, the transit from *on* the boards to *in* the can to *down*-loaded (as well as previously *broad*-cast) marks one familiar declension of "performance" in contemporary playback mode.

But here the vector of progress stalls—or at least lingers—in remembrance over the assaulted membrane of a predecessor medium. For next door to the initial digital projection, in an adjacent gallery within this abandoned museum space, is the "recycling" of celluloid itself: the actual plastic trace from which the DVD transcription was made. Looping around a gallery over rollers guyed by pulleys and passed through a dimly lit editing monitor, the whole performance unwinds less persuasively as filmed play than as the sheer play of film: very sheer, and, after a month's collected dust and abrasion, gradually frayed and scratched on both visual and audial tracks, slowly enfeebled, dying out. Museum-framed in this way, the institutional idea of the collectible is instead, in its very display, gradually effaced, expunged. Indeed, by not being a gallery holding so much as a one-time material installation, preservation time is no longer on the side of the artifact.

The ironies of this, though immediate, also spread wide. The so-called Museum of Mankind, in London's grand but cramped Burlington House, had cabined the ethnographic wing of the British Museum from 1990 to 1997. Between then and its new rehabbed use by the Royal Academy of Art in 2005—midway through almost a decade's languishing in drydock between anthropology and aesthetics—it provided the temporary and wryly chosen home for this museumized piece of modernist psychic ethnography crossed with media archaeology: the multiplatform homage to Beckett's study of human alienation and self-obsolescence. On the way to the gallery space set aside for this "program" by Egoyan, viewers had to pass through corridors of display cases littered with empty film canisters and celluloid strips from a seemingly abandoned archive of ethnographic films and outdated audiovisual equipment, including a curatorial ledger of former exhibits at the museum—all metonymic, in part, for cinema's own lapsed hegemony as modernist form.

Past this clutter and debris, attention is first channeled, then, into that high-definition "screening room" in its typical postmillennial incarnation: running the digital transfer of Egoyan's originally filmed, then televised, production of the Beckett play, with John Hurt in the self-anthropologized solo lead: a reminiscing consciousness looking back at the figuratively unwinding traces and tracks of human impulse. From the viewer's position in front of the digital screen, it is only a few yards, a short historical step, and a full ontological lunge backward to the original film version in its disheveled form as unspooled and criss-crossed "footage," reeled past us in a makeshift chamber of material wear and tear answering to the one conjured in different terms by Beckett's stage set. For in that adjoining "film lab," the overloaded 2,000-foot reel of celluloid—rendered necessary, in a kind of purist medial stunt on the director's part, to record the whole last monologue in one unedited take—has been unreeled and "strung up" in its friable rollercoaster of vulnerability. As if reversing the ordinary logic of screen production, its destiny is to be fed—only at this point, and thus well after the fact of both original broadcast and digital remediation—into the gnashing sprockets of the traditional Steenbeck editing machine (fig. 8). There the film—in the discrete feed of its separate frames, its intrinsic *filmedivision*—is now to be slowly devoured, worn thin, rubbed out.

The title of Beckett's play may well refer in part to the last tape from Krapp's own biographical archive that the title figure chooses to hear, made when he was a younger man in 1939, rather than to the one he is presently to record. The former audio "text" is wheeled round on a dated and clunky playback deck as his older self speaks back to it in rage and regret and then begins recording—in a new monologue (and that alternate claimant for the title spool)—his present dismissive cynicism about youth's spent "fire." In the gallery installation by the punning name *Steenbeckett*, that last tape is—by coiled and unwound association with the outmoded film strip as well, that final spun *bande* of cinematic apparition—not so much archived and museumized as atrophied, frayed raw, over days of exhibition time. No accident, surely, that this transmedial installation, playing between platform and manifestation, finds its cues in the play itself. When Hurt follows Beckett's own original theatrical instructions and all but personifies his aged recording machine during a remembered amorous incident, hugging it like the lost object of desire whose description it can only broadcast, not embody, it is then that a medium, varying the sense of Egoyan's fellow Canadian Marshall McLuhan, submits almost to its own *massage*. But so, too, does celluloid incur its own physical pressure in gallery execution, its own tangible but nonerotic friction. It does so precisely as time runs out not just on a human life and an antiquated magnetic technology but on the signature modernist medium of photomechanical film. Thus has the director materialized in emblematic but tangible surrender his own belatedly plastic footage—Egoyan's last reel—as a symbolic counterpart to the "wearish" man, timeworn and threadbare, mentioned in the first stage direction: scraped raw by time and disappointment like the current fate of the film itself, as opposed to the less (or differently) abradable material support of its afterlife in digital transmission.

Frampton, Broodthaers, Graham, Sietsema, Starling, Barba, Egoyan. Not just the low-resolution 16mm film of avant-garde screenings in the decade after Beckett's "realist" audiotape, but the whole institution of cinema, has become a museum piece—enfolding here the downbeat drama of more than one defeat at the hands of time. Beckett's snarling, guttural Krapp may well seem to incarnate the last rasp and wheeze of modernism, caught for video projection through—and as a last testament to—the film reel's own coiled translucent tape: a spooling anachronistic apparatus aptly cognate with the warhorse reel-to-reel tape deck used by a hero who dotes on the very word "spool."[5]

But even going in circles—as in spooloops—can be a downhill operation, as the further unreeling turns of Egoyan's celluloid mobile make clear. Between one modern screening space in immaculate electronic high-definition and the makeshift slaughterhouse of its preceding medium, where film is flayed alive over frictional time in a rehearsal of its own production (editing machine) rather than exhibition, there is a curious dialectic at work after all, though without any stable synthesis. A theater piece in electronic documentation stands opposed to the model—or celluloid "master print"—in precisely the latter's degeneration. Here are performances of the same text getting poised against each other amid the detritus of documentary (ethnographic) cinema as well across the otherwise airtight compartmentalization of media platforms. The resulting contrast works to return the mobile viewer of the installation to a kind of filmed-theater spectator after all, positioned there in real time before the rehearsed duration of a recorded play in its plastic manifestation. But this dual spectatorial vantage point is made available only when the audience is also directed to view the temporal degradation of its initial and costly 35mm record, as cultivated by the director in the first place to enhance the quality of a commercial video broadcast: a small-screen TV manifestation whose only (displaced) remnant is the editing room monitor in this new and punishing museum setting.

With his stressed footage abutted, a room away, by its own digital successor in the DVD screening—under a yoked contrast typical of Conceptualism 2.0—the traditional film director Egoyan, in this installation departure, has passed the plastic of his medium through the apparatus of production in a way that taps into an earlier moment in radical conceptual practice. In the mode of the late 1960s "Art and Destruction" movement, for instance, experimental filmmaker Jud Yalkut once covered a gallery floor with miles of appropriated celluloid to be trampled on in exhibition—as if in a materialized tactile pun on "footage"—under the title *Destruct Film*, putting any "viewer" (of the room, not the strips) in palpable touch with its underfoot (its underlying) materiality. This 1967 piece then further dismantles the anterior function of film screening by a mere slide show that slowly flashes fixed-frame images of the number cells (1-2-3-4 . . .) on the reel's normal leader, preparatory to the actual projected image in the usual course—and coursing—of the moving picture. In this half-a-century-old installation, reconstructed for the chronological walk-through of the 2016 Whitney exhibition "Dreamlands: Immersive Cinema and Art, 1905–2016," the chance of absorption in any spectacle has been replaced by a confrontation with its material and mechanical conditions instead, unthreaded, decelerated, canceled. Egoyan's much later work evokes, rather, and in light of electronics, the damage inherent to editing and projection themselves, in all their resulting parable of wornout mediation—rather than the more extreme destruction arranged, decades before by Yalkut, to autopsy film's primal matter and mechanics.

Thrice mediated in Egoyan's treatment, from film to video broadcast to digital file, and thus unmistakably transmedial in the force of such conjunction in gallery space, modernist theater returns upon itself, dramatically enough, in the real-time staging—or more to the point, the accelerated rehearsal—of its own obsolescence. This transpires according to the same material conditions that evoke the anagram (and palindrome) of *[spool::loops]*—namely, the intermittence that gets overridden (by engineered *span*) in the muted *snap* between film frames, their elided breach and sprocketed catch-up. Such is the pulsing stroboscopic skein masked by ocular continuity in the typical run of things. But this norm is worn away in Egoyan's installation trope by two *time frames* at once: a century's and a month's, spanning by inference the former hegemony of a medium and the duration of this one strip's installed gradual laceration. Film's symbolic abrasion, that is, is sacrificed to the newer transcription regime as if by ritual scarification. What, one can only ask, might Éric Rondepierre do with the photogrammic victims of this brutal celluloid loop?

Concerning all such ironic interfaces between imprint and succession, our current Scene's threefold discussion has tried coming at this issue from diverse but intersecting directions. We've noted how the variable orientation that relates ocular field to picture plane within the shifting planarity that constitutes the moving picture—the rotary motion behind or beneath its lateral movement—tends under Conceptualism 2.0, whether explicitly (Heinecken, Okiishi, Staehle, Starling, Barba, Arcangel, Lauschmann) or not (Sietsema, Banner, Saunders), to engage with contemporary digital options complementing or replacing the filmic strip. Next, after that chapter on "Pictureplaning," and in contrast to the televisual displacements of Turrell's "Magnetron" fixtures, it is the beam motion of McCall's "solid light films," long after his early place in the first wave of conceptual or materialist filmmaking, that is overtly revamped for a new century, not just by digital projection but—through subliminal computer editing—by the digital execution of a dated laboratory device in the reconfigured postnarrative "wipe." In contrast to these "Lightshown" shapes in McCall, subsuming digital edits to a fluent seamless succession, we've moved back to the forcefully marked *filmedivision* in the counter-cinema of Broodthaers, where the blown cover of continuity is enacted at the primary level not only of refused montage but of canceled animation effects. Attention has then been directed forward to a related transmedial effect, not between photography or painting and motion pictures, but between the latter sequencing of frames and the digital scan. For in Egoyan's work, the laboratory editing of filmic cinema, in its constitutive and divisible frame advance, is palpably obsolesced—before our eyes—by the Steenbeck wreckage of the moving strip, frame by discrete frame, in deliberate counterpoint to the playback of the filmed play's DVD transfer. With Krapp's final tape as reel-to-reel prototype, the theatrics of the absurd are thus recycled in the performance space of an unwound technological lastness conceived transmedium. Here, the aggravated pictureplaning of the scanned strip, in friable tension with the apertures of the editing machine, operates its own undoing from within the former machine of production.

Steenbeckett enacts, in this way, one kind of death drive. We turn next, in an exit piece on cinematic "Endscapes," to another. After such stripped-down materialist precision, sharpened by internal differentiation, as McCall's and Broodthaers's and Egoyan's—respectively: drawing versus sculpture versus "solid light" cinema; cataloging versus paging versus painting versus photography versus screen montage; theater versus film versus broadcast TV versus digital monitor—we move to a very different mode of deflected and renegotiated mediality. In contrast to the antinarrative temporality of timed light "screens," scrims, or "films" in McCall, and in equal contrast to the pending mortal closure of its theatrical source figured twice over by the unreeling spools of timeworn process in the installation *Steenbeckett*, we are next to take up a different case from the same year as McCall's recent Bahnhof exhibit: Michael Haneke's harrowing film *Amour* (2012), whose mortal crisis is off-loaded by art-historical transmediation onto the balked temporality of its own narrative drive, at which point, with shades of Broodthaers's *Voyage*, a throttled cinematic process substitutes painted canvases for celluloid progression.

[timed::out]

How to summarize the temporal emblematics we have so far watched develop under transmedial pressure—and not just in this present Scene of captured motion alone? Certainly Egoyan's work with the transmediation of *Krapp's Last Tape*, from an otherwise narrative filmmaker, fits the model of Balsom's "post-medium/postmortem" designation for contemporary gallery film. In its reflection on lastness itself, of filmic cinema as well as of magnetic tape, the one surviving version of the Beckett performance is the result of a DVD "loop" without spool, only disk. Other reductions are, as we know, more re-visionary yet. If McCall's projections, from the first, are "movies" without pictures, film without cinema, Broodthaers's variant from the same period of ferment offers stop-time imaging without figural animation, a filmic cinema without any motion but that of change itself, linear change over time, which is the medium to begin with of any and all movement in traditional projection and its simulated motor durations. In their thus opposite but still comparable transmediations—respectively, between painting or photography and screen "figuration," between "drawing" and sculpturesque projection—Broodthaers and McCall turn the time-machine of film inside out.

They inaugurate in this way a main thrust of counter-cinema renewed by the conceptualist gestures of projection 2.0 (even, in the latter case, by the same artist himself and his digital editing). This is a tendency in recent art making whose practitioners, as we're by now well aware, are as varied as they are many. In returning to the first ubiquitous commercial dissemination of binary technology in the digital rather than analog clock face, for instance, what Lauschmann's digital exercise in "growing zeroes" does—in another version of the photo/graphic hyporealm (as in Fontcuberta and others), in this case via the underlay of subnumeric modularity—is to render the time-based medium of video an exploration of time itself. But this is time as a manually materialized construct. In the most revealing instances, the medium-specifications of such a transmedial event do not enshrine a single support system; rather, they investigate the difference—via the internal differentiations—it makes. The same is true, in regard to an obvious structural rupture in the audiovisual mix of sound cinema, with the discrepant trajectories of analog soundtrack and morcellated image stream in Arcangel's reductive literalization of *Colors*. Same, too, in regard to time-based projection, with the cross-faded dates of their own filming in the calendrical superimpositions, evoking the intermittencies of the filmic strip itself, in Sietsema's metatemporal *At the Hour of Tea*. Or with the interstitial gaps, from four to eight seconds in length, of Staehle's digital chronologs, from whose video displays, with their own kind of time-based epistemography, the very condition of visibility emerges—and does so against the backdrop of the art-historical challenges as well as inspirations (impressionism, pointillism) recalled in his process as a sampling rather than a continuum. Or same as well with the transmedial soundscapes of Breder's "screenings," which probe to the inner curvature of sound waves themselves in their electronic transfer to an abstracted visual interface. So, too, even as still images, with the cinegraphs from Ruscha to Rondepierre that work to materialize the intermittence of temporal succession in the imprint system known as film—along with the media-historical "end" (Ruscha's titular allusion) that such a system's implicit time frames must oversee. In all this, of course, the "same with" or "so, too" is simply a marker for the variousness of related conceptual materializations when transmediation has, as its object, art.

Across both Scenes of self-splayed and analytically ramified display, our attention has in just this sense sought to define, or has at least tried delimiting, the transmedium condition as a staged (and thus reconceptualized) space between or among media assumptions. In McCall's work, the engaged audience actually in the physical sense *assumes that space*, walks within it, between and among its actual projections: takes on its optical responsibilities, as it were. In Broodthaers, there is only the resisted presumption of any actual space on screen. In the waiting and final example, Haneke's comparable but limited resistance is strategically targeted—and contained, or almost—within the normative phenomenology of a typical narrative film. After so much recent experimentation in the region of the digital (Egoyan and Starling and Arcangel and Staehle), we turn to the art of a still-filmic screen fiction whose implacable narrative drive (toward and including plot's ultimate telos in death) is interrupted by a transmedial collapse into image frames shorn of temporality, stripped of transition, and returned not to a modernist flatness but to their own denaturalized spatial (planar) expanse.

The example is revealing in its very anomaly. What Jameson identified as the true postmodernist "context" (that term a touchstone for Foster and Dworkin as well) in the initiatives of Conceptual art—its decided antimodernist stamp—stems, as we've explored it, from an allegiance not to aesthetic autonomy in the Greenbergian sense but to the "mediatic system" in its artificially installed spatial coordinates. With the tentacles of this system spreading everywhere since, the same "contextual" orientation persists as a shaping influence on works very far from what Krauss would identify as strictly and experimentally "post-medium," as our rounding back to a more traditional narrative format should next show. Under scrutiny in the case of Haneke's *Amour*—a scrutiny enforced by the climactic suspension of diegetic filmmaking within a mediatic realignment of image production—is the momentary crossing (or death) of realist film into a leveling dialectic with romantic painting as well as the latter's own aftermath in photography. This is to say that, in an impacted moment of psychic crisis and interface catastrophe, the bottom drops out of narrative altogether into a hyporealm of transmedial blockage and impasse.

A length of 35mm celluloid is what Haneke's film constitutes as material support; imaging is what it does—and in this case all but transmedially undoes by an exposed intrinsic disjunction whereby a plot that is suddenly *[timed::out]* puts the very temporality of its normal process in doubt, in a manner both abrupt and rupturing. Building on the plot's preceding transmediation between photograph and photogram, this climactic fracturing of continuity evokes yet again, we will find, the transmedial link between single-framed images and the viewed scene devised by cinema's audiovisual mirage of being-in-time. Such evocations have, of course, marked the decisive stress points, the impacted aesthetic labor, of many inspected artifacts in Scene Two, the screenings and even the blank luminous projections—but never more insistently, perhaps, than in what's left for us to view. Certainly Haneke's is one more (and in its own way extreme) planar manifestation that we look to, as well as at, in order to see with—that is, see something else *through*—and thereby reconceive.

Again, then, we confront the uneven development, though manifest dialogue, between conceptualist procedures and mediarchaeology. What brings us from Kosuth's oversized photostats to Rondepierre's outsize photograms—while leading us back to Duchamp and forward through Broodthaers to the likes of Egoyan or Lauschmann or Starling, let alone to a narrative film like *Amour*, with its own structuring summons to the predecessor media of photography and painting—is obviously not some chronological charting of Conceptualism 2.0 in its postmodern emergence and postmillennial escalation. Rather, the purpose is, and has been, to trace and re-estimate, rather than historically track, the broadening base(s) of transmedial experiment, from its low-tech ironies in the 1970s para-films of Broodthaers and McCall through the digital investigations of Staehle or Arcangel and on round, next, to the embeddedness of art-historical (and, more to the point, mediahistorical) cross-reference and disjunction in Haneke's more "conventional" filmmaking.

In this long arc of aesthetic exploration, it isn't that electronics changes everything. It is, instead, that computerized input is one more thing to register when an artifact or installation is cross-purposed, as well as just cross-wired, with other material ingredients and considerations in aesthetic practice. In some attempted wedding of technology and aesthetics, no mere paradigm of "post-medium" digital "convergence" would begin to cover such cultural transformations, especially in a practice keyed to this undeniable technological drift. Internal *divergence* rather—a reflexive diversification and realignment—is the investigative mode, especially in art concerned with audiovisual technologies both dominant and still emergent. As signaled repeatedly by those bifold colons in this discussion's own subsets, the most rigorously impacted transmedium works "split the difference" of their own facture or fabrication in the very event of conceptualization. They are reversibly divided against themselves to conquer the otherwise unexamined through the work of new specification. As such, their inferences are arrowed inward even as they may point beyond themselves to shifts in an instrumentalized media culture on which their various inutilities at least momentarily—and even if only figuratively, from within their own digital facilitation—pull the plug.

Endscapes

For all the interplay of technique and technology explored by the manifold works behind us in these pages, at least one demarcation has been relatively clear-cut from the start: whereas mixed media works (even most multimedia works) are concerned with the material poetics of admixture, transmedium works are drawn to the conceptual logistics of mediation. So one way to generalize the Concept evinced by the perceptual objects we've encountered is to ask what we've *seen* by looking. The broad answer: medial operations under analysis from within their own conflationary display. Whether by the force of overload or understatement in a given aesthetic machination, hesitation leads to re-estimate. What thereby comes under assessment in case after case, through the divergence of potentially competing modes of realization, is a zone of audiovisual investment both occupied and *crossed*: not just acknowledged but conceptually engaged.

The contextualist definitions of "a medium" we began with, from Dworkin and Foster, derived from an implied common query. It could be put this way: by what received or revised understanding does the material of an object become its medium, become *a* medium—or find itself unexpectedly denied that status? The transmedium emphasis, we can now realize, begins with a complementary question, posited and probed from the inside out: what is it about the social as well as technical context of mediality that gets addressed, even baffled, by works of internally divergent material presentation? To recognize a medium, you need to know the network in which it operates; to investigate rather than merely accept that network, you may need to test it against the internal variables of its carrying effects. Where materiality becomes conveyance, the discerned layering of its often-manifold platforms is part of what it delivers. It is in this transitive sense, most potently, that purposes are crossed only in the mode of being attentively traversed.

Crucially, the form of any such second-order delivery system is its tangible conceptualization. This is where the works of the transmedial initiative take their place in a debated lineage of "ideation" in Conceptual art, a movement whose exclusion of traditional aesthetics, as such, is regularly seen as germinal and definitive.[1] But mediation is hardly quarantined along with aesthetics. If it therefore seems hasty, or at best vague, to assert that art after modernism exists in a "post-medium condition," that's certainly not because the thrust—the original breakout—signaled by the term, as illustrated by Broodthaers's initiatives, isn't clear. To be sure, art since conceptualism is no longer policed by a dichotomy between essentialist and dispersed, pure versus mixed, chaste versus promiscuous. But getting beyond the straitjacketing logic of abstract modernism doesn't require tethering all nuances of medium to the sidelined "post" of an overthrown reign of essentialist procedures. Why should a suspended quest for essence vitiate the very question of medium altogether? Recent artists certainly know better. For mediality itself is what many of them set out to conceptualize, often by first confounding its determinations. In graphic art, for instance, this mediacentric stress by no means reflects merely some unfinished business of a lapsed purist regime. It mobilizes, instead, the ongoing vigilance by which visual making may seek to make visible how we see.

The drawback of Krauss's widely circulated term, then, insofar as it may deflect one's attention from the process (rather than the valorized distillation) of medial interplay, is that the license, or simply relaxation, it implies is likely to miss the specific irony of technique in some of the most compelling work now being done. With its counterparts in sound art, this is work addressed to a retinal acquiescence from which such wryly estranging efforts themselves draw back—with their attempted fresh purchase on a social space of hypertrophic mediation. Under the shadow, or in the glare, of ever-new medial prosthetics, the noninstrumental inventions we've reviewed have a way, many various ways, of looking cross-eyed at this global saturation of image technology. Again: *[concept::dual]*. It is the double vision of these material formats—inducing us to *think transmedium*—that makes for the engaged cognitive work of their often-oblique materializations. The tacit procedural reversal in all this is cultural as well as art-historical: where Conceptual art once displaced the medial purism of aesthetic practice by its demediated idea or critique, Conceptualism 2.0, under pressure of new media, takes up as art, in densely material formats, the very idea of a medium. That is why the "Prelim" looked ahead to the objects tabled for discussion not as postmedial but rather, in their intensely worked materiality, as something more like *ultramedial*.

Everything depends, within this heightened interplay of transmissive forms, on the individual balancing act of the composite. To vary a biblical adage in application to such a media rather than a moral economy, and in response to postpurist methods that remain underspecified in particular works rather than aesthetically preformulated: where little is "given," much may be asked. Recognition begins in inquiry. This we've seen—and done our share of. Yet a certain disciplinary irony has shadowed these pages, one never too late to acknowledge head-on. It has probably been hard to miss. Discussion of a growing body and range of new media (or otherwise cross-mediated) art ventures, even though pursued in their local nuance and wider inference by a literary and film critic rather than an art historian, can seem less like an interdisciplinary stretch on his part than a retrenched commitment. Which is one way of saying that this book is as far afield as it seems from anything now going by the name of digital humanities. Certainly hermeneutics (rather than "data interpretation") is no longer the chief field of play, let alone home turf, in humanities scholarship under such a broad-gauged new initiative in archive mining and display. To judge from academic hiring patterns, digital priorities now tend to subsume rather than supplement the agendas of traditional humanities. Confronted, then, with aesthetic ventures bent on transmedial *specification*, such new scales of aggregate inquiry are a natural mismatch. Art-historical scholarship may traditionally have been more often segregated from art criticism and art theory than comparable partings of the ways in literary study, but never so much so as now—when digital "interests" are so often split between matters of facilitation and examined aesthetic constitution, or between the instrumental and the media-theoretical.

In this respect, for transmedial art the burgeoning work of digitized humanist investigation has at least one curious and notable result, less by way of overt backlash than through an unspoken division of cultural labor. After many other sea changes, digital innovations in scholarship (especially of the more statistical or positivist stamp) may lately seem complemented by, rather than concentrated on, actual digital artifacts. Contemporary galleries tend, that is, to house as much investigative work, as much theoretical discourse even—with a deflationary wit and concision unique to display, and often, as we know, denominated "art research"— as do the offices and lecture halls of a former critical bastion. It's not just that the digital ironies of transmedial work may go unnoted by academic commentary; it's that these works' own tacit (or supplemental) commentary on media regimes has more analytic grip and critical bite than a good deal of digital scholarship on any subject.

This is to say that aesthetics, too, like social and economic exchange at large, has its checks and balances, its reaction-formations, its displaced procedures and recouped priorities. With the sometimes amorphous will to electronic scholarship sweeping across the protocols of one discipline after another in claiming an ever "bigger picture" of historical trends, the results are often productive enough on their own terms. Yet a growing proportion of aesthetic analysis per se, and in particular when directed at the computerized audiovisual signal in perceptual culture, falls to artworks themselves rather than to institutional discourse. So it is that elucidations in this line—however strenuously elusive—arrive from practice at least as often as from scholarly comment. If computers can at times seem leading humanists by the nose, computer art often responds by taking an increasingly ignored bull by the horns in the arena of analytic detachment and exaction. As the emergent work of digital humanities tends to zoom out with its new tools, backing away from the inherent contours of textuality (visual or verbal) to broader grids of pattern recognition in regard to genres, sales figures, circulation routes, and the like, Conceptual art's alternate tendency comes all the clearer by contrast.[2] Exploratory electronic constructs in exhibition mode, for instance, together with the parallel work of artists equally freed from canonical medium-allegiance, have moved on their own to investigate precisely the impact of mediations new and old on the human sensorium and its cognitive proclivities.

It isn't the case, then, that Conceptualism 2.0 closes hermetically upon its own new-media terms, or their inevitable digital horizon, in some arcane retreat from the social field. Such art is more and more urgently contextual the more technical it becomes. Where academic scholarship, with its recent drive toward data gathering, increasingly *works* the digital vein, electronic Conceptual art is more likely to worry it, to approach it with a perplexing and user-unfriendly new purposiveness. To put it in terms earlier proposed in connection with the ironies of the "reverse skeuomorph," this art, faced with the latest spate of "data visualization," may seem answering to the lure of computer facilitation by the *inconveniencing* of vision itself. As amply sampled by now, such art sharpens the contemporary edge of a decades-long transformation in conceptual practice that may well appear to have more interpretive traction—and hence a keener grasp of sensory manipulation and its ironies—than analytic projects in the (formerly hermeneutic) fields of scholarly criticism. As we've also seen again and again with such recent art formats, interpretive discourse of some sort is typically requisite not just in contemplation but *in situ*—as if it were all but internal to the cognitive aesthetic at stake in certain exhibition works. It is called upon in order to ground (rather than merely round out) the aesthetic procedure in question: to call up the sometimes invisible complexities of generative functions for a nonetheless reflective and critical recognition. I used to think such works were just too difficult and tricky to assess, even access, without prose backfill. The explanatory gloss seemed frequently essential, though not actually central. I've grown to suspect, instead, the broader analytic ecology I'm here proposing, whereby artists—and not least digital artists—are, if only by default, the new exploratory hermeneuts in an age of electronic positivism, working to this extent against the bitmap grain of their own data feeds in the global cult of information.

It's hard to ignore the fact that many recent art works mobilize a rarefaction and subtlety, a close and deep "reading," increasingly out of fashion in academic exchange. A certain evolution in practice makes itself felt in this way. With the first forays of Conceptual art in the 1960s, there was a tendency toward the narrowing of the aesthetic, in any recognizable mode, to the thetic: to propositional thesis. In contrast, the transmedial dialectic of Conceptualism 2.0 recovers a more palpable attention to the ferrying of idea by form—and often by a formal network witnessing, through irony or indirection, to its own digital input. This electronic presence alone, in gallery or text art, would hardly render marginal the traditional literary or visual critic; that's happening anyway, one hears. But there is a curious compartmentalization afoot when the frequent digital complexities of transmedial art are brought so seldom into contact with the electronically generated templates of humanist or "neohumanist"—or even avowedly posthumanist—inquiry. Even as digital implementation is offered, and advertised, to refocus academic attention at every level, it is left to certain new media constructs themselves—along with nonelectronic works operating in their medium-quizzical vicinity—to deliver both artifact and its supplementary discourse at once, text and explication, instance and principle, *objet* or installation and its analyzed modes of manifestation. If choosing to, of course, the critic may enter the conversation by tacit invitation at any point—but enter it, more to the point, on the work's own proffered terms.

How to determine those aesthetic terms? That's been our question. From a curatorial (rather than a critical) perspective, an indirect clarification in terminology and classification has been recently afforded. The new Whitney Museum's much-debated shift in exhibition logic, for its 2015 move to downtown Manhattan, involves separating exhibited works only by artist and chronology, no longer by medium (reversing the former quarantine of painting from sculpture, from drawing, from photography, and so forth)—and thus respecting the way artists in any given period may work "across media." Such a principled loosening of rubrics is suggestive even for our special purposes. This new dispensation might, in the long run, incline toward an enhanced hospitality not just to such cross-sectional displays but to individually inmixed works operating "across media" in their own formal system—or at least provide a more vividly diversified space for their contextualization. Imagine the yield from showing Heinecken's screen-grab televisual slideshows and enlarged quasi-filmic photographic transparences not just together, but together with works, for instance, like those video/pigment palimpsests by Ken Okiishi previously inserted into the Whitney's own last uptown Biennial. Not to mention displaying these latter chromatic laminations alongside the overpainted photographs (rather than earlier photorealism) of Gerhard Richter. Gathering together such works from the most recent historical periods of experimentation, even though strategically sorted for comment between fixed and moving image, has been, of course, this book's own curatorial principle.

Scene One: the fixed image or plastic form in its transmedial function—whether manually or digitally generated. Scene Two, often staged by the same artists: the time-based image—whether plastic in its support or digital. In each case, the image or form is located, by entirely intrinsic determinations at first, within the scene of its own transmedial context. Now static, now kinetic, the image moves between medial assumptions and supports as its very purport, before moving out to the implicit communal (communicative), environmental, or political impact of its operations. This is the gist of Conceptualism 2.0, each viewed image or construct organizing its own mode of purview, historical as much as technological—and, at the very least, topical by default. Is it any wonder that such objects of and for art, such new purposes in making, cannot help but speak to us—and we back to them, in ways like those attempted here—from a shared social space in which so many hours of our lives are themselves lived across media?

It is in this respect, long after a reflexive modernism, that artists still answer the *call* of their materials—the better to call them out. Such is the continued vocation of even the latest transmedial artists—including Rondepierre in two-way transit, now between filmic study and photography, now between cinema and digital streaming; Fontcuberta between photographic history and visual epistemology; Sietsema and Saunders between painting and indexical record across both their still and their time-based works; Starling between filmic cinema and digital trace, elsewhere between recorded image and its mere computer generation. Such praxis operates always, at one level, in the abstract. This is because the new museum mode of installation "research" is conducted by its ad hoc media historians in their composite (rather than oxymoronic) role as practicing theorists. These new makers or fabricators, these art workers, "search" inward, examining materials and means, for the shared secrets and ludic collusions their own transmedial constructs have brought to our notice. In this respect, the "ouroborus" logic cultivated so steadily (and headily) by Starling can stand as the latest emblem of an entire trend. Time and again, it is through the linked (and often looped) materiality of this conceptual mode's resulting *objets*— its concretized new *objectives* in all their variant cognitive instigations—that such resilient aesthetic making serves to plumb its own medial depth. This, then, is precisely the research *discipline* of these "objects of study" in both senses of that phrase: a study at once intrinsic and solicited, inherent in form and invited from the viewer in response.

A good part of this book's evidence has been amassed to show how electronic art may in this sense foreground the medial flashpoints in one's response to preceding aesthetic ventures (or simultaneous ones by the same artists under different material conditions of experiment). On this score, a conjectural gallery arrangement might be entertained to clarify. For all it would take is to find "Old Media Wing" on a major museum's floor map for us to recognize head-on the crux of temporal periodization in its strictly relative terms—the crux, yes, as well as the retrospective vantage it can broker. If these pages have made good on only one claim, it is, I trust, just this: that thinking of the progressive newness of new media innovation makes us *think transmedially*—and not just about art's latest experiments. We are put, and kept, in mind of the latent and debated material basis of all visual production since the modernist event of paint on canvas was first upset—and set into new perspective—by Concept: by idea rather than isolated medial idealization.

In pursuing recent materially keyed practice in this line of descent, our tandem Scenes of fixed and moving images, framed and frame-advanced respectively—as this very difference is about to come crashing in Haneke— have operated in the conceptualized realm between a plurality and a composite. We have not been preoccupied with new media at large—which are everywhere, if aging by the day. Nor focused on some refortified sectors of purity, of cultivated medium specificity—which are, as they say, history. Attention has been aimed, instead, at local sites of combinatory medial *specification*—marked out either by divergence or conflation or by each in turn. That's been the focus—and in part the basis for any implicit critique concerning the discovered force of the objects under investigation. Certainly the high modernist impetus toward internal coherence, integration, essence, "presence," has inevitably lost a good deal of its communicative force by the time the posthuman subject has been understood as no more than a function of communication technology to begin with: a signal conduit. If we do more than just pass our days in a thoroughly mediated environment—existing, as it were, *in media(s) res*—but find ourselves wholly mediatized in our own neurological right, the task asked of art is mostly that it slow over certain articulated nodes of this assumption long enough to test its manifestation. This happens by resistances *in* the system, rather than *to* it: interferences, alerts, disturbances—not redemptive interventions, just skewed traversals, roughenings, extra recognitions.

And we can step farther back yet in order to compass this. If, according to Systems theory, form in art (in a variant of the "bared device" of early formalism) is what makes mediums make a perceptible difference (and all but defines them in so doing), then the formative work of transmedial art—amid the mass saturation not only of "the media" but of the networked perceptual subject as such—is to select from the field of technological prosthetics some telling moment of analysis rather than of sheer operation. Art becomes a quite delimited effort to seize up the system—if only long enough, if not to size it up, at least to perceive its local coalescences across disparate material supports or conditions: to try knowing for a moment, with some clarity, what's in front of us. So it is that strange conversions and syntheses not only devise new perceptual formations but engage new forms of attention—and less in the mode of spectacle and spectation than, again, of analysis. Historical and technological turning points are often embedded as medial pivots. In turning the track-lined TV image into a line drawing or a woodcut (Celmins, Baumgartner); in turning the archival print of distant violence into a degraded monumental jpeg (Ruff); in turning the canonical painting or photograph into a simulated bitmap and thumb-nail search file (Fontcuberta); in turning the optical plane (erotically veiled '50s TV screen, painted HDTV monitor) into a laminate of analog or digital remediations of previously broadcast images (Heinecken, Okiishi); in turning wall art or sculpture or cinema into the reductive pour or pulse of radiant light alone (McCall, Turrell); in turning the optics of reflective sterling silver into computer-generated polymer sculpture (Mann); in turning found newsprint photos into simulated sculptural environments for recapture in high-definition digital prints (Demand); in turning his own film footage over first to digital storage and then to the reverse editing of gradually eradicating machinic frottage (Egoyan); in turning the image of an already outmoded photomechanical negative into a lackluster update of a nineteenth-century trompe l'oeil painting on a turned-over photo reprint of a post-Impressionist masterwork (Sietsema)—in all such transforms, and more, the effect *turns conceptual* at just the fold(s) between alternate technical manifestations. It is there that the material conflations or competing substrates are seen specifying not *a* medium but the formal irony at stake in each generative field of the in-between.

[grid::works]

In frequent play, as noted, is a kind of triangulation. But this involves vectors that may well become diagonals in a more schematically imagined field of differential force. In so saying, I invoke two previous touchstones of discussion that are now found to intersect. In "Scene One (Image Frames)," with its picturings stilled rather than installed in sequenced motion (and flagged by the reciprocity of *[ground::figure]* as rubric), we saw how Sietsema's *Untitled figure ground study* might help in understanding the refused visual seductions of the same artist's film work. And earlier yet, I had mentioned the debt of my double-coloned formats to Rosalind Krauss on the figure/ground dialectic as it is resynthesized in her view of the modernist grid, rendering moot the difference between foredrop and foundation across an insistently rectilineated surface. We noted there, via Krauss, how the antithetical elements of *[ground::figure]*, or vice versa, speak to each other in terms of the semiotic square, traditionally resolved at the top (in her particular application) into a figural image, and then below in the realm of double negation as the neither/nor (neither figure nor ground) of abstract modernist gridwork—not just as schematic underlay but as the canvas's dominant optic. In this light, a similar pattern—when pushed one level down, as we've been doing ever since, to the material support of the already given image—can help in mapping a viewer's cognitive disposition toward the immanence of one mediating function (or more) in certain complex works.

The latest phase of transmedial art may often seem a mode not merely of Conceptualism 2.0, with digital platforms either as models or as active modes of image support and production. Crossing between media in order to produce a given perceptual effect, including its often elusive affect, the multiplied optics and sonics of transmedial work can seem like Conceptualism[2]—raised to the power of itself, squared into a whole new order of reflex recognition. And so we arrive at the clarifying square (in a nonmathematical sense) of semiotic cross-determination. This is the template anticipated, early on, as lying behind the graphics of those ongoing subheads—as they are invited to widen now, in fuller explication, from the near approximation of a vertical gallery frame to the squaring off of a transmedial sign system: [] ... [ ] ... [::].

According to the bracketed four-point schema central to Jameson's (as well as Krauss's) approach, though never applied by him to the "mediatic system" he designated as key to postmodernist art, one notes how sectors of recognition divulge the transpositions and transits on which they are based. When the horizontal poles of contrariety (categorical "opposites") intersect with the diagonals of contradiction (absolute "negations") on the implied lateral axis defined by the initial binarity (as graphed below for the instigating contrary of image versus its support), flanking terms seem to clarify each other in a momentarily stable fashion to the left and right of the square. At the same time, the upward and downward apex of the remaining parallel quadrants also emerge to complement rather than cancel each other. The immanent *both/and* (as in the phenomenological fusion at the top of the diagram) may in fact depend on the constituent *neither/nor* that underlies it in the fourth quadrant. Say: immanence versus substrate(s). A run of photographic transparencies generates the projected firing of a hand gun at an innocent victim in a cop thriller, and the medium is filmic cinema. If the assault arises from a DVD disc via an electronic bitmap, the medium is then, one could argue, postfilmic cinema—or at least cinema's digital transfer. But with Cory Arcangel's digital scrubbing of such a remediated Hollywood film (the police procedural *Colors*) for its constituent pixel streams (colors), the question of a medium, in any commercially available sense, is referred away to its double negation as a transmedial interplay. Neither celluloid film nor digital copy, neither cinema nor any other representational system, what we find is projection and analysis at odds with each other in the same protracted loop. Operating here is a *substratification* in transit between the now unseen original and its linear unravelment not as plot line but as slit-scan bitstream. And what we see in Sietsema's films, or before them in Broodthaers's—resistant in different ways, as they are, to the coherence or impetus of a moving image—is not a yielding up, in some distilled essence, of the cinematic medium (the both/ and of indexical frame and motion) but rather a motorized transmediation across the registers of textuality, painting, photography, and serial strip.

In such counterplays of conception behind perception, think of it as follows in the framework of a semiotic square (see ex. 1). Arrayed here in the most general binarist terms, the coterminous field of support and image locates—first, foremost, and topmost—the manifestation in question (the mediated event) through its discernible formal markers. So it appears— until reduced (or referred away) on the left to its raw functional matter and on the right to an idealized sense of its disembodied depiction. In the works that have held (held open) our interest, the place and play of mediality underlie both the image and the support together—and certainly hover, waver, beneath any transparent convergence as picture or portrayed scene. This field or function of mediality operates within—and across—the spectrum of visibility but does so beneath any unified vision. It amounts, in effect, to the materialized but subrepresentational features of a sheer and shared medial *provision*, which may well involve a reciprocal transfer between constituent systems. As such, it is a case of an undergirding potential understood differentially, analytically, in the role of a composite *[plat::formation]*. In the uppermost synthesis of the charting below, one graphs the means by which the material support is made to realize the "manifestation" of its image in the process (or not) of cohering as a "representation." The medium per se is what regularly goes unperceived as such in this "materialization" of its material. Such is the status quo, indeed the modus operandi, of standard representation: to keep a recessive mediality in (its) place: active but tacit. Yet this medial provision is just what may seem forced to the surface, in works of uniquely aggravated or conflicted display, by certain transmedial pressures (just as much as by a former mandate of medium specificity and the denigration of the representational urge in its abstractionist bias):

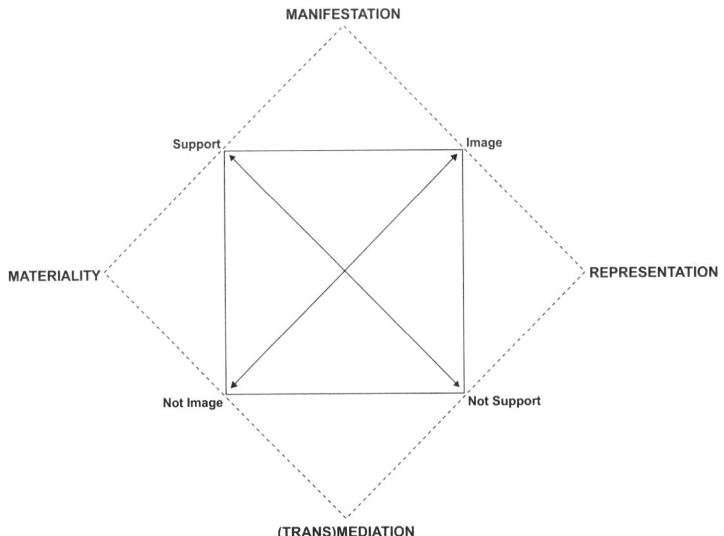

The diagram is its own map of modalities in action. Much depends, of course, both on genre and on level of apprehension. When an image is manifested in a painted surface, for instance, it partakes of application and picture at once, a materiality made visible in its aesthetic function (Luhmann one last time). As sheer representation, however—That's Mt. St. Victoire! Look at that tabletop with fruit!—there is no materiality left in the optic of phenomenological investment. Such is the case even while—appreciating the image as a postimpressionist *treatment*—one may still note, by separate apprehension, the painterly work of picturation very much in play.

This is where we have needed to adjust the emphasis of this so-called square of opposition for the frequently "tensed" nature (both senses again: structural and historical) of transmedial work, where discrepancy may open upon diachrony in a longer view of the seen. Typically, this logical schema is best at capturing exactly such "oppositions" (as between picture and execution) in the lateral and diagonal axes, as these generate the very force field that the square is out to delimit against any presumption of stable binaries. Less commonly stressed in its application, and unmarked in its usual layout, is the vertical interplay between the upper and lower horizontal dyads. The "neither/nor" is not simply the negation of the "both/ and"—but at times its hidden condition. That's why the deployment by Krauss in *The Optical Unconscious*, though borrowed from Jameson's *Political Unconscious*, is more immediately instructive for our purposes than his application. Jameson exercises his cognitive mapping, with this semiotic tool, upon whole swaths of narrative material whose ideological horizon or blind spot is often abstract and unlocalized, pervasive. For Krauss, in contrast, when applying the semiotic method to individual (and indeed often foursquare) painted objects in modernism, the zone of double negation (for her, the neither/nor of figure/ground) stands more obviously in relation to visual "manifestation"—as do the transmedial shuttlings we've pursued—on the loosely psychoanalytic model of "latent" versus "manifest" content (though not spelled out in precisely these terms by her treatment). In the works we've considered, the medial intersection—and often its own tacit archaeology—waits latent, recessive, in the discerned (or puzzled out) image. It rests implicit there not merely as the work's conditioning possibility, as composite form, but as its retinal intent under analysis: the return of its repressed infrastructure from within an often enigmatic congestion of image. Think of it this way: an opacity of manifestation rendering suddenly urgent its composite latency of generation. Recall, for instance, the different "glitchings" or "irresolutions" that characterize the pixelated jpegs of Ruff and the intermittent digital sampling of Staehle. The support is imprinted photographic paper in one case, digital monitor in the other, but that's where the question of "medium" (and its cross-purposing) only begins rather than ends.

Recognition might unfold as follows in the most typical cases. When neither the image (representational or otherwise), nor any stable medium or platform recognized to manifest it, is held in steady focus, attention may shift with (and within) certain works, certain provocations, to that contributory give-and-take that queries image, or its imageering, from the traversed bases of its own multiple—or sometimes overtly deceptive—input. Such is a neither/nor where, short of singling out one material substrate or another as dominant, perception tracks the aesthetic manifestation transmedium. We've seen this called out again and again by that shorthand of the double colon, often around an overt grammatical hinge like *[brush::painting]* (*of* and *by*). A related bifold interplay, for example, is denominated by *[apparatus::theory]* in flagging the inherence of the theory in the machination. Same, for instance, with *[vision::cones]*, where the ocular cone of vision finds its own means of perception represented by metonymy in a conical light show. But these abutted polarities do not just evoke local conflations. They condense a broader proposition about transmedial logistics. Here is just where a foursquare semiotics of means, rather than meanings, helps frame—at its lower edge especially—the dynamized field of play to which our investigations have repeatedly been drawn. With no settling-out as a medium-specific distillation, here again—graphed in schematic form now—is the typical crossfire of reciprocal specification that defines the transmedial interface.

This is why the associated results of the [::] habit—marking the analytic gesture of this book's our subheads—deserve some further audit or tallying: not to solidify an overlooked rigor of method (which it was never meant to boast) but to assess in retrospect its flexion and variety, its deliberately ad hoc cross-plaitings. The format was, after all, broached in the first place to compress, almost rebus-like, what could be fully unpacked only when cumulatively reviewed. The paradigm is scarcely airtight—and was intended from the start as the opposite of a categorical straitjacket. With varying obliquity in their formulated responses to the quirkiness of a given artifact or installation, these subheads nevertheless share a center of gravity in the swivel mechanism of the double colon. Repeatedly, inherently, in the reverb of its implied byplay, such punctuation does more than offer a reversible turnstile between terms. For one thing, this switchpoint often interrupts a staid phrasing (or syllabification) of concept, implicitly breaking it open to a four-point orientation not unlike that of the semiotic grid. No simple "third term" escapes the yoking in a suggestion of clean synthesis. It is rather, as spelled out time and again, the "squaring" of opposition that is invoked by the bonding parameters of the brackets. To pick another example almost at random, *[movie::still]* (Ruscha) locates neither the one nor the other, neither projected movement nor affixed image, but the mutual inherence of each in the neither/nor—and ultimately both/and—of segmented sequence. Elsewhere, the bonding of *[sound::shapes]* plays not on the shaping work of sound alone but, in the new combined anomalies of 3-D printing and voice-recognition software (Brument), on the neither/nor of vocal formation versus spatial form—yet in computerized transfiguration, nonetheless, to the both/and of polymer manifestation. So it goes, never predictable in advance, seldom decidable at a glance.

However intractably mixed the mode in these investigated works of transmedial—and often mediarchaeological—practice, a twofold recognition persists. As with trompe l'oeil painting registered as a matter of surface and of marked illusory depth alike, or cinema as a matter (also elusively materialized) of both separately fossilized film frames and their rotary and serial reanimation, it remains the case that when a manifold artifact is apprehended in such layered terms, the materiality is no longer coherently or exclusively "supportive." Instead, one sensed technical dimension of an abiding effect may become "cited" as such in its manifestation—and perhaps thematized as a result. As we are about to see in Haneke's film work, such is the relation not just of digital video to analog tape in one film, or of early twentieth-century photography to cinema in another, but—across a more radical medial gap—of film frames to canvas planes.

Yet it should aid in approaching all this, with both Rondepierre's and Saunders's celluloid studies again in mind, to see how the pitched contrast of such framing—between painted surface and kinetic projection—can nonetheless seem tacitly modeled on the inherent transmediation between photo imprint and motor image already coded in the estranging notion of the sectioned out and bracketed-off *[photo::gram]*. Indeed, one way to conceive the disappearing act, or say the formative entr'action, of celluloid screen movement—generated from an interstitial traction between fixities—is to situate its categorical slippage by semiotic mapping. Where Krauss builds on Benjamin's "optical unconscious" in respect to bodily motions never before halted for recognition until the historical moment of snapshot photography, there is also the wholesale photogrammic "preconscious" of the frame-sectioned film strip, its imprints no sooner impressed into service than retinally suppressed.[3] For our transmedial purposes, then, when quadratically understood, there is either photography or cinematography, the alternatives only phenomenologically (but not materially) resolved in the once all but oxymoronic function of the "motion picture"—or, more symptomatically, "the flickers." The pure flanking contraries, to the left and right side in this imagined foursquare mapping—namely, photography but not cinematography, cinematography but not photography—would be manifested in the form of photo print and screen image respectively. Finally, the neither one nor the other, yet the generative transfusion of each, would be identified and isolated (*beneath* in the square's bottom sector; *before* in the process) by the arrested transit of the photogram in work like Rondepierre's—and like Haneke's, by a less direct association, in his latest film.

[motion::pictures]

By rotary impetus, motion *pictures* movement on screen by moving single pictures, their separate and divisible existence recessive to projected display. From the start, in planning eventually to clarify the place of narrative cinema (unlike the very different films by Broodthaers or McCall or Sietsema or Starling) as a pertinent exhibit in a book on conceptual media, I knew I would need, in the long run, to make two associated points. Their time has come. As we know, Krauss's terms oscillate between "post-medial *condition*" and a "post-medial *position*"—intending on her own part no apparent distinction. They are alternate terms for the whole innovative program signalized and in part triggered for her by Broodthaers's early 1970s film work. The terms thus waver between a material a priori (condition), more or less ironic in the case of Broodthaers's gestures, and a rhetorical attitude (position) toward the very idea of mediality and its concerted purifications. By way of a closed-circuit middle ground, the initial point that needs insisting on, then, is that the transmedial *disposition*—a typically assertive, self-conscious, sometimes even insolent perspective—comprises both of these categories by definition and at once: positioned in transit between conditions so as to take a position on them.

And there, implicit, is the second point already: by being conceptual before material, the transmedial disposition can even operate from within an apparent single medium so as, in a given passage, to cross in contemplation between alternatives it only conjures rather than instances or activates. That's how our gathering evidence concerning such transmedial installations has taken on a broader interest, in reflection, than could be exhausted in a considered account of their own dual or reversible transpositions, their fused and triangulated materialities, and so forth. The transmedial is an attitude or stance, finally, rather than a technical application—a certain aesthetic leaning and focus, a disposition *toward*—and on the spectator's part, as much as the artist's. It is, as I've kept saying, a mode of analysis, of interpretation: one brought to bear on imaginatively cross-bred, as well as directly cross-wired, installations.

This is the notably the case with a seemingly straightforward late work by an artist earlier preoccupied more openly with transmedial parameters. Three "art house," if by no means "experimental," films in a row by Austrian director Michael Haneke serve to outline, in this respect, a certain gradual tamping down and internalization of mediatic counterplay. Shot in high-definition digital video about covert VHS taping and its initially enigmatic playback, *Caché* (*Hidden*, 2006) has no interest in keeping its optic means in hiding—inserting us, rather, into precisely the cognitive (and ethical) space between perception and its record. *The White Ribbon* (2009) in (back)dated black-and-white—digitally enhanced for maximum saturation and contrast—has its own inbuilt aura of mediarchaeology. In contrast, the realist color treatment of *Amour* (2012) seems farther removed from any such optical reflexivity until it locks down on a climactic moment thereof in the chromatics of mere painted canvas—and moves us, in the process, to rethink its own opening effect of a blacked-out screen (and soon its answering closure) in line with this abrupt shift in perspective from filmed to painted "space." In this way, a dialectic emerges between the not-film (of strictly painted frames, though of course reshot) and the anti-cinema of wholly unexposed celluloid (so-called black leader).

In art-historical terms, even the most obvious contrast—as between Haneke's searing narrative art and the 1970s avant garde—cannot be total. Exhibited along with the unexposed flicker films of contemporaneous experiment, Broodthaers's paradoxical cinema of the paginated still (now a nautical painting, now a photograph) was one reductionist dead end—and conceptualist breakthrough—in an isolation of the image frame. That, we can readily grant. Yet four decades later, a film like *Amour*, busy with matters of life and especially death, can nonetheless articulate them in a moment of transmedial impact (and extreme optical impaction) that revisits in abrupt recoil the entire register of what Stanley Cavell calls, in a definitive formulation of film's ontology, "the world viewed."[4] With an emphasis on verisimilitude rather than documentation, Cavell would seem to mean, in effect, *a* world viewed, but not in the sense that painting can give us, instead, merely pictures of a world. On screen, in Cavell's account, the mediation is more immediate. In a crucial moment under Haneke's lens, however, the typically viewed world of cinema, its narrative space, loses the effect of that immanence altogether—a world present to me, but to which I am not present (in Cavell's paradigm)—and stages, instead, a double absentation.

Yet, in its very negation, the result of this suspended determination of the image plane is, as we're now to see, transmedial through and through—and as internally finalizing in its way as the blank black screens that begin and end Haneke's narrative, between which elapses the flashback structure of a long dying and a nonetheless sudden death (by euthanasia). We may come to think of these canceled filmic moments—the default to painting, the cut to black—as, equally, the endscapes of cinema in complementary forms of absent motion picturing.[5]

The brief late scene I have in mind takes everyone by surprise—by taking, as it were, no one into its detached line of sight. Haneke's bleakly uncompromising plot of domestic mercy-killing stops dead just at its last point of crisis, giving way for what is only a little more than half a minute—though it seems like the nonnarrative eternity it also figures—to decinematized extracts from the archive of romantic landscape painting. The agonized couple on whom the camera has been riveted from one mundane scene of humiliating ministration to the next, she withering in pain, he suffering in anticipation of the worst, are for once nowhere to be seen. Nor seeing. Instead: just pictures at a nonexhibition, given over only to us—but with the full force of our exclusion as well (as example, fig. 9). This shock effect is as muted as it is indisputable. Its affront to beholding within the regime of the visible, its aggressive showing forth—yet stripped of all theatrics in the process—is one that the broader purview of Michael Fried's art history can help bring to focus. On Fried's showing, there is, at one pole, the theatrical model of painting, angled at—and in effect addressing—the viewer through the delegated gestures of its figured subjects, however deflected their sightlines. And then there are paintings that withdraw all such display into the nontheatrical absorption of their figured bodies, by which images we, as viewers, are shifted from specular passivity to our own borrowed, modeled, or at least associated absorption (rather than detached audiencehood). That is at least one blunt outline of a complex theory tracked across many periods, styles, artists, media, and separate monographs from Caravaggio through Courbet down to contemporary photography.[6] In these rough terms, certainly any dialectic installed by the transmedial moment in Haneke's *Amour*—the devolution of cinema into fixed frame close-ups of unmoving painterly scenes—achieves at this level, in semiotic terms, only a negative synthesis. Neither theatrical nor absorptive; neither medium-specific nor exactly metapictorial, these inserted and usurping paintings are just images without a beholder.

The irony compounds itself from within—and in terms spectatorial before mediarchaeological. According to Fried's more closely art-historical or evolutionary template, the given six paintings themselves, in their outdoor romantic topography, are of a decidedly posttheatrical composition, no longer stagily "rhetorical" or histrionic but essentially "realist" in their "natural" self-containment. Only a few human figures are to be seen in them (a pair of travelers on foot in two separate canvases), whose miniature forms are overshadowed by the landscape—so that there is certainly no gesturing outward to draw in a viewer in the fashion of neoclassic bombast. Indeed, the force of all this is entirely the reverse. Those pairs of tiny human figures are no more dwarfed by their dominant scenography than are Haneke's protagonists, Georges and Anne Laurent, shrunken in their mortality before (though not actually in front of) these unseen images of what one can call *vistas without the gaze*. In just this regard (this absence of regard), the couple has been forcibly, if only momentarily, removed from the whole theater of the world—including its pending last act of merciful suffocation. So it is that the only "rhetoric" of these embedded paintings is second-order, in the shock value of an arrested diegesis. They have swallowed up cinema in a doubly distancing figuration: a trope both for the world (as pictured) and for the world's things (pictures) going together unviewed, lost *in prospect* to mortality's final absence.

Even though these made and unreal images take over the film for less than a minute of successive display, cinema as sudden slideshow has become narrative as deconstructed image system. The sheer filing-by of discrete picturation—film in a kind of transmedial parody and implosion at the hands of painting—becomes its own metaphor for the inanimate. With the result that these antifilmic "figs." can at first suggest—as in Broodthaers again, and related as well to those anti-cinematic "pages" in *A Voyage*—a passing catalog of the apartment's own holdings, amidst which a woman lies dying: "plates" of the objects soon to be no longer held in her world, let alone beheld. But that is too thematic, not quite material enough, for the full force of this cinematic default. Not in their genre, of course, but in their evocation of the world's ironic arrest, these landscapes may affect us, in fact, like nature morte. But the affect depends on a more fully transmedial effect of exclusion and removal, as only Haneke's previous digression into a montage of fixed-frame photographic images can help bring out, lifted as they are from the heroine's own life in time.

Such a transmedial stress point is scarcely anomalous in Haneke's recent work—just unprecedented here in its pretechnological reversion. Haneke is a director almost uniquely poised at the definitive medial watershed in contemporary screen narrative between photochemical and postfilmic image production. "Films" don't have to be photochemical at all any longer, or celluloid at base, but are often, instead, digital—and brought to screen (rather than traditionally "screened") not by projection necessarily, but by upload or webcast stream, sent thereby to "displays" no longer public and even increasingly portable. With the result that even new media make an eclipsed traditional cinema look different through the parted curtains of hindsight—and perhaps not least in the latest work of a screen artist who, in *Caché*, had previously vivisected the role of "expanded cinema" in its least aesthetic dispensation: the video regime of surveillance rather than spectacle.[7] Half a decade later, *Amour* pushes the transmedial inquiry even deeper by backdating the contrast to a premechanical moment in image history set into resonance with photography's own operations, as we will find, let alone cinematography's. In doing so within the broader media preoccupations of his career, Haneke's wrenching apart of narrative momentum for a sheer visualization of the unseen invites a brief review of its broader transmedial inferences within the arc not just of the director's own recent filmmaking but of contemporary art practice more generally.

In the electronic "context" (Foster, Dworkin) of Conceptualism 2.0, the exfoliated "mediatic system" (Jameson, writing about an earlier Conceptualist moment) has been irreversibly complicated by digital imaging. One result is that electronic screening can aid in resituating a "reflexive" tenor (Jameson again) of a specifically medial (or again *[plat::formatic]*) sort even in more traditional forms of image making. This is the case even with the least hybrid ventures of artists elsewhere preoccupied more openly with transmedial parameters. Platinum photo prints by Starling take their fullest measure, in regard to a recycling of materiality in manifestation, from his CGI projection of a first computer, nonmachinic photograms (or "frottograms") in Fontcuberta from his digital Googlegrams. In a similar vein, the mediatic impasse we're noting in *Amour* takes its sharpest reflexive charge within an auteurist spectrum whose most marked previous crux is the palimpsest of high-definition digital video and VHS surveillance tape in *Caché*. That film was followed, in 2009, by Haneke's traditional 35mm celluloid reconstruction of that black-and-white optic zeitgeist of the pre–World War I *The White Ribbon*. Shot to resemble the German still photography of August Sander, and stalled over single photographic frames at certain abrupt and disquieting twists in its violent plotline, *Das Weisse Band (The White Ribbon)*, with its narrative fading slowly in from—and then out to—a deep and prolonged black rectangle at each end, seems named in part for the ribbon of variably filtered or blocked light that lets screen picturing seep through (rolling variant of "our white rectangle" in Frampton, as well as in Beckett's [and Krapp's] *Dernière Bande*.)

In this line of declension from an explicit medial thematic, *Amour* may appear to have few of these metafilmic investments in its chronicle of a dying woman—until all that seems left to say about death depends on, and is refigured by, an unexpected transmedial disjuncture between image systems, moving versus still. With its present-day setting, *Amour*'s fairly traditional cinematographic management of the narrative in 35mm color stock, though inflected by the signature jolts and lacunae of Haneke's typical editing style, comes up against its unprecedented impasse and transmedial recalibration only with the filing past of canvas space as sheer surface. Such is the late turning point where the very history of visual representation intercedes, or more to the point intrudes, into narrative with those half dozen detached painted planes: sampled in regress and subtracted from narrative progress as both a prefiguration and an arrest, the one in the form of the other—and by way of triangulation, again, with another form of imaging. It is here that Haneke wants the relation of fixed painted images to moving filmic ones checked against the still frames of indexical photography: film in embryo. This, too, is a not unfamiliar move in his late work. In framing *Amour*'s moment of ferocity and peace in what we might call the film's title scene (love tested to its bleak limit in a spontaneous euthanasia by suffocation with a bed pillow), Haneke draws on two arresting formal innovations in *The White Ribbon*: first, those bracketing fades from and to black at the opening and closing of the plot, a play between visibility and its absence differently (but comparably) manipulated by the syncopation of black leader in *Amour*. Beyond those gapes of non-image, *Amour* also returns to the previous film's arrest of cinematographic sequence by narratively unmotivated fixed-frame inserts. In *The White Ribbon*, indiscriminate episodes of human cruelty are interrupted by identical landscape shots in different seasons, their depopulated frames seeming to anticipate the destiny of these spaces as eventual killing fields in World War I. Two of these are long-distance shots of an unfluctuating landscape, one an actual freeze frame: fixity in two registers, each intrinsic to a *[frame::advance]* medium—yet with their very mode of landscape image to be alienated and medially denatured by the veer from indexicality altogether, under the sign of death, effected by those imaged canvases in Haneke's subsequent film.

[scene::painting]

Even more jarring in *Amour* than the photochemical automaticity of those seasonal freezes in *The White Ribbon* is the irruption of full-frame paintings to mark the inevitability of subtracted human presence. These canvases break ontological stride with plot's narrative realism, doing so, moreover, at the very moment when the eruption of physical violence between the couple—Georges striking Anne—seems a clear harbinger of the inevitable (yet still unspoken) violence of canceled animation of which the pictures so lushly but ominously speak. Defiantly, desperately, Anne spits out the water with which Georges is trying to hydrate her, and after impulsively slapping her face, he says, "If you don't drink this, you'll die. You want that?" The question barely lingers long enough to sound rhetorical before the world goes under anesthesia and the knife in those edited canvas surfaces.

All the film audience has to go on, in the abrupt pacing of these sequenced paintings, is that faint echoing of the early montage in which the couple's apartment is treated like a dossier of cinematographic still lifes, stepping off a kind of time-lapse of desertion across Anne's hospitalization and failed cure, explained only when the rooms are reinhabited on her return from an unsuccessful operation. That sequence involves five prolonged shots (of seven or eight seconds each) of deserted rooms in forlorn half-light, ending with the kitchen we last saw occupied by the couple. Answering these fixed frames at the subsequent turning point, then, and held before us for similar intervals of narrative arrest, are those six screen-engulfing shots of landscape paintings with no ornamental frames included, canvases stretched to the screen's edge, with and without human figures—it hardly matters. Where are they coming from? Who's looking but us? And how can we count on remembering—when they are thrust on us to the exclusion of narrative—that their excision from all framing (except the screen's own) picks up on Anne's passing mention at the start, after a discovered attempt at a break-in, that the attic apartment in their building was burglarized lately as well, with "the most valuable pictures cut right out of their frames." A "professional job," Georges notes at the time. There is a double theft involved an hour later, too, when a slow cascade of painted images is stolen from context and robbed of all gaze.

It is only the next time we see Anne in her bed, the daughter leaning over her, that the camera angle is wide enough, and the shot held long enough, to confirm that the initial canvas in the series—with two women in a forested landscape—is in fact hanging over her bed. And one canvas is later disclosed when, for the first time, we see the wall opposite—at the very moment Georges crosses in front of the picture for his last scene with Anne: a somber cliff, a tiny couple on foot, birds in flight. In a second viewing of the film, two more of the six foregrounded paintings can, if one works at it, be made out on far walls or tucked into the parlor bookcase.

One confronts us in the aftermath of Anne's death, when the daughter returns to the apartment in the closing scene, a pictured located—we may now realize—to the right of the inner set of double doors. One canvas seems to go entirely missing from the household, at least as the camera inventories it. This is just enough to generalize the rest for what they are: not the couple's personal belongings, but anyone's everyday surround—life's normative décor—come home to empty roost at the end of one's days. And, of course, that retrospective tally (five out of six accounted for) is only if we're following the film's tracking shots with obsessive care on second (or third) viewing, ignoring the human action transpiring in front of these painted images. Here, ironically, that action is in fact suspended. This time the paintings come (and go) to represent, we may say, the exclusion of lived duration even in the time of their notice.

Certainly these climactically regrouped and optically inset paintings, typical of romantic salon art, are markedly generic—in a mode neither "theatrical," as we saw in Fried's sense, nor "absorptive." Nor are they absorbed by any one presently looking at them, not even by us, since in their random interchange and implausible artifice they remain just images, their space not only virtual but uninvolving: the opposite of cinematic immersion. Even in characterological terms, they capture and displace a middle-class aesthetic ambience, not a private catalog. The issue, then, isn't ultimately to locate the paintings in the couple's rooms, but to see what they orient us toward in their impacted gathering, what they themselves evacuate—and what they therefore accentuate by negation.

It is in this respect, too, that they enter into that promised "triangulation" with photo frames of a traditional print sort. Eclipsing the cinematic image entirely for a moment, the canvas sequence runs parallel not only to that comparable editing of the twilit empty rooms near the start but to the album of personal photographs that Anne later studies well into her decline. Those images of a real past, however, are reframed by her point of view as she looks at them—and looks back with them—even while she openly resents being "peered at" by Georges (and as if by us, too) while doing so. Page after turned page, this album tracks her life through the decades—along with the evolving life of the photographic medium—in moving from black-and-white to color images. Suddenly, however, she comes upon a missing picture removed from the four-cornered cardboard grips—the routine frame arrangement—into which it should have been inserted in the otherwise uninterrupted sequence. Instead: only black cardboard backing rather than the photo plane. Such a picture gone from its frame, within the album's bio-optic record of a life in time, may thereby anticipate, as if in reverse, the frameless painted images of nowhere soon to round out this motif of secondary mediation. If so, the demarcated black gap would be all the more likely, not just to anticipate these canvas vistas by marked contrast, but also to echo—in a closer graphic match (of solid black absence)—the "missing" images in the comparable black rectangles of suspended film that bookend the narrative.

In between, telescoped into their arbitrary slideshow just a few scenes after Anne's study of her photographed past, those artificial painted land-scapes are pictures, I repeat, at which no one looks: the world not only withdrawn to its similitude but also removed from human attention. If they are meant, in any sense, to offer a narrational respite from the emo-tional and suddenly physical violence of the plot, they are also a further premonition. In their sudden serial punctuation of the film's death drive, these artifacts are not a private collection stripped from its dying owner in an image of relics surviving her. The claustrophobic gallery curated and toured by the very rhythm of narrative deviance at this point has nothing to do with the solace of art. Nor do these pictures evoke otherworlds to which one might flee in imagination, representations of some fantasized counterspace. They are finality itself, emptied of life. After Georges strikes Anne, they appear as imaging's own recoil—as if, in their flattened expanse, they mark the point of no return that the couple has reached (though with no sense of their being "subjective" shots; quite the opposite). Because it is known now for certain (they seem to say in their muteness) what must soon be done, here is the very image of the inevitable: an image of a world without consciousness, of space without recognition. Marking the dead end of screen plot in the rigor mortis of visualization itself, these flush-fit rectangles almost seem to give us death itself under inspection.

At which point two further cognitive—turned conceptual—dimensions of these already full-screen displays bear mention regarding both spatial framing and ocular subjectivity. This is because these linked issues cut to the quick of a cinematic apparatus momentarily transmediated not only with photography but now with painterly representation. First, one thing that painting, unlike photography or photochemical film, insists upon through sheer geometry—and does so, in this exceptional case, by making the film frame rather than the decorative frame its absolute border—is its strict difference from filmic space. "On" screen, there is always an "off," always a tacit off-frame extension to the image, which is thus selected in passing rather than given, pre-established, prestabilized. The index is partial, the wider world presumed beyond this one selected and potentially shifting view. But here in these painted "views," instead, the world, an entirely imagined one, is only mimetically conjured and contained—and then embalmed, not as time captured (on the Bazinian model of "change mummified") but as visual rendering per se. Passing in lock-step before us are wholly virtual spaces preserved in the oil of their own production, owing no chemical (indexical) debt to the real. Once more, then, in the schematography of punctuation in these pages, we trace a move from []—as if inserted sideways as the equivocated image plane of a horizontal canvas ([   ])—to its conceptual opening as [::].

This logic is mapped again here (as in the previous diagram, reconceived and recharted below as ex. 2) so that "materiality" on the left answers to "representation" on the right. Together, these functions delimit the manifested medial synthesis at the top and, by symmetrical reversal, its functional antithesis and potential cancellation—or, in certain cases, transmedial implosion—at the bottom. Again we encounter the content of the form itself—or the depletions of its interface. The abrupt medial violence that turns movie into shuffled canvas sequence derealizes each medium, cinematography and painting, photochemistry and oil, in view of the neutered other. In this extreme conflation of representational history and its modes of visualization, film itself is reduced—in memory of its own photographic alternative and base—to a flat imprinted series without inherent motion, whose status as virtual space is exposed by its forced simultaneous transmediation with canvas imaging:

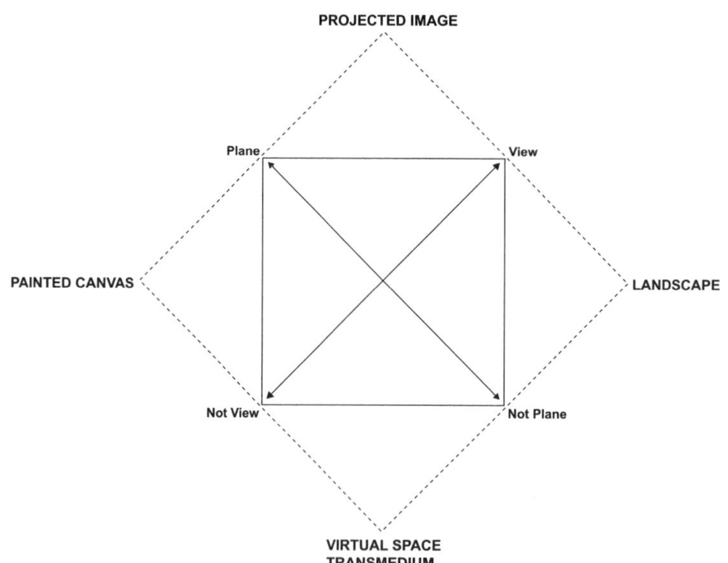

The terms of the previous diagram are readily overlain upon this more specific breakdown of Haneke's film. And apparent again, in this light, is the oscillatory function of our typographic shorthand throughout. In the most unpacked and explicit variant of this sub-sectioning motif, as anticipated in "Prelim," one can understand the semiotic schemata proposed here according to an ultimate interpenetrating binary of support and optical purport. In educing, that is, the latent from the manifest content of certain complex works—and thus in surfacing their (trans)medial unconscious— analysis unfolds within the conceptual bracket of *[platform::manifestation]*. In this way, the structuring dichotomy between recessive support and visual effect yields the effective disclosure of the former in the latter. In an earlier and explicit polarity turned reciprocal, recall the logic broached by *[support::system]*—where the categorical gap between underlay and image field allows at the same time a conceptual recovery of structure from its own resultant surface features.

Once again, then, to read the grid vertically, rather than transversally, is to recognize something implicitly held open by the spacing of those reversible colons that have paced our episodes of analysis. That something, if one may put it this way in sum, is mapped here by association with the interdependence of gestalt above, gestation below: of attempted specular resolution over against—above, but not beyond—its constituent dissolution into the self-operated analysis of contributory means. These are means whose definitive latency only a default in normal manifestation tends to reveal. In Haneke's wrench to cinematography at this impasse of the image, what surfaces is an abrupt meld in the planar interface between film and canvas. In another manifestation of the Duchampian *inframince*—that ultrathin conceptual differential introduced by Dworkin's *No Medium*—there is no actual betweenness to measure. In the case of Haneke's frame-displacing paintings, the result can be identified as "virtual" precisely by the simultaneous evacuation of "actual" space from both aspects of these intersecting and coincident ocular planes, celluloid and oil, indexical and representational. In what Simon Starling might well call a "collapse" of mediations, the standard demarcation of the canvas plane is mechanically deframed in *Amour* through its sudden limbo of manifestation as filmed surface: not a "virtual world," but a strictly virtual ocular field. In the diagrammed fourth quadrant, therefore, this zone of registration is marked as a virtual space inherently subtended by the only real thing about it: the transmedium juncture that brings it to view.

An emphasis on frame rather than sightline is, then, the first of the two anticipated conversions from cognitive to conceptual effect that are staged—or better to say detheatricalized—by Haneke's plot-rending episode. Pursuing the second, and apropos of this same jump-cut withdrawal from world to its flattening virtualization as transmedial image, we recall the twofold terms for screen investment in the film theory of Christian Metz. In brief, Metz's "primary identification" with the camera, in its only quasi-embodied and thus subjectivized access to visible space, is regularly devolved in narrative cinema onto a secondary identification with characters.[8] We align our attention first with looking, that is, and then with personified lookers. Remove both at once, as Haneke does, in a moment that is neither a scene nor a localized seeing—where suddenly no one is looking, and where the camera seems not so much pointed as co-opted, denied, and exceeded all at once—and suddenly this double theft of identification has birthed, from imminent death in the narrative, a purely desubjectified image-without-the-gaze.

Imminent—and all but immanent, that death. Beyond either cinema or painting, and thus transmediated into sheer virtuality by their collision, here is a perverse Deleuzian time-image of action's eternal absence. Or call it a case not just of death idiomatically, and all too palpably, *in view*, but of mortal absence actually rendered up *in plane sight*. On the optical spectrum thus educed—involving a *[dis::junctural]* continuity across discrepant art forms—Haneke's film operates so that the painterly furnishings or appendages of "the good life" have become the markers of its absence, not supplemental landscapes but endscapes. In this collapsing—or drastic telescoping—of cinema's metahistorical categories, temporality's own action is placed, by displacement, under house arrest. The accoutrements of bourgeois domesticity turn *unheimlich* on a dime. In the process, or say in this processual blockage, the nature of motion picturing, contemplated again as pictureplaning—one microsecond of *[exposure::time]* after another—has instead been caught up short in the figuration of final stasis by being dropped back into a dead zone between continuity and arrest, duration and its final suspension. An abyssal bottomless scenography defines the intransigent *[scene::painting]* of this held moment: now film scene, now merely painting, now both and neither at once. In the gap between primary and secondary identification, it is as if not-being-there were the true condition of visuality at stake in this seeing *through* of a fatality in more than the dead-ended sense: this thinking through of death both transmedium and by sheer force of image as such.

In this film's mediacentric knot of photography/film/painting, a director who is no stranger to transmedial tension (between HD camerawork and VHS replay in *Caché*; between digitally enhanced black-and-white cinematography and pre-WWI German photochemistry in *The White*

Ribbon)—no stranger to its narrative estrangements, in particular—has brought such tension, the pressure of such process itself, to bear even more openly on a cinematographic break point. There is, however, something implicitly film-historical as well as mediarchaeological about this unsutured open wound, with ocular signals pulled in opposite directions—and thereby abandoned in transition—between pictorial regimes. Highlighting this aspect may be part of the point in alluding early on to stolen paintings sheared from their frames—indirectly summoning, by contrast, exactly that different terminological sense in which the photogrammic "frame" is self-contained, its perimeters unmarked beyond the edges of its own image. If so, the inference returns to interpret what is sprung from the moment of Georges slapping Anne—in anticipation of a greater violence coming.

Entering a transmedial vortex that may well call back to mind such terms as "metamedia" (from Starre) or "metamorphology" (from Starling), film overleaps its own more familiar stop-action reflex to excavate a deeper history of removed human presence, where the screen subject is severed from any ongoing plot and subsumed to seized image. This is to say that at the dead center of *Amour*'s climactic crisis, Haneke has installed an optical trope comparable to the italics of the freeze frame so prominent in the European New Wave of the 1960s and inherited by the New American Cinema of the next decade, and which he himself pillaged for macabre effect at the end of both the Austrian and the American versions of *Funny Games* (1997, 2007), as well as, less stridently, in those inserted "frozen" landscapes midway through *The White Ribbon*.[9] This is the stop-frame iteration of the same photogram used as an italicizing marker for violence or death in nullified bodily motion—or, by a narrative rupture of a different sort, for an open-ended closure. In *Amour*, instead of freezing on the chilling moment of (or just after) Georges' slap ("…you'll die. Do you want that?"), Haneke inserts a sequence of precinematic, even prephotographic image planes that operate not in the least like a skeuomorph for pause (invoking celluloid function via an older sense of "plastic arts" like easel painting), let alone a reverse skeuomorph for the cinematization of oil on canvas, but rather as a full-scale reversion to a predecessor medium unaffected by its secondary imprint on film, yet stripping the latter of its diegetic agency. Such is the proleptic figure of mortal absence—certainly as ultramedial as it is "post-medium"—achieved at the interface of self-canceling determinations, film track and facture, viewer and viewed, in the lapsed capture of inhabited space.

Many of our considerations are rehearsed and digested here. I began by suggesting that this was a book about why, in the museum context, we still look—*for* what, that is: for what *reasons*, in search of what, as well as at what. And, as the argument developed, about *how* as well: through what discursive as well as optical prisms. Evidence has shown the means by which a good deal of recent Conceptual art—as well as the suspension of plot by concept in Haneke's more traditional screen form—speaks in this way to vision itself, as well as, on another wavelength, to audition. Haneke's reduction to sheer silent visibility without embodied sight or occupied scene—his probing the optics of a transmedium vacuum in the most desubjectified of contexts—is only our final, scarcely our first, example of the contemporary image in isolation from any coherent view. Six times in a row with this climactic idea in *Amour*, we get the very picture of visibility when doubly stripped from presence: at each end of the ocular axis, the absence of world and viewer alike. With *Amour*'s balked montage of canvas interchange, everything collapses into a momentary tunnel vision without any vanishing point in the real. But its aggravated slow-down in frame-advance finds thereby a further connection to the black leader that marks, before and after, another kind of rupture in the cinematic world viewed. Two kinds of cinematographic negation, the nonfilmic and the invisible, are here triangulated in interrogation of screen presence itself in its transmedial constitution by the shuttled photogram.

Now it might seem trivial to claim that this book's final example from a widely distributed and Oscar-winning screen narrative epitomizes the conceptual inclinations of both still and moving images in the broader scope of experimental practice. This would be a closural gesture woefully forced, that is, if it were not otherwise so obviously true (to the main tenets of this study) that any complex artifact is liable, under certain circumstances, to plumb the transmedium basis of its own manifestation. It is in just this sense that each of the two preceding Scenes of still and moving gallery emplacements have been trifurcated across separate chapters in ways that can here be merged to characterize—across those same linked registers—the unabashed transmedial crux of Haneke's *Amour*. Without, in fact, straining the issue, just to say so is to begin seeing how. All traditional cinema, exceeding even the photorealist canvas in the "lifelike" aspect of the 2-D "hyperreal" of virtual presence (1), may nonetheless tend to lay bare at times its own "hyporealm" of dependence on the still-image substrate (2). This is the case even when the entire screened moment is "derealized" in its *mise en scène* (3) by being displaced, in the case of *Amour*, onto frameless painterly representations of an unreal but nonetheless "external" world from which the claustrophobic interior of the narrative's plotted space has long been implacably excluded (after an early sequence of theater-going and home-coming). At the same time, as in Scene Two's continuing threefold breakdown, the "pictureplaning" (4) of any and all normative cinematic projection—especially in the case of a film that punctuates itself early and late with the black frames of absentation-as-death—renders almost tangible the "lightshown" aspect (5), versus flat black, of its realized *mise en scène*. For in *Amour*'s first quick-cut glimpse into underlit and untenanted space (with the doors of the deserted post-mortem apartment broken open by a fire crew), editing per se, in its earliest shock cut, articulates the definitive "filmedivision" (6) generated much later, from flush-framed artificial vistas, in a manifest internal counterpoint between paint and photochemical imprint—as if in a dilated parody of the photogram chain on which all editing depends. Such an effect is all the more tightly conceptual when one senses that this jump-cut fixed-frame "divisiveness"—in its climactic figuration of film's own lifeless and, to be sure, *invisibly* framed succession (the photogram's edge only an internal limit, not a border)—is conceptually routed by Haneke through its own exacerbated cancellation, there again at the end, by an instantaneous lapse to black leader.

Alternately, to sum up by way of paired Scene rubrics rather than their six chapter titles (when those rubrics are shifted now into the familiar typography of those chapters' dialectic subdivisions), we note how Haneke's ocular rupture arranges for us to sense how (and why) the film's singular *[image::frames]*—at this dilated moment of "collapse"—serve to isolate, to *re*frame in conceptual terms only, certain prephotographic *[motion::captures]* in their inevitable arrest. They do this in the mode of a pictorial declension from screen to canvas surface—each field of view analyzed by the other as a comparably opaque plane. One needs only to imagine, in pinning this down, what "cinephotographer" and sometimes frame painter Rondepierre might do—on the roughened opaque medium of paper—in executing an acrylic copy of one single photogram lifted from each of these six canvas shots in *Amour* and then, after destroying these (derivative) originals, as with certain of his own *Annonces* works, offering up their reprinted photos on a transmedial strip.

To close round on the full provisional entitlement of this study—by further enlisting a typography previously withheld for this keynote phrase—let me summarize the ultimate *[object::art]* interplay we have found acted out across certain manifold tutor works. In squaring the hermeneutic circle of interpretive reinvestment in the grips of certain *[plat::formatic]* dismantlings—as we've done for a wide array of image fields as well as for Haneke's film in particular—the correlation has grown clear, I hope, between the upper quadrant of synthesis and the lower zone of analysis in that semiotic template. Above: the offered image. Below: manifestation divested of its passive allure and subsumed, by nonetheless aesthetic means, to the reciprocal rethinking it affords, its braided latencies raised to view in a perceptual climate of mostly unexamined audiovisual data. Nothing less can keep acquiescence at bay in a technosphere where, through the exponential surfeit of interface, electronic permeation has become a kind of universal *permediation*.

So that one may say, finally, that the transmedial field of force locates less the scene of generated effect than a discipline of attention in its own generative right, more transactive than just composite. In a culture of steadily coursing visual data, wired spectacle, and computerized retinal inundation, it is becoming harder all the time to imagine zeroing in, for either production or reception, on anything like the "autonomous" art object, to say nothing of encountering any autonomous human agent. Yet despite this (as well as because of it)—through a conceptual vantage point, rather than just an angle of cognition, that gets cued transmedium by many contemporary works—there remains, even still, the self-investigated object art. This is why we keep looking—and listening—even while in Conceptualism 2.0 it remains, first of all, the materialized thought that counts.

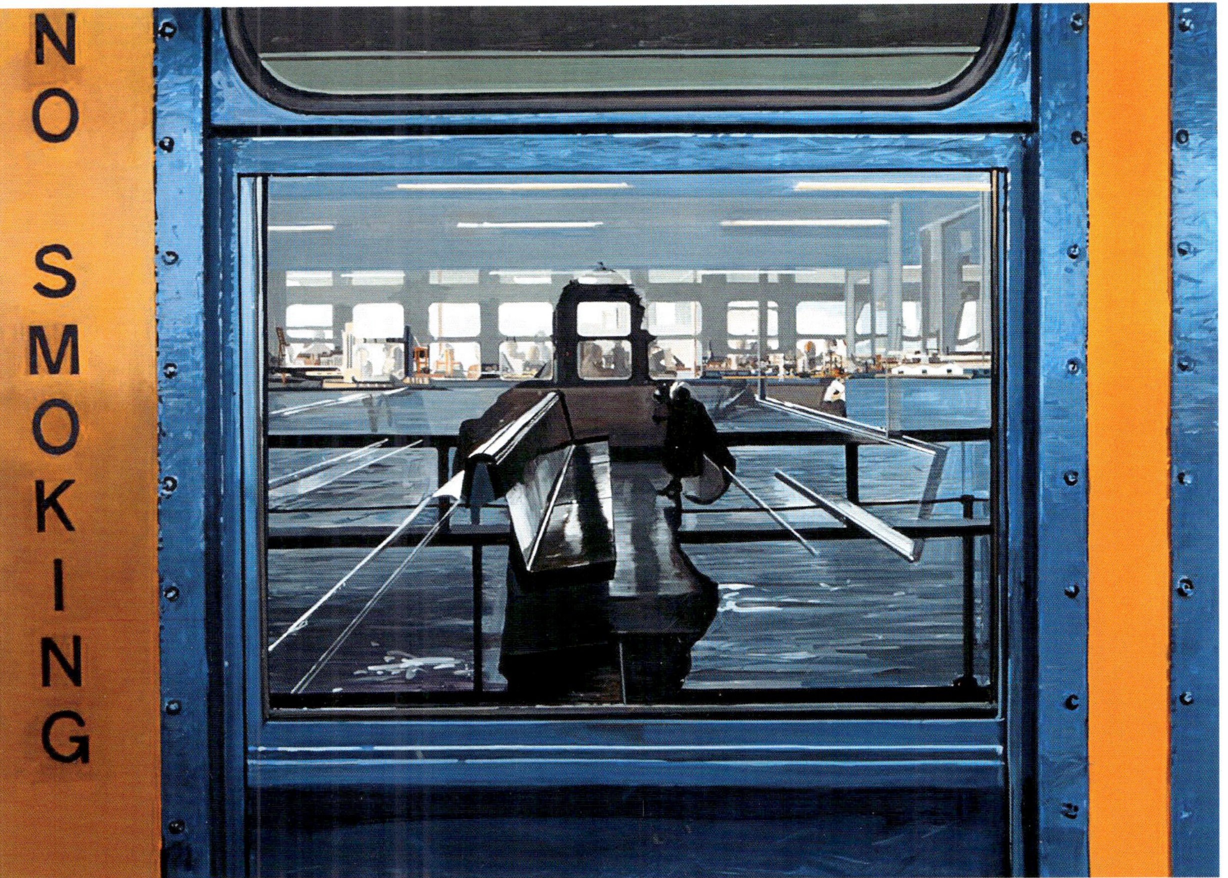

CHAPTER ONE [HYPERREAL]
Fig. 1. Richard Estes, *Self-Portrait*, 2013. © Richard Estes, courtesy Marlborough Gallery, New York.

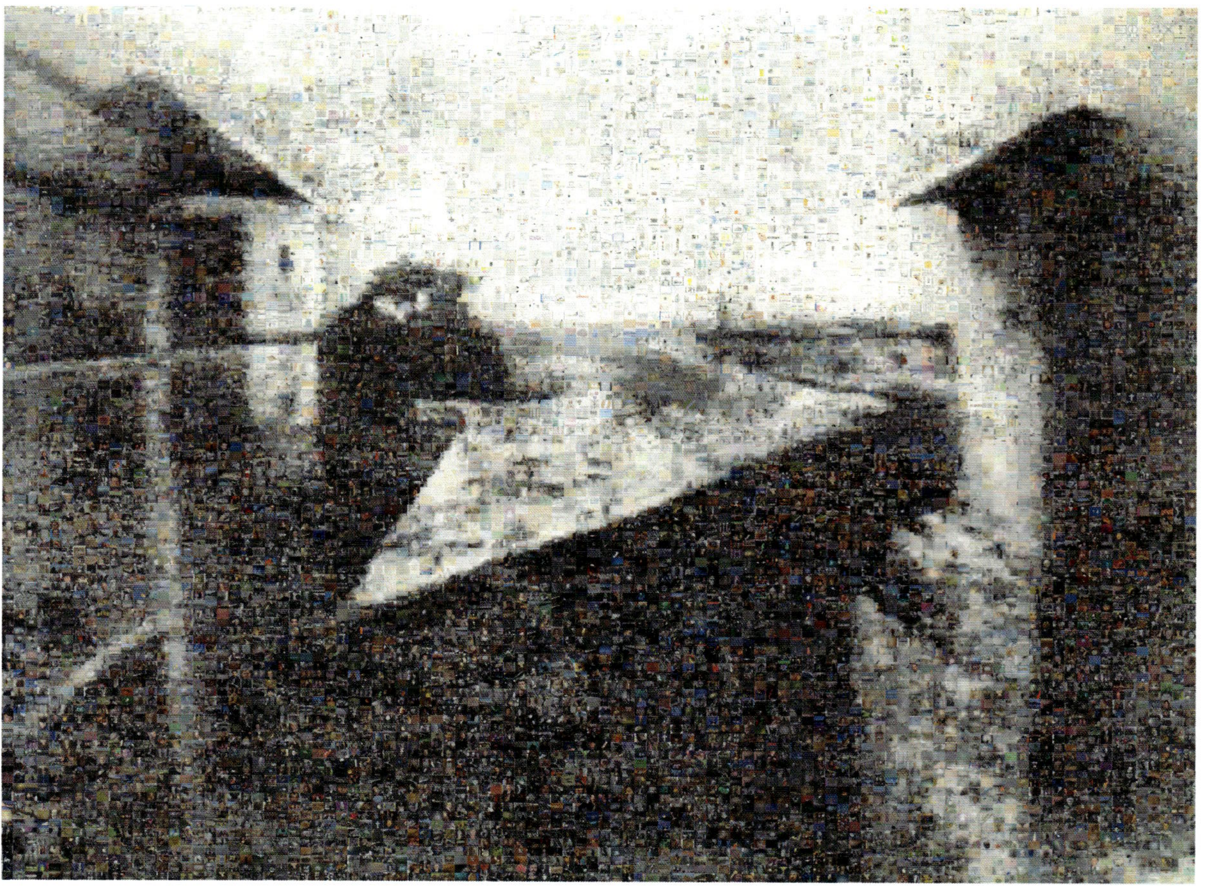

CHAPTER TWO [HYPOREALM]

Fig. 2. Joan Fontcuberta, *Googlegram: Niépce*, 2005. © Artists Rights Society (ARS), New York/VEGAP, Madrid.

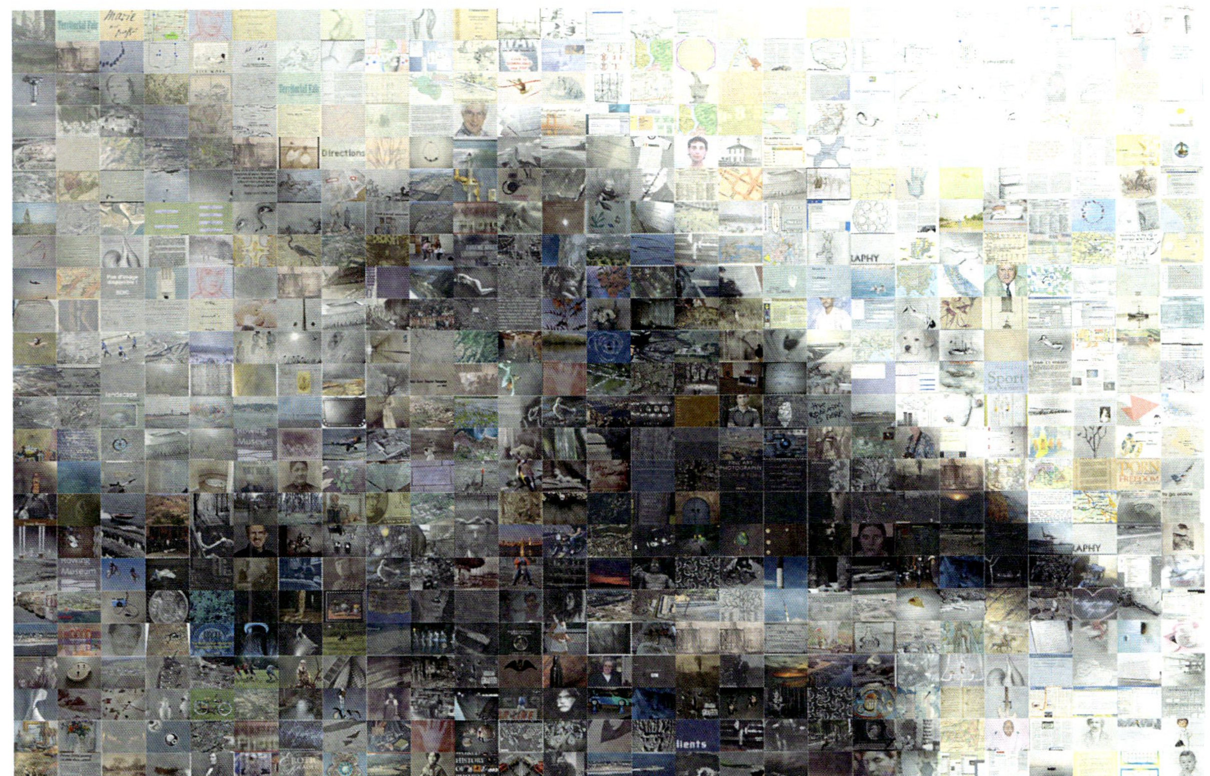

Fig. 3. Joan Fontcuberta, *Googlegram: Niépce* (detail), 2005. © Artists Rights Society (ARS), New York/VEGAP, Madrid.

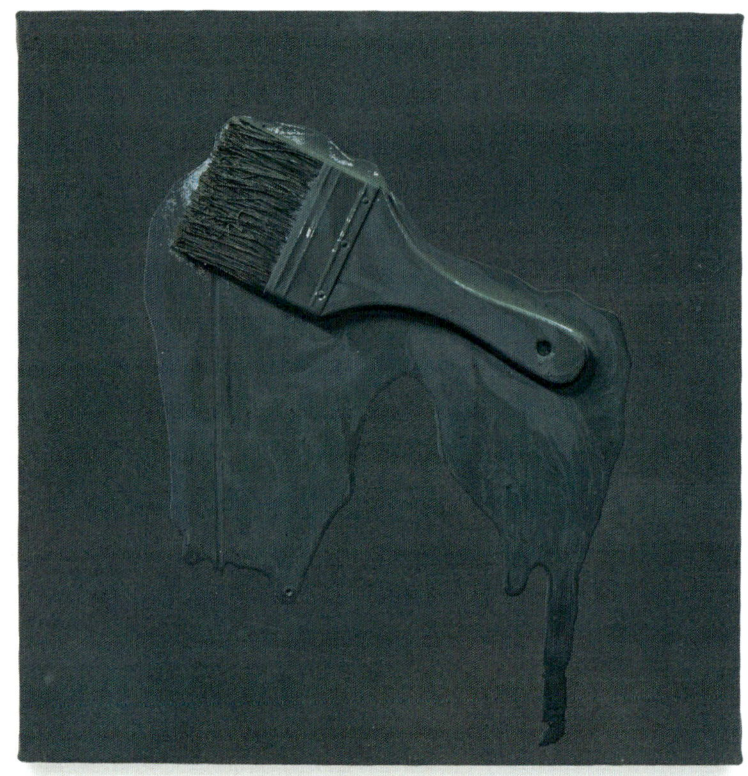

CHAPTER THREE [DEREALIZED]   Fig. 4. Paul Sietsema, *Brush Painting (green)*, 2012. Enamel on dyed canvas. 26½ × 27 inches (67 × 69 cm). © Paul Sietsema, Courtesy Matthew Marks Gallery.

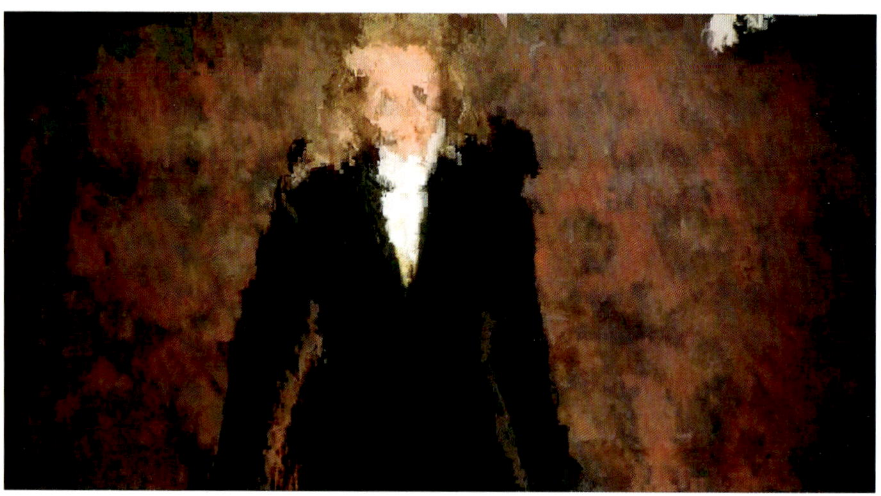

[ENTR'ACTION]   Fig. 5. Éric Rondepierre, *DSL no. 4*, 2011. 50 × 90 cm. Courtesy of the artist.

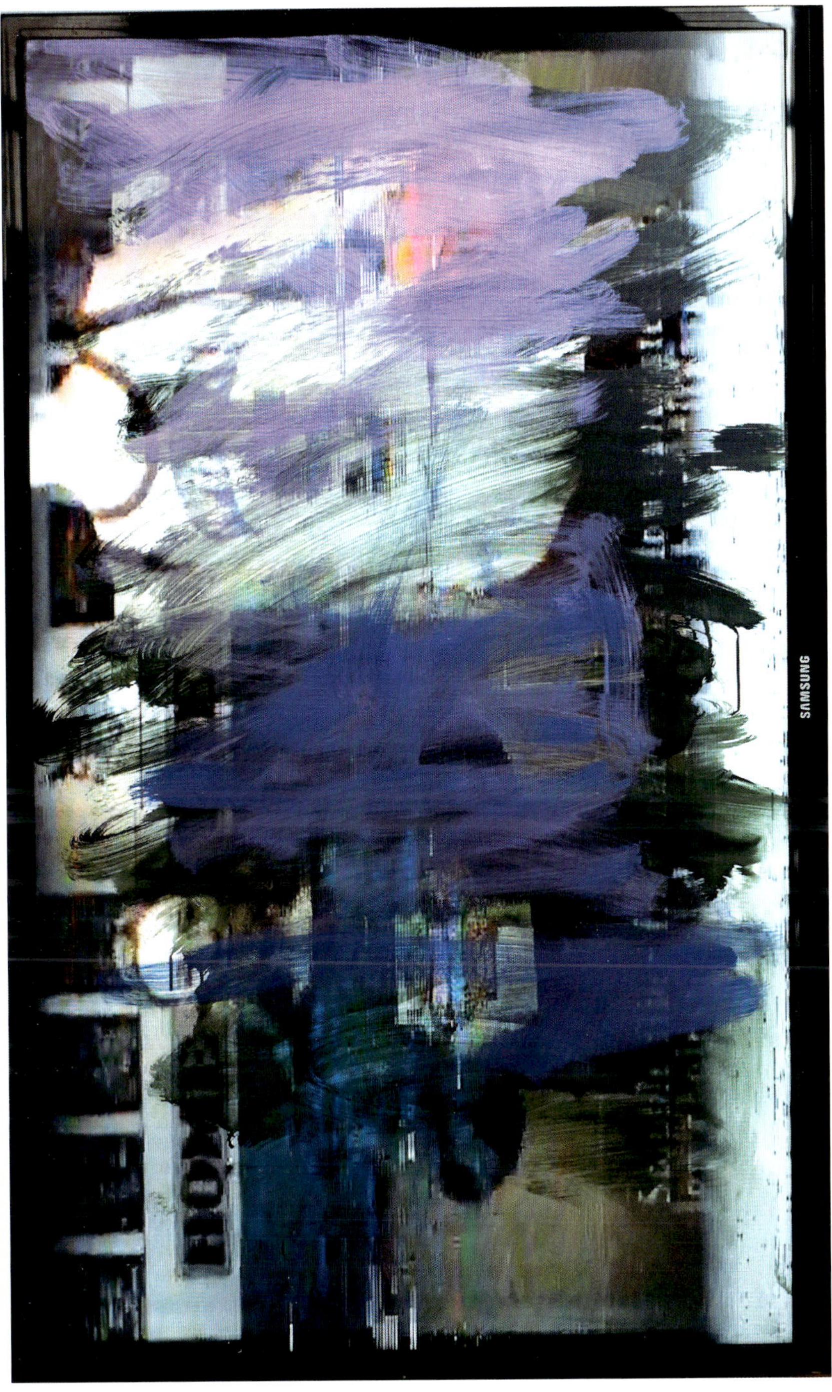

CHAPTER FOUR [PICTUREPLANING] Fig. 6. Ken Okiishi, *gesture/data*, 2013. Oil on flatscreen, VHS transferred to .mp4 (color, sound), 35 5/16 × 21 × 3 11/16 in. (89.7 × 53.3 × 9.4 cm). Collection of the Whitney Museum of American Art, New York; purchase, with funds from Richard Mishaan. © Ken Okiishi. Image courtesy of the artist, Reena Spaulings Fine Art, New York, and Pillar Corrias, London.

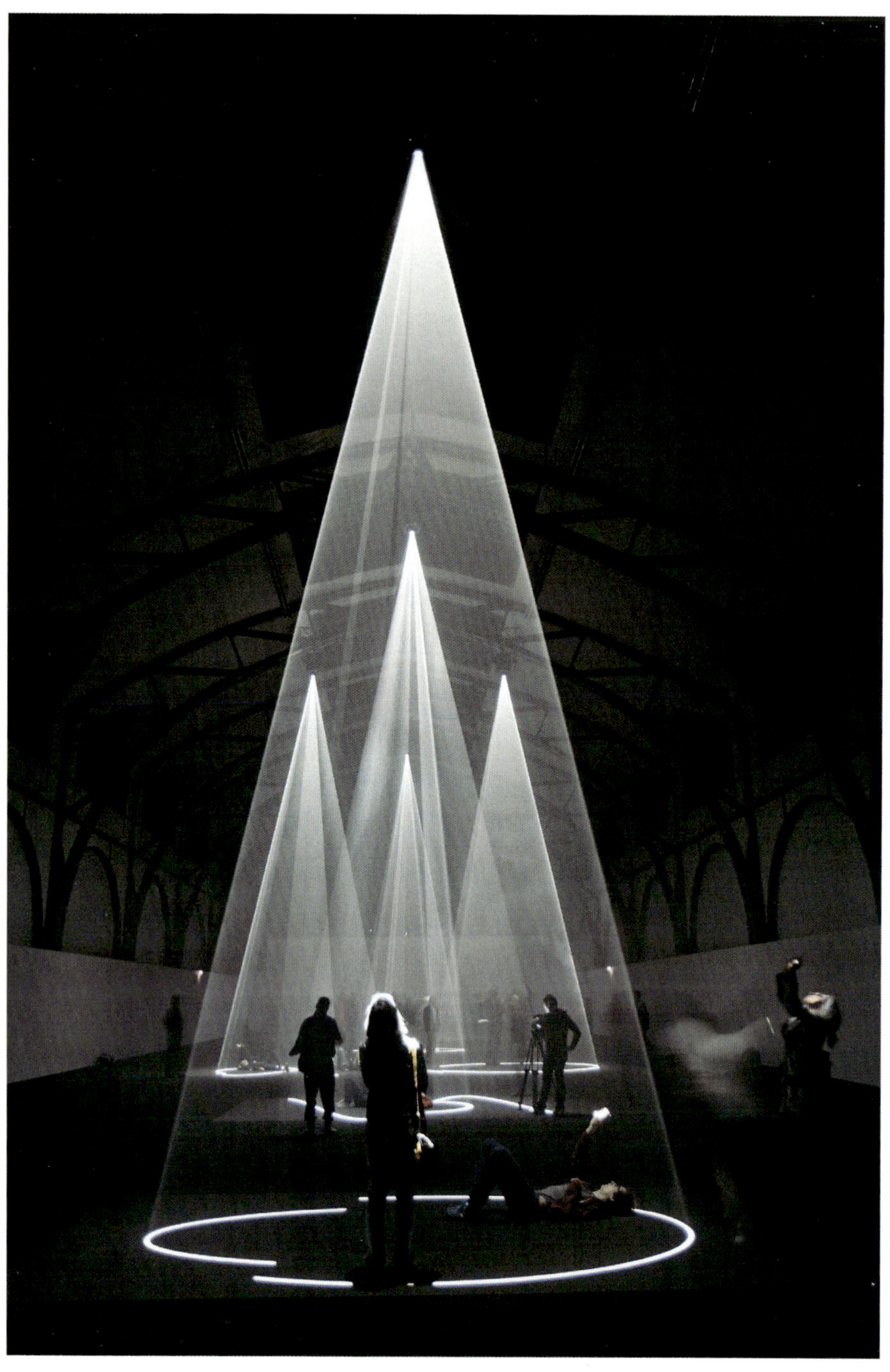

CHAPTER FIVE [LIGHTSHOWN]   Fig. 7. Anthony McCall. "Five Minutes of Pure Sculpture." Installation view, Nationalgalerie im Hamburger Bahnhof—Museum für Gegenwart—Berlin, 2012. From front to back: "Meeting You Halfway," "Breath III," "Between You and I," "Coupling." Photograph by Sean Gallup/Getty Images.

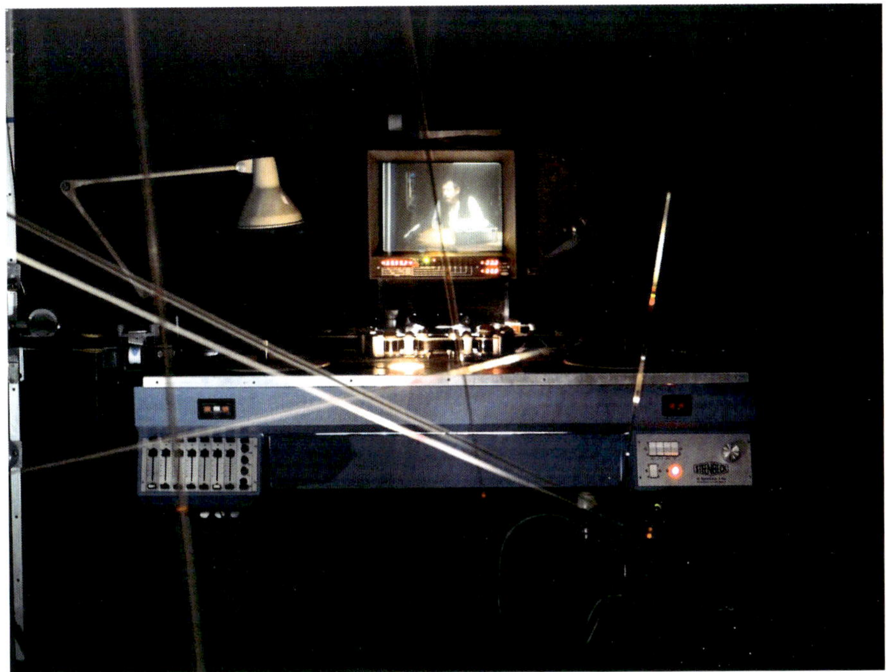

CHAPTER SIX [FILMEDIVISION]   Fig. 8. Atom Egoyan, *Steenbeckett*, 2002. Installation view, Museum of Mankind, London. Courtesy of the artist.

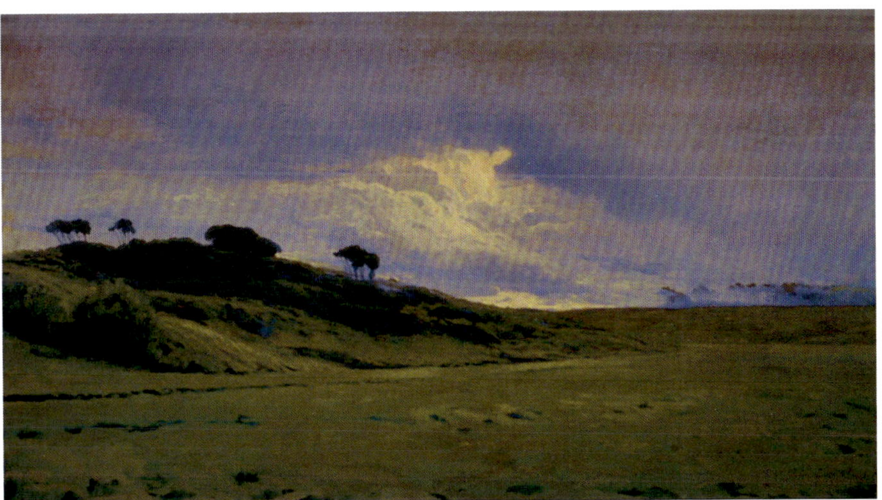

[ENDSCAPES]   Fig. 9. From *Amour*, 2012.

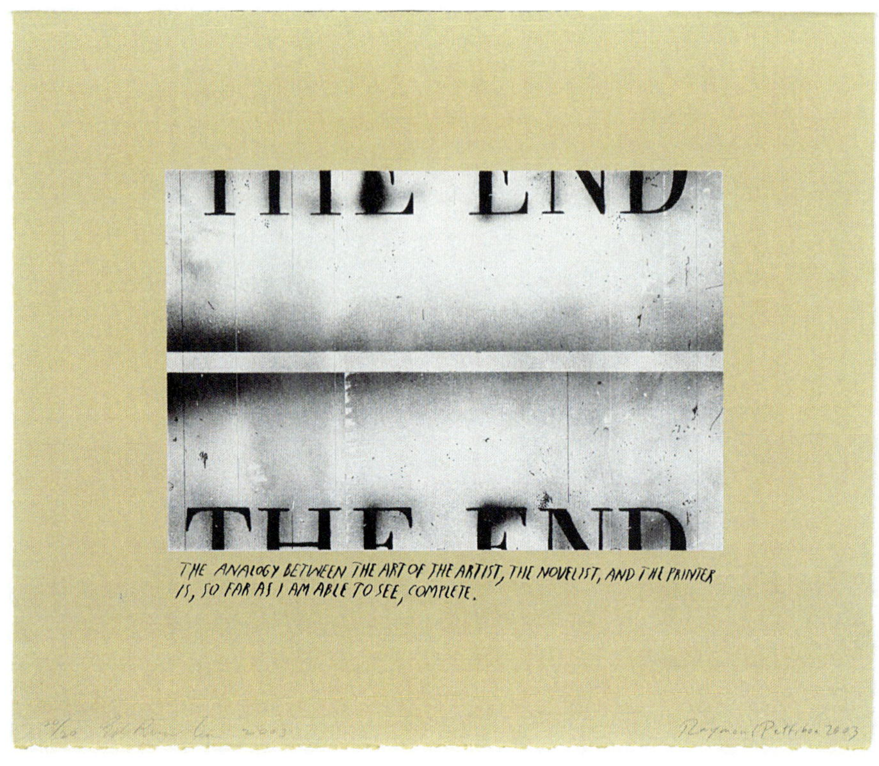

Fig. 10. Ed Ruscha and Raymond Pettibon, *The End (State I)*, 2003. Lithograph. 17¼ × 21 inches (43.8 × 53.3 cm). Edition of 20. © Ed Ruscha and Raymond Pettibon. Courtesy of the artists, Hamilton Press, and Gagosian.

Notes

PRELIM

1. David Trotter, *Literature in the First Media Age: Britain between the Wars* (Cambridge, MA: Harvard University Press, 2013). As an intriguing complement to this launching citation, Trotter has a searching essay, in the same year, on the contemporary British painter Vanessa Hodgkinson in connection with his own writing on techno-primitivism in modern fiction. Without invoking the category itself, he encounters there the logic of transmediation in noting the artist's painstaking overlays of gouache upon a deliberately retro egg-tempera, the latter with its long drying times—as originally used on gesso panels before the innovation of oil painting on canvas. Trotter further sees this media-archaic gravitation to a time-based process, once "edited" by another overlying medial application, as a temporally privileged "filming" of pigment in (inter)action: at the very least, a transmedial process in a kind of transhistorical material homage. See Trotter's online analysis at http://www.thewhitereview.org/art/techno-primitivism/.

2. Registered there is one of many generalizations invited by the multiplicity of effects in an art now of mechanical seriality, now of lexigraphic dominance, now of numerical multiplication per se. Among the numerous (mostly retrospective) commentaries on its leading separate agendas and practitioners, see Tony Godfrey, *Conceptual Art* (London: Phaidon,1998), published in the "Art and Ideas" series as if it were a parenthetical subtitle, and then, from the same press over a decade later, Peter Osborne, *Conceptual Art* (London: Phaidon, 2011). As brought out this time under the "Themes and Movements" rubric, and bringing out in its own right the topoi and separate programmatic directions of such work, a general history of the "movement" like this also invites, in turn, the present consideration of its more recent moves under the spreading digital shadow. And of particular bearing on the recent works considered in Scene One below, see the anthology *Photography after Conceptual Art*, ed. Diarmid Costello and Margaret Iversen (Oxford: Blackwell, 2010).

3. See Fredric Jameson, the chapter on "Space" ("Utopianism after the End of Utopia") in *Postmodernism, or the Cultural Logic of Late Capitalism* (Durham, NC: Duke University Press, 1991), 154–80.

4. Without the deviant typography of double colons, a comparable thinking informs my previous book on visual imagery, *Closed Circuits: Screening Narrative Surveillance* (Chicago: University of Chicago Press, 2015). A distinction that might have been

marked, in the format here, by *[surveillance::cinema]* becomes, in one screen manifestation after another, a term "telescoped" (optically as well as verbally) into the impaction of *surveillancinema*—though refusing to stay put as such: reversing subject positions, as we watch, across the interplay between full and inset screen, between narrative montage and narrated espionage.

5. Dworkin's approach in *No Medium* (Cambridge, MA: MIT Press, 2013) is to be compared here with that of Hal Foster in *The Art-Architecture Complex* (New York: Verso, 2013).

6. Forster's definition seems as deliberately layered and purposefully wordy as the issue is manifold and thickly discursive (rather than strictly technical). And with one tacit but obvious result for critical practice. If the medium is "contractual," then it can be refused or disputed, especially when image is encouraged to exceed all engagement with the potential inhabitant as spectator instead, as in the most showy landmarks of recent architectural design critiqued in his book. Hence the position staked out by Foster, a polemic and a rallying cry at once—and to whose positive exemplars in the "solid light films" of Anthony McCall (as singled out by Foster) we will be turning in Scene Two. Thus Foster: "This book is written in support of practices that insist on the sensuous particularity of experience in the here-and-now and that resist the stunned subjectivity and arrested sociality supported by spectacle" (xii). The "support" it offers is in part through specifying the use to which a material support itself is put as part of its medium.

7. In driving home this point, Dworkin's extended opening example, drawn from Jean Cocteau's film *Orphée*, is a poetic volume called *Nudisme* consisting simply of blank pages stapled together, and thus equivocating between textual undress (rather than address) and its representation. As such, these are uninscribed surfaces that could well be said to "analyze" rather than merely assume the sine qua non of both codex form and poetic license.

8. As focused on the image and film work of Marcel Broodthaers in *Voyage on the North Sea: Art in the Age of the Post-Medium Condition* (London: Thames and Hudson, 2000), this is an important argument on which the evidence in Scene Two below will come bearing down.

9. Yet while there is no intent in this discussion to recover some reductive version of medium specificity in the canonical Greenbergian sense, there is every reason not to want this position itself treated reductively. As Foster himself is moved to acknowledge, this medium-specific view of things "mirrors" its supposed antithesis and overthrow in the interart camp of mixed media. And something like that mirroring, when gone internal to a given work, is our ongoing concern.

10. I have in mind here, on the one hand, the video artifacts extensively analyzed by Mark B. N. Hansen in *New Philosophy for New Media* (Cambridge, MA: MIT Press, 2004), in a context expanded since by his subsequent books about the mediatized corporeal subject, as well as, on the other hand, the writings of Alexander Galloway, Lisa Gitelman, and others that our discussion will later, if obliquely, cross paths with: approaches whereby the templates of media history and communications theory, rather than aesthetics, would organize any analysis of digital thinking in new media display. It is by way of alternative that one doesn't want to absorb Dworkin's emphasis too soon to the "post-medium condition" that, as mentioned, it "roughly" resembles. In his study of negated means within a still communicating function, from silent vinyl record to

erased paper drawing, the works explored in *No Medium* are hardly *beyond* all medial concerns, defiantly "post," independent at last in their material indeterminacy. Rather, they offer an intensified comment on mediality per se in its most strenuous test cases.

11. Jameson, *Postmodernism*, 160.

12. What Jameson does say is that this conjunction of romantic landscape and sculpted earthen plot involves not the reincorporation of the world, the real, by a no longer hermetic modernism, but rather the very "grave of Nature" (170) in the artifice of a wholly virtualized sphere: again, more a "spatialization" than a real space. Not organized by a vertical idea, the Concept here is for Jameson entirely lateral, where one thing refers to the other by way of deferred shared terms in the knowingness of no longer discrete mediations.

13. A further benefit of the term "transmedium" (even in the adjectival form of a phrase like "transmedium gesture") is that it may help circumscribe the integrated activity of a single artifact in contrast to such attenuated usages of the more typical modifying form in, for instance, the punningly subtitled *Lego Studies: Imaging the Building Blocks of a Transmedial Phenomenon*, ed. Mark J. P. Wolf (London: Routledge, 2014), where the force of the epithet is primarily to suggest the openness to other product incorporations in a commercial assemblage model.

14. See Jay David Bolter and Richard Grusin, *Remediation: Understanding New Media* (Cambridge, MA: MIT Press, 1999).

15. I am applying here the well-known term from Gérard Genette's *Paratexts: Thresholds of Interpretation* (Cambridge: Cambridge University Press, 1997) at two related levels—or interpretive "thresholds": first, to the encroaching texts that tend to edge out all (other) visual material from the most aggressive gambits of Conceptual art and then, decades later, to the peripheral curatorial comment that has become, when accompanying so many complex transmediations, the necessitated "internal supplement" of any full perception, hence complementing the already analytic work of the aesthetic structure itself. This second aspect of the issue is different from the trajectory noted in Ruth Bernard Yeazell's historical survey *Picture Titles: How and Why Western Paintings Acquired Their Names* (Princeton, NJ: Princeton University Press, 2015), 260–62, where the fairly late advent of titles for paintings—as a device for either cataloguing or thematic highlighting—devolves, much later yet, into the sheer wordworks of Conceptual art, characterized at times by no more than a *nonmedial* tension between worded title and words within the frame. Still more recently, in the discursive hypertrophy of Conceptualism 2.0, the appellation, when more than *Untitled*, is often less important in clarifying what we see than is the explicative gallery text that backs it up, with captions thus trumping titles in the spotlighting of purport.

16. See John Roberts, *The Intangibilities of Form: Skill and Deskilling in Art after the Readymade* (London: Verso, 2007), as discussed at length in Garrett Stewart, *Bookwork: Medium to Object to Concept to Art* (Chicago: University of Chicago Press, 2011).

17. Lucy Lippard, *Six Years: The Dematerialization of the Art Object from 1966 to 1972* (New York: Praeger, 1963).

18. Rosalind Krauss, *The Optical Unconscious* (Cambridge, MA: MIT, 1993), 27–29, spelling out her methodological debt to Fredric Jameson, *The Political Unconscious: Narrative as a Socially Symbolic Act* (Ithaca, NY: Cornell University Press, 1981).

19. An early modeling of this process above, in the *m*-melded dyad *[platform::manifestation]*, is already tacitly glossed, in the pages since, by subsequently bifurcated—but at the same time fused—subheads in which *medium* is conjoined in process with its materialized *specs*, *process* with its manifested *art*, or *support system* made to parse itself into clarity by separating out the former from the latter: material facilitation from orchestrated aesthetic phenomenon, physical support from visual system. Both as a coordinate process and as a division of labor within it, both as a merger and its underlying risk to coherence, a formulation like *[support::system]* is thus typical of the tension—and test—indicated througout by the toggle of this book's double colons. The difference between a medium and its specular manifestation in a given transmedial work, for instance, lurks there in the tacit specs of the work's very materiality.

20. "Remediation" is of course the more familiar term, and thus deserves a word more. Its emphasis is indeed technological more than (or before) aesthetic. Think of cinema transferred to and thus remediated by VHS tape—or then again remastered for DVD issue. One medium seemingly disappears only to be reincorporated, its former content finding a new transmissive mode. In contrast, transmediation preserves in some sense the medial energies it supplements or even supplants.

21. No borders merit strenuous policing here. In the later collage work of Romare Bearden, for instance, from the 1960s, his assorted images of African Americans drawn from the new proliferation of glossy magazines and other outsourced facets of a racialized image culture address stereotypes of the media as much as they borrow them for a new sympathetic figuration. So the *trans*medial can be a potential subcategory of the *mixed* at any given turn. Nothing need seem categorically murky about this. It just, as we say, depends.

22. Niklas Luhmann, *Art as a Social System*, trans. Eva M. Knodt (Stanford, CA: Stanford University Press, 2000), 109. Luhmann stresses (with an implicitly fourfold distinction) the variable definition of a (1) medium in terms of the malleability of its (2) formal manifestations in their shaping of (3) content within a given (4) communicative context (this last sense of context so definitive for Dworkin and Foster as well). Luhmann sums up his position this way: "In contrast to natural objects, an artwork's material participates in the formal play of the work and is thereby acknowledged as form" (109).

23. If a medium makes form possible and is then manifested in it, according to Luhmann—so that form alone makes the medium functionally visible—it is then that form, in turn, is the flashpoint for any openly deliberated (rather than masked) transit across media, between material templates. This is to say that, in the work of transmediation, form is often the place—in *immediate* response to platform—where medium is manifested in the manner (because matter) of a wry and estranging inquest rather than a demonstration.

24. During the last weeks of a Leverhulme Visiting Professorship in 2015, for which I have my host and host institution, Matthew Rubery and Queen Mary, University of London, to thank most warmly—and under whose auspices my three public lectures were the seed of this study—it happened that a BBC radio program mentioned "skeuomorph" as its "word of the day," questioning callers on its application. Aesthetic refunctioning wasn't part of the aired range of reference, but David Trotter (see n. 1 above) is revealing on just this point in his discussion of Hodgkinson's work. About the manifestation of

"techno-primitivism" in her tempera treatment, in connection with the newer chromatic machinations of four-color printing, he speaks of an aesthetic of "subtraction" in her most transmedial venture, titled "You're Just a Headline to Me" (C,M,Y,K), from 2012: "In each panel, one of the four colours (cyan, magenta, yellow, and key, or black) used to test the ink in a printer-cartridge has been subtracted from the complete set, and left to its own devices. The depleted colour-chart sits in state—pure ceremony, it tests nothing—above the real action, which takes place beneath it, the shuttling to and fro of its own supplement." Trotter goes on to characterize this relation of an optically rippling supplement to its technological trigger as that of an "anti-skeuomorph." Identifying the design norm as the case in which an "element of structure returns as decoration," he gives as one of his examples of the straightforward skeuomorph "that functionless click your digital camera emits to encourage you to believe that you have indeed taken a 'photograph.'" It is a case of atavism as "reassurance," whereas the actual art of techno-primitivism—keen to "exploit any available slack in the system"—has therefore an opposite purpose in mind. Rather than an acculturation to the new via the old and cozy, it produces what is best understood as the sudden *inconveniencing* of response.

25. If for Henry Jenkins, in *Convergence Culture: Where Old and New Media Collide* (New York: NYU Press, 2006), "the one-to-one relationship that used to exist between a medium and its use is eroding" (10), that is because a given medium, say the photographic still or the moving image, can these days have different "delivery technologies" (13). But if the "use" value is conceptual rather than pragmatic, or say aesthetic rather than instrumental, the "one-to-one" match-up may return—and in the form of a transmedial uniqueness within competing parameters.

26. Alexander Starre, *Metamedia: American Book Fictions and Literary Print Culture after Digitization* (Iowa City: University of Iowa Press, 2015).

27. Such effects are by no means exclusively the province of new cultural iconographies. In Renaissance paintings, for instance, there was the grisaille imitation of sculpture in painted altarpieces as a pre-easel form of religious iconography seemingly more rounded, more embodied, than in subsequent surface treatment, its idealities more fully incarnated. Call it an earlier version of the skeuomorph (in a nonutilitarian context) as well as a foundational case of trompe l'oeil. In contemporary aesthetics, this can happen in forward or reverse chronology, either one: the photograph, digital and otherwise, invoking the texture of a painting, the painting or drawing simulating the look of a photograph.

28. In one of the more blatant instances of skeuomorphic irony in recent gallery practice, there is the 2009 laminated plastic sculpture of an antique, tall-carriage 1940s tabletop telephone built up layer upon layer, by British appropriation artist Rosie Leventon, out of discarded and then flattened cell phones that are thus repurposed—or not even, quite—as the material basis of their own unworkable sculpted predecessor. Communications history in reverse: the mobile contraption as stable aesthetic fixture—and this appearing for display under a title, *Sub-Text*, that jokes in part on the sedimented, and thus buried, e-text function of this throwback reassemblage.

29. As a point of comparison with this book's stress on a 2.0 phase of transmediation's longer aesthetic run, see the recent collection of texts about the "beyond" of a lapsed postmodernist paradigm, *Supplanting the Postmodern: An Anthology of Writings*

on the Arts and Culture of the Early 21st Century, ed. David Rudrum and Nicholas Stavris (New York: Bloomsbury, 2015). There, a chapter-length excerpt is given over to each of eight separate coinages rising to address this sense of aftermath, including "remodernism," "performatisim," "hypermodernism," "renewalism," "altermodernism," and "metamodermism." The two remaining neologisms are more directly concerned with global computerization, though only "digimodernism" asserts this terminologically. "Automodernism" (the preferred rubric in the excerpt from Robert Samuels) speaks instead, by etymologically loaded prefix, to a supposed "autonomy" won back by "personal" computing from postmodernism's "death of the subject." As a practice tapping transmedial energies both preceding and outlasting the claims for postmodernity, then, I would wish to append "Conceptualism 2.0" to the anthology's eightfold roster of regrouped considerations in our subsequent century. Its own framework somewhat more skeptical than that of Samuels, the eponymous excerpt under the category of "digimodernism" from Alan Kirby's *Digimodernism: How New Technologies Dismantle the Postmodern and Reconfigure our Culture* (New York: Continuum, 2009) is closest to the attention frequently paid in my pages to the cross-media impact of digital aesthetics on a variety of fields. Though Kirby's book ranges from blockbuster cinema through reality TV to electronic innovations in radio and videogames, the scope of analysis (with his title's sense of "culture" concentrated in mass entertainment) does not include works of Conceptual art that have taken on—and often onboard—such new technology in a spirit of investigative critique rather than mere display.

CHAPTER ONE

1. Michel Butor, *Inventory: Essays by Michel Butor*, trans. Richard Howard (New York: Simon and Schuster, 1968), 55.

2. It is in respect to just this terminological distinction between the de- and the trans-mediated that these outsize painted *bibliobjets*, appearing two years after my study of similar sculptural bookworks, can offer a bridge, concerning the variable registers of mediation, between the present chapters and *Bookwork*, in which light Ruscha's blank pages also revisit and textually eviscerate the conceptual tradition I had previously explored, under the category of "lexigraph," in *The Look of Reading: Book, Painting, Text* (Chicago: University of Chicago Press, 2007).

3. See Geoffrey Mann's website, http://www.mrmann.co.uk/.

4. http://www.mrmann.co.uk/natural-occurrence-series-shine.

5. What results is almost a turning of the artifact in the poet's own refashioning hand, all that euphony and metaphor at his fingertips. With Brument's *Vase*, in contrast, enough guttural *urs* may turn into an urn through merely the least grunt of intonation. No words cross aesthetic borders to conjure the *objet*. It is a case, instead, of ex-phrasis: an arbitrary pulsional association taking contingent form. The rhetorically shaped artifact of the poem itself in Keats, matched by its rounded internal double in the Grecian artifact, has become instead, two centuries later, the move from sonic reception to a fashioned receptacle. Any "please do not touch" has been outplayed by the automatically push-button manifestation of a once hand-tooled craft.

6. Nothing could be more, as it were, purely conceptual in its materialization—

with the exception, perhaps, of the piece of furniture, the furniture piece, displayed there at MAD along with Brument's voice sculpture: a *Brain Wave Sofa* (Lucas Maassen and Dries Verbruggen, 2010) contoured to the graphic EKG patterns accompanying the mere (wired) *thought* of rest and relaxation—rather than of any actual ergonomic form. The fantasy of mind over matter has come perversely true in this furnished realization of synaptic connection. Yet the rippling arbitrary contours of this object could tolerably couch no human form. The brainwave printout has been too unfiltered, not passing through an engineering idea at all, but short-circuited in a directly transferred oscillation without functionalist constraints. Mind and matter are not such compatible mediums after all—as this one attempted breakthrough serves to expose. Putting it another way: to operate transmedium produces in this case not a product, an instrument as potential everyday commodity, but only a conceptual artifact.

7. See the most recent survey of this work and its contemporary legacy in John Russell Taylor, *Exactitude: Hyperrrealist Art Today* (London: Thames and Hudson, 2009).

8. Michael Fried, *The Moment of Caravaggio* (Princeton, NJ: Princeton University Press, 2011).

9. Patterson Sims, "Richard Estes' Realism," in Sims, with Jessica May and Helen Ferrulli, *Richard Estes' Realism* (New Haven, CT: Yale University Press, 2014), 16.

10. In high modernism, the battle of painting against photography is waged once more on related terms. It takes the form there, under the flag of medium specificity, of a belligerent purism of means: an entrenched position closing ranks in part against the mechanics, per se, of a competitor medium—rather than, as in the earlier impressionist turn, trying to best its rival's powers by certain revised facets of its own ocular craft. But time is often on the side of the machine. In charting photography's rising aesthetic stock under postmodernism, Walter Benn Michaels notes how, in a kind of double bind or Catch-22, the work of photography had earlier fallen victim to modernist medium specificity, narrowly understood, as determinative of aesthetic status—with the quite specific automatism of photography, its own insistent medial essence, tending to exclude it from the category of art according to then-reigning standards. This is among the paradoxes and reversals tracked in Benn Michaels' book on neoliberal aesthetics, *The Beauty of a Social Problem* (Chicago: University of Chicago Press, 2015)—where, apart from specificity, for instance, fabrications that refuse to be commodified thus refuse to be considered art (100). On the particular score of mechanical reproduction, it is only as a critique of "art as such" (18), suggests Michaels in solidarity with Michael Fried, that the indexical parameters of photography lay claim, ironically enough, to full aesthetic status in a postmodern ethos. In a more complex way—when subsuming the specificity of photography to brushwork, if still at the risk of degraded aesthetic valuation—the transmedium effort (and affront) of photorealism or hyperrealism makes a more intrinsic (because cross-material) move against aesthetic purism. We've seen just some of the adulterations and redoublings that result.

11. To compare this tendency, as manifested in *Toms River*, to Haberle's tour de force of photogravure in *The Changes of Time* (1888) is to see at once the difference. Haberle represents a carved wood frame of American presidents in etched vignettes surrounding a cabinet door affixed with US banknotes representing several different engravings of the same dignitaries. Continuous with the craft of these illusionist depictions is a

carte de visite photo of a woman at the upper left and, at the very bottom, surmounting a self-addressed envelope, a small passport-like snapshot of the painter—also dispatched in the mode of his "signature" precision. Although the "counterfeit" bills lend an extra irony to the nearby photorealist forgeries, the whole assemblage is an orchestrated testament to representation rather than, as in Peto, the case of a visible upper hand given to pigment over photochemistry. Transmediation can, in these ways, both close and open hierarchical gaps in even the most conventional of easel work. In Haberle, painting has reabsorbed its rival in photography on the brushstroke's own terms. In Peto, the battle seems still being fought.

12. This effect is answered elsewhere along the Guggenheim ramp by works of Christian Megert's, including *Mirror Box* (1967), an expanse of wall-hung miniature mirrors, and, from earlier in the decade, his fanned-open book in fractured mirror and glass called *Mirror Shard Book* (1962). Here is a quintessentially "demediated"—and then transmediated—*bibliobjet* in which transparency and reflection are displayed as the alternative wavelengths of reading across the implied phenomenology of textual access, now directly available in its offered world, now answering to external desire by an optic parable of reflective identification. For a further sense of such "demediation," see Stewart, *Bookwork*.

13. Catalog essay by Kerry Brougher, from Brougher, Russell Ferguson, Dario Gamboni, *Damage Control: Art and Destruction since 1950* (New York: Prestel, 1913).

CHAPTER TWO

1. But other and more central media genealogies are also inscribed. The pornographic legacy asserts itself only at first disconcerted glance. In Fontcuberta's systematic override of the organic by the machinic, his process also has a way of recovering the discourse-heavy bias of early Conceptual art from the contemporaneous ferment out of which photorealism also arose. True to the transmedial electronics of these Googlegram works in general, his puzzle-piece image of the Courbet doesn't resort to the overt microcosmic or fractalized build-up of separate nude shots in a wholly geometric—and exponential—erotics. Instead, with a conceptualist bias toward displacement and word-play, and triggered by Courbet's own generalizing title, *Origin of the World*, the piecemeal plane of optic fragments (10,000 strong, with some of them strictly visual frames, some others illegibly small text blocks) has been motored into frozen and printed view by the triangulated search criteria of "Big Bang," "Black Hole," and "Dark Matter," the first two sexual puns drifting over to the metaphysical, the copulative become cosmic. What the overall look of this Courbet redux thus serves to figure, digitally to configure, is a wholesale break from anthropocentrism, where the primacy of desire—carnal desire in its role as species reproduction—has been subordinated to a diffused epistemophilia, digital rather than genital. This new *Origin of the World* suggests that the dominant form of origination in our day, sheer combinatory association, is marked not by interrupted menstrua but by intercepted data streams.

2. In other work, less strictly photographic, to which we next turn, Fontcuberta's use of optical software in the interception of found images happens to anticipate, again in homage to *Blow Up*, a 2015 video work on display in the 2016 exhibition "Public, Pri-

vate, Secret" at New York's International Center for Photography. Offering a comparable twist on the vexed epistemology of Antonioni's film, this is the *Portrait Landscape* by John Houck, named paradoxically for its conflation of art historical genres as well as for its digital transmediation. For Houck has applied rapid-fire face-recognition software to excerpts from *Blow Up*: a program that spots and brackets mostly misrecognized human features in bushes, peeling walls, fabric folds, fences, and the like—singling them out in miniature square frames, sometimes almost at the search rate of 24 per second, a contrapuntal film within the film. As does the hero in Antonioni's narrative, the software suspects what it cannot more closely inspect. It does all this, however, while—in the ultimate irony—*not* zeroing in for "framing" on the famous corpse, even "in person," given the supine and oblique angle of its features. In its forensic irrelevance here as "surveillance" software, and in this respect inverting the drive of the narrative film's scopophilia, Houck's computerization thus falsely humanizes the inanimate while ignoring the organic death mask. Transmediated between algorithms and celluloid in such repurposing, the optic frame dismantles its own cogency.

3. Illustrated on front and back cover of the *Iowa Review* (Winter 2014), to accompany my essay "Transmedium."

4. Joan Fontcuberta, "Landscapes of Landscapes, or Art as Map," in Fontcuberta, *Landscapes without Memory* (New York: Aperture, 2005), 6.

5. Kaja Silverman, *The Miracle of Analogy or The History of Photography, Part 1* (Stanford, CA: Stanford University Press, 2015), with discussions of the Niépce image and Fontcuberta's uptake running, respectively, 55–60 and 60–65.

6. The technological regress involved here is one that Silverman might well have stressed more fully in the terms of her larger framework—as if the whole procedure, from Niépce through Gernsheim to Fontcuberta, were backing up toward an allegory of her own point about the cultural afterlife of the image—in the cognizant eye of subsequent viewing. Pace Silverman, one might think to grant separate indexical status to most of the 10,000 microbit images when examined closely: the faces, objects, spaces once present to a camera, or perhaps, as well, the non-mechanical photograms in contact only with lit things, depending on what the artist's word searches on *foto* and *photo* have turned up. Still, their multiplied indexical contribution here to a single image base—a transmedial reinterpretation, so to speak, from webstream to rectilinear collage—operates only when each foursquare and often color index is rendered *analogous* to some differential shading in the greyscale of the original light tracing. Each subsidiary unit of imaging thus becomes an emblem of the overall nonindexical gestalt of the famous (and artificially legible) Niépce "photo" in its archival reworking by a cellular watercolor aggregate, pinpoint by pinpoint.

7. I am alluding here, though it was summoned in a different context for his study, to the separate etymological backstory of the two terms, *craze* and *pixilated*, given in Dworkin, *No Medium*, 97.

8. Another early variant of Fontcuberta's cameraless work, from the end of the 1990s, sheds a further (and literal) light on his view of conceptualism as a third term between document and formal shape, evidence and abstraction. In a variant of the photograms, and again avoiding the camera, the presence of blood on microscope slides—from anonymous "donors," in this way patrons of the arts—is treated in one sense as if

it were part of a photographic slide when projected through a magnifier onto photosensitive paper, where the image leaves a negative trace that is later reversed to positive in the photo lab. Without the medium of camerawork in these *Hemograms*, the newly foregrounded "medium" of blood goes directly into representation like a new kind of indexical portrait (oblique predecessor of the thumb-swipe portraits by Evan Roth mentioned in chapter 6). And in other works in the photogram vein, Fontcuberta returns to the pencil-rubbings (*frottage*) of Max Ernst in coining the portmanteau term *frottogram* for objects not just passively traced on light-sensitive paper but scraped across it: doubly evidentiary—and all the more conceptual—in their transmediation between the passive automaticity of shadow and the aggressive handiwork of engraving.

9. See especially, amid many approaches to this technological phenomenon in his work, Friedrich Kittler, *Gramophone, Film, Typewriter*, trans. Geoffrey Winthrop-Young and Michael Wutz (Stanford, CA: Stanford University Press, 1999), as well as the further development of this theme in Kittler, *Optical Media*, trans. Anthony Enns (Malden, MA: Polity Press, 2010).

10. Early in 2013, in advance of nearly a dozen gallery exhibitions of Baumgartner's work that year in England and on the Continent, the artist gave a suggestive interview about her just-concluded three-month residency and exhibition in once war-torn Hanoi, her show there called "Woodcut-in-the-Digital-Age." Blogged by the Goethe Institute of Vietnam, the interview explains her starting point (and crafted destination) in the low-grade fidelity of the "video still": "When viewed close up the lineation seems abstract, almost like reading an information line; the farther one is away from the picture, the more recognizable it gets." And further: "The time factor is important to me and the contrast between the slow time-consuming technique of cutting in wood and the motifs, which are often related to speed, such as highways and airplanes." But it's not just the time of the represented objects and the time of their drafting, their crafting, that are palpably at odds in these artisanal "throwbacks." Brought into relief, with a systemic tension characteristic of Conceptualism 2.0, is also the rendered military (or surveillance) activity in contrast to the initial rendering time of its television transmit: one "information line" at a time in an almost instantaneous horizontal delivery, slowed by carving to the pace of sculpture rather than broadcast.

11. See n. 24 in the "Prelim" for David Trotter's exploration of this concept.

12. See Régis Debray, "The Three Ages of Looking," trans. Eric Rauth, *Critical Inquiry* 21, no 3 (1995): 529–55, where Debray outlines a metahistory in which the Logosphere of the divine Word, once followed by a graphosphere leading from print through the evolution of realist painting to cinematography, was succeeded, from broadcast TV forward, by the videosphere. This is the domain of the free-floating image per se, rather than the word or picture: an increasingly ambient and permeating sphere of contemporary culture that transmediation, rather than affordance and application, tends to resist.

13. For a fuller discussion of computerized combat, in its links to surveillance, see Stewart, "Digital Reconnaissance and the Wired War," chap. 6 in *Closed Circuits*.

14. See David Campany on this aspect of Ruff's jpeg works in relation to the classic modernist grid, http://davidcampany.com/thomas-ruff-the-aesthetics-of-the-pixel/.

15. And since then, a decade later, as seen in a 2014 one-man show at the Camden Arts Center in London, Ligon has begun working with similar verbiage in neon—as it,

too, threatens to reduce or falsify black experience in a mode associated more immediately with public signage and its hype. Verbiage—or its erasure. For at the same time, in another new work shown in London, Ligon drops out all speech from a video record of Richard Pryor's famous 1982 *Live on the Sunset Strip* performance, so that only the articulateness of body language remains legible in sampled, digitally edited visual poses: no jokes in this "found footage" stand-up, just stance and gesture and the stereotypes these, too, enact even when mocking. The audiovisual archive of African American celebrity is thereby dismantled from within, by elliptical editing, in the speaking silence of analytic montage.

CHAPTER THREE

1. See my fuller treatment in *Bookwork* of Roberts, *The Intangibilities of Form*, 56–58, 63–65

2. Under the distant shadow, perhaps, of Ezra Pound's high modernist emphasis on art as "news that stays news," the post-Cubist pseudo collage of newspaper sheet among other found objects in Sietsema's work has, as anticipated, a specific lineage in Conceptual art as well. I think of Robert Gober's "simulated," twine-bound copies of the *New York Times* in recyclable stacks from the early 1990s, which are in fact "ageless" photo-lithographic reproductions of the same in (further) unfading yet useless perpetuity. In the instance held by the Walker in Minneapolis, Gober has hand-painted a three-quarter-page ad of himself in a bridal gown with the tagline (in a casual and personalized but fully commercialized cursive intimacy) "Having it all" flourished across it in exuberant (yet as if newsprint-reproduced) longhand. Ironies congregate. Here is the identificatory power of advertising—in transgendered projection—isolated by a transmedial piece of mass-print self-portraiture. The same artist whose earlier installation prompted Jameson's remarks on "the mediatic system" has in this case subsumed his own body to it.

3. Discussed in *Bookwork*, 119.

4. On frontality and its medium-specific "facingness," see Michael Fried, *Manet's Modernism: Or, the Face of Painting in the 1860s* (Chicago: University of Chicago Press, 1999).

5. Casting such procedures in terms of a systems theory approach to a social modernity that constructs its world by a reflexive reporting on itself, the literary critic Mark Selzer, in *The Official World* (Durham, NC: Duke University Press, 2016), takes up briefly Demand's attraction to "control centers," though not instancing the specifically political Stasi photo among his examples, as producing "a sort of secondary virginity"—with art's crisis of representation seemingly displaced onto its negative double in social oversight, "twin sides of the same formation" (87–88).

6. See Craig Dworkin on Duchamp and the "inframince" ("ultra thin") in his chapter on "The Logic of Substrate," in *No Medium*, 17–18.

7. See *Art in America* interview with Aimee Walleston, titled "Photo Finish: Q+A With Paul Sietsema," *Art in America*, May 13, 2011, in which Walleston introduces the artist's remarks with the general claim that his purpose is to "excavate sites of image production," with such a metaphor again lending itself to media-archaeological inference. http://www.artinamericamagazine.com/news-features/interviews/paul-sietsema-matthew-marks/.

8. Sietsema's interviews repeatedly stress his role as "maker" more than "artist," or rather as an artist whose leading question to himself is about what remains to be made, and how—made, or (via appropriation) remade. In Walleston's interview, Sietsema begins by addressing the subterfuges of technological simulation in his work—the indeterminacy, for instance, between photographic and drawn plane—as an explicit equivocation (and, in effect, transmediation) between "man-made" and "machine-made," a difference that Sietsema moves to make heuristically interchangeable.

ENTR'ACTION

1. For this apparently ambiguous sentence in context, see Stewart, "Contra Modernism: From the Mediatic to the Transmedial," *Affirmations: of the Modern* 2, no. 1 (December 2014): 3. http://affirmationsdev.library.unsw.edu.au/index.php?journal=aom&page=issue&op=view&path[]=4.

2. For helping me to shore up this broader sense of "demediation" as a subclass of defunctioning at large, and for the reminder of Gober's sink installations as example, I am grateful for Paul Fry's remarks after a public lecture of mine preceding the Yale seminar mentioned above.

3. Jameson, *The Political Unconscious*, 237.

4. Jameson, *Postmodernism*, 162–65.

5. On the general phenomenon of "nostalgia film," see Jameson's marathon discussion, "The Existence of Italy," in *Signatures of the Visible* (New York: Routledge, 1992), 155–230. The volume's earlier essay, "Historicism in *The Shining*," 82–98, with its argument about a retro subtext in Stanley Kubrick's contemporaneous setting for his return-of-the-repressed plot, can be read as a tacit companion piece to the more influential claims about a reified nostalgia of period style (rather than cinematic stylistics) in films from the preceding decade.

6. On the retro mediatrics, as it were, staged by Coppola's later *Dracula* adaptation, see my discussion of "Film's Victorian Retrofit" in *Between Film and Screen: Modernism's Photo Synthesis* (Chicago: University of Chicago Press, 1999), 225–64.

7. This last is in part the subject of my recent book *Closed Circuits* (Chicago: University of Chicago Press, 2015), with its subtitled focus on "Screening Narrative Surveillance," where those potentially separate "watch"-words are nonetheless meant to indicate a tendency toward simultaneous functions in recent cinema. Under analysis are screen narratives variously responding to a global "technopticon" in which optics and ballistics have converged at scales unimaginably remote from the eyeline match of bow-and-arrow or pistol. Fiberoptic and satellite imaging, with their own particular grain and tenor, are a central part, as well, of the second-wave conceptualism that is my present topic, even when no dominant electronic stress centralizes their ironies.

8. See my discussion of Khan's work in the "Endpapers" section of *Bookwork*, 225–26.

9. The 2015 catalog of Rondepierre's work, accompanying, among other venues, his winter retrospective at the Maison Européenne de la Photographie in Paris, bears the bifold title *Images Secondes*—secondary traces of split-second captures. It contains an appreciative essay by film philosopher Jacques Rancière, "What the Eyes Have Never Seen," in which Rancière stresses the theoretical force of Rondepierre's anti-cinema in

exploding the "Oneness" of the image by "ceaselessly separating it from itself" (87).

10. See Philippe Dubois, "Working with Photograms (Between Spot and Texture)," in *Éric Rondepierre* (Bretigny sur Orge: Espace Jules Verne/ Galerie Michèle Chomette, 1993), 28–35, as reproduced unpaginated on Rondepierre's website, from which the citations here are drawn: http://www.ericrondepierre.com/pdf/en__philippe__dubois.pdf. I have engaged more fully with the transitions (and theoretical ramifications) in Rondepierre's career, as with Dubois' nuanced appreciation of his work to that point in the 1993 exhibition, in "Dredging the Illegible: Phoneme, Photogram, Ph...Ontology," *Amodern* 6 (2016), noting that "illegible" is Dubois's word, too, for what is anomalously italicized by Rondepierre's frozen segues. In particular, but by broader extension, Dubois is referring to the "textually illegible" in the fractured trailers, but this as representing the general blind spot of cinema's transitional mechanism, brought to notice only by its spotting (or blotching) in the other sense. From this perspective Rondepierre is not content simply to isolate the photogram as such, the "stain" (Dubois) at the heart of the motion effect, but sets out to capture it in its own lapsed contribution to sequence. This is the flawed photogram caught in the act of exposing its very law—or, in Dubois's way of putting it, "a sort of squared photogram (a stain of a stain)."

11. This, too, is the collective thrust of a later traveling exposition, begun in Lyon (at the Gallerie Réverbère 2), that Dubois curated under the title *L'Effet Film: Figures, matières et forms du cinéma en photographie*, with Rondepierre given pride of place in the 1999 catalog copy, followed by several other artists concerned at least implicitly with the transfilmic at its double interface of optic trace and serial strip, celluloid transparency and projected frame line.

12. It is tantalizing to imagine these works responding, at the end of the decade in which Dubois first celebrated the *Annonces* images (n. 10 above), to the critic's sense of a Freudian palimpsest at work in the infratext of those blurred trailer frames: namely, the famous trope of the mystic writing pad—in Dubois's terms "the Wunderbloc, or 'magic notebook'"—as Freud's figure for the sequentially expunged impress(ions) of the unconscious in action. The possibility is raised by Dubois in his speculative closing section, with its interrogative subhead "A Metaphor for the Psychic Apparatus?" To this question, Rondepierre's answer would certainly seem affirmative, delivered some years later in formalized (rather than formulated) material shape with what we might call the wonder-*livres* of the "Loupe/Dormeurs" series—sleeper cells of the dreamwork indeed. In this mode can Rondepierre be understood to have encountered, interface-on, the locus classicus of the illegible in modern thought.

13. On this work by Spinatsch, in the broader context of Swiss nationalism, see the probing seventh chapter by Katie Trumpener, "National Vistas, Peripheral Vision: War and the Making of Nations in Alpine Panoramas," in *Viewing Platforms: Perspectives on the Panorama* (New Haven, CT: Yale University Press, forthcoming).

CHAPTER FOUR

1. Niklas Luhmann, *Art as a Social System*, trans. Eva M. Knodt (Stanford, CA: Stanford University Press, 2000), 18–20, on language as communications model for all art.

2. In the broader spirit of reflexive film experiment, *At the Hour of Tea* replays in its own way the evolution of moving images in their relation to the fixed picture. And, more specifically, if Lichtenstein lurks unmistakably in the background of Sietsema's *Brush Painting* (Scene One), so all the more obviously yet is Hollis Frampton's *Nostalgia* (1971) the intertext for *At the Hour of Tea*—at least in the two artists' comparably evoked lag-time between description and a sense, rewarded or not, of pending visualization. The latter is entirely balked in Sietsema when no image ever answers to, let alone coincides with, its prolonged annotation.

3. See as canonical checkpoints Gilles Deleuze, *Cinema 1: The Movement-Image*, trans. Hugh Tomlinson and Barbara Habberjam (Minneapolis: University of Minnesota Press, 1986), and *Cinema 2: The Time-Image*, trans. Hugh Tomlinson and Robert Galeta (University of Minnesota Press, 1989).

4. In the larger arc of cultural reception, of course, both modernist abstraction and cinema have, for many "viewers," rendered aesthetically "invisible" the accomplishment of any such dated painting, even in the most observant interpretive description—and even in this devoted mock-epistolary communication to the film's own audience of its line, balance, thrust, form, color, and the rest. There lies the further and final irony: that such graphic analysis serves to reduce classic verisimilitude and its modeling to (or toward) the abstract shaping of cubist modernism after all, with the play of image parsed and rationalized to a farethewell. Either way, however, as homage to classicism or disassemblage under scrutiny, the descriptive (strictly inscriptive) result hovers between imprint medium—alphabetic, then filmic—and a phantom realist image in a verbal depiction resisting all picture. The horse frozen in its iconic pose, the rider poised for motion, enter the narrated space of time and change—as with that calendrical superimposition that clocks the film's own production—only through the lap dissolve of formal notes and envelopes that make for no familiar "motion picture," or even the picture of a suspended dramatic motion, but that hollow out all spectacle from within the rigors of a reported spectation.

5. On the more than self-referential, the actively circuitous, conceptualism inflecting many of Starling's works, see mention of the recurrent "ouroboros" motif in Dieter Roelstrate, *Simon Starling: Metamorphology* (Chicago: MCA Monographs, 2014), 16, 22: an irony of self-ingestion that could apply as well not only to the Starling's metahistorical loop of computerized celluloid, *D1 - Z1* (22,686,575:1), as discussed next, but (also pending) to the self-feeding cogs of the editing deck in Atom Egoyan's *Steenbeckett* (chap. 6) and the self-sampling frame captures of consumed and regurgitated duration (ahead here) in Wolfgang Staehle's digital chronophotography.

6. In a more recent variant of his platinum print series, in 2011 Starling exhibited giveaway multiples based on the China Clay mines of Cornwall, whose rare yield is used in the production of high-gloss photographic paper. Yet such paper is used here in replicating only its own material origin—not in some photogenic vista or pictorially privileged landscape but, again, as with *One Ton II*, in what comes across more like a featureless *landscrape*.

7. In a Barcelona version of his platinum mine prints, Starling juxtaposes a supposedly conservation-friendly fuel cell with other such high-definition photo prints,

noting (in paratext, of course) the irony that the platinum necessary to the makeup of the battery, not to mention the photo-emulsions, vitiates its own supposed environmental contribution. Indeed, a generalized "media ecology" might be said to pervade Starling's "research" and execution both, even at its most flamboyant and fantastical. And certainly in his moving-image work as well. As another self-described experiment in "collapsed time and space," Starling organizes a computer-savvy team of motion-control camera technicians for a distended, time-traveling shot, tracking and temporally backtracking as well, through the austere Duveen galleries of the Tate Britain ("Phantom Ride," 2013). The result, the "special effect," is to revisit (by partly digital reconstruction) certain once hung or installed masterworks of contemporary art—including a recent and no longer extant piece by Fiona Banner: one of her "caged" (or indoor) fighter planes that had to be digitally reconstructed for credible implantation in Starling's time-tunneling process. Again, media ecology—here as both historical "collapse" and reparation at the same time, with Banner's once-material, if conceptual, appropriation "recycled" by Starling through a technology future to it.

8. It may be a further circular turn in this irony of obsolescence that the film itself must revert to its predecessor in photography in order to be reprinted in another endangered medial form, as art book rather than e-text, under a title borrowed from the freeze-frame montage of Chris Marker's futurist/retro *La Jetée* (1963, "un photo-roman" in its credits) as repackaged by subtitle as a "ciné-roman" when published in still form by Zone Books in 2006. See Mike Davies and Simon Starling, *black drop - ciné-roman* (Milan: Humbolt, 2013).

9. In another outmoding of the wheel as human tool, all that's left is a going round in circles that no longer projects any relevant trajectories. In conjunction with Barba's work, Oppenheim's canny transmedium gesture is perhaps the one that most vividly pictures—graphically, visually—the new digital dominance, even if only as passed through the transition of analog video. This chain of associated descent is accomplished, that is, when optically invoking the crudest and grainiest of early digital projection simply by low-res association with a transitional format. Oppenheim educes this suggestion when thirty years of Christmas Eve TV broadcasts of a yule log as simulacral hearth are reshot in a second-generation image (then third, etc., with steadily declining resolution) and edited together for filmic projection against a brick wall. From this roughly rectilinear surface, the image's faux fireplace seems carved out in a steadily more low-fidelity, blotchy, and toward the end vaguely gridded or *pixelated* (rather than just striated) abstraction: the disintegrated fire of filmic cinema dying out (dying of the light itself) before our eyes.

10. Upon entrance to this Camden exhibit, the spectator is greeted by one of two camera obscura presentations, recalling a distant precursor of electric projection. There, beamed upon a black wall opposite the closeted space in which their originals are mechanically turned, the smooth spin of detached bicycle wheels appears by an inverted image opposite three small-scale apertures of "projection." These illusory wheels, not their metallic models opposite, are seen swirling in a superimposed balletic rotation that offers a synecdoche for the entire evolution of an all but species-deep rotary technology (for the wheel-using animal) en route to its recent outmoding. And once past this camera obscura of metonymic reeling, once entering the forest

of projectors mounted on benches, pedestals, and shelves, there is another historical checkpoint awaiting—this when one of the 16mm loops thrown on the almost kaleidoscopic gallery walls, like crowded images in a nineteenth-century painting salon, alludes to Muybridge's protocinematic motion studies of horses on the run. It does so by tracking a donkey ridden in slow motion across a small town square. Filmic cinema thus sputters out in this case upon its own graduated and staggered photo-processural origins.

11. Erika Balsom, *Exhibiting Cinema in Contemporary Art* (Amsterdam: Amsterdam University Press, 2013).

12. Without citing Balsom, Thomas Elsaesser has since made a similar point in *Film History as Media Archaeology: Tracking Digital Cinema* (Amsterdam: Amsterdam University Press, 2016): "While cinema has also migrated and relocated to other sites and platforms since the 1990s, its passage and entry into the contemporary art museum has often taken the form of appropriation, self-reference, and re-enactment whose media archaeological alignment can best be described as a revaluation of *obsolence as the new authenticity* of the avant-garde" (22).

13. Nothing marks the divergence between Balsom's emphasis and mine more clearly than a helpful footnote of her own gathering up, on the sidelines, artists concerned less than centrally with the "senescence" of photomechanical projection. What she "brackets" demarcates exactly the topic repeatedly at stake in my pages: "This chapter will bracket a consideration of cross-medium remakes that serve to illuminate medium-specific characteristics through hybrid formations of cinema/new media (such as Cory Arcangel's *Colors* [2006]) and cinema/painting (such as Sam Taylor-Wood's *Still Life* [2001] and *A Little Death* [2002]). Instead, it will examine how strategies of remaking serve to set up a relation to cinema as a social institution that functions as a cultural vernacular and a reservoir of shared experience" (112–13). Our present Scene of investigation is often focused instead—and with *Colors* as one of its signal examples, in fact—on precisely that "cross-medium" *slash* ("cinema/new media") in the recurrent form of the contrapuntal *[::]*—where any ready "cultural vernacular" is bothered or obviated from within the taut play of mediations.

14. This emphasis derives from Balcom's stress on the social context of projection (see note 13) in the shift from popular theatrical exhibition to gallery display. There is no question that one force of screen practice, first filmic, then digital, issues from its social determinations: exactly the cultural "context" within which cinema comes across as a "medium" to begin with, initiating a communicative circuit between (mostly narrative) message and its mass reception. But with the ascendency of the digital, the consequent museumization of the celluloid substrate, along with its mechanical facilitation in the wheeling reel, have entered upon new modes of reflexive salience. Under such isolated scrutiny, mechanics and plasticity, rather than group spectacle, are at a new diagnostic premium in a mix of medial exegesis and elegy. An emphasis like mine on the transmedial estimate of filmic obsolescence, in variously explicit play either between still photography and the photogram strip or between celluloid and computerized imaging, is thus a functional complement—in approaching the same gallery installations—to Balcom's emphasis on the abrogated sociality of outmoded reception protocols.

15. Jean Epstein, *The Intelligence of a Machine*, trans. Christophe Wall-Romana (Minneapolis, MN: Univocal, 2014), 10.

16. Ibid. This sense of the cellular, the piecemeal, the discontinuous, is the burden of my argument in *Between Film and Screen* about the photogram/mar of screen motion, as contrasted with the digital advent explored in *Framed Time* and *Closed Circuits* (see n. 8 in the "Prelim," above).

17. And there is a pop-culture equivalent of these "intertextual" effects—almost a tacit nod to Arcangel's in particular. This hint of a subsequent (uncredited) uptake returns the effect of deconstructive abstraction back into the diegetic mise en scène of mainstream cinema, however abstracted and undermotivated in its own right. For in Christopher Nolan's 2014 sci-fi blockbuster *Interstellar*, the three-dimensional rendering (in 2-D film) of so-called fifth dimensional space that constitutes a revelatory gravitational "translation" (or quantum leap) across galactic portals—such is the unusually baroque SF argot—is not unfamiliar to avid museum goers. Certainly plot's tesseract finale involves (in a variant of the same computerized "slit-scan" process) a cascading linear rainbow-effect that cannot fail to put Arcangel's *Colors* in the mind's eye of anyone who knows it. If the latter work were even more famous, Nolan's effect might be called a knowing allusion. Perhaps the British director actually saw Arcangel's piece at the Tate. In any event, here is a putative case of new media art co-opted by the bigger budgets of Hollywood, as were installation laser graphics by Stanley Kubrick for the renowned Stargate sequence in *2001: A Space Odyssey* (1968). In this visual materialization at the climax of *Interstellar*, no plausible reason emerges for these streaming walls of digital color in slatted freefall—except perhaps to evoke in oblique form the less obviously digitized surfaces (known as VF/X spectacle) we've come for and that here surround, in heady recession, these abstract panels.

18. The lapsed function of mechanical gears and the differential force is explicitly on the mind of this artist. Before the camera and its spool, the wheel was of course the first tool, serviceable well along in its career to the rotary printing press developed after Gutenberg—until the Industrial Revolution itself was born of the wheel's refinement in the gear, enhancing the transferable force of circular motion. Now, in the wake of photomechanical reproduction altogether, Lauschmann's *Contemporary Gear Box* (2009) screens from a slide projector—sprockets and reels no longer needed, but returned here to a predecessor "lantern" effect that is itself outmoded—a computerized simulation of meshed cogs made by digital software rather than industrial hardware: iterated ridged edges from what resemble optically multiplied cardboard boxes (hence the wordplay of the title). The "contemporary gear box" for the new media artist—and toolkit as well, each a dead metaphor (think of a nostalgic, or skeuomorphic, term like "Photoshop" for the artist's updated workbench as keypad)—has become CGI animation itself, the current prime mover of the image.

19. Steven Cairns, untitled review of the show at Mary Mary Gallery, Glasgow, *Frieze Magazine* (October 28, 2009), http://www.frieze.com/shows/review/torsten__lauschmann/.

20. I extrapolate here from the point made by Tom Gunning in "The Play Between Stillness and Motion: Nineteenth-Century 'Philosophical Toys' and their Discourse," in *Between Stillness and Motion: Film, Photography, Algorithms*, ed. Eivind Rossaak (Am-

sterdam: Amsterdam University Press), 27–44, where Gunning's evidence suggests that it was in particular the separation of image from its (spun or wheeling) substrate in the optical toys that was the true ocular precursor of a motion effect in cinema—as engineered by, yet visually detached from, its generative material underlay.

21. This is the same Graham, it is worth remembering, who did the lightbox version of a superannuated photo store (pre-"Photoshop") from the late thirties (chap. 2) and who elsewhere projects film images of such other superseded technologies as electric rather than electronic keyboarding—this in a 35mm film in which an IBM typewriter is lost gradually to view in a simulated snowbank composed of white flour. Here is a triple metahistorical obsolescence: filmic projection, carriage return, and non-lab illusionism in the age of digital special effects. But let the audiovisual misfit of that *Phonokinetoscope*, in its very portmanteau formulation, perform its own *medi-archaeological* allegory: technical escalation often out of sync, out of phase, unevenly developed, in the march—and revolutionary turns—of mediation. Perhaps indebted to the logic of this Tiergarten "spin" is a 2010 audiovisual work called *Lover's Discourse* by San Francisco artist Mauricio Ancalmo, winner that year of the SECA Award from SFMoMA. As if named for the audiovisual intimacy of two rotary mechanisms, the work consists, by material designation, of "16mm film projector, turntable, LP record, amp, speakers, rope, found footage." A 16mm projector is hung, slowly twirling, from the ceiling—and leashed in turn to a phonograph turntable. The installation thus alternates between a resulting artificial remix of vinyl sound and the intermittently thrown image of the strip as it flashes into motion on the gallery's own enclosure as a sudden panoramic screening room. In this way, two appropriated and altered forms of decalibrated rotation fracture both each other's continuity and the media-historical axis between them in the standard cinematic gestalt of audio and image. The (tacit background) fact that streaming digital imagery has no such material vulnerability in its detachment from the audio track, indeed no such tangibly shared origin in the wheel, is one conceptual horizon of this analog recovery act in the throes of its own twinned defaults and conjured obsolescences. As in the case with certain mixed-media collages more interested in the means of received representation than in the composite picture, it is this that tilts an unmistakable multimedia work like Ancalmo's in the direction of the actively—the analytically—transmedial.

22. See Kittler, *Optical Media*, where film as "hybrid medium" is said to operate only as it "combines analogue or continuous single frames with a discontinuous or discrete image sequence" (161). It is work like Éric Rondepierre's, of course, that, in returning sequence to the single imprint (photogram, then photoprint), renders this "hybrid" manifestly transmedial. Further, in the paragraph here endnoted, my own license for evoking filmic operation in the wordplay of such interstitial phonemic skids comes in part from recognizing how Kittler's anomalous emphasis on "alphabetization" as the internalizing function of oral pedagogy circa 1800, iterated throughout his earlier study *Discourse Networks: 1800/1900*, trans. Michael Metteer, with Chris Cullins (Stanford, CA: Stanford University Press, 1992), may well derive almost by back-formation, linguistic as well as historical, from the more commonly used noun "digitization."

23. Quoted in Nancy Princenthal, "Prolix: Fiona Banner's Word Works," *Art on Paper* (May–June 2000): 40.

CHAPTER FIVE

1. Foster, *The Art-Architecture Complex*.

2. Foster would seem to agree. Linking the artist's visual studies to the Ganzfield ("entire field perception") of the Gestalt school, Foster quotes Turrell's demurral from the project of either minimalism or conceptualism, stressing that his is instead "perceptual work" (ibid., 209). In this respect, Turrell is aligned with artists of "opticality" rather than "medium"—like Robert Irwin, who turned from a minimalist emphasis on epistemology to the atmospherics of phenomenology. For Foster, all of this tends, even if it only indirectly leads, toward the new international style in built space: an architecture of visuality rather than visible structure, a site of mostly virtual dimensionality. For us, this is precisely what recontextualizes such paracinema as Turrell's or McCall's in newly useful terms.

3. For Dworkin's comments on Arcangel's *Colors*, with its effect like "test patterns," see *No Medium*, 95.

4. William Faulkner, *Absalom, Absalom!* (New York: Vintage, 1990), 15.

5. McCall's Web lecture, on the occasion of the newer work, "Between You and I," https://www.youtube.com/watch?v=3ODbdXy5UPs.

6. See my discussion of this early moment in cinema, where the "Animatograph" was replicated en abyme by "lightning cartoonists," in the on-line survey BRANCH, http://www.branchcollective.org/?ps__articles=garrett-stewart-curtain-up-on-victorian-popular-cinema-or-the-critical-theater-of-the-animatographAnimatograph.

7. See "Sculpture-in-Motion" in Vachel Lindsay, *The Art of the Motion Picture* (1915; New York: Modern Library, 2000), 65–74.

8. See discussion of Frampton's theory of filmic subtraction from the all-white plane of projection in *Between Film and Screen*, 194.

9. Hollis Frampton, *Circles of Confusion*, found in Frampton, *On the Camera Arts and Consecutive Matters* (Cambridge, MA: MIT Press, 2009), 125.

10. In commenting on the anomalous curvatures of sheer luminescence produced by the immaterial surfaces of McCall's beams, Giuliana Bruno, in *Surface: Matters of Aesthetics, Materiality and Media* (Chicago: University of Chicago Press, 2014), describing their effects as a "haptic transitivity" (71), quotes as a point of reference Roland Barthes's "On Leaving the Movie Theater," from *The Rustle of Language*, trans. Richard Howard (New York: Hill and Wang, 1987), 347, about the quite different effect of fictional cinema. InBarthes's wording, the "imperious jet" of a projector's beam operates "exactly as if a long stem of light had outlined a keyhole, and then we all peered, flabbergasted, through that hole." Instead, only the sketched rim exists in McCall, no voyeuristic aperture. The only space opened is the one we're already in, the scene of viewing rather than the recessed space of the gaze.

11. See Sean Cubitt, *The Practice of Light: A Genealogy of Visual Technologies from Prints to Pixels* (Cambridge, MA: MIT Press, 2014), with its subtitle's telltale across-the-

board media plurals. In Foster's quoting McCall on the search for the "ultimate film" that would be "nothing but itself," and granting that "this ambition is in keeping with the modernist project of artistic reflexivity and autonomy" (168), Foster's further gloss on this underlines an axiom of art practice that is expressly brought out in such works of transmediation. In the actual manifestation of McCall's "search," the goal is never that of a stringent reduction, for "what is disclosed here is less any essence of film than the recognition that mediums do not operate in this way—that they are not so many nuts to crack, with a meat to eat and a shell to discard" (168). Rather, in a contextual and social understanding on Foster's part shared, as we know, by the premises of Dworkin's *No Medium*, as well as by Balsom's work on the superannuation of film in the dialectics of gallery display, media come to definition as a complex of instrumental options (variable, "expandable"): "a matrix of technical conditions and social conventions in a differential relation to the other arts" (Foster, 169–70). Which leads one to add that rarely has the "differential relation" been less passively assumed, more immanently negotiated, than in McCall's case by this transmedial convergence of intangible sculpture, "solid light film," and kinetic drawing.

12. On the technical basis and aesthetic ambitions of such intercepted and interlaced image signals, as a kind of appropriationist "remix," see the 2014 paper by Thomas Y. Levin, as part of the Cologne Media Lectures, called "Datamoshing as Syntactic Form" (the process named for a recent dance craze, but suitably evoking "data mushing" as well), at https://www.youtube.com/watch?v=iuIu-LlRO7Y.

CHAPTER SIX

1. Early on in her extended lecture, then book, on Broodthaers's oblique conceptual work, *A Voyage on the North Sea: Art in the Age of the Post-Medium Condition* (London: Thames and Hudson, 2000), Krauss sums up the drive behind cinema's once much-debated "apparatus theory" as an instance of medium specificity (in the broader context of reception as well) thus pursued in a more capacious sense than Greenberg's for painting. In widening beyond solely material preoccupations of surface and its coterminous support in the fashion of Greenberg, apparatus theory served, for the temporal medium of film, as a definitional bridge between process and product, projector and (in the other sense of "projecting") the "subjected" and identifying spectator. A bridge—and thus, when the standard working of the apparatus was impeded in some way by avant-garde resistance—a site for congestion, friction, contestation. This is the kind of resistance, she stresses, that was found thriving in alternative cinema screenings during the early 1970s, of which McCall's work would also have been a part.

2. Broodthaers's transitional moment, in the shift from poetry to conceptual book sculpture, is discussed in my *Bookwork*, 166–67.

3. In Krauss's backcast, Broodthaers's move from archived figures to projected ones typifies the historical moment of post-1960s aesthetic ferment. She sees the conceptual talents gathered, for instance, in screenings at New York's Anthology Film Archives (among other underground venues) as spearheading a major backlash against Greenbergian purity in and beyond easel painting—and this with no loss of concern for the differential specificities of an already more complex and hybrid medium like

film, where "flatness" alone (one of Greenberg's rallying cries), even in silent screening, could scarcely seem exhaustive, given the fuller opticality of cinema's retinal framings. The high-structuralist project denominated by the term "apparatus"—meant to indicate its machinic as much as ocular essence, yet including as well its psychological entailments—saw, as Krauss reviews it, "the medium or support for film being neither the celluloid strip of the images, nor the camera that filmed them, nor the projector that brings them to life in motion, nor the beam of light that relays them to the screen, nor the screen itself, but all of these taken together, including the audience's position caught between the source of the light behind it and the image projected before its eyes" (Krauss, *A Voyage on the North Sea*, 25). But in McCall, as we know, working out of the same early 1970s moment, the spectator is not "caught between" but is found, freed from illusion, moving *amidst* and between—yet still bound by this fundamental understanding, according to Krauss, of cinema's "aggregate condition" (24). This is the case even when, years later in McCall's retooled light works, the digital file replaces all photographic animation at the point of origin.

4. Krauss, *A Voyage on the North Sea*, 51, where this (subdi)vision is precisely what she has modified in a borrowing from Walter Benjamin to call the "optical unconscious" in her earlier eponymous volume (see n. 18 in the "Prelim" above). Instead of the eyes "dilated" in passive spectacle, the image itself opens to the idea of its own subliminal generation. This disclosure of constituent increments runs counter, as it happens, to the privileging of an "open whole" in Deleuze's film theory, where for him the inconsequential flicker (so vividly noted by his predecessor and otherwise model, Henri Bergson, in the earlier philosopher's resistance to the artifice of cinematic duration) is entirely suppressed in the idea of "mobile sections" rather than a more inherent segmentation (see my discussion of this photogrammic crux in *Between Film and Screen*).

5. He does so, one must assume, not just for its ameliorative echo of "stool," though that seems part of the black comedy when he first picks up the mic and has next to nothing to say but his enthusiasm for that elongated noun: "Nothing to say, not a squeak. What's a year now? The sour cud and the iron stool. (*Pause.*) Revelled in the word spool. (*With relish.*) Spooool! Happiest moment of the past half million." Not just this scatalogic recommends the echoing assonant association, but also, perhaps, the latter word's mimetically drawn-out anagrammatic relation, as both noun and verb, action and its object, to the unspoken circular palindrome "loops." The immediate transmedial context of *Steenbeckett* would have everything to gain from this association, and much with which to repay its passing suspicion.

ENDSCAPES

1. In the seemingly paradoxical effort to locate a Kantian aesthetics in the supposedly anti-Kantian as well as antiformalist procedures of Conceptual art, one retrospective theorist of this movement can help us summarize—concerning Conceptualism 2.0 and its object, art—the way an *idea of the aesthetic* is aided by a return, as if chiastically, to the "aesthetic idea" in Kant. This is a complex notion defined as "a presentation of the imagination which prompts much thought, but to which no determinate thought whatsoever, i.e., no concept, can be adequate, so that no language can express it completely and allow

us to grasp it." See Diarmuid Costello, "Kant after Lewitt: Toward an Aesthetics of Conceptual Art," in *Philosophy and Conceptual Art*, ed. Peter Goldie and Elisabeth Schellekens (New York: Oxford University Press, 2007), 92–116, quoting Kant's *Critique of Judgment* (#49, 289, Ak 314). Without putting pressure on the difference between "idea" and "concept" in this very passage when quoted, Costello nonetheless charts a convincing middle ground on which the energy of ideas generated in "response" to the discernible material properties of Conceptual art confirms its relation to the ideational fallout of aesthetic force in Kant, even without hewing to conventional formalist determinants. One might say that Costello's whole nuanced argument is thus anticipated by approaching Conceptual art, as he does, from the vantage of what is often termed *reception aesthetics*, with emphasis on that second noun in this case. Our more circumscribed emphasis, of course, has been on the closed circuit in which the aesthetic *ideas* thus generated are reflexively focused on a *concept* of "aesthetics" per se—and, in the 2.0 phase, on the technology of mediation in its own conditioning right.

Kant understood the sensory power of art, its perceptual forms, as a kind of affective way station leading to, or helping to make sensible and manifest, the realm of rational (rather than merely aesthetic) thought—helping, as it were, to *make sense* of it. In contrast to, but also in a certain circuitous derivation from, this position, the aesthetic "ideas" rendered—and often literally spelled out—by early Conceptual art tended to round (and close) upon themselves to become *concepts about aesthetic form per se*, often negatively couched. Transmedial art follows suit in a 2.0 mode. To put it chiastically, again, in response to their involute method: what these latest works can be thought to achieve in regard to the history of mediation is to have achieved "thought" itself ("i.e. . . . concept")—in the form of medial *reconception*—about their own formal aptitudes and operations. The Kantian aesthetic template: "concept" versus (even if via) the uprush of unparaphrasable "ideas," the latter making potentially sensible the grounds of the former. Neither circular nor tautological in its reversal of priorities, the transmedial derivation: "aesthetic ideas" generated by formal intersections leading on to the very thought (or concept) of variable mediation.

2. Concerning digital databases rather than reflexive artifacts, certain rough parallels in the realm of art history to, for instance, corpus stylistics in literary scholarship, or to aggregate distribution charts in cinematic reception studies, grow unmistakable under the shared category of "information science." Alongside the incontestable value of digitized image banking and the availability of online catalogues raisonnés, the "computerization of knowledge" in aesthetic research casts a vast net. It can include everything from, at the prevalent macro level, provenance archives for single oeuvres or digital mappings for the national proliferation of a period style to, at the micro scale, radiographic dossiers on single restoration projects under magnified analysis. And all of this electronic dissemination is properly celebrated as enhanced "data presentation": sufficient unto the day being new display tools rather than pursued interpretive conclusions. No one can complain of local results in the stockpiling of such immediately, or even just potentially, illuminating data. In the discipline more broadly, however, inquiry certainly stops short if electronic process is detached from anything like media study to become merely a study aid. What certain digital artists themselves are doing, by contrast, deserves in a different sense the same rubric, "digital art history." This happens

when—in the case of digital video, for instance—they place their own medium's latter-day emergence into relief against an implied archaeology of visualization ever since the immaterial image as such was first sprung free from the fixed picture in the run-up from optical toys to cinema.

3. See my stress on the photogrammic stratum as the "preconscious," rather than the unconscious, of film reception—generative in a more immediate and less displaced sense—in *Between Film and Screen*, 114.

4. Stanley Cavell, *The World Viewed: Reflections on the Ontology of Film*, enlarged ed. (Cambridge, MA: Harvard University Press, 1979).

5. In this respect, the self-conscious meditations on the history of painting or the evolution of celluloid stock in the later films of Godard, in particular the play between cinematography and tableau in *Passion* (1982) or between b&w and color footage in *Eloge de l'amour* (2001), may come to mind as well, their "mixtures" being subtly *trans* in various ways. But no pressure point between media regimes in these films carries anything like the immediate narrative charge of *Amour*'s "collapse" (to borrow Starling's rubric) of moving celluloid into stretched canvas.

6. Fried's is a career-long argument begun most explicitly with *Absorption and Theatricality: Painting and Beholder in the Age of Diderot* (Chicago: University of Chicago Press, 1980).

7. With the once constituent photogram in mind, even though never wholly in view on screen, and attempting to mark out a conceptual interspace within the requisite throw of light and shadow, *Between Film and Screen* was my late-century effort at singling out the quintessentially modernist "photo synthesis" (subtitle) of cinematic manifestation. Pointed up by the main title's prepositional phrase, as well, is the dialectical tension between frame capture and moving frame: a generative tension made possible by optical afterimage and inducing upon succession the third term of visible movement rather than just motor(ized) image. The place of surveillance in relation to the subsequent digital transition of record and projection, as captured, for instance, by the texture of Haneke's *Caché*, is the broad subject of my more recent book on "surveillancinema," *Closed Circuits*.

8. See Christian Metz, "Identification with the Camera," *The Imaginary Signifier*, trans. Cecilia Britton, Annywl Williams (Bloomington: Indiana University Press, 1982), 49–52.

9. In *Funny Games*, the freeze effect is already digitized by association with the "control" mania of one of the two teen killers in his TV-fixated and channel-surfing distraction, where even his murder by the wife of the family they are torturing can be rectified, impossibly, by the surreal work of a mere rewind button on the TV's remote control. When a freeze frame finally suspends the next round of brutality at a subsequent household by closing down on the other boy's coy, malicious smirk, it reads less like a cinematographic disclosure of the photogram strip than like the self-imposed pause button in an ongoing chain of mayhem: a transmediation between screen protocols linked to Haneke's familiar critique of televisual violence.